MUSICAL

IMPROVISATION

MUSICAL IMPROVISATION

ART, EDUCATION, AND SOCIETY

EDITED BY
GABRIEL SOLIS
AND **BRUNO NETTL**

UNIVERSITY OF ILLINOIS PRESS

Urbana and Chicago

© 2009 by the Board of Trustees
of the University of Illinois
All rights reserved

Library of Congress Cataloging-in-Publication Data
Musical Improvisation : art, education, and society /
edited by Gabriel Solis and Bruno Nettl.
p. cm.
Includes bibliographical references and index.
ISBN 978-0-252-03462-6 (cloth : alk paper)
ISBN 978-0-252-07654-1 (pbk : alk paper)
1. Improvisation (Music)—History.
2. Improvisation (Music)—Social aspects.
3. Music—History and criticism.
4. Music—Instruction and study.
I. Solis, Gabriel, 1972–
II. Nettl, Bruno, 1930–
ML193.M87   2009
781.3'6—dc22   200805474

CONTENTS

PREFACE

Bruno Nettl

We probably never should have started calling it "improvisation." *Webster's Third New International Dictionary* (1981) doesn't give the term a positive spin, quoting Willa Cather about a cook who hastily improvised a supper, a Canadian government report about a team of surveyors being housed in improvised and obviously uncomfortable quarters, and a fisherman who had forgotten his equipment improvising a fishing hook and line. A person not familiar with the term as we use it in music might expect to hear a violist who forgot to bring his music "improvise" by somehow following along using a combination of imperfect memory and acquaintance with the style, or of a cellist who forgot to bring an extra string "improvise" by making do with three. And should musicians make much of the fact that they can play without preparation, that would only support the stereotype of musicians as improvident and unreliable people.

But "improvident"? Duke Ellington (quoted by Derek Jewell, 1977) famously said, "Improvisation? Anyone who plays anything worth hearing knows what he's going to play, no matter whether he prepares a day ahead or a beat ahead. It has to be with intent." In that sentence, at least, Ellington was saying he didn't think one needed the *concept* of improvisation. And the lack of preparation? Giving a different perspective, Yehudi Menuhin in *Theme and Variations* (1972) wrote, "Improvisation is not the expression of accident, but rather of the accumulated yearnings, dreams, and wisdom of our very soul." It's music making with a special immediacy. But then, in the words of a colleague on a panel in 1985: "Improvisation is something that simply cannot be explained." For him, improvisation is a mystery.

Preparation, immediacy, mystery. I'm not sure whether any of these soundbites grasps the essence of improvisation. They certainly present it in three very different lights. But in all three, we're far from the host improvising a dinner. In our everyday lives, improvisation is a kind of emergency measure; but in music, and in the other performing arts, it has a place of honor, but of mystery. The worlds of music lovers and of scholarship seem often to be asking: Can this complicated work of art we're hearing really be the product of a merely improvising mind? Or: This complex performance must be improvised; or could it possibly have been memorized in all its details? Yet in the last 50 years I've detected a change from dismissive judgment to the feeling that improvisation is something grand, magnificent, if also inscrutable. Ellington, Menuhin, and my anonymous colleague tell us that we're really talking about a lot of different things.

⤚

We should consider the studies in this volume in the context of the history of scholarship on improvisation. For ages, musicians have thought that improvisation was on the way out. Jan Adam Reinken is quoted by Karl Geiringer in *The Bach Family* (1954) as saying to Bach, in 1720, "I thought this art was dead, but I see it lives on in you." Musicologists writing about the 20th century sometimes lament the passing of the old days, when improvisation was more significant. Nevertheless, we—the musical culture of the United States, maybe of the world, if such a concept is imaginable—have in the last few decades become increasingly aware of the existence and significance of improvisation. Either there is a lot more of it, or musicians are more willing to admit that improvising is what they're doing, or they're more inclined to think that the term helps to explain certain commonalities. And in musicology too, one encounters the term with increasing frequency. I maintain that we haven't found ways to study improvised music as efficiently as we do music composed and recorded in writing or memory.

Certainly in the last two decades, the study of improvisation has made great strides. Compare, for example, the treatment of improvisation in the 1942 edition of *Grove's Dictionary of Music and Musicians*—it's included under "extemporization"—with that in the latest, and you will observe exponential growth. Incidentally, even in its earlier editions, *Grove's* has had trouble deciding on which side to come down. The 1886 edition: "The power of playing extempore evinces a very high degree of musical cultivation." 1942: "The art of composing and performing music simultaneously; it is therefore the primitive art of music making." It's interesting that in musicological literature, improvisation first found its role in association with performance practice studies, then as a kind of component of aural composition as suggested by Albert Lord in his influential book *The Singer of Tales* (1960), and eventually as the opposite of composition. The concept suggested taking liberties with tempo and dynamics. Ernst Ferand, who in 1938 published the first large book (*Die Improvisation in der Musik*) in which the word appears in the title, gave it far more dignity, but tended to look at improvisation as essentially one kind of thing, emphasizing the commonality of oral composition, Baroque improvisation, and the 19th-century extempore playing of organ fugues. Later, it became an increasingly common musicological practice to ask whether this genre or that practice—paraphrasing voices in a gamelan, jazz solos, Persian avaz—were truly improvisation, and perhaps to try to measure the degree of their improvisatoriness.

But it has gradually become clear that the things that we call improvisation encompass a vast network of practices, with various artistic, political, social, and educational values. It concerns everything from the organist who can make up a Bach-like fugue on the spot to the keyboardist who plays literally without having much of an idea of what will come out of his instrument. It encompasses the Native American shaman who composes as he sings, so at least we think, in a trance. It includes the Carnatic musician who always gives you something new, selecting from and recombining a limited stock of melodic, rhythmic, motivic building blocks. It includes the jazz musician who learns his art by listening to and memorizing recorded improvised solos, and the composer of classical music who played something, found that he liked it, and quickly wrote it down. It's music by amateurs and professionals. It's the music of certain cultures in which nothing is consciously memorized or otherwise recorded, and also of cultures in which a sharp distinction is made between what is precomposed and what is created in the course of performance. Its value differs by culture: in 19th-century European art music it was merely something of a "craft," compared with the "art" of composition, but in the classical music of Iran, it was (and is) the central musical activity, surrounded by lesser, composed genres. The many things we call improvisation have come to be greatly respected, as certain musics in which it plays a major role—the classical traditions of south Asia and the Middle East, the jazz traditions, branches of new music—and the improvisatory elements of precomposed music, the classical cadenza, and the ornamentation in Baroque instrumental and vocal music have all increased their visibility in Western musical culture, and finally perhaps also in the world of music scholarship.

⌒

It is now largely accepted that if there is contrast, there is also a close relationship between improvisation and composition, that the two are different faces of the same process, that it is hard to know where one ends and the other begins. The mainstream discourse of scholarly literature about improvisation has revolved around three questions: (1) whether something is properly improvisation, and how we can find out; (2) the relationship between some point of departure learned by an improvisor and the product that is created in the course of performance; and (3) the methods of combining, juxtaposing, and otherwise arranging building blocks to create music. These are essentials. But we—the editors and authors of the essays in this volume—believe it is important also to follow another perspective: the study of improvisation in a variety of contexts. The papers in this volume follow three paths: improvisation in the context of society and politics, improvisation in its various relationships to the concept of education, and of course, improvisation in the context of music making and art

In musical cultures that distinguish between improvised and precomposed music, the improvisor—or groups of improvisers—is inevitably making a statement: It may be that by following the freedom of improvisation, we are fighting for personal and political freedom; it may be, as I once heard from one of my teachers in Iran, that in improvising you share your personality in ways that the composed genres don't permit; it may be that group improvisers relate to each other differently and more closely than musicians in other ensembles. Or it may be that a subculture shows its individuality by specializing in improvised music. We examine the gestures in human and group interrelationships that improvisation reflects and supports. We wish to see what the concept of improvisation signifies, in human cultures and histories, and in the history of European and American thought and whether it is, as for Yehudi Menuhin, the accumulated yearnings, dreams, and wisdom of the soul, or whether it is what various kinds of "others"—we've heard it said about Asians, African Americans, Jews, rural people—do in their slapdash approach to music making, because they lack the capacity for disciplined composition. In any event, improvisers are, as Ingrid Monson notes in the title of her book *Saying Something* (1996)—saying something simply by engaging in the act of improvising. And in their discourse about improvisation, musicians, the audience, and scholars are saying something about social relations and the manipulation of power.

In accordance with our second theme, we provide studies of how musicians (and others) learn to improvise music—how processes of improvisation are used in some musical cultures to provide the essential window to the entire musical system—or, as Patricia Campbell writes in these pages, improvise to learn music. We know that Indian musicians learn exercises; that Persian musicians memorize the long musical corpus known as the radif and then use it, as it were, to improvise upon; and that jazz musicians have a large repertoire of learning and teaching techniques. We wish to know what these building blocks have in common, and how the differences among them reflect fundamental guiding principles of their cultures. How does one learn to deal with risks that have musical as well as social consequences? We wish to know how this knowledge can help us in teaching music, and we wonder whether we can bring back into our musical culture some values, such as improvisation, that seem to have receded.

Our third theme follows paths already well worn by scholars of improvisation, but with greater emphasis than before on the Western classical tradition (seen simply as one of the world's musical traditions). We wish to learn more about how the minds of improvising musicians work, and to look at improvisation in the context of other music-making arts, and of musical creation at large. Musicologists, and particularly scholars of jazz and of south and west Asian music, have done a good deal of that by analyzing improvised performances by different musicians based on the same tune, the same raga, the same Persian dastgah, the same maqam. But there are still those, quoted by Paul Berliner, who think jazz musicians pick notes out of thin air; and I remember a jazz educator beginning an address by saying that improvisation was a process that simply could not be explained. But I guess our job as -ologists is to find ways of explaining, and we benefit from the cross-fertilization of studies relating and comparing composed (or "precomposed") music and improvisation, comparing improvised performance with the performance of extant music. The work of composers can often be seen to be informed by processes related to those of improvisation; the compositional methods identified by music historians can be traced in the work of improvising musicians. Among the authors of papers in this volume are scholars who have devoted themselves to explaining, if I may put it that way, how Beethoven's, Mozart's, and Wagner's musical minds worked and how they engaged in the creative process, studying sketches and successive versions of their works There are ways of following the same analytical procedures for improvised music—for some improvised musics—but, except in the field of jazz, they haven't been applied very much. We try to follow new directions, perhaps to see how musicians, as Stephen Blum wrote in *In the Course of Performance*, "respond appropriately to unforeseen challenges and opportunities" (1998) in ways that parallel or contrast with those of composers.

↢

In its attempt to provide studies of three contexts, this collection hopes to move scholarship on musical improvisation in new directions. We must be modest in our claims of innovativeness. Our intellectual ancestors, as usual, were already aware of some of the cherished innovations that now excite us. Mindful of the importance of knowing the history of our scholarly discipline, the authors of these essays frequently take advantage of a historical perspective. Significantly, our intellectual godfather, the Hungarian Ernst Ferand, born in 1887, began his career as a music educationist, studied the methods of Emile Jaques-Dalcroze, and went on to write the first musicological dissertation explicitly dealing with improvisation. His combination of interests in music history, music education, and dance, the relationship of these three fields buttressed by their mutual dependence on improvisation, became an inspiration for the organization of the present work.

In important respects, this collection is a successor to the earlier collection of studies mentioned above, *In the Course of Performance* (edited by Bruno Nettl with Melinda Russell, 1998), which undertook, perhaps for the first time, to bring together some 15 studies approaching the subject from various ethnomusicological perspectives. The present offering had its origins in a conference held at the University of Illinois in Urbana in 2004, sponsored by the Division of Musicology and supported by many units of the institution. The present group of essays shows that the scholarly study of improvisation has made important strides, as the combination of studies by scholars in historical musicology, music education, ethnomusicology, and the world of practical music making reveal a common cause, and studies from the related disciplines of folklore and dance make important contributions. The tripartite focus readily demonstrates, as does the sharpening of focus in the new studies by those authors who also contributed to the 1998 volume, that the study of improvisation in music has been making substantial progress.

Let me close with three quotations that may serve as leitmotifs for this collection of essays, statements that encourage us to continue with a critical perspective of our subject, by three major figures in the history of improvisatory contemplation. All insist that improvisation is a central part of the musical enterprise. Our spiritus rector, Ferand, writing in 1938 on the dangers of rigidity: "The boundaries are fluid, as we note that much of the creative work of Chopin, Liszt, Schubert is the written fixing of improvisations" (1938). Feruccio Busoni, in his *Sketch of a New Aesthetic of Music*, on the tangled relationships of composition to improvisation and inspiration: "Notation is to improvisation as the portrait to the living model" (1907). And Paul Berliner, in his grand study *Thinking in Jazz*, on the magnitude and the magnificence of the endeavor. "For jazz musicians, a performance can also be likened to a symbolic miniature version of their life's pilgrimage: their overriding musical activities, creative processes, and life goals" (1994). The understanding of improvisation—or should we find a more providential term?—is basic to the comprehension of music as a fundamental metaphor of life, society, and culture.

↜

Gabriel Solis and I wish to take this opportunity to express our gratitude. The essays in this collection are substantially revised and expanded versions of papers and lectures delivered at a conference, "New Directions in the Study of Musical Improvisation," held at the University of Illinois at Urbana-Champaign in April 2004 and supported by many academic and administrative units of the campus, particularly the School of Music, the College of Fine and Applied Arts, and the Provost's office. We are grateful to the authors for permitting us to include their work here. In the preparation of the manuscript, we received support from the Campus Research Board, which we gratefully acknowledge. We wish, finally, to thank three graduate students in musicology who provided important editorial help: Marie Rule, Anne Oleinik, and (now Dr.) Jennifer Fraser.

MUSICAL
IMPROVISATION

INTRODUCTION

Gabriel Solis

Improvisation—in the broadest sense, the practice of making compositional decisions in the moment of performance—is part of virtually every musical tradition in the world. Yet an informal survey of people who listen to and make music, at least in the American collegiate setting, will elicit an assortment of odd and wildly contradictory ideas about improvisation, which, taken together, make it seem something altogether distant and unknowable, as well as impracticable by all but a very select few.[1] For instance, many students who begin instrumental or vocal instruction in the Western classical tradition during childhood are never encouraged to improvise in the narrow sense, to play without a prescribed piece in mind, because it is somehow seen as a secondary, quite specialized art. It is something to be learned only after one has developed mastery over the instrument, if then. This holds true long after students pass out of childhood. Conservatories of music are filled with college-aged virtuosi who, despite remarkable technical ability, are at a total loss when faced with the task of improvising. That said, something like the opposite holds true for ideas about jazz improvisation that are in current circulation. Not only does it appear to be an exceptional skill, but there is a primitivism characteristic of reigning ideas about improvisation. Even highly trained classical musicians often find themselves at a loss when listening to jazz. Those who are unable to follow what is happening in jazz improvisation often assume that it is random or "natural," and not the product of study, training, and intellect. That is, either improvising musicians just "play whatever" or they play entirely on instinct, without really knowing why they play particular things.

How can a musical practice be at once a highly specialized, difficult skill and the natural, mindless outpouring of some blessed (or perhaps cursed) few? The answer is that it is neither. It is a skill cultivated more or less consciously by many kinds of musicians around the world and throughout history—one that disappeared from the Western classical tradition only recently. The essays collected in this volume represent the work of scholars from musicology, ethnomusicology, and music education, and of improvising musicians from a number of traditions dedicated to providing better explanations of improvisation in music than those currently prevailing. Together the selections explore improvisation as a mode of musical creativity that varies cross-culturally and through time. Unlike previous works dealing with improvisation, which have tended to take a single methodological perspective (historical, music-theoretical, sociological, ethnographic) and focus on a single tradition (Hindustani music, jazz, Baroque keyboard music), this volume approaches the problem from a number of methodologies and includes many of the world's musical traditions of the present and the past. In this way we aim to represent a more complex, richer picture of improvisation's variety.

If this orientation runs the risk of creating a collection that lacks a single, unifying viewpoint, we propose that such diversity is as much a strength as a weakness. Instead of a monolithic approach, we have chosen to select voices and themes that interrelate to form a web or network. Three main themes ground the essays: improvisation in social and political processes, that is, improvisation as a key feature of the ways music binds people to one another (and at times drives them apart) as groups and individuals; improvisation and the educational process, that is, investigations of "improvising to learn and learning to improvise," as Patricia Shehan Campbell so neatly puts it; and finally, improvisation and the creative process, that is, improvisation in the moment, constituting one of many tools creative musicians use to make new music. This organization around three main themes distinguishes this collection from previous studies of improvisation and is one of the collection's strongest qualities. No new grand theory of improvisation will be found here, but rather an expansion in many directions of the possibilities to be found in a concerted approach to the practice. The three main themes have often been seen as the respective purviews of three or four separate fields of inquiry: ethnomusicology, music education, and musicology or music theory. By grouping them in this volume as parts of the study of improvisation, we are suggesting that they are highly compatible and have much to learn from one another.

Perhaps the first question one would expect the introduction to a volume of this sort to ask is, what is improvisation? An answer is not necessarily or readily forthcoming, however. There are dictionary definitions, of course. Merriam-Webster Online, a workhorse of its genre, and the more rarefied Oxford English Dictionary agree substantially that *improvise* derives from a Latin word meaning "unforeseen" and that it means "1. to compose, recite, sing, or play extemporaneously; 2. to make, invent, or arrange offhand; 3. to fabricate out of what is conveniently at hand."[2] In the grossest sense these definitions, or at least the first of them, will suffice as a starting point. The notion of creating music extemporaneously is reasonable, and though the notions of convenience and offhandedness in the second and third are problematic, the practice of making the most of what is at hand does resonate with respect to many improvisatory practices. Still, do these definitions really answer more detailed questions about improvisation? Are the jazz musician from 1927 who ornately elaborated and ornamented a melody, the free improviser of today who creates collective sound spaces, the Baroque keyboardist of the 17th century or today who preludes, and the sitarist who plays an alap really all doing the same thing? All create new music using models known and in some way agreed upon beforehand, but the nature of the models, the degree of departure, the context for interpretation, the interactive frameworks, and the meaning those creations take on among the musicians and audiences are all distinct. It is the purpose of this volume, then, not so much to offer an answer, another pat definition of improvisation, or to begin with a single point of view, but rather to investigate the many possible permutations of musical practice that might be called improvisation. If this approach seems to skirt the general ontological question, it is because like the question, what is music? it can be a diversion from questions that ultimately offer more satisfying answers without actually yielding more at the end of the discussion than one had at the start.

Why study improvisation? A collection such as this raises the question of whether there is something to be learned from studying improvisation in its many varieties and contexts that could not be found by studying these various contexts separately without an explicit focus on improvisation. We propose that both perspectives are vital, but that improvisation has often been neglected in studies of the second sort, and that a collection such as this suggests that far from being a minor, mystical, exceptional practice, improvisation is a basic part of most musical activity. Moreover, the perspective afforded by a look at improvisation in many kinds of music can actually uncover a number of things about music making across various traditions that might otherwise not come to the surface. The most radical proposition embedded in this collection is that such a focus on improvisation can make music making central to the ways we study all music. By extension, other aspects of musical traditions—musical works, reception, historiography, and so on—might be understood in relation to music making. We certainly are not suggesting that these areas of inquiry ought to be abandoned in favor of the micro-level ethnographic study of musical performance; rather, as Christopher Small suggested many years ago, we can come to a better understanding of improvisation cross-culturally if we remember that music is, in the first place, an activity and not an object or an idea, and that it becomes objectified and idealized only after its making (1998a, 1998b).

There is a substantial background literature on improvisation on which the authors in this collection draw. If improvisation has been underrepresented recently in those areas of study and practice where the modern Western classical tradition is focal or paradigmatic, and in traditions where it operates in an unacknowledged way, such as Anglo-American folk traditions, it has been studied extensively in both theory and practice in jazz, early music, Middle Eastern music, and Indian classical music, among other types. There are also significant primary sources on improvisation in the Western classical tradition from earlier periods.

The practical literatures dealing with these traditions have generally been written for performers or aspiring performers and have been exhaustive in mapping out the options open to an improviser in the particular styles. Massive tomes such as Robert Donington's *The Interpretation of Early Music* (1989) and Frederick Neumann's *Ornamentation in Baroque and Post-Baroque Music with a Special Emphasis on J. S. Bach* (1978) (the latter of which dedicates 11 somewhat short chapters to the application of trills in what is ultimately a fairly limited repertory) demonstrate the immense complexity and sheer volume involved in systematically presenting the options available to an improviser working even with as idiomatically limited a practice as 16th- and 17th-century instrumental ornamentation.

Donington, Neumann, and others writing contemporaneously on the revival of early music differ from their historical counterparts in one particularly interesting way. They are very much of their time inasmuch as their writings treat musical performance, including improvisation, as a technical problem exclusively. The writers they draw upon, such as Johann Joachim Quantz and C.P.E. Bach, also dedicate themselves to the exhaustive discussion of the minutiae of improvisation and ornamentation (Quantz, for example, provides 29 tables showing the possible ways of "varying" such figures as a repeated note, a rising third, or a descending tetrachord, with each table including as many as 20 or 30 options; see Quantz 1966, 136–61); but, following 18th-century practice, the aesthetic and technical discussion is framed within a discussion of ethics, of the qualities necessary in a person who wishes to become a "truly learned musician" (Quantz, 14). These qualities include natural gifts and talent, but also, significantly, dedication to hard work and *wissenschaft*, or scientific contemplation (Quantz, 11–27).

Jazz, too, despite its origins as an oral-traditional music, boasts a wealth of published instructional literature on improvisation. Early examples exist, but in the past 40 years teachers of the music have produced countless variations on chord-scale theory, the dominant model for instruction in post-bop improvisation. They teach aspiring jazz players to manipulate licks, or melodic patterns, slowly discovering more and more complicated, generally more and more dissonant, and more and more piquant relationships between chord types and scales in which the licks fit. At the same time, improvisers learn gradually more sophisticated chord progressions, generally as substitutes for traditional changes, which can then be used in improvisation and composition. Professors in major university jazz programs—particularly Indiana University and the University of North Texas—have been key in making this the dominant model for jazz improvisation training. David Baker's and Jerry Coker's theories, first articulated in the 1960s, laid the groundwork for this tradition, along with Jamey Aebersold's thriving series of "play-along" recordings (Baker [1969] 1983, 1971; Coker 1964, 1970, 2002). Both draw heavily on George Russell's "Lydian Chromatic theory" of jazz (1959), which outlines a concept of scalar and harmonic interrelation based on chromatic alterations of the Lydian scale. As Ingrid Monson has noted, although Russell's theory is chiefly concerned with formal relationships between pitches (in scales and chords), it is intended primarily to move students toward musical freedom rather than toward musical standardization; and inasmuch as it is about the struggle for freedom, Russell's theory encapsulates a spiritual philosophy that goes far beyond formalism (1998, 154–56). That the language of the spiritual journey surrounding Russell's work was not incorporated by his (mostly white) conservatory education–oriented followers should come as no real surprise. David Ake has critiqued the dominant model of chord-scale theory in jazz education as one that becomes a search for mastery but has no place for the struggle for freedom in "Jazz 'Traning: John Coltrane and the Conservatory," from his book *Jazz Cultures* (2002, 122–27, 144–45). It should be pointed out that although Ake may be quite right that the easily gradable quality of orthodox chord-scale theory has made it the most common classroom jazz theory technique, it is neither the only thing discussed by Baker and Coker nor the only approach to the study of jazz improvisation practiced at present.

The literatures of Asian classical traditions stretch back many centuries, though older texts in particular tend to be more philosophical and theological than practical, concerned more with musical structure than with its application. In Indian and Middle Eastern music, as in jazz, much of the practical instruction in improvisation has remained in the oral tradition. Early manuscripts in India, from the fifth to the thirteenth centuries, discuss such topics as the spiritual and cosmological dimensions of music, the place of music in human life, organology, elements of compositional structure such as *raga* and *tala*—melodic and rhythmic modes—and music's relationship to emotion. The *Sangitaratnakara* from the 13th century does include significant sections on ornament and improvisation, incorporated into a larger chapter on music and dance performance (Rowell 2000, 35). Because the tradition of scholarship was conservative and served to reinforce canonical ideas, treatises from the 14th century on often treat improvisation and ornament in some fashion as a nod to the authority of works such as the *Sangitaratnakara* (Simms 2000, 44). Interestingly, despite their philosophical bent, these treatises—somewhat in line with our work here—tend to speak more to the practices of music making (as an ethical as well as an aesthetic activity) than to the improvised musical objects that might result. More recent works, particularly those in the 19th and 20th centuries, typically deal with improvisation in practice, but even now most practical instruction in Indian music of any sort remains oral.

Historical treatises on music of the Middle East exist in abundance, particularly in Arabic and Persian, though many have yet to be reproduced in adequate numbers or translated into European languages, so knowledge of them in the West remains limited (Neubauer 2002, 364). Nonetheless, some material from these traditions is known widely. Perhaps even more than is the case for south Asia, older scholarship on Arabic and Persian music tends to be extremely philosophical, dealing with the practical aspects of music making secondarily (Caton 2002, 131). Consequently, the bulk of learning about musical improvisation in these traditions was orally transmitted until the 20th century.

Instructional writing has generally had less to say about the creativity involved in improvising than about techniques—how, that is, to move from knowing what is possible to developing a feel for what is *right* in the moment. This is often treated as ineffable, or just something that comes with time and practice, and that therefore is not worth addressing in any detail in instructional literature. For instance, toward the beginning of *Improvising Jazz*, which purports to be a theoretical primer in the art, Jerry Coker says, "The absorption and utilization of theory and techniques, which are the improvisor's tools, can in no way guarantee an interesting musical personality. Each jazz player will find his own musical style and will be subject to the criticism of the listener. . . . The style of the individual player is affected by his personality, his intelligence, his talent, and his coordination, all of which are beyond the scope of this text" (1964, 2). Even in works that do attempt to address the nature of good improvising, such as a pamphlet on extemporization at the organ written by Sydney Nicholson for the Royal School of Church Music, there is a tendency to make the art seem out of reach for all but the chosen few. Nicholson's first words are "It is often said that the good extemporist is born, not made, and this is to some extent true; it is given only to the favored few to excel in this branch of the art" (1969, 3).

More academic, theoretical works have tried to pierce the veil, so to speak, in order to understand what makes great improvisation work, describing past performances more than prescribing future ones. Beyond the technical considerations of what is correct or incorrect, there has been an attempt to understand why some improvisations sound so right. Key to this work has been a focus on social-interactive systems—the idea, commonly drawing on the work of Pierre Bourdieu, that great creative moments usually happen in the context of improvisatory social spaces, either between musicians or between musicians and audiences, or (most likely) both. Far from suggesting that the technical skills discussed in the practical literature do not matter, theoretical studies generally take it as a given that those skills will have been mastered before the broader considerations are likely to even emerge.

The drawback of a disciplinary ghettoization of the study of improvisation to those musical situations where it is marked as the central activity is that it has limited our understanding of musical improvisation in general. As far back as 1974, Bruno Nettl suggested that improvisation is better seen as one end of a continuum that has as its other end what we generally gloss as interpretation (6). The implication is that to study any music in performance is to study a phenomenon that is somehow linked to improvisation—or, better, that the study of improvisation is fundamental to, though properly a subset of, the study of musical performance as a whole. Others have suggested that improvisation and composition (often seen as antitheses, polar opposites of a sort) are actually linked processes, perhaps even different registers of the same sort of activity—what Paul Berliner describes as two sides of an ongoing dialogue (1994).

The most substantial volume on the subject of improvisation in general, which is to say the most important precedent for the present volume, is Bruno Nettl and Melinda Russell's *In the Course of Performance* (1998). In the introduction to that volume Nettl gives a fairly complete survey of the literature on improvisation up to the time, determining that in spite of a small offering of quality work, it is nonetheless "an art neglected in scholarship" (1). The central premise of *In the Course of Performance* is that, first, academic musicology has largely ignored improvisation or treated it as a skill of only minor importance and, second, scholars who wish to deal with improvisation in detail have precious few models to draw upon. The book offers much in the way of addressing both concerns, providing a mix of essays highlighting the importance of improvisation in various traditions (almost all of them from the realm of "world" music) and others providing theories that could be applied broadly (and some, of course, doing both).

Around the time of publication of *In the Course of Performance* and afterward a number of works have appeared dealing with improvisation—with a notable explosion of jazz scholarship—such that it is now hard to claim that improvisation is neglected in scholarship. It remains somewhat neglected in the scholarship of the Western classical tradition, perhaps because of the extent to which it remains neglected in the practice of that music and because of the extent to which the study of that music remains work-oriented. There has also been a recent flourishing of interest in studying improvised music in practical ways in academia. Jazz performance programs, which were certainly on the rise throughout the 1990s, have become even more common in the 2000s; more and more universities offer opportunities to play gamelan or to learn Indian classical traditions, for example; and "new music" ensembles offer students the opportunity to improvise in the Western classical tradition. As a barometer of these changes, the most recent version of the *Grove Music Online* dictionary offers a much expanded entry on improvisation, much of it written by Nettl, that incorporates many of the premises of *In the Course of Performance* (1998). Nevertheless, as suggested earlier, the newfound academic respect for and understanding of improvisation has not trickled down as effectively as it might into common understandings of the practice, nor has it impacted the field as Nettl seemed to hope it would in 1998, when he wrote, "Changing the values as fundamentally as these paragraphs suggest may indeed require a reinvention of musicology" (6).

Echoing that bit of a manifesto, I suggest that we stand at a moment when studies of improvisation can be useful in shifting the discourse in the field in general. The "new musicology" (now more than a decade old) has been important in moving the focus to a more "cultural" account of music, as has a shift in the subdiscipline of ethnomusicology in the past two decades; the focus on music making that Christopher Small proposed (in his words, a focus on "musicking," 1998b) and that we follow here can be the core of a new musical scholarship that moves beyond the division into a historical musicology that focuses only on the Western classical tradition and an ethnomusicology whose purview is the rest of the world. What would this mean in terms of the study of improvisation and of music, generally, if we follow out its logic? This is, to some extent, an open question, but one can at least suggest some possible answers. Without question, it would mean that the study of performance per se—the study of music making—would have to take on a more central role in all of musicology, not just certain areas of ethnomusicology, and that improvisation would have to become central to the teaching of music more generally, and not just in jazz, for instance. Such a shift could have a truly radical outcome: a profound change in the way we think about the canon in Western classical music. At present the canon of musical works is *the* object of study, except in a handful of cases. Even when the focus of study is not canonical works—the study of obscure 18th-century symphonies, for instance—the canon operates in the background, setting the agenda for investigation and, in any case, orienting our efforts toward the study of musical works necessarily.

This problem, the force of the canon in our field of study, has often been treated as a political problem as much as one of substance. We have acted as though solving the problem may be as easy as admitting marginalized musics or people into the canon. Although the canon as a discourse clearly comes out of and incorporates values of a discriminatory system, acknowledging this and expanding the canon, though necessary, does not mitigate the ideas that underlie it. What is more, as sophisticated as works such as Lydia Goehr's *The Imaginary Museum of Musical Works* (1992) are in explaining how we got into the intellectual cul-de-sac of focusing exclusively on canonical works, they offer little advice on how to get out. A thorough-going commitment to the study of improvisation, of the creativity that rests in all the choices performers make ad libitum, in the moment—from lesser matters of phrasing, intonation, timing, and the like, to overarching matters of melodic and harmonic composition, form, and so forth—might lead us not to forsake the study of works and the various canons of the music we study, but to put such study in its place as one portion of larger, living musical traditions. Ironically, to the extent that we succeed in shifting this focus, this book ensures its own obsolescence. If we are right, as I think we are, then the study of improvisation will ultimately melt into the basic paradigms of musical study, so that there may no longer be a rationale for studying it as distinct from the rest of music making.

Toward that end, this collection offers much that is new. First, by bringing together scholars from a breadth of inquiry and musicians from a number of traditions, we have given serious attention to bridging the close analysis of musical sound with social and historical investigation. This, of course, is a common goal of late but one that is not always achieved. By focusing on performance, as the topic of improvisation all but requires—that is, focusing on music making as much as on music made—this collection necessarily moves back and forth between musical sound and musical meaning. Because of the desire to communicate to one another, as well as to a broad audience, authors who might otherwise have taken a restricted view have risen to the challenge of addressing multiple concerns.

One further benefit of this experiment in speaking across disciplinary boundaries is that a focus on music making recasts the basic premise that we are studying repertories that might be placed in some kind of hierarchy. Rather, we are studying traditions of music making and listening, looking at the ways those traditions work and, to the extent that we do comparative work, at the ways they are similar and are different. So jazz, the Western classical tradition, Asian classical traditions, and European folk forms can do more than coexist in a single volume; they can each influence the ways we understand the others.

↬

The organization of this volume into three parts, each anchored by a longer essay, is to some extent heuristic, since many of the essays could have gone in any of the three sections; nevertheless, it does allow certain themes to emerge that might otherwise have remained obscure. The first section addresses the social domain of musical improvisation. The writers in this section interpret the idea of the social or political variously, but ultimately all are somehow concerned with the ways musical improvisation is meaningful in interpersonal relationships. Ingrid Monson's essay connects the musical and social realms of meaning (that is, the aesthetic and the political) in jazz and west African balofon music by considering both in terms of practice theory. The theory is broad enough to allow for lots of different ways in which music and society can be connected, one of the most important of which is through metaphor. Monson's use of practice theory provides a robust understanding of the ways individuals navigate the social structures in which they live (sometimes without explicit awareness, but often with it). Structures and discourses tend to change very slowly, Monson suggests, but nonetheless people find remarkably creative ways to assume some agency in engaging them. Like society, improvised music requires both structure and freedom in order to be pleasurable and comprehensible. In her essay, Monson sets the tone for this collection by coupling a sustained analysis of musical phenomena with a concern for meanings that transcend the moment of performance, technical aspects of musical form, and even the aesthetic domain.

The essays that follow take up the basic problems articulated by Monson and find other ways to relate the social and musical worlds. Although the issue of "music in culture" has generally been the purview of ethnomusicology, it need not be exclusively so. Sabine Feisst addresses the topic by looking at John Cage's storied relationship to improvisation. Famously, Cage sought ways to make music that was at its core unpredictable and truly new, but he spurned improvisation. In particular, he distanced his "indeterminate" music from the kind of improvisation characteristic of jazz and other African American traditions. Cage was interested in removing the ego entirely from musical expression, and as he saw it, improvisation in jazz amounted to an extreme case in which musical and personal expression overlapped. Later in his life Cage embraced improvisation but, as Feisst shows, did not by extension embrace jazz-like practices in his own music. Rather, he found a place for improvisation in his work in the context of conditions under which the outcome of a performer's actions will be truly unforeseen—just the opposite of the sort of improvisatory practice envisioned by most jazz musicians.

Natalie Kononenko and Anne Rasmussen offer examples in which improvisation is part of people's relationship to the metaphysical. Kononenko deals with Slavic folk culture, one of the classic cases for the study of musical improvisation. She worked with lament singers in rural Ukraine. The lament tradition is, on the face of it, similar to the epic tradition, in which singers memorize poetic and musical formulae and improvise performances that are relatively similar but not identical. It is possible, for instance, to demonstrate the existence of bits of lament text used in the present that are found in essentially the same form in folkloric collections from nearly a century prior. However, the singers Kononenko worked with were adamant that they do not improvise—a term that for them (as for John Cage) implies the use of stock materials and relatively patterned modes of expression; rather, they simply allow their grief to pour out naturally and without artifice. Just as every funeral instance is distinct, so, too, every lament will be unique. Such is necessary, in fact, for it is only in this highly unusual form of performance that people can express their grief and desire for the deceased's return without risking the danger of creating unrest in the spirit world. Rasmussen, in her study of Koranic cantillation in Indonesia—the sung performance of text from the Koran—finds a different set of ideas about improvisation. In that context singers practice so that text and an Arabic modal system for melodic improvisation will become deeply ingrained. As this becomes part of the performers' (and listeners') "habitus," it creates opportunities for them to experience divine inspiration.

My own essay deals with the problems that have arisen in attempts to write the history of an improvised tradition. Histories of the arts—art history, music history, literary history, dance history, and so on—tend to be based on the idea of an evolving canon of works. Jazz fits uncomfortably in this model, as it is an art that is informed by both canonical high art and oral-traditional practices of creation. By looking at the "genius" concept as it has been applied to jazz, I argue that standard historiographic models both reveal and conceal necessary aspects of jazz's past.

Thomas Turino's essay in this collection considers the limits of improvisation in participatory music making. He writes about three different traditions that are based on the formulaic variation of relatively small amounts of thematic material. In each case some improvisation can be useful, to maintain interest in the music, but very much improvisation can be a problem. In each of the cases Turino discusses the guiding principle is social: the goal is to create a musical experience that draws the largest possible proportion of participants into an active, creative role. Too much improvisation can alienate potential participants, violating ethical as well as aesthetic aspects of the performance.

The second section shifts the focus to improvisation and musical education. Patricia Shehan Campbell's keystone essay sets the tone for this section, outlining a number of ways that learning, improvisation, and music can be approached. As she puts it, one can study "learning to improvise music," "improvising to learn music," and "improvising music to learn." Like other contributors to this book, Campbell sees musical improvisation as a special skill, but also as an important part of the ways people in many, if not all, societies engage each other and the world around them. Campbell's examples extend this set of ideas principally through an engagement with academic music education in the United States, but point to the significance of musical improvisation and educational processes in many contexts.

The essays that follow Campbell's represent a number of case studies that explore the potential for valuable insight from understanding improvisation and learning cross-culturally. Robert Levin and Charlotte Mattax Moersch look at aspects of improvisation in the Western classical tradition. Both come from the perspective of performer-scholars, writing on improvisation in repertoires they have played extensively, researched, and taught. Levin argues for the reintroduction of idiomatic improvisation into the education of instrumentalists. Learning such a skill can radically transform the act of performing from re-creative to creative, and "invest performances with spontaneity and danger." Mattax Moersch presents an account of the ways a Baroque player would have learned aspects of improvisation and, by extension, how these skills might be taught to today's players. This analysis becomes particularly resonant in relation to descriptions of other traditions found in the following chapters.

John Murphy, Bruno Nettl, and Stephen Slawek have each provided studies in which learning to improvise is a fundamental part of learning a tradition, an act of enculturation with social and aesthetic consequences. Murphy's study takes an explicitly ethnographic tack in seeking to advance understanding of institutional jazz education, a topic that has been much discussed, in print and more informally, by jazz scholars, musicians, and critics. Having taught jazz studies at the University of North Texas and conducted extensive research with students and faculty there, he argues that far more goes into learning jazz there than can be found in official classroom curricula. It is, his interlocutors say, a process that occupies their whole selves and that continues, despite its institutionalization, to incorporate much of an older oral-traditional model. Nettl discusses the ways learning to improvise in the Persian classical tradition differs from learning in either of the other two major Middle Eastern traditions, Turkish and Arabic. Nettl's teachers in Iran told him that they could not teach him to improvise; they could only teach him the Radif, and the Radif, in turn would teach him improvisation. In a remarkably expansive fashion the Radif teaches techniques, general principles of music, and general principles of social life. Next Slawek, who has much experience playing sitar as a disciple of Ravi Shankar, returns to his first musical home, the Italian American jazz guitar scene of south Philly, to see what lessons can come from a cross-cultural examination of learning to improvise. Although Ravi Shankar is adamant that improvisation in Hindustani music and improvisation in jazz are fundamentally different, in terms of technique and aesthetics, Slawek finds some compelling similarities in both ways of learning and "family"-style relationships between gharanas—schools of Hindustani music associated with particular lineages—and teacher-student lineages in south Philly.

The second section ends with an essay by John Toenjes on musical improvisation for modern dance classes. Here we have a close examination of a musical tradition that is almost entirely improvised and that, although an art in itself, is exclusively and intimately tied to a pedagogical context. This essay is groundbreaking because traditions such as this—totally improvised, contemporary, Western, non-avant-garde music—have been almost completely ignored by music scholars of all types. The music is hard to study using contemporary methods because it produces almost no works to speak of. This sort of music making (akin in some ways to the work of the improvising church organist) is basically invisible except to scholars and musicians interested in improvisation.

The final section of this collection is dedicated to musical improvisation and the creative process. Stephen Blum, writing on representations of improvisation, sets the tone for this section. Drawing on an exceptionally wide set of examples, he writes on the frameworks that different people at different times have used to understand improvisation in relation to other kinds of musical creativity, particularly the tripartite division into composition, performance, and improvisation. Lawrence Gushee takes up the terminological question, looking into how jazz musicians, composers, and writers described the act of improvisation in the 1920s and 1930s. He finds a remarkable wealth of terminology that does not obviously map, in a one-to-one manner, onto musical practices. Rather than look for that mapping in fine-grained nuances of practice or dismiss it as so much meaningless jargon, Gushee suggests a neat historical explanation. He finds that the terminology encodes an increasing abstraction in the conceptualization of improvisation that sets the stage for the major overhauling of the solo improviser's role in the music around 1940.

Robert Hatten, William Kinderman, and Nicholas Temperley all take up the question of improvisation's relationship to composition and performance in aspects of the Western classical tradition. Hatten shows that understanding the improvisational values inscribed in certain 19th-century works helps reveal them as "manifestations of vital music-cultural practices." Rather than museum pieces valuable for their universality and disembodied character, they become connected to an aesthetic world in which the work is only part of the story. Kinderman shows that an adequate understanding of Beethoven's piano music requires knowing how Beethoven himself improvised. Like so many other composers—Bach, Mozart, and Chopin being only the most obvious examples—Beethoven was exceptional at improvising and did so in performance often. Kinderman shows that even after Beethoven retired from concert life he continued to incorporate aspects of his improvisational style into his composed pieces. Rather than take the position that Goehr does in *The Imaginary Museum of Musical Works*—that Beethoven is representative of the moment in Western music when a deep line is drawn dividing improvisation from composition—Kinderman proposes that the two kinds of musical creativity remain intimately intertwined in Beethoven's work. The same is true of Chopin, as Nicholas Temperley writes. Temperley suggests that to fail to understand the ways Chopin's preludes relate to a history of improvisational preluding at the keyboard in the 18th and 19th centuries is to fail to understand them at all. Rather than an homage to Bach's preludes from the *Well-Tempered Clavier* (WTC) or a self-contained, internally coherent cycle, Chopin's collection reflects the varied possibilities that he might have drawn on to improvise preludes to pieces in performance at the time. As Temperley says, Chopin's collection is analogous to the preludes in the WTC only inasmuch as it "sums up a tradition of improvised preluding and completes its transformation into a form of premeditated composition that became a model for others."

Ali Jihad Racy, like a number of other writers in this collection, is a scholar-performer, renowned equally in the fields of ethnomusicology and Arabic classical performance. In his essay for this collection Racy asks why improvisation is so important to the creative process of Arabic classical musicians. Like a number of others, Racy gives answers connected not only to the themes of the final section, but to themes of the whole book. Improvisation in this tradition, he says, is central because it satisfies both aesthetic and emotional desires. Racy shows that, as noted by many of the writers in this volume, improvisation becomes the most intense and highly valued musical experience in the Arabic tradition because it most clearly involves musicians in a "dynamic of introspection and externalization," a process often connected with transcendence and the divine. In this regard, the taqasim genre, especially in its textless, vocal form, becomes imbued with the broadest expressive significance.

The division into three areas of focus—education, social relationships, and creative processes—in this collection is reminiscent of Alan Merriam's tripartite model for the study of ethnomusicology: sound, behavior, and context. As in his justly famous formulation, the three areas all impact one another. The essays in this volume show that learning to improvise and improvising to learn are inherently activities that are embedded in social networks, and are activities that profoundly impact the creative process of musicians regardless of their particular genre or tradition. Improvised music's social efficaciousness is intimately bound up with its creative process, and works in large measure because that creative process constantly engages our ability to continue to learn. Answers to questions about the creative process in music rely on the fact that music is a learned art and a learned behavior, and ultimately social. So each of the essays tells us something not only about musical sound, but about musical meaning, which is necessarily an interpersonal domain. The greatest strength of this collection is found in the juxtaposition of these disparate concerns.

NOTES

1. This may or may not be true elsewhere. It is my impression that it holds true at least throughout the West, but I can speak only from the perspective of people educated in music in American settings.

2. Definition taken from Merriam-Webster Online (*www.webster.com/dictionary/improvising*) and Compact Oxford English Dictionary Online (*www.askoxford.com/concise_oed/improvise?view=uk*).

REFERENCES

Ake, David. 2002. *Jazz Cultures*. Berkeley: University of California Press.

Baker, David. [1969] 1983. *Jazz Improvisation: A Comprehensive Method of Study for All Players*. [n.p.]: DB Music Workshop Publications. Rev. ed. Bloomington, Ind.: Frangipani Press.

———. 1971. *Techniques of Improvisation*. Chicago: Maher Publications.

Berliner, Paul. 1994. *Thinking in Jazz: The Infinite Art of Improvisation*. Chicago: University of Chicago Press.

Caton, Margaret. 2002. "Performance Practice in Iran: *Radif* and Improvisation." In *The Garland Encyclopedia of World Music*, Vol. 6: *The Middle East*, edited by Virginia Danielson, Scott Marcus, and Dwight Reynolds. New York: Routledge.

Coker, Jerry. 1964. *Improvising Jazz*. Englewood Cliffs, N.J.: Prentice-Hall.

———. 1970. *Patterns for Jazz*. Lebanon, Ind.: Studio P/R.

———. 2002. *Clear Solutions for Jazz Improvisers*. New Albany, Ind.: Jamey Aebersold Jazz.

Donington, Robert. 1989. *The Interpretation of Early Music*, new rev. ed. London: Faber.

Goehr, Lydia. 1992. *The Imaginary Museum of Musical Works: An Essay in the Philosophy of Music*. New York: Oxford University Press.

Monson, Ingrid. 1998. "Oh Freedom: George Russell, John Coltrane, and Modal Jazz." In *In the Course of Performance: Studies in the World of Musical Improvisation*, edited by Bruno Nettl with Melinda Russell, 149–68. Chicago: University of Chicago Press.

Nettl, Bruno. 1974. "Thoughts on Improvisation: A Comparative Approach." *Musical Quarterly* 60(1): 1–19.

Nettl, Bruno, ed., with Melinda Russell. 1998. *In the Course of Performance: Studies in the World of Musical Improvisation*. Chicago: University of Chicago Press.

Nettl, Bruno, et al. "Improvisation," *Grove Music Online*, edited by Laura Macy (accessed March 7, 2000), *www.grovemusic.com*.

Neubauer, Eckhard. 2002. "Arabic Writings on Music: Eighth to Nineteenth Centuries." In *The Garland Encyclopedia of World Music*, Vol. 6: *The Middle East*, edited by Virginia Danielson, Scott Marcus, and Dwight Reynolds. New York: Routledge.

Neumann, Frederick. 1978. *Ornamentation in Baroque and Post-Baroque Music: With a Special Emphasis on J. S. Bach*. Princeton, N.J.: Princeton University Press.

Nicholson, Sydney H. 1969. *The Elements of Extemporization*. Croydon, UK: Royal School of Church Music.

Quantz, Johann Joaquim. 1966. *On Playing the Flute*, 2nd ed., translated by Edward R. Reilly. New York: Schirmer Books.

Rowell, Lewis. 2000. "Theoretical Treatises." In *The Garland Encyclopedia of World Music*, Vol. 5: *South Asia, the Indian Subcontinent*, edited by Alison Arnold. New York: Garland Publishing.

Russell, George. 1959. *The Lydian Chromatic Concept of Tonal Organization for Improvisation*. New York: Concept Publishing.

Simms, Robert. 2000. "Scholarship Since 1300." In *The Garland Encyclopedia of World Music*, Vol. 5: *South Asia, the Indian Subcontinent*, edited by Alison Arnold. New York: Garland Publishing.

Small, Christopher. 1998a. *Music of the Common Tongue: Survival and Celebration in Afro-American Music*. Hanover, N.H.: Wesleyan University Press.

———. 1998b. *Musicking: The Meanings of Performing and Listening*. Hanover, N.H.: University of New England Press.

PART ONE

SOCIETY

ᕲ 1 ᕲ

JAZZ AS POLITICAL
AND MUSICAL PRACTICE

Ingrid Monson

In this article I wish to address the perennial question of the relationship between music and society—a question that is inevitably tied up with the politics of that relationship. On the one hand is the relationship between music and the big social questions: power, ideology, hegemony, globalization, economics, modernity, history, colonialism, race, sex, gender, and doubtless many others; on the other hand is the relationship between the act of making music and more local social issues such as the construction of communities, aesthetics, political resistance, kinship, and symbolic meanings.

In the first case—the domain of the big question—our scholarly voices tend to become abstract and disembodied as we find ourselves situating Music (with a capital M) in relation to other mediums of cultural practice—literature, visual arts, dance, and the various disciplines of the academy from sociology to cultural studies. In the second case, the connections we seek to describe are more intimate—those that bind music to relationships that are up close and personal—from romantic relationships to intracommunal debates over whose music is the most poignant symbol for communal identification, from kinship ties emerging from wedding celebrations to rancorous inter-cultural debates over the power relations among groups whose communities have disparate levels of social power.

To deal with these issues, I divide this essay into three parts: (1) a theoretical section that sets up a framework to explore why the legacy of practice theory continues to be important in ethnomusicology, (2) a section that illustrates the utility of the concept of practice at a musical level and (3) a section on the politics of race illustrating the utility of practice at a political level.

THEORY

As an ethnomusicologist, I have frankly been confused and bewildered over how to make sense of the full range of interconnections in which music is embedded, without spending an excessive amount of time talking about the interconnections and too little time talking about what drew me to the field in the first place, that is, the music. This is a particular problem in the interdisciplinary world of the academy in which many of us work or study, where the discrete boundaries among fields have been collapsing for years.

The field of ethnomusicology has often defined itself, at least since Alan Merriam, as the study of music as culture. But lately I have been tempted to describe it as the interdisciplinary study of music as cultural practice, in order to emphasize a practice-based anthropological conception of culture, which seems to me to be one of the principal differences between our discipline and the fields that have come to be called cultural studies, popular music studies, media studies, postcolonial studies, and globalization studies. In the past 20 years the field of ethnomusicology has moved from one in which "non-Western musics" or "folk musics" were the taken-for-granted subject matter, to one that has increasingly incorporated studies of popular musics, globalization, recording technologies, politics, identity, and gender. Indeed, ethnomusicologists tend to have very individualized interdisciplinary configurations, depending on the repertories they study.

This interdisciplinary expansion of ethnomusicology has been exciting, but I have noticed a reduction in the number of studies devoted to musical process. Indeed, in the last 10 years or so, close attention to musical sounds has even become *suspect* in our field. Since I began a joint appointment in the departments of music and African American studies three years ago, my interdisciplinary colleagues in African American studies often ask me for explanations of how musical processes work, while my colleagues in music tend to ask for my thoughts on cultural theory, politics, race, and gender. If people in music have become less interested in talking to each other about music (since we seem to take our shared knowledge about this subject area for granted), the public at large is clamoring to understand more about what they hear as well as what it means. This is particularly true of the mysterious process of improvisation, which so often is taken as one of the central points of difference between Western music and the repertories more typically explored by ethnomusicologists. Part of what we have to contribute as musical intellectuals is the capacity to make the musical process understandable to a broader public, something I believe we can do without dismembering its social connections.

In the effort to chase away my confusion and finish my book *Freedom Sounds,* which is about the impact of the civil rights movement and African independence on the history of jazz in the 1950s and 1960s, I have spent a great deal of time trying to make the text speak to the big social questions (power, race hegemony, etc.) and at the same time addressing the up close and personal aspects of music making and society. In the end I settled on a framework for organizing my thoughts that consists of three parts: discourse, structure, and practice. In a nutshell, I am interested in the ways social and musical practices weave interconnections between the more disembodied domains of discourse and structure.

Like all frameworks and analyses, this one is incomplete. It is something like a lead sheet that must be improvised upon, expanded, changed, trans-mogrified, or even abandoned in the course of breathing life into what might otherwise be a dull and plodding set piece. By discourse I mean ideas, ex-pressed most typically in language, that are deployed in the process of fram-ing arguments and justifying positions, and that possess the authority and prestige to shape how people think about the world at a particular moment. The big ideas such as modernity, race, power, and gender are included here, as well as local discourses constructed around particular genres, includ-ing aesthetics, symbolic value, and political meaning. This is discourse with Foucault as the point of departure, but not as the final landing place.

By structure I mean the social categories, laws, and economic systems that define the terms of social experience for large groups of people. The demographic categories used in social analysis such as race, gender, class, ethnicity, sexual orientation, educational level, and place of residence form one dimension of structure. Legal codes governing what is permitted/pro-hibited to members of various social groups and the system of economic exchange also form durable yet malleable configurations that shape what is possible for individuals. Although structures, as Anthony Giddens (1976, 61) and William Sewell (1992, 4) remind us, change over time in the process of social reproduction, they change far more slowly than social practices.

That leaves practice as the remaining term, the wild card, for it is what people choose to do given the particular structural and discursive configura-tions in which they live. Practice is about agency, that is, the implementation of cultural ideas, values, and structures through various kinds of social ac-tion. Practices can take many forms—musical, economic, sexual, ritual, and others—but key to their difference from discourse is their stress on embodied knowledge and action. Pierre Bourdieu, a central figure in the development of practice theory, stressed that every society transmits embodied patterns learned by emulation of the actions of others (rather than conveyed by dis-course) that serve in the development of "practical mastery" of social life (1977, 87–88).

Bourdieu had in mind the practical competence necessary to navigate everyday life within a particular culture, but its extension into the practicing of musicians is not hard to see. The activity of practicing—mastering scales, rhythms, harmony, patterns, repertory, and style by repeating passages over and over again—is simply part of what it is to be a musician. Once musicians have this musical knowledge "in their fingers" (and ears), they may no longer need to think consciously about the faculties they have drilled into their bodies through practicing. Thus mimesis and repetition—of live or recorded sources—lead to embodied knowledge and the freeing of the conscious mind for creative aesthetic discovery and expression.

But agency is never solely individual; existing social structures empower individuals differently, according to their place in a configuration of social hierarchies and institutional organizations. As William Sewell has noted, "the agency of fathers, executives, or professors is greatly expanded by the places they occupy in patriarchal families, corporations, or universities and by their consequent authority to bind the collectivity by their actions" (1992, 21). This is another way of arguing that positionality with respect to social constraints must always be accounted for. Social theory's idea of practice as social action, which has developed and expanded considerably since Bourdieu's *Outline of A Theory of Practice* (1977), is particularly useful for moving beyond deterministic understandings of how social structure and hegemonic discourses shape social life.[1] Although the social categories one occupies may be given—black, white, man, woman, rich, poor—through the creative deployment of various kinds of practices, an individual might succeed in doing many things that are not predicted by the social categories to which they belong. Indeed, aesthetic practice in 20th-century America—and musical practice in particular—has been extremely important in the vision of a society freer than the one we inherited. I am resuscitating a word that may sit uncomfortably on the tongues of many ethnomusicologists, musicologists, and anthropologists—aesthetic—not for its ability to describe sensibilities that fit well with the expected relationships between social categories and practice, but to provide a space for those that do not. An aesthetic as used here is simply a set of evaluative criteria deployed by some collective of individuals to argue for what is good or bad or who is inside or outside the communal circle.

Cultural and social anthropologists who developed the idea of practice theory in the sense used here have used it to move beyond the concept of culture as bounded and holistic to one that sees culture as emerging from hybrid practices and performances that are (1) contested and disputed, (2) overlapping with those of other cultures and (3) not bound neatly to space or geography, but rather mediated by recording, print, and broadcast media. The work of Sherrie Ortner (1996), Jean and John Comaroff (1991, 1997), and William Sewell (1992, 1999) has been particularly influential in this conceptual shift, in addition to a number of musical scholars whose collective work adds context and meaning: Steven Feld (1981, 1982, 1984, 1994), Sherrie Tucker (2000, 2001–2002), Jocelyne Guilbault (1993), Chris Waterman (1990a, 1990b, 1991), Bruno Nettl (1974, 1998), Travis Jackson (1998, 2002), Louise Meintjes, Paul Berliner (1994), Guthrie Ramsey (2003), John Chernoff (1979), Judith Becker (1981, 1996), Timothy Taylor (1997), and Charles Keil (1966, 1972, 1995). Like any list, this one is incomplete.

MUSIC AND PRACTICE

Consider the opening of John Coltrane's solo on "Wise One," recorded on April 27, 1964, with McCoy Tyner on piano, Elvin Jones on drums, and Jimmy Garrison on bass. Note the way the solo begins with humble whole notes and proceeds to the drama of a 16th-note-based rhythmic motive that becomes a key part of the larger shape of the solo (1964, 4:46–6:11).

There are many things that can be said about this musically, including the slow build, the careful reaching of registral high points, the clave-based time-keeping pattern by Elvin Jones, the relentlessness of the motivic development, the quasi–pedal point feeling of the bass line, and the dance between Tyner's comping line and Coltrane's melody. What is most interesting, however, in this context, is a mode of listening that can be called perceptual agency or perceptual practice. Perceptual agency is the idea that what we hear in a particular performance depends, in part, on where we focus our attention. It is somewhat analogous to the figure/ground problem in visual perception. In teaching students how to listen to jazz, I often ask them to listen from the bottom of the band up, focusing first on the bass line, then on the ride cymbal, then on the comping of the piano, *before* they listen to the soloist. Focusing listening on different parts of the ensemble, in other words, yields different experiences of the music.

This practice of shifting one's focus of attention is something that not only enriches the listening experience for audiences and consumers of recordings, but is an integral aural skill for improvising musicians, who must be able to locate themselves temporally and spatially and with respect to rhythm, harmony, melody, and the calls and responses of the other members of the band. The better one knows the tune, the less conscious attention needs to be focused on the basics of the tune, and the more attention can be freed up for taking improvisational risks and aurally scanning other parts of the band for moments of improvisational opportunity. Perceptual agency as embodied practice is an aural skill central to improvisers in many genres. Finding creative ways to illustrate this musical skill to broader audiences is something that musical scholarship ought to do.

Yet to listen to John Coltrane, one of the most iconic figures in jazz history, is to be embedded in a set of aurally indexical relationships that point to contexts of interpretation, history, and meaning well beyond the given recording. This is what I argued in *Saying Something* (1996), through the idea of intermusicality—that people hear music over time as well as in time; that is, they listen in relation to all the musics they have heard before, recognizing in particular performances similarities, differences, quotations, allusions, and surprises that contextualize their hearing in the moment. They also relate these aural signs and markers to a web of ideas and discourses they may have encountered—with respect to Coltrane, spirituality, genius, freedom, originality, African American consciousness—as well as to their understanding of history. They may hear the classic Coltrane quartet performance of "Wise One" in relation to the historical moment in which it was recorded—during the fervor of the civil rights movement and amid debates about black nationalism—and consider why Coltrane was one among many to be presented as a shining example of black excellence in a society reluctant to grant the most rudimentary rights of citizenship to African Americans. It is in this sense that music itself is discursive—a world of sonic interrelationships created through music making and listening practices that are part of the construction of webs of larger social and cultural meaning.

NEBA SOLO

Perceptual agency, on the one hand, can lead to thinking to about the web of interconnections between musical practice and larger arenas of discourse and history, but also significant is its potential utility in musical analysis at a more microscopic level.

In this regard, pianist Vijay Iyer's dissertation on cognition and embodiment is particularly useful in developing an in-depth view of the relationship between sound, body, and social practice. Based on recent work in cognitive science, Iyer urges us to move beyond viewing perception as the raw experience of sensation. Instead, he argues that "what is commonly called 'perception' should be viewed as a practice—an open-ended, intentional activity that is accomplished actively by the musical participants, while profoundly influenced by the perceiver's social context" (1998, 100). Recent research on auditory perception seems to support this observation. Reinier Plomp (2002, 1–3), for example, argues that the process by which our hearing system translates complex acoustical phenomena into perceptual images involves a combination of passive and active auditory processing.

The idea of perception as being partially volitional works well to explain the concept of perceptual agency: that what you hear in a particular performance can vary widely depending on which part of a multilayered texture you choose to focus your attention. The key to the perspective Iyer calls "embodied cognition" is to treat cognition and perception as something structured by the body and its contextual placement in the social environment—that is, viewing sensory processes and motor processes as "fundamentally inseparable, mutually informative, and structured so as to ground our conceptual systems" (1998, 24). The relationship between mind and body, abstract logic and sensory perception, it seems, is not one of hierarchy but one closer to mutual interaction. As Iyer has put it, "the functions of situated or embodied cognition neither replace wholesale, nor obey blindly, but rather supplement and complement the abstract, symbolic cognitive processes that we usually associate with 'thinking'" (70).

As an illustration, consider a musical pattern I learned when I went to Mali in 2002 to study with balafonist Neba Solo. Neba Solo is a Malian of Senufo ancestry whose gifts as a musician have earned him the title of "genius of the balafon." His full name is Souleymane Traoré, and he grew up in a small village not far from Sikasso, Mali, known as Nebadougou. Solo is short for Souleymane, and as his reputation spread, people began referring to him as Solo from Neba.[2]

The pattern presented in Figure 1.1 is one I had much difficulty learning and performing, especially when Neba Solo asked me to maintain it as an accompaniment figure for his improvisations. In terms of motoric skill, it really should have been the easiest, because it consists of four beats of eight notes, played by alternating hands. There are no abrupt leaps in either hand, so the technique of the pattern should be no obstacle. The figure shows the composite pattern with the sticking pattern for the right-handed player.[3] It is the core pattern of a composition by Neba Solo's father, Zano Traoré.

Next, I have rewritten the composite to illustrate the individual patterns being played by the right and left hands, respectively. Finally, I show the notes that Neba Solo emphasized as the melodic core of the pattern, by doubling these notes an octave below as I attempted to maintain the pattern. Even

FIGURE 1.1. Melodic pattern from a Senufo balafon piece as
played by Neba Solo. (Transcribed by Ingrid Monson)

though my ear had been directed to the left-hand melody (by my teacher
reinforcing this melody at an octave below), the right hand was crucial to
keeping the time together. Consequently, I found that the longer I played
the pattern, the harder it was for me to keep from turning the time around.
When I explained to Neba Solo that listening to my left hand made me lose
my right hand, he laughed and said that is always the way with the balafon.
Indeed, the process of mental focusing and the ability to switch vantage points
given increasingly complicated musical patterns seem to be among the key
pleasures of playing the instrument.[4]

When Neba Solo improvises on this composition, he often plays the composite pattern with the right hand alone as he improvises (virtuosically) with
the left. This becomes the home base from which he departs and returns
with extended stretches of improvisation. The relevance of this illustration
to the larger argument about discourse, structure, and practice is twofold:
first, the patterns of embodiment and the patterns of cognitive focus in the
process of listening can be, and often are, in counterpoint with one another;
and second, the idea of perception as practice is useful in considering the
connections of music not only to macrosociological issues and discourses,
but also to those micro-level issues of musical analysis that are so key to
understanding improvisation.

THE POLITICS OF RACE: SOUND STEREOTYPES

But what about the thornier questions such as those that pervade the study
and history of jazz: race, Jim Crow, hybridity, appropriation, and essential-
ism? How does a framework that uses practiced-based conceptions of cultural processes to mediate between discourse and structure assist in making
sense of the complexities here? The example of racial sound stereotypes in
jazz is illustrative. There is perhaps no topic more certain to elicit firestorms

of invective and counterinvective in jazz than the idea that there is a white sound and a black sound in jazz. Jazz, after all, as one line of argument goes, is universal—an art music open to all who master its repertory, improvisational mode of musical creation, and demand for individuality and originality. But, as others quickly point out, it is a music whose origins are in African America, and whose most central aesthetic components are rooted in the blues and that elusive thing called swing. To erase that aesthetic history in the name of universalism, many argue, whitewashes the history of the music in a way that allows non–African Americans to appropriate and profit from black cultural forms with impunity.

The basic terms of this debate have been part of the discursive air in jazz since at least the swing era, when Benny Goodman became the King of Swing, and Ellington and Basie were the Duke and Count. But the problem is much, much older, dating to when the enslaved first arrived in the 17th century, and white Americans began to notice the musical activities of the new arrivals. During the Great Awakening and the era of the camp meeting, missionizing evangelizers commented mostly on singing, declaring the slaves to have melody in their souls and an ear for music "above all the human species" (Epstein 1977).

In the early to mid-twentieth century, African American jazz musicians self-consciously took up the discourse of the modern artist as a means of legitimating their music and as part of a broader transformation of African America from rural to urban, and with it came the inexorable demand for full citizenship and inclusion in modernity's promise of equality and justice for all. Bebop musicians and the civil rights pioneers alike mobilized the language of merit, universal justice, and transcendence to demand entreé and recognition in mainstream American society, one in the language of art and the other in the language of politics. Yet, as in all things pertaining to race in the United States, the idea of the modern artist is a double-edged sword. If it enabled African American musicians to partially break out of a race-based, second-class citizenship by appealing to merit and genius, it also provided a rhetoric through which white musicians could insist that the music be understood as colorblind, and those who emphasized its African American history dismissed as reverse racists, or in more recent terminology, essentialists.

I use the following framework in my courses to move the discussion beyond the discourse of blackness and colorblindness, to the version of social constructionism I have been building here, and the idea of aesthetic practice, or aesthetic agency. By aesthetic agency, I mean the process by which performers draw from a multiplicity of aesthetics, not only those considered to be definitive of their home cultural or social category or categories. The big question is how do we talk about musics that are hybrid; musics that draw upon several overlapping aesthetic and generic sensibilities, without losing our ability to talk about the power relationships within the mixture—that is, without flattening the politics of intermixture and cultural borrowing within a feel-good version of multiculturalism that does not deal with a long history of racial tension? My historical point of departure is the debate over black and white sounds in jazz in the 1950s, cool jazz versus hard bop, aka West Coast versus East Coast.

The first issue to consider is defining an African American cultural aesthetic in music. The three most influential definitions of African American musical aesthetics have been Albert Murray's "blues aesthetic" (1976), Olly Wilson's "heterogeneous sound ideal" (1992), and Samuel Floyd's "ring shout" aesthetic (1995). Although practical limitations do not allow full elaboration of each author's perspective, there are four points on which the authors seem to agree.

1. The importance of the blues and what Olly Wilson calls a vocalization of sound in melodic sensibility. Of particular importance is timbral contrast and inflection in both singing and instrumental music. Included here are the blue note, the moan, the shout, and the imperative of making a horn talk.
2. Swing or groove, a sensibility that emerges from rhythmic organization at multiple levels, including rhythm section–soloist relationships, call and response, and riffs and other repeating patterns of various periodicities.
3. The interplay between the sacred and secular, and the sense that even secular music when performed at its highest level is concerned with the spiritual.
4. Embodiment, that music is closely connected to dance, motion, and participation.

It is not hard to find recorded examples that illustrate each of these musical dimensions and that most observers would accept as exemplifying African American musical aesthetics as defined by Murray, Wilson, and Floyd. The transition from sermon to song on the Georgia Sea Island Singers' recording of "Sign of the Judgment" (1998), the interplay between voice and guitar on Muddy Waters's "Walking Blues" (1950), and Ornette Coleman's bent and smeared notes on "Blues Connotation" (1960) all illustrate the centrality of vocal and timbral expressivity in African American music. The groove on James Brown's "Soul Power," Aretha Franklin's call and response with her band on "You're All I Need to Get By," and Lee Morgan's trumpet solo on

"Moanin'" likewise illustrate the importance of call and response and rhythmic organization at multiple levels. Ray Charles's "Come Back Baby," Charles Mingus's "Wednesday Night Prayer Meeting," and Kanye West's "Jesus Walks" are just a few examples of the interplay between the sacred and the secular in African American music.

There is no parallel literature aimed at defining the musical characteristics of a white mainstream musical aesthetic, but the ideas of what sounded white in 1950s jazz can be said to stem from two main aesthetic streams: the American popular song and classical music. Further, like the definitions for African American aesthetics, a combination of vocal style, preferred instrumental timbres, and rhythm is applicable here. Consider as examples Bing Crosby and Frank Sinatra, whose crooning singing styles were central to the American popular song of the 1940s and 1950s. Crooning generally refers to a round, smooth vocal tone; the use of expressive vibrato; and a sentimental emotional tone. If, as Olly Wilson has noted, African American musical aesthetics have tended to prefer a "heterogeneous sound ideal" that emphasizes timbral contrast, the smooth crooning styles of Crosby (1936) and Sinatra (1956) on their recordings of "Pennies from Heaven" illustrate a more homogeneous sound ideal. The smoothness and consistency of the vocal timbre, plus the sweetness and sentimentality of the delivery, are central to the appeal of this style. But by this definition we would also have to include African Americans Billy Eckstine and Nat King Cole among the crooners. Eckstine's recording of "Blue Moon" and Cole's recording of "Sweet Lorraine" (1957) illustrate their mastery of this style.

The mention of Nat Cole and Billy Eckstine is not intended to suggest that their music is somehow "less African American" because it shares aspects of aesthetic style with popular white singers of the day, but to make a different point: however central the black aesthetic in music, as defined by Wilson, Murray, and Floyd, has been in highlighting the distinctiveness of African American music, it is also true that it does not describe the full range of music making practiced by African Americans.

The debate over West Coast jazz and hard bop in the 1950s often centered on saxophone styles. White musicians such as Stan Getz, who was voted the top tenor saxophonist from 1950 to 1959, and Paul Desmond, who became the favorite alto saxophonist after Charlie Parker died in 1955, both had saxophone styles that were described as light and smooth in timbre, and that often contrasted with the edgier and bluesier hard bop saxophone sound. Getz's recording of "On the Alamo" and Paul Desmond's of "Pennies from Heaven" both revel in a sweet, smooth timbral palate and relaxed time feel. But the complexity of the sonic relationships among black and white musicians is considerably complicated by the fact that many of the 1950s white saxophonists modeled themselves on African American saxophonists of the previous generation—more specifically on Lester Young and Johnny Hodges. A similar timbral lightness can be heard on Lester Young's "Tickle Toe" (Count Basie 1940) and Johnny Hodges's "Day Dream" (1940). Would anyone really suggest that Lester Young and Johnny Hodges sound "less black" because non–African American saxophonists modeled their sounds on them, rather than on the saxophonists of hard bop, such as Sonny Rollins and John Coltrane?

The big question lurking behind all these examples is, what is the relationship among sounds, social categories, and individual choice and how malleable is it? In the late 1940s and early 1950s jazz musicians drew upon a multiplicity of aesthetic perspectives in fashioning individual sounds, including the African American vernacular aesthetics, the aesthetics of the American popular song, the aesthetics of classical music, and, for some artists, Caribbean sounds such as Cuban music (remember the mambo craze) and calypso. Individual musicians, regardless of their ethnic home base, can and did infuse their playing with musical aesthetics from both within and beyond their expected social categories.

Consequently, there were more than enough musical examples for Leonard Feather to use to confound Roy Eldridge in a blindfold test in 1951. Eldridge had assured Feather that he could tell whether a musician was black or white simply by listening to his or her recordings. But Feather, playing for him examples in which the white musicians sounded particularly bluesy and the black artists smooth and sentimental, proved Eldridge wrong in more than half of the cases. According to an article by Feather titled "Little Jazz Goes Colorblind," Eldridge was forced to concede in print that he couldn't tell the difference between white and black artists by listening to recordings alone, and that that Feather had won the argument.

But did he? If musical sounds aren't wholly determined by social category, does it follow that ethnic background, social location, and cultural socialization have no bearing on aesthetics whatsoever? American music is far more mixed aesthetically than its makers are socially. In other words, the hybridity and intermixture that can be heard in various musical examples is not accompanied by a similar intermixture in where people live, where people go to school, where they worship, where they work, and whom they marry. Indeed, it often seems that the only aspects of African American culture that non–African Americans really want access to are the fun parts: music, dancing, sex, and sports. As Greg Tate has suggested, it's as though white

Americans want "everything but the burden" that comes with being black in a racially stratified society.

The larger point here is that regardless of how well a white American or other non–African American may master the sonic parameters of African American musical style, as long as a racially stratified social structure exists, she or he will have a different social relationship to the music than will an African American. This is not to say that the relationship is less real, less musical, inflected by class, or less important, but only to say that structural and historical issues beyond our individual agency make it different. To say this in another way: the structural legacy of our racially stratified society establishes a particular configuration of social positions that gives us a particular point of departure based on where we were born, where we were raised, how affluent our family was, what color our skin is, what gender we are, and other conditions. This is an especially important issue for those of us who are white to think through. To not acknowledge the different social configurations, which is another way of denying the existence of white privilege, is disrespectful to the history of the African American music we claim to love.

In the debate over ethnic particularity and colorblindness in jazz of the 1950s and 1960s, the greatest difference between black and white musicians in the 1950s was that white musicians had access to the structural privileges of whiteness, no matter what their relationship was to the blues and African American aesthetics more broadly, whereas black musicians experienced racial discrimination, no matter what their relationship was to Western modernism and mainstream culture. American Jim Crow social structure and the music industry, with its de jure and de facto segregation of "black" and "white," ensured this.

The key here is acknowledging one's positionality within a social structure not of one's making, and this is far more complex than simply thinking about race. For race is inflected by gender, class, shade of color, sexuality, ethnicity, and national origin in various proportions.

When Leonard Feather insisted at the end of his blindfold test that Roy Eldridge admit that music was colorblind, he was asking Eldridge to forfeit his claim to having a special connection to black music by virtue of being raised as an African American. He was asking him to say that race and history don't matter; it had become everybody's music now. This was the situation despite the fact that the white bands had become the public face of swing music and that Eldridge had recently faced many racial problems with accommodations and theaters while touring with a white band (Artie Shaw). What other ethnic group is asked so regularly to do the same? Are Italians

decried as essentialist if they express a feeling of special relationship to Italian opera and the various Italian cultural values and practices in which it is
historically embedded? Are women asked not to feel a special relationship
to menstruation, childbirth, and the experience of sexism? Are Irish Americans asked not to feel a special relationship to St. Patrick's Day even though
it has become a generalized American event? So when whites feel excluded
when African Americans claim to have a special connection to the history
and culture of African American music, are they being fair? Such a reaction
seems especially churlish given the history of economic relations between
white and black performers.

The position being articulated here is something like what Paul Gilroy in
The Black Atlantic terms "anti-anti-essentialism," an anti-essentialism that
does not deny the lived experience of race, but rather views "racialised subjectivity as the product of social practices that supposedly derive from it" (1993,
102). For Gilroy this is about imagining a solidarity that is not transmitted
through fixed essences, but rather is constructed and transmitted through
everyday interactions and ruptures—in other words through a set of social
practices. What this ultimately means is that there are structural limits to
aesthetic agency and practice. Even though individuals in the jazz world can
reach beyond their sociologically defined categories through practical acts
of imagination, emulation, and creativity, their social relationship to styles
not of their home social categories is, frustratingly, shaped by the continuing
race, class, and gender, hierarchies in American and global society. A white
person might sound convincingly bluesy, a woman swing hard, and an African American excel in classical music, but they still carry the advantages and
disadvantages of their various respective social positions, whether they like it
or not, and they are symbolically interpreted against the social categories that
are assumed to be most socially relevant to them. This is not to say that over
time our efforts to move beyond the rigidities of social categories don't have
a cumulative effect, but only to argue that the larger structural configuration
changes much more slowly than aesthetic and musical practice.

This basic framework of discourse, structure, and practice has enabled
me to construct an analysis that lies somewhere between the social determinism that remains in many of the macro-level theories of globalization,
postcolonialism, and poststructuralism, and the overly loose ideas of free-
floating signifiers, limitless individual agency, and pastiche that undermine
the liberatory and utopian aspirations of postmodernism. I do not offer it
as the only way to think through these problems, but as one option that has
been particularly helpful to me. That the music itself, in all its improvisational,

aesthetic, and technical complexity, is a central part of this flexible concept of culture as practice, is the parting thought I leave.

NOTES

1. Indeed, Bourdieu's own determinism has been critiqued in these further extensions of practice theory. See Calhoun et al. (1993).

2. I am doing a larger project on the music of Neba Solo. Excellent recordings of his compositions that are available in the United States include *Kene Balafons*, *Kenedougou Foly*, and *Can 2002*.

3. The tuning illustrated here is approximate.

4. These points are consistent with many of those made by John Chernoff (1979).

REFERENCES

Becker, Judith. 1996. "Trance Talk for Kalamazoo." Unpublished manuscript.

Becker, Judith, and Alton Becker. 1981. "A Musical Icon: Power and Meaning in Javanese Gamelan Music." In *The Sign in Music and Literature*, edited by Wendy Steiner, 203–15. Austin: University of Texas Press.

Berliner, Paul F. 1994. *Thinking in Jazz: The Infinite Art of Improvisation*. Chicago: University of Chicago Press.

Bourdieu, Pierre. 1977. *Outline of a Theory of Practice*. Translated by R. Nice. New York: Cambridge University Press.

Calhoun, Craig, Edward LiPuma, and Moishe Postone, eds. 1993. *Bourdieu: Critical Perspectives*. Chicago: University Chicago Press.

Chernoff, John Miller. 1979. *African Rhythm and African Sensibility: Aesthetics and Social Action in African Musical Idioms*. Chicago: University of Chicago Press.

Comaroff, Jean, and John L. Comaroff. 1991. *Of Revelation and Revolution: Christianity, Colonialism, and Consciousness in South Africa*, Vol. 1. Chicago: University of Chicago Press.

———. 1997. *Of Revelation and Revolution: The Dialectics of Modernity on a South African Frontier*, Vol. 2. Chicago: University of Chicago Press.

Epstein, Dena S. 1977. *Sinful Tunes and Spirituals: Black Folk Music and the Civil War*. Urbana: University of Illinois Press.

Feld, Steven. 1981. "'Flow Like a Waterfall': The Metaphors of Kaluli Music Theory." *Yearbook for Traditional Music* 13: 22–47.

———. 1982. *Sound and Sentiment: Birds, Weeping, Poetics, and Song in Kaluli Expression*. Philadelphia: University of Pennsylvania Press.

———. 1984. "Sound Structure as Social Structure." *Ethnomusicology* 28(3): 383–409.

———. 1994. "Aesthetics as Iconicity of Style (Uptown Title); or, (Downtown Title) 'Lift-Up-Over Sounding': Getting into the Kaluli Groove." In *Music Grooves: Essays and Dialogues*, edited by Charles Keil and Steven Feld, 109–50. Chicago: University of Chicago Press.

Floyd, Samuel A., Jr. 1995. *The Power of Black Music: Interpreting Its History from Africa to the United States*. New York: Oxford University Press.

Gilroy, Paul. 1993. *The Black Atlantic: Modernity and Double Consciousness*. Cambridge, Mass.: Harvard University Press.

Giddens, Anthony. 1976. *New Rules of Sociological Method: A Positive Critique of Interpretation Sociologies*. London: Hutchinson.

Guilbault, Jocelyne. 1993. *Zouk: World Music in the West Indies*. Chicago: University of Chicago Press.

Iyer, Vijay. 1998. "Microstructures of Feel, Macrostructures of Sound: Embodied Cognition in West African and African-American Musics." Ph.D. dissertation, University of California, Berkeley.

Jackson, Travis A. 1998. "Performance and Musical Meaning: Analyzing 'Jazz' on the New New York Scene." Ph.D. dissertation, Columbia University, New York.

———. 2002. "Jazz as Musical Practice." In *The Cambridge Companion to Jazz*, edited by Mervyn Cooke and David Horn, 83–95. Cambridge; New York: Cambridge University Press.

Keil, Charles. 1966. *Urban Blues*. Chicago: University of Chicago Press.

———.1972. "Motion and Feeling Through Music." In *Rappin' and Stylin' Out: Communication in Black Urban America*, edited by Thomas Kochman, 83–100. Urbana: University of Illinois Press.

———. 1995. "The Theory of Participatory Discrepancies: A Progress Report." *Ethnomusicology* 39(1): 1–19.

Matory, J. Lorand. 1999. "The English Professors of Brazil: On the Diasporic Roots of the Yoruba." *Comparative Studies in Society and History* 41(1): 72–103.

Monson, Ingrid. 1996. *Saying Something: Jazz Improvisation and Interaction*. Chicago: University of Chicago Press.

Murray, Albert. 1976. *Stomping the Blues*. New York: DaCapo.

Nettl, Bruno. 1974. "Thoughts on Improvisation: A Comparative Approach." *Musical Quarterly* 60(1): 1–19.

———. 1998. "Introduction: An Art Neglected in Scholarship." In *In the Course of Performance: Studies in the World of Musical Improvisation*, edited by Bruno Nettl with Melinda Russell, 1–23. Chicago: University of Chicago Press.

Ortner, Sherry B. 1996. *Making Gender: The Politics and Erotics of Culture*. Boston: Beacon Press.

Plomp, Reinier. 2002. *The Intelligent Ear: On the Nature of Sound and Perception*. Mahwah, N.J.: Lawrence Erlbaum Associates.

Ramsey, Guthrie P. 2003. *Race Music: Black Cultures from Bebop to Hip-Hop*, Music of the African Diaspora No. 7. Berkeley: University of California Press.

Sewell, William H., Jr. 1992. "A Theory of Structure: Duality, Agency and Transformation." *American Journal of Sociology* 98(1): 1–29.

———. 1999. "The Concept(s) of Culture." In *Beyond the Cultural Turn: New Directions in the Study of Society and Culture*, edited by Victoria E. Bonnell and Lynn
Hunt, 35–61. Berkeley: University of California Press.

Taylor, Timothy D. 1997. *Global Pop: World Music, World Markets*. New York: Routledge.

Tucker, Sherrie. 2000. *Swing Shift: "All-Girl" Bands of the Forties*. Durham, N.C.:
Duke University Press.

———. 2001–2002. "Big Ears: Listening for Gender in Jazz Studies." *Current Musicology* 71–73: 375–408.

Waterman, Christopher. 1990a. *Jùjú: A Social History and Ethnography of an African
Popular Form*. Chicago: University of Chicago Press.

———. 1990b. "Our Tradition Is a Very Modern Tradition." *Ethnomusicology* 34(3):
367–80.

———. 1991. "The Uneven Development of Africanist Ethnomusicology: Three Issues
and a Critique." In *Comparative Musicology and Anthropology of Music: Essays on
the History of Ethnomusicology*, edited by Bruno Nettl and Philip Bohlman, 169–86.
Chicago: University of Chicago Press.

Wilson, Olly. 1992. "The Heterogeneous Sound Ideal in African-American Music." In
New Perspectives on Music: Essays in Honor of Eileen Southern, edited by Josephine
Wright with Samuel Floyd, Jr., 327–38. Warren, Mich.: Harmonie Park Press.

DISCOGRAPHY

Brubeck, Dave. 1955. "Pennies from Heaven." *Brubeck Time*.

Cole, Nat King. 1957. *After Midnight*. Hollywood, Calif.: Capitol W-782.

Coleman, Ornette. 1960. "Blues Connotation." *This Is Our Music*. Atlantic 7567–
80767–2.

Coltrane, John. 1964. "Wise One." *Crescent*. Englewood Cliffs, N.J.: Impulse! IMPD-
200.

Count Basie and His Orchestra. 1940. "Tickle Toe." New York: Columbia; reissued
on *The Essential Count Basie, Vol. 2*, 1987. Columbia CK40835.

Crosby, Bing. 1936. *Best of Bing Crosby*. MCA Records MCAD-11942.

"Georgia Sea Islands." 1998. *Southern Journey Volume 12*. Cambridge, Mass.: Rounder
CD 1712.

Getz, Stan. 1950. "On the Alamo." *The Roost Quartets*. New York: Roulette CDP 7
96052 2.

Hodges, Johnny. "Day Dream." *The Great Ellington Units*.

Sinatra, Frank, and Nelson Riddle. 1956. "Songs for Swingin' Lovers!" Capitol CDP
7 46570 2.

Waters, Muddy. 1950. "Walkin' Blues." *The Real Folk Blues*. MCA Records/Chess;
088 112 822–2.

JOHN CAGE AND IMPROVISATION:
AN UNRESOLVED RELATIONSHIP

Sabine M. Feisst

Improvisation, a neglected phenomenon in Western art music in the early 20th century, has been reconsidered by many composers since the 1950s. John Cage, a key figure and catalyst in the avant-garde movement, was among the first to embrace the indeterminate and unpredictable elements of a musical process—which are characteristics of improvisation. Yet, throughout most of his career, Cage displayed ambiguity and adversity toward improvisation and warned performers against improvisatory performances of his own scores, challenging his society's well-worn concepts of free music making and improvisation. Cage's skepticism toward improvisation was symptomatic of avant-garde composers and sheds light on the complexity of improvisation, particularly in the context of new music. This article examines Cage's reasons for his definitions and dislike of improvisation and how Cage circumvented, toyed with, or used improvisation in his works.

EARLY CONSIDERATIONS OF IMPROVISATION

Cage's views of improvisation changed in the course of his career many times. In the early 1930s he took an improvisatory approach to composition when he chose "an entirely different way of composing, which was through improvisation, and improvisation in relation to texts" (Fleming and Duckworth 1989, 16). He explained, "My inspiration was carried along on the wings of Aeschylus and Gertrude Stein. I improvised at the piano and attempted to write down what I played before I forgot it" (Kostelanetz 1993, 29). Most of this music did not survive. Dissatisfied with the "glaring weakness of this method," Cage studied Ebenezer Prout's music theory but continued to consider improvisation as an element of composition (29). In 1935 he composed "Quest" for amplified small sounds and piano solo, which is among his earliest surviving pieces incorporating improvisation. Written for the dancer-choreographer Martha Deane, the first of the two movements, involving amplified sounds of mechanical toys and other small objects, was an improvisation and devoid of a score.

After 1935 he began to conceptualize the four main aspects of his newly acquired compositional processes: material, structure, method, and form. According to Cage, musical material consists of sounds (including noises) and silences. Structure is no longer based on functional harmony, but on temporal divisions and proportions. Method refers to the note-to-note procedure, and form is the "morphological line of the sound-continuity" (Kostelanetz 1968, 78–79). The element of improvisation is not completely absent within these categories. During the late 1930s and 1940s, when Cage created his all-percussion works and compositions for prepared piano based on the so-called macro-microcosmic temporal structure, he reflected on the possibilities of improvisation within his compositional processes. He explained that "three of the four components could be improvised, form, material and method, and that three could be organized, structure, method and material. And the two in the middle, material and method, could be either organized or improvised" (Charles 1981, 36). The only category from which improvisation was excluded is structure. This implies that for him structure was the foundation of a piece, and after the structure was organized, improvisation could be used as a compositional means, and material and method could be handled more freely. Form generally depended on the outcome of the compositional process. Cage viewed "form as the aspect of mystery in which the life of an organism sometimes cloaks itself. If you attempt to organize it, you kill it" (Charles 1981, 36).

In his influential essay "The Future of Music: Credo" (circa 1940), Cage also points out that the temporal structure in music could become the basis for group improvisation: "Methods of writing percussion music have as their goal the rhythmic structure of a composition. As soon as these methods are crystallized into one or several widely accepted methods, the means will exist for group improvisations of unwritten but culturally important music. This has already taken place in Oriental cultures and in hot jazz" (Cage 1961, 5). Hence, as early as around 1940 Cage already predicted the phenomenon of collective improvisation and the emergence of improvisation groups such as Musica Elettronica Viva, The Scratch Orchestra, and Nuova Consonanza in the 1960s. Moreover, he saw certain affinities between his methods of rhythmic structuring (square root form), Hindu tala, and hot jazz (Kostelanetz 1993, 63).

Even though such views seem speculative, they derive from his early consideration of improvisation, non-Western music, and New Orleans jazz (21–22). Cage's interest in jazz can be linked to his exploration of percussion sounds, favored in jazz (and non-Western music), and his performances of William Russell's jazz- and Latin-influenced all-percussion works.[1] During the early 1940s, when Cage stayed in Chicago, he not only attended jam sessions and taught group improvisation in his experimental music class at the Chicago School of Design, but he also toyed with jazz idioms in works such as "Third Construction" (1941), "Credo in Us" (1942), "Ad lib" (1942) and "Jazz Study" (circa 1942) (Revill 1993, 75; Kumpf 1976, 92).

IMPERSONALITY

Starting in the late 1940s Cage studied south and east Asian philosophies, and his aesthetic ideas about composition and improvisation changed. Influenced by the Indian art scholar Ananda Coomaraswamy and his book *The Transformation of Nature in Art* (1934), Cage became fascinated with the idea of art as "the imitation of Nature in her manner of operation" and opposed to art as an expression of emotion. He began to reject artistic self-expression. A paramount concept in 19th-century Western music, self-expression is also a fundamental aspect of improvisation. Improvisation often involves the expression of a personal style, emotions, likes and dislikes. Even if carried out in a passive manner—for instance, as a kind of "automatic writing"— improvisation reflects the performer's musical baggage, his subconscious musical experience, motor patterns, and idioms. If understood as an aurally transmitted complex creative act involving the use of well-rehearsed patterns, consideration of rules, and assessment of the ongoing process, improvisation appears as a respect-commanding autonomous activity. It highlights the improviser's artistic abilities, subjectivity, and virtuosity. Hence improvisation frequently tends in the direction of personality cult. Nothing could be farther from Cage's new aesthetic, as he emphasized: "Improvisation is something that I want to avoid. Most people who improvise slip back into their likes and dislikes, and their memory, and they don't arrive at any revelation that they're unaware of" (Turner 1990, 472). He dismissed improvisation because it is generally descriptive of the performer and not descriptive of what happens (Kostelanetz 1987, 222).

CHANCE OPERATIONS AND EXPERIMENT

In the early 1950s Cage began to instill works such as the "Concerto for Prepared Piano and Orchestra" and "Sixteen Dances" (both 1950–1951) with compositional impersonality by using vertical charts (i.e., collections of sonorities) and employing concentric circles and squares as a means to select sounds from the charts. He therefore limited free compositional choices in the note-to-note process. In a further step, in addition to charts containing sounds, silences, durations, and so on, he applied chance operations involving the 64 hexagrams of the *I Ching*, the Chinese "Book of Changes," and tosses of coins to free sounds from his personal taste and let the sounds be themselves. Later Cage let chance enter his compositional processes by employing imperfections of paper, star maps, and other sources to determine the nature and succession of sounds. Through such procedures, he eliminated deliberate relationships between sounds and created a novel type of abstract musical continuity largely "free of individual taste and memory (psychology) and also of the literature and 'traditions' of art" (Cage 1961, 57–59). This new kind of objectified musical continuity seemed to counteract all types of communicative improvisation based on common practice idioms or phraseology as they are found in jazz. And indeed, Cage stated, "The form of jazz suggests too frequently that people are talking—that is, in succession—like in a panel discussion or a group of individuals simply imposing their remarks without responding to one another. If I am going to listen to a speech then I would like to hear some words" (Kostelanetz 1991, 162). Further, Cage preferred chance operations to improvisation since for him "chance operations are a discipline, and improvisation is rarely a discipline" (Kauffmann et al. 1966, 46). Yet both chance operations and improvisation, if interpreted literally, aim at the unpredictable or *unforeseeable*.

Besides chance operations, Cage embraced and redefined the terms "experiment" and "experimental music," which were often used as a negative description for novel and strange compositions. An experiment connotes trial, unpredictability, failure, success, scientific research, and proof, but Cage defined it as a compositional act the outcome of which is unknown (Cage 1961, 69). His primary goal became exploring the unforeseeable and making discoveries. Chance operations undoubtedly became an ideal device for creating experimental works and transcending imagination and inspiration, as Cage himself acknowledged: "Chance, to be precise, is a leap, provides a leap out of reach of one's own grasp of oneself" (162). Cage's notions of experiment and improvisation are not compatible, due to his belief that improvisation "does not lead you into a new experience, but into something with which you're already familiar" (Darter 1982, 21). Many other composers and improvisers, however, see experimentalism and improvisation as related to one another.

Compositions based on chance operations can lead to works in which every sound aspect is determined, leaving no interpretive flexibility to the performer. This was the case in "Music of Changes" (1951). In fact, this work's sound material and the system to which chance procedures were applied yielded a very complex score, an "object more inhuman than human" according to Cage (1961, 36). And it induced him to introduce the compositional dimension of indeterminacy with regard to performance, granting the performer a certain degree of creative freedom. Although one can observe indeterminacy in many works of the performing arts through the centuries, the word was not part of the music vocabulary until the late 1950s. And Cage was one of the first to use this term in musical contexts. In his essay titled "Indeterminacy" he presented and explained compositions that were indeterminate with respect to their performance, such as Bach's "Art of the Fugue," which lacks specific instrumentation (35). By means of novel and ambiguous notation, Cage achieved indeterminacy in manifold ways, leaving various aspects of sounds and their combination for the performer to choose. Compositions such as "Concert for Piano and Orchestra" (1957–1958) and "Variations I–VIII" (1958–1978) reveal a high degree of indeterminacy. The question, however, arises of whether Cage's indeterminate scores invite the performer to improvise. Improvisation, in fact, is often defined as the difference between notation and the sound product.

Answers to this question can be found in the realizations of David Tudor, pianist, composer, and Cage's most important artistic associate, for whom many indeterminate works between 1952 and the mid-1970s were written. Far from using these indeterminate scores as invitations to improvise, Tudor followed Cage's instructions and prepared by means of measurements and calculations practical performance scores, "second texts" derived from the composer's scores (Holzaepfel 1994, viii). These performance scores, which specified the musical content, but also contained devices to bring about unpredictability, were generally works "perpetually in progress"; it was, according to Cage, "in David's nature not to repeat what has been done" (Charles 1981, 178). Thus Cage expected from all of his performers a similar attitude

and presupposed discipline and compositional decisions within the framework he designed. Performers were expected to work out all or part of the
score ahead of the performance from materials and directions Cage provided.
Performers have to strive for impersonality and nonintention and engage in
situations with unknown outcome. Sometimes they need to employ chance
operations. Cage stated once that his indeterminate pieces "resemble cam-
eras that don't tell you what picture to take, but enable you to take a picture"
(Campana 1985, 109). This explains further why Cage distanced himself from
improvisation. He did not want to encourage common habits, subjective and
ultimately predictable acts, among improvising performers.

Among Cage's most significant indeterminate works is "Atlas Eclipticalis"
(1961–1962) for orchestra, whose notation Cage derived by placing trans-
parencies with staves over star maps and interpreting the stars' positions
as notes. There are 86 individual parts for the symphony orchestra's instruments, including 12 mostly unspecified percussion parts. There is, however,
no master score for the conductor, only a "road map." The number of parts
and passages to be played, the order of the sections, and the duration of the
whole work, for instance, are left to the performers' choice. The work can
be performed in whole or part in any ensemble (from chamber to orchestral), simultaneously with specific other compositions by Cage if desired.
The notations are ambiguous, and performers need to find the perfect balance between discipline and choice by using objective strategies such as coin
tosses to overcome their personal taste and remove value judgment from the
decision-making process.

The performance history of "Atlas Eclipticalis" and numerous other works
by Cage proves that his suspicion about improvisation was justified. In 1963
Leonard Bernstein chose to present "Atlas Eclipticalis" together with works
by Morton Feldman (" . . . Out of 'Last Pieces'") and Earle Brown ("Available Forms II") at the New York Philharmonic concerts of February 6–9,
1964. Perhaps because of Bernstein's perception of a certain "improvisatory"
quality in the chosen works, he decided to include a separate free orchestra
improvisation. Unhappy about Bernstein's decision, Cage wrote him four
months before the concert:

> Dear Lenny, I ask you to reconsider your plan to conduct the orchestra in an
> improvisation. Improvisation is not related to what the three of us are doing in
> our works. It gives free play to the exercise of taste and memory, and it is exactly
> this that we, in differing ways, are not doing in our music. Since, as far as I know,
> you are not dedicated in your own work to improvisation, I can only imagine

that your plan is a comment on our work. . . . Surely there must be some less provocative way to conclude the program, one which will leave no doubt as to your courage in giving to your audiences the music which you have chosen to present. With best wishes and friendliest greetings, John Cage.[2]

The concert lived up to Cage's worst fears: not only did Bernstein lead the orchestra in an improvisation preceding "Atlas Eclipticalis," which was performed as a live electronic version simultaneously with "Winter Music" (for 1–20 pianos), but the orchestra also improvised freely in Cage's piece.[3] The orchestra members disregarded their parts, played scales, quoted melodies from other works, talked, experimented with the contact microphones attached to their instruments, and even trampled on the electronic devices. This behavior, however, seemed partly beyond Bernstein's control. During the performance he did not assume the traditional role of a conductor (a clock-like mechanical device in front of the orchestra was used to indicate time), and in the rehearsal process he seemed indifferent. When he reprimanded the orchestra for their conduct afterward, however, the damage had been done. This experience largely explains why, for a long time, Cage viewed his concepts of chance operations and indeterminacy as incompatible with improvisation.

IMPROVISATION—NATURE—POLITICS

In the 1970s, during a period in which Cage became involved with the writings of Thoreau, ecology, and politics, he reconsidered improvisation. He even used improvisation emphatically as subtitle and title for a number of works. "Child of Tree" (1975), "Branches" (1976), "Inlets," and "Pools" (both 1977) are subtitled "Improvisation 1a," "Improvisation Ib," "Improvisation II" and "Improvisation IIa," respectively. Cage continued this series in the 1980s with two pieces titled "Improvisation III" and "Improvisation IV" (1980, 1982), which were followed by "Improvisation A + B" (1986) and three "c-[C]omposed Improvisations" (1987–1990). But now his goal had become to free improvisation from taste, memory, and feelings, as he explained: "The reason I didn't want to improvise was that I would be expressing my feelings. I do want a music in which I don't do that. So when I use improvisation now, it must be in situations where I have a low degree of influence" (Cope 1980, 21). He also stressed that he wanted "to make improvisation a discipline" and that it would involve "doing something beyond the control of the ego" (Kauffmann et al. 1966, 46). In pieces such as "Child of Tree," "Branches," and "Inlets" the players have to make discoveries with unfamiliar materials. Both "Child of Tree" and "Branches" are percussion works requiring "instruments" such as pod rattles from a Mexican poinciana tree and cacti amplified by contact microphones. Cage pointed out that in these pieces "the instruments are so unknown that as you explore, say the spines of a cactus, you're not really dealing with your memory or your taste. You're exploring. As you play you destroy the instrument—or change it—because when you make a spine vibrate it begins to lose its same pliability" (Holmes 1981, 3). The temporal structure of these pieces and the "instrumentation" of each section have to be determined by the performer through chance operations ahead of time.

With "Inlets," for three performers using water-filled conch shells and a fire, live or recorded, Cage introduced a second type of improvisation, which he also classified as "music of contingency" (Cope 1980, 21). The players moving the conch shells have no control over the occurrence of the gurgles and their rhythms since they cannot see the water passing through the shell's chambers. Here the music results from a separation of cause and effect, and the players cannot rely on personal taste or memory (Cage 1993, 43–45). He also called this new improvisational concept "structural" improvisation, explaining

> What delights me in this thing . . . is that the performer, the improviser, and the listener too are discovering the nature of the structure. . . . Improvisation . . . that is to say not thinking, not using chance operations, just letting the sound be, in the space, in order that the space can be differentiated from the next space which won't have that sound in it. (Cage and Reynolds 1979, 581)

It seems that natural materials were the ideal source of the conditions Cage sought in his music: unpredictability and uncontrollability. In improvising with natural materials, discovery replaces the expression of ideas or emotions. Works such as "Child of Tree," "Branches," and "Inlets" also reveal an ecological quality, where humans do not control nature but accept and try to discern her laws.

In works written in the 1980s such as Improvisation III and Improvisation IV, performers operate cassette players. In the former work, four musicians play identical cassettes with sound of a single kind. During the course of the performance each player is allowed to "improvise" one crescendo. In the latter work, musicians use cassettes with three types of sound materials and "improvise" one change of the playback speed on variable-speed cassette players designed by John Fulleman. In contrast, the three "c-[C]omposed Improvisations" involve the use of traditional instruments: a snare drum, a

Steinberger bass guitar, and one-sided drums with or without jangles. Cage provided highly indeterminate scores and gave the improvisers a variety of problems to solve, including instructions for the use of chance operations. These new approaches to improvisation, which seem to have nothing in common with the conventional idea of improvisation, actually come very close to its etymological meaning: "to bring forward the unforeseeable."

In the 1970s and 1980s Cage also wrote some socially and politically motivated works that involve elements of improvisation. His concepts of individualist anarchy and freedom coincide with improvisation in, for instance, "Etcetera" (1973), for orchestra, three conductors, and taped nature sounds; and "Etcetera 2/4 Orchestras" (1985), for four orchestral groups, four conductors, and taped city sounds.[4] In these works "anarchic," uncontrolled, and improvised situations are contrasted with "governed," controlled, and determined ones. Performers can be improvising soloists realizing indeterminately written parts, or they may play more conventionally notated materials in conducted groups. Cage characterized the differing roles of improvisation in these two works as follows: "In *Etcetera 1*, the musicians begin by improvising, more-or-less, and they leave the situation of improvising and go to one of the conductors, and then they play fixed music in those situations. And then they go away, and go back to improvising. In *Etcetera 2*, they begin by playing with conductors and they leave the conductors to go and improvise. So the pieces do the same thing, but in opposite ways" (Turner 2003, 5–6).

CAGE'S PERFORMANCE OF HIS TEXT PIECES
AND THE QUESTION OF IMPROVISATION

A similar metamorphosis of Cage's attitude toward improvisation can be found in his recitations of his linguistically idiosyncratic and innovative writings, revivals of the defunct form of the solo literary recital.[5] His text "Indeterminacy," of 1959, for instance, consists of 90 very short stories to be read at varying speeds depending on the story's number of words so that each story would take no longer than one minute to finish. The time constraint prevents the reciter from improvising the intonation, yet involves a certain degree of unpredictability. From the nonhierarchical assemblages of narrative and linear short stories, Cage progressed in the 1970s and 1980s toward nonsyntactic prose "written through" other authors' texts. A mix of letters, syllables, words, phrases, and sentences, "Mureau" (standing for "Music" and "Thoreau," 1970) was drawn from Thoreau's remarks on sound and silence in his *Journal* and composed by means of chance operations. As Cage gradually "musicalized" language, he developed his vocal skills further. and his readings of his texts became chanted performances. While preparing for a recitation of "Mureau," he seemed to have stumbled upon improvisation: "I discovered that I could improvise, but only along the same lines! . . . When I improvised by myself, I used all the resources of my voice and all the elements of language without falling back upon known words or a syntax. I found this experience thrilling" (Charles 1981, 113). Yet, when asked whether he improvised in public performances of his texts, Cage answered, "I feel best when something happens to my voice that is not normal that perks up my ears like a loss of breath or a loss of tone in other words some deviation from the expected" (Cage 1990, 216).

Improvisation also played a limited role in the creation of some of Cage's mesostic poetry, visually structured poems displaying series of vertically organized words. Besides using chance operations and other artistic choices, he found himself in some instances "working by improvising and trying to find out what the words wanted, how they wanted to work" (Retallack 1996, 64). For the performance of some of his mesostics, Cage developed—by reading them aloud and improvising—a specific kind of notation indicating pauses and stresses. In mesostics such as "Art Is Either a Complaint or Do Something Else" (1988) and "I-VI" (1988–1989) a space and apostrophe signify a new breath, and syllables printed in boldface indicate that they should be accented. In his performance instructions for "Sixty-two Mesostics re Merce Cunningham" (1971, printed in about 730 different typeface and type size variations) Cage points out that the "type face and size differences may be used to suggest an improvised vocal line having any changes of intensity, quality, style." Yet he cautions the performer against "following any conventional rule" and against searching "to establish any pronunciation rule" (Cage 1971, preface).

For the performance of his last text piece, "One^{12}" (1992) for a lecturer, featuring a score with 640 numbers between 1 and 12, Cage gave himself "a problem in improvisation which was not easy to do" (Retallack 1996, 270). Whispering or vocalizing the letters of the alphabet, he had to come up with and speak a "full word" (noun, verb, etc.) each time he came to the number 12 and an "empty word" (conjunction, pronoun, etc.) each time he came to the number 1. Number 7 required Cage to choose any seven letters and give them pitches. These conditions, plus the fact that this piece's duration is indeterminate, have led to a variety of unpredictable moments largely independent of taste and memory. Cage's performance of a 30–minute version of "One^{12}" in June 1992 during the Quaderni Perugini di Musica Contemporanea in Perugia, Italy, was described as diatonic, soft, continuously different and "radiating a quiet and beauty of its own."[6]

If Cage changed his attitude toward improvisation in the 1970s, what was his view of jazz, which had undergone many changes and become freer since the 1950s? His opinion on jazz does not seem to have changed at all. Cage commented on free jazz as follows: "Everyone tells me that jazz is free today. But when I listen to it, it always seems to me to be confined within a world of ideas and musical relationships. . . . And what is called free jazz probably tries to free itself from time and rhythmic periodicity. The bass doesn't play like a metronome any more. But even then, you still get the feeling of a beat" (Charles 1981, 171).[7] In an unusual turn, however, in June 1986 Cage appeared in concert with the legendary free jazz composer Sun Ra. This event, which took place in a noisy amusement park environment under the title "Sideshows by the Shore" on Coney Island (New York), might appear to be Cage's ultimate reconciliation with jazz. Yet rather than a collaboration, only a meeting was promised—the concert being called "John Cage Meets Sun Ra." In the concert the two took turns: Ra improvised on his Yamaha DX7 and presented his own poetry, accompanying himself, and Cage alternated with softly spoken-sung excerpts from "Empty Words" (1973–1974), stretching vowels and observing long pauses between syllables. The musical meeting, however, grew into a brief duet at the end of the concert, where Ra subtly punctuated Cage's recitation with a few bell-like sounds. Otherwise each of the two kept "improvising" in his own way.[8] Cage later emphasized that "they had not played together" (Szwed 1997, 356–57). While Cage remained cautious in his rapprochement with jazz, many jazz composers and representatives of (free) improvised music—including AMM (whose music has been dubbed "John Cage Jazz"), Carla Bley, Anthony Braxton, Malcolm Goldstein, Joëlle Léandre, Musica Elettronica Viva, and John Zorn—absorbed some of his ideas without sacrificing self-expression (Wilson 1991).

CONCLUSION

Cage's complex relationship with improvisation sheds light on its many connotations. Cage dealt with improvisation on various levels, using it as a precompositional and compositional tool and employing it as a dimension pertaining to performance. In the course of his career, his idea of improvisation underwent a considerable transformation. He embraced improvisation in the 1930s and 1940s, rejected it vehemently in the 1950s and 1960s, and approached it again under new premises from the 1970s on. Intriguingly, his disapproval of improvisation coincided with a reduction in compositional control, yet it also accompanied a rationalization of the creative process. This has created much confusion and misunderstanding. Cage's indeterminate notations often require performers to prepare written realizations prior to performance. The act of performing an indeterminate score thus seems to go beyond execution or interpretation. And despite the performers' greater role in the creative process, their performance is equivalent to neither improvisation nor composition. Yet everything depends on how the terms *execution, interpretation, composition,* and *improvisation* are defined. Cage rejected improvisation because many of its implied meanings contradict his aesthetic principles. These connotations include intuition, self-expression, memory and taste-based utterances, discursiveness, predictability, and repetition. He embraced solely one rarely achieved and often illusory etymological meaning of improvisation: to do something unforeseeable. And it was this denotation which led him to reconsider improvisation later in his career without making any aesthetic compromises. He undoubtedly created a greater awareness of the implications of improvisation and shed light on the challenges and illusions of improvisation. In his search for the encounter with an unexpected experience or revelation, he provided new creative opportunities for his performers. Whether Cage fought against improvisation or embraced it, throughout his prolific career he found manifold ways of dealing with the *imprévu,* the unforeseen.

NOTES

1. In the 1950s, when Cage became critical of jazz, he still held Russell, then active as a jazz musician and historian, in high regard: "Jazz per se derives from serious music. And when serious music derives from it, the situation becomes rather silly. One must make an exception in the case of William Russell. . . . His works, though stemming from jazz—hot jazz—New Orleans and Chicago styles—were short, epigrammatic and entirely interesting" (Cage 1961, 72).

2. J. Cage to L. Bernstein, letter of October 17, 1963. Bernstein Collection, Library of Congress, Washington D.C . See also J. Cage to W. Hinrichsen, letter of October 18, 1963. Archives of C. F. Peters Corporation, Glendale, N.Y.

3. Tudor performed "Winter Music." His participation was a last-minute decision, with the use of electronic equipment and Bernstein's reluctant cooperation posing considerable problems. For details on this performance see Miller (2001). This inglorious performance is available on CD: *The New York Philharmonic—Bernstein Live*, New York Philharmonic Special Editions, NYP 20012/13 (2000).

4. To Cage individualist anarchy meant that people and sounds were free to be

themselves: "We need first of all a music in which not only are sounds just sounds but in which people are just people, not subject that is to laws established by any of them, even if he is 'the composer' or 'the conductor'" (Kostelanetz 1987, 257).

5. Cage performed primarily as a pianist, percussionist, and conductor until the early 1950s. Thereafter he focused on performance with live electronic equipment and voice. From the early 1970s on he gave almost exclusively vocal performances of his own writings.

6. See "Quaderni Perugini di Musica Contemporanea," *Neue Züricher Zeitung*, July 11, 1992. This premiere was to become one his last performances, for he died just seven weeks later.

7. In a thought-provoking article, George Lewis contends that Cage's "radical emphasis on spontaneity and uniqueness" was influenced by bebop, which first explored these features and "structural radicalism." He claims that Cage rejected jazz and improvisation and chose his own "eurological" approach and terminology to distance himself from "afrologically" oriented concepts and the influence of non-white sensibility. According to Lewis, Cage's reluctance to give credit to "the other," that is, jazz composers/performers, reveals "whiteness as power." However, Lewis does not take into account Cage's early interest in improvisation, his positive remarks on hot jazz in the 1940s, and such experimental works as "Quest" (1935) and "Imaginary Landscape No. 1," (1939), which predated bebop (1996, 99–100).

When Cage turned to chance operations and indeterminacy, he rejected not only jazz but also self-expressive European classical music, including Beethoven. He never embraced "spontaneity": "It is at the point of spontaneity that the performer is most apt to have recourse to his memory. He is not apt to make a discovery spontaneously" (Kostelanetz 1987, 222). His dismissal of jazz and improvisation must be seen in the context of his new aesthetic, which excludes self-expression, and as a strategy to prevent inadequate performances of his own indeterminate works. Yet Cage clearly distanced himself from the black protest movement and "the idea of black power" expressed in American music in the 1960s: "I have nothing against black, but I have everything against power" (Amirkhanian 1992, 69).

8. This concert was recorded and released as an LP without editing on Meltdown Records in 1987.

REFERENCES

Amirkhanian, Charles. 1992. "'The Universe Should Be Like Bach, but It Is Like Mozart': John Cage and Conlon Nancarrow in Conversation." *World New Music Magazine* 2: 47–70.
Cage, John. 1961. *Silence*. Middletown, Conn.: Wesleyan University Press.
———. 1971. *Sixty-two Mesostics Re Merce Cunningham*. New York: Henmar Press.
———. 1990. *I-VI: The Charles Eliot Norton Lectures, 1988–89*. Middletown, Conn.: Wesleyan University Press.

————. 1993. *Composition in Retrospect*. Cambridge, Mass.: Exact Change.

Cage, John, and Roger Reynolds. 1979. "A Conversation." *Musical Quarterly* 65(4): 573–93.

Campana, Deborah. 1985. "Form and Structure in the Music of John Cage." PhD dissertation, Northwestern University.

Charles, Daniel. 1981. *For the Birds*. Boston: Marion Boyars.

Coomaraswamy, Ananda. 1934. *The Transformation of Nature in Art*. Cambridge, Mass.: Harvard University Press.

Cope, David. 1980. "An Interview with John Cage." *Composer* 10/11: 6–22.

Darter, Tom. 1982. "John Cage." *Keyboard* 8(9): 18–29.

Fleming, Richard, and William Duckworth, eds. 1989. *John Cage at Seventy-five*. Lewisburg, Pa.: Bucknell University Press.

Holmes, Thom. 1981. "The Cage Interview." *Recordings* 3(3): 2–5.

Holzaepfel, John. 1994. "David Tudor and the Performance of American Experimental Music, 1950–1959." Ph.D. dissertation, City University of New York.

Kauffmann, Stanley, John Cage, and W. Alfred. 1966. "The Changing Audience for the Changing Arts (Panel)." In *The Arts: Planning for Change*, 23–52. New York: Associated Councils of the Arts.

Kostelanetz, Richard, ed. 1968. *John Cage*. New York: Praeger.

————. 1987. *Conversing with Cage*. New York: Limelight Editions.

————. 1991. *John Cage. An Anthology*. New York: Da Capo Press.

————. 1993. *John Cage: Writer. Previously Uncollected Pieces*. New York: Limelight Editions.

Kumpf, Hans. 1976. "John Cage und der Jazz—Werkstattgespräch mit John Cage." In *Postserielle Musik und der Free Jazz. Wechselwirkungen und Parallelen. Berichte—Analysen—Werkstattgespräche*. Herrenberg: Musikverlag G. F. Döring.

Lewis, George. 1996. "Improvised Music after 1950: Afrological and Eurological Perspectives." *Black Music Research Journal* 16(1): 91–122.

Miller, Leta. 2001. "Cage, Cunningham and Collaborators: The Odyssey of *Variations V*." *Musical Quarterly* 85(3): 549–50.

Retallack, Joan, ed. 1996. *MusiCage. Cage Muses on Words, Art, Music*. Hanover, N.H.: University of New England Press.

Revill, David. 1993. *The Roaring Silence. John Cage: A Life*. New York: Arcade.

Szwed, John. 1997. *Space Is the Place. The Lives and Times of Sun Ra*. New York: Pantheon.

Turner, Steve Sweeney. 1990. "John Cage's Practical Utopias—John Cage in Conversation with Steve Sweeney Turner." *Musical Times* 131: 469–72.

————. 2003. Cage Interview No. 3, Almeida Contemporary Festival, London, 1990. *Frankfurter Zeitschrift für Musikwissenschaft* 6, http://www.fzmw.de.

Wilson, Peter Niklas. 1991. "'Wider das tödliche Gleichmaß.' John Cage, der Jazz und improvisierte Musik jenseits des Jazz." *MusikTexte* 40/41: 84–87.

~3~

WHEN TRADITIONAL IMPROVISATION
IS PROHIBITED: CONTEMPORARY UKRAINIAN
FUNERAL LAMENTS AND BURIAL PRACTICES

Natalie Kononenko

Improvisation is important not only in music but also in the verbal arts. Many forms of oral poetry are improvised, and studying how improvisation works in a text sheds light on all improvisation. Albert B. Lord's work (1960) was seminal in this regard. He showed that a folk performer learns a vocabulary of poetic lines and half-lines, which he then uses to "speak" in verse. The "lexemes" of oral poetry, which Lord called formulas, differ from words—the basis of normal speech—in that they are macro-units, consisting of groups of words that fit the meter and the content. In an oral narrative, formulas are grouped by larger units that Lord called themes, essentially scenes from the story being told. The sequence of the themes, in turn, is determined by a traditional narrative plot. The system of units Lord identified explains how traditional stories can be improvised in performance. His work proves that complex texts need not be created in advance in written form. His oral theory advanced the understanding of the verbal arts and also helped us see how improvisation works in general.

The aim of this essay is much more modest. By looking at folk verbal arts in contemporary Ukraine, I hope to contribute to our understanding of attitudes toward improvisation. Improvisation can be viewed positively or negatively. It can be seen as the purest form of artistic creativity or as a lesser art, one not as "high" as the more static and immutable artistry produced on paper prior to performance. My work with Ukrainian laments, a genre closely related to the epic poems on which Lord based his theory, shows that attitudes toward improvisation depend on context; it is not just a matter of a particular culture's understanding of what constitutes good art. Ukrainians cherish the artistry of good improvisation in some contexts. Yet, in other situations, striving for artistic excellence is viewed ambiguously. People insist that practicing to improve one's ability to lament or drawing on traditional formulas to produce a good text is inappropriate to an emotional situation such as the death of a loved one. Furthermore, they expect all affected by a death to lament, although, in practice, it is mostly women who do. Other traditions, such as the Karelian one described by Tolbert (1990, 1994), entrust lamentation to people who are especially skilled at performance. This is not the case in Ukraine. Yet, even though they ask ordinary people to produce unrehearsed text, Ukrainians criticize a performance that is not sufficiently artful. This contradiction stems from beliefs about death and the relationship between the living and the dead rather than from attitudes toward artistry. It is also influenced by the nature of the Ukrainian funeral. Work with Ukrainian laments shows that it is important to examine context and cross-genre relationships. In the case of the Ukrainian funeral, laments, the improvisational genre, are in dialogue with funeral psalms, a written and seemingly static art form that has been largely overlooked. When a static genre appears in the same ritual context as an improvisational one, it can affect the way improvisation is viewed. In short, both genre proximity and ritual function can influence how improvisation is perceived.

For the purposes of this study, improvisation will be defined following Lord: it is the use of traditional poetic structures to make up a new text at the moment of performance. In rural Ukraine, where oral traditional song still flourishes, improvisation is viewed as a good thing in most contexts and the ability to improvise is valued. During the wedding, for example, the bride's entourage exchanges taunts with the groom's. The bride's druzhka, or maid of honor, or one of the other girls can accuse the groom's party of gluttony, saying that they ate an entire steer at the wedding banquet, not leaving a single bone. Someone in the groom's party is expected to respond. One way to do so is by accusing the druzhka of being thin as a rail and wearing a borrowed shirt instead of her own (field recording 1998). In this exchange of wedding taunts, a singer is expected to use traditional wedding song formulas and to produce verses everyone at the banquet will recognize. At the same time, if a person can innovate and vary the wedding formulas or combine them in a new way, making up a verse or a stanza that captures the specific situation or the particular individuals involved, perhaps by adding descriptive details, that person advances his or her reputation as a performer and gains status. Good performers are known by their fellow villagers and sought, especially for public occasions such as weddings. In Velyka Burimka, a village in the Cherkasy province of central Ukraine, Mariia Velychko told me that her nephew Vitia was such an effective improviser that he had been asked to serve in various official capacities at over 30 weddings (field recording 1998). In Velkykyi Khutir, another village in the same region, Mykhailo Koval, himself a recognized performer, said that, if encouraged by a receptive audience, a good singer could go on for hours.

In some contexts improvisation is viewed negatively. When it comes to lament, people feel that the singing should be spontaneous rather than artful. It is not the creation of a new text that is deemed inappropriate; it is the use of traditional poetic structures. The lament is a genre alive in the Ukrainian village today. Contemporary laments are long and complex poems which can span several hours (field recording 2000). They are composed at the moment of performance using traditional formulas. Yet villagers claim that laments are spontaneous, that they are not improvised using a traditional poetic vocabulary of lines and half lines. Lament is not a unique form in terms of how it comes into being; it is, however, unique in terms of the public's attitude toward its composition. Why do the folk view it as different from other living oral genres?

Lamentation is taken very seriously and is a component of funerals and funeral-related events exclusively. Lamenting is expected between death and internment, at commemorations of the deceased 40 days and a year after death, and on "ancestor days," calendar holidays that honor all those who have come before. Wedding laments, like the ones mentioned by Tolbert (1990, 1994) or the laments collected in Russia, are not attested in Ukraine though singing mournful ballads during the wedding is acceptable (Barsov [1872] 1997). A lament can be a virtuoso performance, but people capable of such singing do not perform for tourists, as has happened among Tolbert's Karelian refugees in Finland. Again, this prohibition affects laments only. Other genres, ritual songs included, are routinely taken out of context and performed for outsiders. Fake weddings, usually with a comic element, are a regular form of entertainment at outdoor museums such as the one at Piro- hovo, outside Kyiv. Ritual songs connected with the calendar are also sung at staged reenactments in this and similar venues (Kononenko 2004). Just as laments cannot be sung outside the funeral setting, they cannot be used to mourn a loss other than death, such as the way Tolbert's subjects used laments to bemoan their refugee status. In Ukraine expressions of sorrow and loss not connected with death must be voiced using other genres, such as the personal narratives collected by Noll (1999).

Laments were fairly extensively collected in the late 19th and early 20th cen- turies from ordinary villagers. However, because improvising poems of this length and complexity seems very difficult, scholars including Sventsits'kyi

(1910a, 1910b, 1912) assumed that laments were once performed by specially trained professionals, just as epic poetry is typically performed by minstrels (Kononenko 1998). Lament is a demanding form. The performance can go on for hours, as I have personally witnessed. The structure is stychic: the text is built line by line, although rhyme, especially in couplet form, is frequent, just as in Ukrainian epic poetry.

Imagery is striking and virtually identical to that found in the classic lament collections recorded in the late 19th and early 20th centuries: the coffin is compared to a house without windows and doors, where the sun does not shine and the wind does not blow (*khata bez vikon, bez dverei; tam sonyshko ne prohrie i viter ne provie*); the deceased is asked about the roads that he or she might travel on the journey to the land of the dead; the passage of time is expressed in holidays; birds are catalogued as potential messengers that might bring news from the departed (Kolessa [1938] 1983). Sharing Sventsits'kyi's perception that lament must be difficult to improvise and probably falling victim to what Wilce (2006) calls the postmodern anthropologist's tendency to "mourn" the loss of traditional expressive forms, my field partner Olesia Britsyna of the Ryl's'kyi Folklore Institute in Kyiv and I, while preparing for our collecting trip in 2000, assumed that lamentation was a dead art. Thus, we made up a questionnaire asking people if they remembered seeing villagers lament in the past, and we wrote out lines from laments in printed collections such as Chubinskii (1877) to see if people could recall ever hearing those verses, or variants of them. During fieldwork, we both conduct interviews and try to observe as many funerals as we can. To our surprise, at the first funeral we attended, a number of people lamented (field recording 2000). The same thing occurred every time that we were present at a village burial rite.

Britsyna and I are both interested in oral composition and the transmission and improvisation of oral texts. When we observed actual lamentation, we thought we had found a wonderful and unexpected opportunity to investigate truly complex oral poetry. Thus, we decided to modify our fieldwork plans: instead of asking about recollections of oral composition, we thought we could investigate the phenomenon itself. Once we set out to gather data on laments and lamentation, we discovered that although people are quite willing to talk about improvisation in connection with genres such as ballads, wedding songs, and calendar songs, laments are a totally different matter.

Ideally, field study should begin with investigation of the target genre in context, and, indeed, we did try to record laments as they were being sung. Recording laments during a funeral proved impossible, however. We could not get decent sound quality without being offensively intrusive into the lives and the sorrows of the persons performing the funeral rite, and we chose the dignity of our subjects over data collection. Since we always supplement our observation of rituals with interviews, we decided to get our data on laments there and to request that respondents perform laments for an audio recording. We thought that, in those cases where people could not produce lamentation without prompting, we could use our original questionnaire to solicit expansions on the verses that we had taken from earlier collections.

Contemporary laments are strikingly similar to published ones. When we asked our subjects if they had heard certain lament lines that we had taken from the classical collections of the late 19th and early 20th centuries, they not only knew the lines but were able to add at least a few, and sometimes as many as 10 or 12, more. The lament section of our interview with Motria Perepechai, for example, lasted for almost an hour, with her providing appropriate quotations of lament excerpts from various recent funerals (field recording 2000). When we encouraged Perepechai and others to continue, performing a lament as they would at a funeral, they either refused or dismissed us, implying that we should know better than to make such foolish requests. We then started asking people about the material that we had already solicited. How had they learned the lines that they had just recited? This elicited some rather unusual responses. All respondents admitted to having heard the lines or expressions that we quoted, yet they denied the existence of a lament tradition. A vocabulary of standard lament lines and half lines that were regularly used in performing a lament did not exist, they claimed. They were especially insistent that learning lamentation was simply not done. They said that laments were spontaneous and should be completely spur-of-the-moment performances. No learning or training was involved; this was something that just did not happen. Of the many functions attributed to laments by Wilce (2006) and by Rosenblatt and others (1976), the respondents acknowledged only one: helping the lamenter feel better through the release of sorrow. Laments, they continued, are an expression of people's feelings at the time of someone's death; they could not be traditional. If a person died young and everyone was very upset, many people would lament and they would lament at length. When an old person died, this was a common occurrence and there was not a great deal of lamentation. We asked people about the content of this supposedly spontaneous lamentation, hoping they would acknowledge, or at least recognize, that this was stable, traditional, inherited material. But they said that the circumstances dictated content: you sang what was appropriate to the person in question and to the feelings that you had; you did not draw on the laments of the past or the verses that you had heard at other funerals.

Claims of total spontaneity and the implied avoidance of traditional material directly contradicted the field data we collected from the very same informants. To us, if people know all of the traditional formulas that have appeared in the collections of the past, and if we hear these same people and their neighbors use the verses at funerals, then laments are a traditional genre, just like other ritual songs. The evidence for tradition was strengthened by the fact that lament formulas were known and used not by isolated performers, but by every person we interviewed on this topic.

There were other pieces of evidence indicating that laments are traditional and that a certain body of material accompanies all funerals, that the absence of traditional poetic vocabulary claimed by our informants is more a matter of perception than of fact. Although no one claimed that honoring the deceased was requisite, lack of lamentation, even lamentation that was insufficiently artful, was criticized as bad behavior. We were told that lamentation depended on the degree of sorrow and that old people need not be lamented at length, yet we were witness to an instance where a woman was chastised for not marking her elderly mother's death with laments of sufficient artistry and length. Several village residents complained, to each other and to us, that the daughter did nothing more than exclaim, "Oh, Mother, oh, Mother." She should have found something elaborate and meaningful to sing, they explained, because the deceased was, after all, her mother (field recording 2000). The fact that the deceased was well on in years did not seem to matter, contrary to what we had been told in interviews. Villager statements implied that the daughter should have been better versed in traditional lament formulas and better equipped to perform her filial duties. Their comments implied that laments were important to the deceased as well as the mourner, though such a function was not explicitly acknowledged.

Interestingly, an almost identical situation was described by Ivan Benkovskii in an article published in *Kievskaia starina* more than 100 years ago (1896, see esp. 251–52). He attended a funeral in the village of Hryhorivka and listened to the comments of women walking back from the graveyard after interment. The deceased had two daughters, and both were present at the funeral. According to Benkovskii, one daughter was so upset by her father's death that she was literally rendered speechless: all she could do was to choke back her tears. The other daughter was in better control of her emotions. She did not cry at all—but she did lament at length and in elaborate form. To

Benkovskii's dismay, it was this expression of sorrow that villagers praised. He considered the silent daughter to be more genuinely and deeply distraught by her father's passing. And she may have been, but although villagers claim to value depth of emotion, it was the effective lamentation that they actually prized. In both Benkovskii's experience and ours, good lamentation was valued regardless of its relationship to a mourner's feelings. Good laments, with the appropriate blend of music, words, and weeping, as described by Tolbert (1990, 1994) and others, were important and even necessary. By implication, laments with effective word choice were needed because they had the magico-religious power to help the deceased make the transition to the other world. Even though the degree of the lamenter's sadness was supposed to be the operative factor, if deep sadness did not produce good text, then the mourner was subject to censure, no matter how poignant his or her other expressions of sorrow might have been.

While good lamentation is expected, developing the ability to perform well through practice is not allowed. In fact, an account that we recorded from Ol'ha Trush of Ploske shows that lament practice can be patently dangerous (see Tolbert 1990). When she was a girl in her teens, and thus quite foolish, Ol'ha had a frightening experience. She and a group of her friends were working in the fields picking strawberries. When it came time to take a break and rest, the girls started fooling around. They told Ol'ha to lie down and they started singing laments over her. Trush, who recounted this incident some 60 years after it happened, still remembers how good the laments felt. As the other girls sang, she said, she felt at peace and grew progressively sleepier. Suddenly an adult, the gardener, came along and started scolding the girls, telling them to stop what they were doing or they would sing their friend to death (field recording 2000).

In our fieldwork, it was striking that denials of learning and practice characterize discussions of laments only. When questioned about any other folk genre, no one denied learning it or practicing the songs, tales, or verses. I have been collecting data on weddings and birth customs, in addition to data on funerals, since 1998, and when I discuss the appropriate songs with the people I interview, they willingly volunteer information about learning the genres in question. Women describe attending parties and weddings and listening to the songs. They recount practicing the songs, often in groups. During the 2000 collecting trip, when Britsyna and I asked the same people who denied practicing laments about practicing other songs, they would readily admit that this indeed was done. Many villages have a community group that is interested in oral poetry, what I call village culture keepers. The group collects local songs, sometimes writing them down, and they gather regularly to practice singing. Such gatherings are social occasions and are enjoyed by the participants (field recording 1998, 2005).

To understand the peculiar position that laments hold relative to other genres, it is necessary to examine them in context. We need to see at which points in the funeral laments are performed and what other songs accompany ritual burial. Ukrainian village funerals, even today, are elaborate. They would be deemed effective mourning by Rosenblatt and colleagues (1976), for they are both public and circumscribed in time, helping the living to accept the loss of those dear to them. People prepare for their own funerals, although some say that only women can carry out this task, and that it is a woman's responsibility to prepare for the death of her husband or that of a brother who has no wife, such as a widower (field recording 1998, 2000). At about age 50, people put aside a complete set of clothing, including undergarments, shoes, and headgear, such as a scarf for women; a cap or a hat for a man is optional. They get the cloth that will line the coffin and a length of gauze or tulle that will be used to cover the body. It is traditional to have two crosses, one for the hands and another to wear around the neck, and a "passport" to the land of the dead. This is a printed prayer that is folded and placed in the hands of the deceased. Candles for the funeral service, usually 12 in number, are set aside, as are towels and kerchiefs that will serve as gifts for the people who help the family perform the burial ritual.

Once a person dies, his or her body is washed by postmenopausal women who are among the family's neighbors and friends; relatives are not allowed to touch the body until it has been prepared. The body is dressed, tied down to prevent it from moving when rigor mortis sets in, and placed either directly on the bench under the icons in the icon corner or in the coffin, which is then set on the same bench (Kononenko 2006). Lamentation begins at this point. After family members and anyone else who wishes to express his or her feelings have had a chance to lament, things quiet down toward evening and everyone leaves except the family and the same elderly women who washed the deceased. The deceased is supposed to spend at least one night, and preferably three, in the home before interment. During the night, the elderly women and any family members who feel that they have the strength to do so keep a vigil over the body. There is usually no lamentation, but one of the women reads the Psalter (Kononenko 2006; field recording 2000). Burial takes place in the afternoon because it is believed that everyone must return from the cemetery before dark. Afternoon burial also leaves the morning free for mourners to make preparations for the wake.

The funeral proper begins with a service in the home, although a service in church is preferred, if the family can afford one. After the service, the family is left alone with the deceased to bid their farewells. As they do so, many family members, and especially women, lament. The coffin is then removed from the home. If there is to be a church service, it is carried to the church. If not, the coffin goes directly to the cemetery. The coffin travels in a procession, usually one of considerable size, including the priest, a church choir called the pivcha, the family, the men and women who help with the funeral, friends of the deceased, and as many residents of the village as feel obliged to accompany the departed. The procession down the streets of the village is a solemn ceremonial occasion, and this is where lamentation is universal. Lamentation can take place during the entire course of the procession, as I saw occur in Iavorivka in 2000, or it can be performed at crossroads only (field recording 2000). The procession must stop at all crossroads and there must be a minimum of three stops; therefore, a stop not at a crossroad is added, if necessary. At each such stop the pivcha sings the Lord's Prayer and family members lament. There is usually another, smaller religious service at the graveside, after which family members kiss the deceased and lament some more. The coffin is then lowered into the grave, each family member throws in three handfuls of dirt, and the gravediggers quickly fill the hole. All lamentation must cease as soon as the grave is covered over (Sventsits'kyi 1912).

After the burial, the family and friends of the deceased go to the home for a wake. No laments are to be sung at the wake, and any crying for the deceased henceforth is to be a private affair. Extensive mourning is discouraged. Excessive tears are said to fill the grave with water, making the deceased uncomfortable, and too much lamentation is said to disturb the dead person, preventing him or her from resting in peace (field recording 2000).

Singing does occur at the wake. Relatives are supposed to be silent, but the pivcha performs. As the meal draws to a close, the singing of religious verses called psal'my begins. This is not an oral genre. Psal'my are written out and transmitted from one pivcha member to another in written form. Pivcha members all keep notebooks with handwritten texts and copy these from each other. Because psal'my exist in writing, they have not been collected by folklorists and they have not been studied by anyone. Literary scholars are not interested in them because they see them as the writings of lesser poets. Scholars of religion also ignore them because they are deemed folk, rather than church, religion. Sventsits'kyi (1910a, b), one of the few people to say anything about funeral psal'my, claims that they are based on the hymns of Ephraim of Syria and that they were added to the funeral to balance and counteract the many pagan references in laments. Any relation between contemporary psal'my and the hymns in question is not apparent, however, and it is just as likely that psal'my were composed by seminarians using a variety of sources rather than a single model. Voropai ([1966] 1991) mentions that ordering a psal'ma from a seminarian was standard practice for Ascension Day and other commemorations of the dead, such as Provody. I also made no special effort to record psal'my at first, though I did ask for and receive a copy of a written text in 2000. In 2005 I was able to make a follow-up trip, during which I specifically requested psal'my. I photographed the notebooks, requested information about psal'my, and I asked people to sing psal'my for me.

Psal'my proved to be the opposite of laments. People were quite willing to perform them outside the funeral context. Groups of women would readily gather and sing them for me. They would let me record them, and they were anxious to hear how they sounded on the recording (field recording 2005). They did not deny rehearsing in situations similar to the ones in which they performed for me, and they willingly admitted that they did so to sound good and to please God, their neighbors, and themselves. Interestingly, some acknowledged an economic motive, although attributing it to others rather than to themselves. They said that singers wanted to achieve artistic excellence so that the priest would take them to funerals, allowing them to earn the gifts of food and kerchiefs that were typically given to singers. Pivcha members in other villages, they claimed, would even refuse to share notebooks, not wanting other people to learn their best songs (field recording 2005).

In terms of composition, psal'my are again the opposite of laments. Because they are in written form, psal'my are not supposed to be spontaneous. Quite the opposite: they are supposed to be fixed, immutable texts, copied from a written original. I tried hard to ascertain where the original came from but could not. The priest in Ploske, who had formerly been quite chatty, went to see his superior and then became reticent about giving information. If anyone was willing to identify any source, it would be the seminary. Seminarians, they said, wrote psal'my, which then circulated among the people (field recording 2005; see also Voropai [1966] 1991). Interestingly, just as the supposed spontaneity of laments was more a matter of belief than of fact, so the psal'my were hardly fixed texts. I photographed a number of psal'my, which allowed for detailed comparison. I can now document that psal'my vary from notebook to notebook. It may also be true that psal'my are improvised in performance, at least to an extent. I specifically asked about improvisation and was told that it is appropriate to change the psal'ma depending on the gender of the deceased (field recording 2005). The performers were not aware of any other variation. Once singing began, however, most women put their books aside. Under such circumstances, improvisation is entirely possible.

Laments and psal'my are not simply opposites. In the context of the funeral, they are in complementary distribution. In terms of time, laments are appropriate for the period from death to interment. Upon interment, singing is restricted to the psal'my. In terms of musicality, laments are not tuneful. They are performed in recitative mixed with weeping. Psal'my, on the other hand, are quite musical. They are stanzaic and are closer to lyric songs than to church chant. As for the performer, laments are sung by individuals whereas psal'my are performed by a group. Laments are believed to be spontaneous and created on the spur of the moment with fluid content dictated by the specific situation. Psal'my, on the other hand, are said to be fixed; they exist in written form and are transmitted by copying. But this balance alone does not explain why people believe laments must be free of the stable, traditional formulas that are actually there. An examination of folk beliefs about death and the afterlife is necessary.

Lament content emphasizes the performer's desire to have the deceased stay among the living. Although the belief that lamentation is a duty and the prohibitions against practice imply that laments help the deceased fall into eternal slumber and make the transition to the world of the dead, the words of laments call the dead person back; they do not guide him or her to the other world. In laments, the mourner literally asks the deceased to return. After describing the coffin as a windowless house, as mentioned earlier, the singer chides the deceased for selecting it as his or her new abode and forsaking the home where all of the relatives dwell. The lamenter asks the dead person to look upon the pain of the living, to pity their plight, and to reconsider leaving them. Mundane problems are presented, such as feeding the children and mowing the hay, and the deceased is asked to help with such household tasks, especially in this time of need. When the dead person is called to return, the paths that he or she should travel are specified, and these are usually actual paths in the village. The mourner may include recollections of walking the paths with the deceased and ask if he or she would consider walking the paths once more. The mourner asks if the deceased has departed because he or she is angry with the living and then promises never to offend the dead person if only he or she will return.

The lament performer asks the deceased to rejoin the living, but such a return is not truly desired (Kolessa [1938] 1983). Ukrainian culture is quite wary of the return of the dead. If a dead person does not make a smooth transition into the other world, this is an indication of problems (Kononenko 2006). It means that something has gone wrong and is preventing proper passage into the afterlife. The problems can be seen in very concrete terms. Anne Ingram (1998) recorded an account from a woman who made the mistake of burying her daughter in high-heel shoes. The daughter appeared to the mother in a dream to complain about the difficulty she was having walking around in the afterlife and to request that low-heel shoes be placed in the coffin of the next person to die so that he could pass them on to her. Similar memorates tell of deceased men coming back because they were buried in shoes too small for comfort in the hereafter. In Ingram's field materials and in my own interviews, other reasons that the dead cannot rest include failure to bury a prosthesis or eyeglasses along with their owner and forgetting to put ritual towels into the grave. In all cases, the problem demands a solution. This can be placing the needed item in the coffin of the next person to die, as mentioned above, or giving it to the poor, who are seen as intermediaries between this world and the spirit realm (Kononenko 1998, 189–91). As much as someone may want to maintain contact with a dead family member, the actual appearance of the deceased is seen as a violation of the cosmic order that needs to be remedied. Sometimes the problems of the living are so great that the deceased is forced to return and help, just as the laments ask. This supposedly happened when a woman could not locate her internal passport, a situation that could have gotten her into trouble with Soviet authorities. Her recently deceased husband helped her find the missing document. Having solved the problem, he disappeared (Ingram 1998).

Memorates are accounts of personal experience. In more developed narrative forms such as legends, the return of someone from the land of the dead is presented as truly dangerous. In legends, the dead are summoned by crying and tears; interestingly, words are not mentioned. Thus, there are stories of women who die in childbirth and then come back to nurse their infants when they cry. Most frightening are stories where excessive adult crying forces the dead to return to the world of the living. The inconsolable mourner is often a wife who misses her dead spouse so severely that she manages to call him back. The dead husband returns as an incubus, visiting his wife at night and causing her to weaken day by day. The way to restore order and get the deceased to stay in the other world is by an ostensible violation of order in this one. Thus, wives being visited by their husbands after death are supposed to dress up and wait for the next arrival of the deceased. When questioned about their attire, they are to say that they are going to the wedding of a brother and a sister. The deceased will then object that the marriage between siblings is improper. The person being visited must counter by saying that it is no more out of order than the return of the deceased after death. In most legends, the dead visitor responds that, if order in the world of the living has become so topsy-turvy that siblings can wed, then it is not worth being a part of this world. The deceased then chooses to remain in the land of the dead (Hnatiuk 1912b, 5–8).

Direct prohibitions against excessive lamentation complement the legends about summoning an incubus through too much mourning. Ukrainians explicitly warn that expressions of sorrow, if carried too far, will actually force the deceased to return, as in the legends. This is not to mention that too many tears can cause the dead discomfort by making them lie in water, as noted earlier. People chide their friends and neighbors against excessive crying not only at funerals, but also at the other events where laments are accepted, namely annual commemorations of the dead. One such commemoration falls on Ascension Day, and when we attended this celebration at the graveyard in Iavorivka, we witnessed just such an event. An older woman was visiting the grave of her daughter with her grandson, the son of the woman in the grave. She lamented passionately at the graveside, expressing pity for both herself and for her grandchild, until some of her fellow villagers reminded her of the dangers of such extreme expressions of sorrow (field recording 2000).

In Ukrainian culture, then, we have both a fear that excessive lamentation might force the dead to rejoin the living and a lament tradition where expressions of grief and loss are couched as requests to be reunited with the deceased. The sentiments expressed in laments are both a natural reaction (Rosenblatt et al. 1976) to the death of a loved one and, as our interviews indicate, a culturally sanctioned one. In fact, as both Benkovskii (1896) and we witnessed, the absence of elaborate lamentation leads to censure. But why would a culture expect mourners to call back the deceased while believing that such calls threaten the social, and even the cosmic, fabric? Filaret Kolessa ([1938] 1983), following Potebnia, provides one answer. He argues that summoning the dead is a remnant of earlier beliefs. Kolessa speculates that, in the past, ideas about the finality of death were different and mourners made a concerted effort to rouse the body through verbal magic. Only when this failed did they accept death and proceed with burial.

It is difficult to ascertain what past practices and beliefs were truly like. It would be good to know how 19th- and early-20th-century collectors managed to record laments. Was the attitude toward singing lament verses outside the context of the funeral different from what it is now? If so, perhaps attitudes toward the return of the dead have changed, although all 19th- and early-20th-century publications present the same attitudes as here. Earlier scholars tell us a great deal about lament poetics, but nothing about how the texts were recorded. They give the place where the lament was collected and publication information, if the lament had appeared in print earlier, but nothing more. Most texts in earlier collections, such as Sventsits'kyi's (1910a, 1910b, 1912), were supplied by correspondents, school teachers, and clergy; they were not recorded by professionals. Furthermore, except in a few cases, most texts are quite short. They could not have filled an hour or more of time, as did the laments we witnessed, albeit what we heard was quite repetitive. This leads me to suspect that published laments were texts heard by the various correspondents during actual funerals and written down afterward from memory.

It is not necessary to reconstruct the past to understand contemporary lamentation. We can make sense of laments by examining them in a way in which they have not been examined before, namely in relationship to psal'my. Laments and psal'my, if viewed together, form a ritual dialogue. Psal'my address the same issues as laments, often in the same vocabulary, as if they are answering the complaints of the mourner. Many of the same images appear: the coffin as a house without windows and doors, the long path from which there is no return. But while the laments say that the choice of a house without windows is a bad one, the psal'my acknowledge that this is so—and then add that it is inevitable. In them, the deceased admits a desire to keep on living, but says that this cannot be. The deceased even revels in the hard work and other physical activity of the past, but accepts that his hands now rest on his chest instead of being used for daily tasks. Every lament sentiment that calls the deceased back is balanced by a psal'ma trope that reaffirms the inevitability of death. In fact, one of the psal'my I collected in Iahotyn states explicitly that the deceased will not return.

It is understandable why the dialogic relationship between laments and psal'my has gone unnoticed. For one thing, as already noted, in the funeral these two genres are in complementary distribution. Laments are sung from the time that the body is laid out to interment. After interment, only psal'my are appropriate. While laments and psal'my are not performed in proximity to one another, viewing them as addressing each other is revealing. For one thing, dialogue is the poetry typical of ritual. The wedding taunts between members of the bride's party and the groom's cited earlier are but one example of such dialogue. Other examples are the songs addressed to various members of the wedding party, such as the mother of the bride, who must give up her child, and the mother of the groom, who must accept a stranger into her household. There are even songs addressed to and sung on behalf of inanimate objects, such as the stove. During the preparation of the wedding bread, or korovai, women call upon the stove and ask it to receive the product of their labor. The stove "responds" through their voices, expressing its readiness. Outside the wedding, verses, albeit in recited rather than sung form, are exchanged between the birth parents and the godparents at baptism. In yearly cycle rites, most songs require singing back and forth between two groups, as documented by Voropai ([1966] 1991) and others (see Kononenko 2004).

Another crucial point is that funerary dialogue is different from other ritual conversations in terms of group versus individual speech. In most ritual dialogue, whether the group or the individual speaks does not matter. Thus, particularly gifted individuals, such as the wedding singers Vitia and Mykhailo mentioned earlier, usually start the singing, perhaps improvising the first two lines of a stanza; then others join in, repeating those lines and adding traditional refrains. The verses themselves can be addressed to a group, such as the groom's entourage, or they may be directed at an individual, such as the mother of the groom, or his svitylka. When an individual such as the svitylka responses, she can theoretically sing her own retort to the teasing from the bride's friends. In most cases, however, the group, often led by a wedding singer, responds for her. Group and individual blend in performance.

A very different situation characterizes the funeral. Here there are certain songs that are clearly individual and others that are group songs and group songs only. Laments are always sung solo. Many people may recognize the words of a lament as it is being sung, but they will never join in the singing. The psal'my, on the other hand, are always sung by a group—the pivcha—and those present may join in, if they so choose. I have never heard psal'my performed by a single person, but even if this were to happen, the fact that the performer would be singing from a written text would remove any semblance of individual expression.

The funerary dialogue, then, is between the individual and the group, a situation that resolves the conflict within Ukrainian beliefs about the dead. This polarization into the one versus the many allows the expression of the sentiments aroused by death without threatening the social fabric. In laments, individuals can give voice to their pain and sorrow by asking the deceased to rejoin the living. But such expressions are those of an individual and not the group. All group songs, the psal'my, reaffirm order by saying that death is right and inevitable. Death is a part of life, they say. We all will die one day, and the departure of the deceased into the afterlife is proper and the way that things should be. Polarization into group and individual expression, I believe, demands the perceived spontaneity of laments that is the subject of this investigation. Laments cannot be seen as traditional because they must be viewed as the spur-of-the-moment wishes of a single person. Tradition implies social sanction and, as much as laments may be expected, the request that the dead rejoin the living cannot be viewed as anything other than the wish of an individual, the result of deep sorrow that will pass. The spontaneity and artlessness attributed to laments is underscored, of course, by making the other pole, psal'my, set and fixed. They are not only transmitted in writing; they are associated with religious canon, both through the name of the genre, derived from the word for the religious psalm, and its performers, a group associated with the church, the pivcha.

There is another interesting juxtaposition of the individual with the group, and this one occurs entirely within psal'my. Psal'my are group poetry, sung by a choir, yet the voice in these songs is that of an individual: the deceased. The deceased speaks through psal'my, calls upon relatives and neighbors to come and bury the body, bids farewell to those left behind, and makes all the other statements characteristic of psal'ma content. Even more strikingly, the deceased speaks in the first person. Having the deceased speak on his or her own behalf is remarkable under any circumstances, but doubly so in a culture that is ambivalent about the return of the dead. The factor that permits the deceased to "speak" is precisely that a whole group does so for him. The voice of the deceased is not put in the mouth of a single person who might be identified with the dead person in some way. This prevents any possibility of the deceased returning to animate the body of someone among the living, a possibility against which there are many safeguards, including prohibitions against naming children after those recently dead. Furthermore, the words of the deceased, as expressed in psa'lmy, are written and set. They are the antithesis of the spontaneous and certainly not the individual voice of the particular dead person being buried in a particular funeral.

In terms of Ukrainian folk belief, it is important that the deceased stop being an individual and become one with the group. As Ingram (1998), following Zelenin ([1916] 1995), has shown, after death a person is remembered as a specific individual for one year. At that point, the dead person becomes one with the ancestors. When a person becomes an ancestor, he or she is no longer viewed as an individual and commemorations tied to the anniversary of death cease. From one year onward, the deceased is remembered only on the memorial days dedicated to all the dead, such as Ascension and Provody. If the normal course is for the dead person to merge with the group, then psal'my can be said to foreshadow this process. They use first-person speech, but it is sung by the group. It is telling that the sentiments expressed by the deceased in psal'my are entirely right and proper; they are all socially approved sentiments. The speaker accepts death. He expresses no desire to return, just a desire to be remembered. This allows, by contrast, the call for the return of the dead found in laments. The first-person speech found in psal'my has not been commented on, perhaps because these songs are so little studied, but this phenomenon is striking and central to the funeral complex.

Further support for the importance of the balance between the individual and the group can be found in the psal'my sung at commemorative feasts (field recording 2005). One of the most prominent memorials for the deceased comes 40 days after death. This is the point where the soul is believed to have completed its journey through the 40 mytarstva, the tollbooths on the way to heaven, and to have entered into the spirit world (Kononenko 2006). The singing that occurs on this occasion is again psal'my, but not the ones sung at the funeral, though these, too, may be performed if the family requests them. Rather, the pivcha sing special 40-day songs. These are sung on behalf of the living, and the living are presented as a group. They are addressed to the deceased as an individual, but there is no effort to summon the dead person, as occurs in laments. Rather, 40-day psal'my say things like "we remember you, mother, and the things that you did for us as children." Just as the 40th day after death marks an important milestone in the deceased's passage into the category of ancestors, so 40-day psal'my can be seen as an important step in the acceptance of death by the living. In them, the mourners begin to blend with the group and make peace with their loss, even as they still cling to painful memories.

Death is a difficult and upsetting event. It arouses many conflicting emotions. There is a sense of loss and a desire to reverse the loss, to somehow return the deceased to life. There is anger at the deceased for dying and creating the vacuum produced by his or her absence. And there is fear of death and of the unknown and apprehension that death will claim yet another. The existence of two diametrically opposed genres, the lament and the psal'ma, helps the bereaved deal with this conflict. It allows the expression of conflicting emotions and beliefs within the space of funerary ritual. There are many senses in which the funeral differs from other rituals, but the personal and societal loss that occurs with death is, of course, the most distinctive feature. The existence of both laments and psal'my allows full expression of the pain of loss without threatening the social fabric. Expressions of loss—the laments—are viewed as personal and spontaneous, composed at the moment of performance. These expressions must be viewed in this way, no matter how traditional they may actually be, so that the dead person can be released, can be allowed to leave this world and journey to the next. Just in case there is any doubt, the deceased is given voice through something that is the opposite of the spontaneous and the fluid: the psal'my sung by the pivcha. These answer all of the traditional complaints of the lament and assure everyone that death is necessary, no matter how painful it may be.

REFERENCES

Barsov, E.V. [1872] 1997. *Prichetan'ia severnogo kraia,* edited by B.E. Chistov. St. Petersburg: Nauka.

Benkovskii, Ivan. 1896. "Smert', pogrebenie i zagrobnaia zhizn' po poniatiiam is verovaniiam naroda." In *Kievskaia starina,* Vol. 9, 229–61, n.p.

Chubinskii, P. 1877. "Rodiny, krestiny, svad'ba, pokhorony." In *Trudy entografichesko-statisticheskoi ekspeditsii,* Vol. 4. St. Petersburg.

Hnatiuk, Volodymyr. 1912a. *Pokhoroni zvychai i obraidy, Etnografichnyi zbirnyk,* Vol. 31–32, Part 2. L'viv: Naukove tovarystvo im. Shevchenka.

———. 1912b. *Znadoby do ukraiins'koi demonolohii, Etnografichnyi zbirnyk,* Vol. 34. L'viv: Naukove tovarystvo im. Shevchenka.

Ingram, Anne Marie. 1998. "The Dearly Not-Quite Departed: Funerary Rituals and Beliefs about the Dead in Ukrainian Culture." Ph.D. dissertation, University of Virginia.

Kolessa, Filaret. [1938] 1983. *Ukraiins'ka usna slovesnist'.* L'viv. Reprinted Edmonton, Alberta, Canada: Canadian Institute of Ukrainian Studies.

Kononenko, Natalie. 1998. *Ukrainian Minstrels: And the Blind Shall Sing.* Armonk, N.Y., and London: M.E. Sharpe.

———. 2004. "Karaoke Ivan Kupalo: Ritual in Post-Soviet Ukraine." *Slavic and East European Journal* 48(2): 177–202.

———. 2006. "Folk Orthodoxy: Popular Religion in Contemporary Ukraine." In *Letters from Heaven, Popular Religion in Russia and Ukraine,* edited by John-Paul Himka and Andriy Zayarnyuk, 46–75. Toronto: University of Toronto Press.

Lord, Albert B. 1960. *The Singer of Tales.* Cambridge, Mass., and London: Harvard University Press.

Noll, William. 1999. *Transformatsiia hromodians'koho suspil'stva: usna istoriia ukraiins'koho selians'tva 1920–30 rokiv.* Kyiv: Rodovid.

Rosenblatt, Paul C., R. Patricia Walsh, and Douglas A. Jackson. 1976. *Grief and Mourning in Cross-Cultural Perspective.* New Haven, Conn.: HRAF Press.

Sventsits'kyi, Ilarion. 1910a. "Pokhoronne holosine i tserkovno-relihiina poeziia." In *Zapysky naukovoho tovarystva imeni Shevchenka,* Vol. 93, 32–33. L'viv.

———. 1910b. "Pokhoronnyi kanon i dukhovni virshi." In *Zapysky naukovoho tovarystva imeni Shevchenka,* Vol. 94, 26–39. L'viv.

———. 1912. "Pokhoronni holosinia." In *Etnografichnyi zbirnyk,* Vol. 31–32, Part 1. L'viv.

Tolbert, Elizabeth. 1990. "Magico-Religious Power and Gender in Karelian Lament." In *Music, Gender, and Culture*, edited by Marcia Herndon and Susanne Zeigler, 41–56. Wilhelmshaven: Floran Noetzel Verlag.

———. 1994. "The Voice of Lament: Female Vocality and Performative Efficacy in the Finnish-Karelian Itkuvirs." In *Embodied Voices: Representing Female Vocality in Western Culture*, edited by Leslie C. Dunn and Nancy A. Jones, 179–94. Cambridge: Cambridge University Press.

Voropai, Oleksa. [1966] 1991. *Zvychaii nashoho narodu: Etnohrafichnyi narys*, Vol. 2. Munich: Ukraiins'ke vydavnytsvo.

Wilce, James M. 2006. "Magical Laments and Anthropological Reflections: The Production and Circulation of Anthropological Text as Ritual Activity." *Current Anthropology* 47(6): 891–914.

Zelenin, D(mitrii) K. [1916] 1995. *Izbrannye trudy. Ocherki po russkoi mifologii: Umershie neestestvennoiu smertiu i rusalki*. Moscow: Indrik.

FIELD RECORDINGS AND INFORMANTS

Field Recordings: 1998

Village of Velyka Burimka, Chornobai region, Cherkasy province
Informants:
Mariia Ivanivna Velychko, born 1919
Stepanida Oleksiivna Krasenko, born 1912
Agafiia Artemivna Chumak, born 1914
Village of Krut'ky, Chornobai region, Cherkasy province
Wedding of Oleksii Oleksiiovych Artemenko, born 1969, and Liubov Ivanivna Shchepak, born 1973
Informants:
Antoniia Vasylivna Ihnatenko, born 1993
Kateryna Andriivna Ustymenko, born 1944
Ol'ha Andriivna Tymoshenko, born 1950
Halyna Ivanivna Palash, born 1941
Sofiia Ivanivna Voropai, born 1920
Village of Velykyi Khutir, Drabiv region, Cherkasy province
Mykhailo Dmytrovych Koval', born 1943
Mariia Ivanivna Koval', born 1921
Oksana Fedirivna Kryvorit, born 1918
Village of Svydivok, Cherkasy region, Cherkasy province
Evdokiia Fedosivna Krasovs'ka, born 1931
Village of Den'hy, Zolotonosha region, Cherkasy province
Ol'ha Oleksandrivna Hirka, born 1919
Village of Iabluniv, Kaniv region, Cherkasy province
Tetiana Stepanivna Pidhaina, born 1927

Village of Iablunivka, Bilotserkva region, Kyiv province
Antonina Mykolaiivna Shtyka, born 1927

Field Recordings: 2000

Village of Iavorivka, Drabiv region, Cherkasy province
Funeral of Hryhorii Pavlovych Novak, age 72
Iavorivka informants:
Paraskoviia Iakivna Latysh, born 1927
Vasyl Ivanovych Latysh, born 1934
Nina Oleksandraivna Basans'ka, born 1940
Kateryna Pylypivna Latysh, born 1941
Village of Ploske, Nosiv region, Chernihiv province
Funeral of Hanna Petrivna Mateiko
Ploske informants:
Motria Andriivna Perepechai, born 1923
Hanna Serhiivna Litoka, born 1915
Ol'ha Romanivna Trush, born 1920
Evdokiia Serhiivna Kompanets, born 1914
Zina Ivanivna Litovka, born 1938
Hanna Demidvna Slisarenko, born 1916
Village of Mryn, Nosiv region, Chernihiv province
Funeral of Ivan Zakharovych Dolych
Mryn informant: Tetiana Mykhailivna Boiko, born 1948
Village of Pluzhnyky, Iahotyn region, Kyiv province
Funeral of Mykola Romanovych Shekenia
Village of Dobranychivka, Iahotyn region, Kyiv province (adjacent to Pluzhnyky)
Ol'ha Mykhailivna Kobets, born 1941
Halyna Korniivna Paz', born 1937
Tetiana Mykiolaiivna Zavalii, born 1934
Tetiana Hryhorivna Kulyns'ka, born 1926

Field Recordings: 2005

Village of Iavorivka, Drabiv region, Cherkasy province
Nadiia Hryhorivna Bezvikonna, born 1952
Hanna Oleksandrivna Iankova, born 1956
Liudmyla Iakivna Vasylenko, born 1971
plus follow-up interviews
Village of Ploske, Nosiv region, Chernihiv province
Ol'ha Ivanivna Iarosh, born 1955
plus follow-up interviews with Motria Andriivna Perepechai, Evdokiia Serhiivna
    Kompanets, and Zina Ivanivna Litovka
Village of Dobranychivka, Iahotyn region, Kyiv province
Follow-up interview with Ol'ha Mykhailivna Kobets

ᔒ 4 ᔒ

THE JUNCTURE BETWEEN CREATION
AND RE-CREATION AMONG INDONESIAN
RECITERS OF THE QUR'AN

Anne K. Rasmussen

RECITATION AND MUSIC

Peoples and cultures of the Muslim world have sometimes been mischaracterized in the popular imagination of the contemporary West as homogeneously "music-phobic." This generalization is due in part to the regulation of musical activity in various contexts and historical periods; see Sawa (1985, 1989), Al-Faruqi (1979, 1985), Lambert (1997), Nasr (2000), Farmer (1929), and additional literature cited in Danielson and Fisher (2002).[1] Rather than being excised from religious and social culture, however, Arab musical techniques and aesthetics are actually preserved and promoted throughout the Islamic world community (*umma*) through performances of the melodically recited Qur'an and a multitude of devotional and ritual practices, ranging from prayer to song, that feature the performance of religious language. Among Indonesian reciters, for example, the goal has been to master an Egyptian style of melodic recitation sometimes referred to with the descriptor *mujawwad* or as an entity, *tilawah*. When performed, or experienced as sounded behavior, *tilawah* features such aspects of recitation as Quranic Arabic (governed by the system of *tajwid*); the intervallic structure, intonation, and melodic shapes that are characteristic of the Egyptian modal system (the *maqamat*); the timbre of nasality (*ghunna*); the singing of unvoweled consonants (such as *nnnn*) sustained through melismatic phrasing; intense vocal production (produced by forcing the chest voice to the top of the vocal register without breaking into a chest voice); extreme range; and the predictable rhythm of a familiar if variously understood text. All of these sounded qualities reference the Islamic ideal and the original site of Arab Islam with multisensory efficacy, both for those who practice and for those who don't.

The preservation of the technique and style of recitation is ensured by a set of rules comprising two interrelated systems, one for language and another for melody. Isolated analysis and practice of the individual components that make up each system (for example, the production of vowel sounds, the elision of consonants, breath control, melodic phrasing, particular ornaments, precise intonation) characterize the teaching, learning, practicing, judging, and evaluation of recitation. In the "course of performance" however, recitation is improvised.

BETWEEN COMPOSITION AND IMPROVISATION: LEARNING ARAB MAQAM

To get at the juncture between composition and improvisation in Quranic performance I describe four scenarios: three teaching sessions and a performance. At the Institute for the Study of the Qur'an, a women's college where I spent a total of one and a half years as a visiting scholar, classes that focus on learning melodies and their application to the Quranic text in the *mujawwad* style of recitation are offered as a part of the required curriculum. In my experience studying melody—*lagu al-Qur'an* (Indonesian), or the Arabic term that is also used, *nagham al-Qur'an*—I learned that a musical genre referred to as *tawshih* was used to teach the catalogue of phrases that make up the progression of a particular *maqam*, "where it goes," so to speak. Ideally a *tawshih* includes the opening gestures and closing cadences, the best or most typical melodic phrases and riffs, any accidentals and variations that are common, and even the spirit (*ruh*, Arabic) of a particular *maqam*.

For example, below are listed the names of the progression of musical phrases, each of which corresponds to a line of text for the *tawshih* entitled "*Ashraq in-Nur*," often referred to more simply as *Tawshih Rast*.[2] Indonesian reciters never refer to notes with letters (A, B, C, etc.), with numbers (1, 2, 3, etc.), or using any solfége system (do re mi, etc.); and they do not describe or demonstrate scales or even tetrachords or pentachords (Arabic, *ajnas*, s. *jins*) in sequential order, a common aspect of Arab music theory in both written documents and oral discourse about music. Rather, reciters express *Maqam Rast*, a mode that has the scale C D E half-flat F G A B half-flat C (where the tonic is relative), as a series of phrases, each of which has a specific name: (1) *Rast Asli* (real *Rast*); (2) *Rast 'ala Nawa* (*Rast* on the fifth degree, G); (3) *Salalim Su'ud* (stairs that go up); (4) *Salalim Nuzul* (stairs that go down); (5) *Rast 'ala Nawa* (*Rast* on G); (6) *Shabir 'ala Rast*; (7) *Zanjaran*; (8) *Alwan* (colors) or *Varasi Rast* (*Rast* variations).

Discussing and performing *maqam* was an interest I shared with consultants and classmates in the recitation world, and we explored our common
interest in the process of formal classes and informal sessions with individuals
and groups, during which I sometimes activated an exchange of information
by demonstrating on the *'ud*, the Arab short-necked fretless lute. The building blocks I introduced were all encompassed in the acoustico-physical act
of playing the instrument: intervallic relationships, intonation, tetrachords,
and directionality. It soon became clear, however, that what defines *maqam*
in the reciter's mind is not the intervallic structure of the *maqam* or even
the stepwise catalogue of notes, but rather the characteristic phrases and
variations, activated only when put into play by the human voice.

The performance process they enacted and that we dissected in our
analysis sessions was difficult to classify. The Indonesian word *jalan* (as a
noun, "street or path"; as a verb, "to go") was certainly used in the course
of explanation, but I never ran across a normative term in either Arabic or
Indonesian—like *seyir* (path), for example, the Arabic and Turkish term
used in practice and in theoretical writings to describe archetypal modal
progression (see Marcus 1989, 674). It seems to me, however that notions
of path or progression are germane to the way in which reciters teach and
describe what a particular *maqam* "does." Of course, there is no recourse
to plotting pitch and duration on a grid, like the Western staff, in order to
"track" melodic progression. Nor is "capturing" the notes and fixing them
in cipher notation an option, although cipher notation is commonly used in
Indonesia, not only for gamelan music but also for an array of musics ranging
from songs for school children, to church hymnals, to lead sheets for pop
musicians. Rather, as mentioned above, description of what a *maqam* "does"
occurs by demonstration.

It may be that the praxis of learning the Arab *maqam* system is precisely
what enables it to be so portable. Writing on Arab modal theory, Scott Marcus
reminds us that although "each mode has a characteristic melodic progression
that the performer and composer must follow when presenting a *maqam*"
(1989, 650), "for musicians, the individual modes are generally understood
by the way they occur in practice, that is, in existing compositions and improvisations, new and old" (2002, 33).

I. Intonation and the Mastery of a Phrase

It could well be the case that for the vocalist, the linguistic apparatus for describing melody is too general. A vocalist has no recourse to the spatial and
visual aids of an instrumentalist—the fixed pitch of an idiophone, the open

strings or holes of a chordophone or an aerophone, and reliable fingerings on either of these instruments. In an attempt to discover an "ethno-theory" that is shared among these vocal specialists the analyst might well end by giving up: "Well, that's oral tradition." But do reciters get any closer to or more specific in defining the parameters of these variations—the way the *maqam* works, so to speak?

Well, yes, actually, they do. In a session I recorded in 1996 with the main consultant for this project, Maria Ulfah (southeast Asia's premier female reciter, or *qari'ah*)—Ibu Maria, as she is called by her students and friends—demonstrated and explained *Zanjaran*, commonly known in Indonesia as a variation of *Maqam Rast*.

MARIA ULFAH: "You have to be strong." (*Harus kuat.*)

She demonstrated the variation immediately using the passages from the Qur'an we had been working on during that session (see Figure 4.1).

Chapter 95 verses 1–3
95:1—*Wa at-tini wa az-zaytuni*—By the fig and the olive
95:2—*Wa thuri sinina*—And the Mount of Sinai,
95:3—*Wa hatha al-balad al-amin*—And this peaceful (secure) land (city).

MARIA ULFAH: "It has to be like that." (*Harus begitu.*)
ANNE: "Ya, and what can't you do?" (*Ya, dan tidak boleh apa?*)

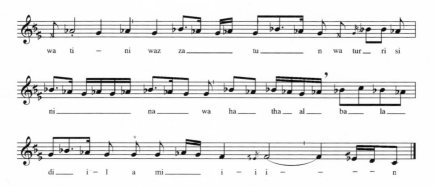

FIGURE 4.1. A transcription in musical notation of Maria Ul-fah's demonstration of the variation she calls *Zinjaran*, known in Indonesia as a variation within *Maqam Rast*. In this instance she demonstrates what *to* do. (All transcriptions by Anne Rasmussen and Bridget Robbins.)

MARIA ULFAH: "You can't descend. You can't . . ." (*Tidak boleh menurun, tidak boleh . . .*)

She demonstrated again, this time showing me what *not* to do: specifically, to rise to the fifth, as in the phrase demonstrated earlier, but then to descend (*turun*) too soon, in this case by the end of the first segment of text on the syllable *ni* of the *zaytuni* (see Figure 4.2).

MARIA ULFAH: "You can't do that." (*Tidak boleh begitu.*)
ANNE: "Ahh, you can't descend and then rise up again!" (*Ahh, tidak boleh turun terus naik lagi.*)

At this point Ibu Maria demonstrated the phrase again in a rendition similar, if not somewhat more ornate and spread out, to her first "correct" phrase. When she finished, she commented, "you have to do it like that." She remarked that her colleague Pak Asyiri would say, "otherwise it is weak" (*melema*). She moved on to identify the aspects of the *qaflah*, or cadence, that also characterize *Zajgaran*. For the *qaflah* she landed on the fourth degree, held it, and then descended to the tonic. She also pointed out the way in which she ornamented the phrase with *ketaran*.

"Also you have pay to attention to the end."

MARIA: "*Ketaran*. If you don't have a lot of 'shaking,' like this and this and this, it's not *Zanjaran* (lit. 'its name is not Zanjaran'). [It is just] pure *Rast* only." (*Harus begitu. Ya Ketaran. Zengaran. Kalau tidak berketar begini, gini, gini namanya bukan Zenjiran, Rast asli (s)aja.*)

Clearly, Maria Ulfah knows how to identify, activate, isolate, demonstrate, repeat, correct, and describe what she refers to as *Zanjaran*. To isolate the ornament that is the hallmark of the *qaflah* she employs an effective descriptor, namely the term *getar* (*ketar*, *ketaran*), which can mean shake, tremble, vibrate, or quiver. This is an ornament that some singers might identify as lying somewhere between a wide vibrato and a trill.

wa   ti   ni   waz   zay_____   tu_____   ni   wa   tu   ri   si

(*tidak boleh begitu*, you can't do it like that)

FIGURE 4.2. A transcription of Maria Ulfah's demonstration of what *not* to do, namely descend to the tonic note C too soon.

In this and countless other pedagogical situations, she engages her students in a process of what Pressing refers to as "overlearning" in his explication of improvisation as a system of expertise (1998, 47). Pressing writes, "Another tool for improvisational fluency arises from the creation, maintenance, and enrichment of an associated knowledge base, built into long-term memory. One difference between experts and non-experts is in the richness and refinement of organization of their knowledge structures. . . . Part of the effect of improvisational practice is to make motorically transparent by overlearning what has been conceptually mastered" (1998, 53).

Maria Ulfah develops her students' expertise by offering them several versions of the variation or, alternatively, by repeating, with astonishing precision, long, intricately embroidered phrases that they are then expected to repeat perfectly in collective mimesis. Once her students can do the same on their own—but without precisely imitating her example—the intervallic shapes, phrasing, and ornamentation of *Zanjaran* will be added to their musical bag of tricks for spontaneous application in what Racy has referred to in his discussions of improvisation as "the artful use of familiar modal material" (2003, 94). By practicing musical ideas until they become "natural," students have some hope of letting divine inspiration take over at the moment of performance, a subject to which we return momentarily.

II. Collective Mimesis, Melodic Precision, and the Identity of a Gesture

Several years later, during a training session in June 2003, Maria Ulfah prepared two contestants (*peserta*)—one male, Abdul Hamid, and one female, Isa Siswatika, both 20 years old—for the national competition to be held the following month.

Many reciters even as young as Isa Siswatika and Abdul Hamid are seasoned competitors. They study with officials such as Maria Ulfah as a strategy for success in the competition. Prior to and concurrent with this precontest training season, professional reciters such as Maria Ulfah are in demand constantly, requiring them to fly around the archipelago to choose and train promising contestants. When Maria Ulfah's schedule is too full to permit her to leave Jakarta, reciters from the provinces are sent to her house so that she can coach them on a daily basis, as time permits—sometimes not until 10 or 11 in the evening, when she has returned from her long days of professional responsibilities.

As in the scenario above, Maria Ulfah demonstrated a modal variation; this time it is *Husayni*, an extension of, or variation within, *maqam Bayyati*, the scale of which is: D E half-flat F G A B (flat or half-flat) C D. She illustrated again what to do and what *not* to do as well as the importance of mastering this musical phrase. Before her demonstration Maria Ulfah explained, "The judges will be really happy if you employ the variations of Mustafa Ismail [the legendary Egyptian reciter], because the reciters (usually) use the variations of Mustafa Ismail or those of Sheikh Mutawali [another Egyptian reciter]. But if you reproduce the variations of Mustafa Ismail you will get higher marks."

She continues, addressing both the contestants and me specifically. "Because it is like this *Ibu* Anne, every reciter has [his or her] own special qualities (*ciri khas*). There are those who follow Mutawali; there are others who follow Ismail. They follow these reciters, why? Because the voice indeed has a precise character. If the character of the voice is like Mustafa Ismail and they follow the style of Mutawali, [it is] too easy; [his voice is] lighter. But the character of Mustafa Ismail is heavier. So if your voice is heavy, *this* is the reciter you should strive to imitate. Our teachers call this *Bayyati Husayni*, for example. Here's the example."

Maria Ulfah then recited a line employing the variation *Bayyati Husayni*, attributed to the Egyptian reciter Sheikh Mustafa Ismail.

> Chapter (*Surah*) 21: *Al Anbiya'*, Verse (*Ayah*) 2
> 21:2 *Ma ya tihimu min thikrin min rabbihim muhdathin il istama'hu wa hum yal'aabuna.*
> (21:2 Whenever any fresh admonition comes to them from their Lord, they listen to it and make sport of it.)[3]

As in Arab practice Maria Ulfah's performance of *Husayni* emphasizes the fifth degree (A) above the tonic (D) as opposed to the fourth degree (G), which is conceptualized and heard as the usual "dominant" of *Bayyati* in musical practice of the Eastern Arab world or *mashriq*. The sixth degree of the scale, B flat, is always in the higher half-flat position in *Husayni* or *Bayyati Husayni*.

In this rather formulaic variation we hear a sequence of ascending thirds beginning on the fourth degree of *maqam Bayyati* (G), which also uses the B half-flat (see Figure 4.3). This is a common gesture in Arab music and is heard, for example, in the ever-popular song by the Egyptian composer Zakariyyah Ahmad titled "*Ya Salat iz-Zayn*."

She recited: *Al Anbiya'* (21:2).

Then she urged: "Try it! La la la la . . ." (*Coba! La la la la . . .*). At this point she isolated the sequence of rising thirds that are a signature of *Husayni* (and indeed the song "*Ya Salat iz-Zayn*") and vocalized on the syllable "la." Isa

ma ___ a ya' tiy ___ him min dhi – k ri m mir ___ ra b bi

him – m – m – m – m – muh da th in il – ll las sta ma 'u hu wa ___

hum _____ yal _____ 'a bu _____ u ___ u n

FIGURE 4.3. A transcription of Maria Ulfa's demonstration of a gesture in the *maqam Bayyati Husayni*. Note the sequence of rising thirds beginning on the note G and the syllable "muh."

Siswatika, the female contestant, recited the same line but didn't treat the sequence of rising thirds as clearly as is desirable. Isa ornamented each cell too extensively (see Figure 4.4). By way of constructive criticism Maria offered further commentary.

MARIA ULFAH: "If you add an extra tail (*ekor*) it is less sweet (*kurang manis*), less elegant/neat/handsome (*kurang anggun*)."
ANNE: "What is *anggun*?"
MARIA ULFAH: "Like your clothes. Sometimes people wear clothes that are less than elegant, less than beautiful."

Maria continued demonstrating: "Not like this . . . it's not necessary (*tidak usa*). Just like this, like . . . (*begitu saja*)" (see Figure 4.4).

Isa Siswatika tried the phrase again.

tail (ekor)   tail (ekor)

la la la _____ la la _____ la

(*tak usa*, it's not necessary)

FIGURE 4.4. A transcription of Maria Ulfa's demonstration, sung on the syllable "la," of the sequence of rising thirds (the gesture that begins on the syllable "muh" and the note G in the previous figure) with too much ornamentation or inappropriate "tails."

la_____   la a_____   la   la   la
(*gitu 'aja*, just like that!)

FIGURE 4.5. A transcription of Maria Ulfa's demonstration of
the correct way to sing the sequence of rising thirds, sung on the
syllable "la," without inappropriate "tails." This is the gesture that
begins on the syllable "muh" and the note G in Figure 4.3.

Among the many things that I found interesting during this session, not
all of which can be detailed in the clumsy descriptors of prose language, is
the way in which Maria Ulfah demonstrated *maqam* or *lagu* on the syllable
"la." The act of singing "la, la, la, laaa" isolates "pure" melody as something
that stands on its own, independent of the text it usually carries. In performance, text and melody are one and the same, a connection that is described
in language with the Indonesian term *irama* and the Arabic/Persian *talhin*.
In practice, however, text and tune can be separated, analyzed, evaluated
and reworked. Second, Maria Ulfah comments on the individuality of the
voice (*ciri khas*), which is honored for any unique aspects or limitations,
including tessitura, range, and timbre. Third, she teaches her students that
by employing the particular "riffs" associated with hallowed reciters, such
as the Egyptian heroes Sheikh Mustafa Isma'il and Sheikh Syed Mutawali,
reciters can demonstrate their technical expertise and their knowledge of the
depth of the tradition while simultaneously paying homage to the revered
artists whose status and style is unchallenged. The point of these variations
is the beautification of the Quranic text, but such gestures will not be lost on
those who are "in the know." Fellow reciters, judges, and even connoisseurs
will respond to such moments of artistic competence in the way that only a
jazz expert will recognize—similar to, for example, the clever quotation by
an improvising pianist of a Fats Waller lick from his well-known tune "Ain't
Misbehavin.'" In this session Isa Siswatika and Abdul Hamid are taught not
only "how to do it" but what "it" means.

III. Cultivating Aesthetic Sensibilities

In the next scenario we hear from Ustaz Asyri, a grand old gentleman of
recitation. Asyri's aesthetic sensibility is decidedly Cairene in orientation,
due to his time studying there, as well as his work with Egyptian reciters and
his love of Egyptian music. In social gatherings and *haflat*—sessions where

reciters gather, socialize, and exchange recitations and singing—as well as in more formal performances involving both music and recitation, I observed the ways Asyri was moved by recitation, singing, and instrumental music. He took great delight in expressing what I would call "musical emotion."

In May of 1999, Asyiri trained contestants Junaidin (who turned out to be the male adult winner that year) and Iis Sholiha (a female front-runner) for the upcoming competition in June. Junaidin presented a lengthy recitation that was both prepared in advance and created in the moment. Asyiri set the mood and egged Junaidin on with dramatically delivered formulas of spoken—in fact, shouted—praise and encouragement.

ASYIRI: *"Allah, Allah, Allah . . . Ya Salaam*!! (God, God, God, Oh Peace!)
Allah Ya Sallimak! (Oh God, [may] peace be on you!)

Junaidin recited *Surah Al Ta Ha, Ayah* 120 (translation: "So we warned Adam: Satan is thy enemy and the enemy of the companion, so let him not drive you out of the garden, lest each of you come to grief." Later we read, "So they ate of the tree and their nakedness became manifest to them and they began to cover it up with the adornments of the garden.")

Asyiri responded to Junaidin's exquisite marriage of tune and text (*talhin*) with punchy, perfunctory exclamations: *"Ah Ya Salaam*! *Musik*! Try to perfect it even more! It's good! *Musik*! Try it again. It is long (*panjang*)! (Here he refers to the length of the phrase.) It is good. It is music! Allah Allah!"

Junaidin recited the same passage. Asyiri interjected: "Ah, yes, perfect, Allah! *Satu, dua, tiga.* (One, two, three.) *Tekan*! (Lean on it!) *Turun*! (Descend!) *Naik*! (Ascend!) *Ankap*! (Grab it, hold on to it!)"

Later on in his recitation Junaidin employed a sobbing, chopping, quasi-yodeling ornament heard in some Arab singing but taken to extremes in Indonesia by the most popular and active reciter, Mu'ammar Z. A.

Asyiri was visibly and audibly moved by Junaidin's modulation to *maqam Sikah* as well as by this young reciter's rendering of a melodic shape that is narrow in range and almost static in movement (in contrast to the Olympian range, length, and notiness of the lines recited moments ago). Asyiri repeatedly offered praise and encouragement during the recitation, particularly at the points where the sobbing-like ornament (*nangis/menangis*, or crying) was employed.

ASYIRI: "Allah, Allah, Allah, hey, *nangis* (cry), *nangis*, . . . *ya nangis*, oh, oh, oh, *Ya Rabb* (Oh Lord!). . . . He has a voice where every time it falls, it is tasteful. Like . . . a person from Cairo!"

IV. Putting It All Together in the Course of Performance.

In our quest to discover what is original about a performance, we might ask questions such as these: What is improvised? What is spontaneous? Where do we differentiate between precise reproduction and fresh invention? But in addition to querying the performer and his or her performance, we should also consider the ways in which an audience improvises.[4] Through explanation and his own behavior, Asyiri conveys how recitation is inspired and inspiring. Unlike Maria Ulfah, Asyiri offers very little in the way of specific technical direction. Rather, he conjures the atmosphere of the performance event during which an audience would be expected to observe the performance and react to it with behavior that is culturally and contextually appropriate.[5]

The historiography of Arab and Middle Eastern Music is replete with commentary on audiences and the ways in which their behavior reflects and contributes to the affective power of music.[6] A leading scholar on this topic, A.J. Racy, has devoted his life's work to understanding the transformative power of Arab music (2003, especially Chapter 5). Ethnographic experience and historical documents inform his discussion of the interactive dynamics between performer and audience and the effect of this synergy on the musical performance itself. Racy's work on *tarab* music and culture establishes the importance of the audience's "initiation" into the performance culture: their expectations and dependence on what the author describes as "creative listening" (131). Although we may "translate" to the Indonesian context many aspects of Arabic language and Islamic custom, in many instances no direct correlation exists between Arab and Indonesian expressive culture, even when it does pertain to the Islamic religion. So, for example, in spite of the long-standing prestige of the Arab aesthetics in Indonesia (Rasmussen 2005), the complete cultural package of the *tarab* world as Racy describes it among perfing singers, instrumentalists, and audiences has not migrated to Indonesia. Nevertheless "creative listening" is a crucial aspect of Islamic performance among this community of reciters that seems to enable an experience of participation with the divine, something I aim to illustrate with the next ethnographic scenario.

In August 2003, at the enormous "Islamic Center" mosque in north Jakarta, the country's premier reciter, Mu'ammar Z. A., was featured as the last performer of a lengthy program called *Haflah al-Qur'an*. While most recitations, as well as the Islamic song genres presented (*tawshih* and *sholawat*), were about 10 minutes in duration, Mu'ammar's performance was remarkably longer: a single, solo recitation lasting about 20 minutes. Extraordinarily long

single-breath phrases (anywhere from 30 to 70 seconds) featuring alternation between rapid melodic movement (often at the beginnings and ends)
and extremely long, held notes characterize Mu'ammar's style. Such phrases
drive the participating audience to impassioned shouts of encouragement
and exclamation.[7] Audiences participate further in the recitation by singing "Allaaaaah" on the final tone of a reciter's phrase (where the reciter is
pausing to breathe and to get ready for the next phrase). Other hallmarks
of Mu'ammar's style include the indulgent and dramatic use of the "sobbing
ornament," which may be described as a register-breaking, regularly oscillat-
ing yodel. He also employs dramatic shift of octave register and purposeful
positioning of the handheld microphone, which he moves from directly in
front of his mouth to a foot or two away to the right or left side and back
again, creating an effective fade and shift in intensity and volume (from
fortissimo to pianissimo and back again).

Although considered the ultimate performer of the evening, Mu'ammar
actually breaks many conventions of performance that have been carefully
codified and canonized by teachers and judges of recitation in Indonesia.
In competition, for example, a reciter could never hold a particular note
for more than six beats (*harakat*); the sobbing ornament would have to be
curtailed, and the inventive shenanigans with the microphone would never
do. The strict canon of rules exists and is upheld precisely because reciters are
supposed to re-create an ideal performance with the practice that has been
passed on in an unbroken chain of oral tradition since the moment of original revelation itself. On the other hand, the practice of recitation is divinely
inspired and divinely inspiring, and accepted conventions of practice admit
spontaneous individual creation that may come not only from individual
humanly cultivated talent but also from mystical experience. Recitation is
not a musical setting of a chosen text; it is the animation in sound of the
word of God. It should not be planned; rather, it should emanate naturally
through a vessel (the reciter), who channels the melodies (*lagu al-Qur'an*)
that are already there.[8] Improvisation, then, which is based on these ancient,
specific, sacred melodies, which one works to manage but can never quite fix
precisely in an "ur"-recitation, may be opposed to memorized reproduction,
something that is unquestionably a human product.

IRAMA, INSPIRASI, AND THE PRACTICE OF THE SACRED

One of the practical lynchpins of recitation that ensures the spontaneity
of the melodic component is the continuous practice of prosody. Whereas

an amateur reciter will be able to render popular verses (*ayah*, sing.) or the shorter, more frequently heard chapters (*surah*, sing.) of the Qur'an (see Sells 1999), a professional will be able to start anywhere and link up appropriately, as context demands, passages from one chapter to passages in another. A truly seasoned reciter needs no lead time at all and can successfully render anything with perfect *tajwid* and in the musical *mujawwad* style.

In his review of Persian and Arabic sources, Blum notes that the term *talhin* can describe the kind of spontaneous composition that takes place in the presence of listeners as well as that meant for performance at a later time. *Talhin*, Blum writes, "sometimes denotes composition in this broad sense, embracing various arts of combination and conjunction—above all, those that coordinate text and tune—but also such common problems as how to move from one component to another within the modal system" (1998, 31).

In the context of their teaching I have heard reciters use the term *talhin*, whose meanings include "to chant," "psalmodize," "to intone," "to strike up a melody," "to set to music," and "to compose" (Wehr 1976, 862), but only rarely. However, I suspect they recognize the term from the Arabic root *lahn* (the letters *lam ha nun*), and especially from the oft-quoted hadith *Iqra' al-Qur'an b'il-lahun al 'Arab* ("Read the Qur'an with Arab melodies").[9] The term Indonesian reciters do use consistently is *irama*, a Javanese word. For gamelan musicians, *irama* is a "keyword" that describes tempo and density levels in instrumental performance. In the reciters' parlance, *irama* has a rather specialized meaning.[10] Scholars of Javanese language and music have helped me to approach and understand the way in which reciters might be using this term. Richard Wallis suggests (and Alec Jensen concurs) that *irama* is related to the Javanese *wirama*, meters of old Javanese poetry that "prescribed patterns of long and short syllables as well as other factors, including melodic shape" (personal comment). Dane Harwood takes the term back even further, deriving it from the Sanskrit *rama*, which is "associated with a number of adverbs and verbs that mean to be delightful, pleasing, and gratifying" (personal communication).[11]

Both terms *irama* and *talhin* get at the marriage of tune and text, which is effected necessarily by a human agent who improvises, setting text (both the sound and melody of it) to melody in the moment of performance. This, however, is an ideal of recitation praxis, and reciters consistently acknowledge the gap between the ideal and the real (see also Rasmussen 2001 and Gade 2004). "There are many people who don't (understand the meaning)" Maria Ulfah told me. "Kids don't. Even Arab people don't always know the meaning. People are trying to remember the melody; they are just thinking about the variations. Like if I were going to sing a Western song, I would sing it but I wouldn't know (think about) the meaning of the words. But it is recommended to understand the meaning because you are supposed to synchronize the meaning of the text with the feeling of the melody. For sad passages you use (*maqam*) *Hijaz* or *Nahawand* . . . for example, if you have done wrong and meet retribution. These verses are sad and serious. If you use *Rast* this is not allowed because *Rast* and *Sikah* are for happiness" (personal comment).

While children who grow up hearing excellent recitation will naturally internalize Arab *maqamat*,[12] the melodies or *lagu-lagu al-Qur'an* are imported. Their fixed and foreign origin ensures prestige and authority that is not subject to alteration.[13] The "agreed-upon-rules-of-performance" (Titon 1996:4) are precisely taught and enforced first and foremost so that the meaning of the Qur'an is preserved. This is particularly important in Indonesia, where Arabic is more of a liturgical code than a spoken language. Reciter Mu'ammar Z. A. goes so far as to suggest that if you recite badly and ruin the meaning (*merusakkan makna*), you can bring on sin (*dapat dosa*). This is an aspect of recitation that discourages experimentation and privileges *re-creation*. In other words: if you can't improvise yourself, it is better to stick to the model, to copy someone else.

Balancing the overpowering incentive to, as Gade puts it, "get it right" is the second rationale for learning the rules: to indulge in the aesthetic beauty of the recited Qur'an. The repeated practice and experience—for some from cradle to grave—of the intervallic relationships, specific intonation, tetrachordal shapes, specific phrases, cadential clichés, along with the ability to move from mode to mode, and so forth, prepares the reciter to improvise and be ready to respond to or even to ensnare that supernatural moment when divine inspiration drives human action. Not only are reciters prepared by their mentors for *inspirasi*, but so is the audience, who learn—either through assimilation or, more likely, through their own experience as students—why and how recitation is aesthetically and spiritually moving. Judith Becker expands our notion of sound-experiencing practices with the concept *habitus of listening*, something that "is learned through unconscious imitation of those who surround us and with whom we continually interact" (2004, 70). While this kind of "natural" acculturation certainly occurs in the community I describe, there is also a degree of conscious "orchestration" of musical performance and emotional response that continuously pushes the reality of recitation toward an ideal based in profane practice but realized in sacred inspiration.[14]

Reciters with whom I have worked are quite frank in their assessment of the real and the ideal in the world of recitation. Anyone who practices recitation will acquire God's blessing (*dapat pahala*), so even the most mundane mimesis is worthwhile. While "practice makes perfect," both the "rehearsal" and the "show" are processes of performance; and although there is a conceptual differentiation between practice and performance, both acts can be devotional in nature. Peacock, in his discussion of the sacred and the profane, argues that sacred performance is a conundrum, a contradiction in terms: "The term [sacred performance] is an oxymoron. Sacrality implies, at least in the salvation religions dominant in Western and Near Eastern history, a meaning rooted in a cosmic frame that transcends any immediate sensed form. The sacred cannot, therefore, be 'performed.' Any reduction of meaning to form deprives that form of meaning. To perform the 'sacred' necessarily is to profane it. Yet the sacred becomes real only as embodied in form" (Peacock 1990, 208).

For the community I describe, God's word may be understood in collective study and individual contemplation, but it is experienced in praxis. This community of believers accepts the "profaning" of the sacred through practice—and here I mean practice as work (as when you practice the high jump or the trombone)—that is rewarded by the divine. For it is disciplined and continuous practice that enables a reciter to, at the perfect moment of divine inspiration, unite individual creativity, technical competence, and an informed aesthetic sensibility, and to beautify, melodically and musically, the word of God.

NOTES

1. Part of this neo-Orientalist exercise includes the regarding of Islam as a monolithic entity with its own singular personality.

2. Teaching Arab melodies using *tawshih* texts is institutionalized at Jakarta institutes and disseminated throughout the archipelago by its many graduates; however, this technique is not practiced by *every* reciter in the country.

3. The preceding verse, 21:1, an antecedent thought to *Al-Anbiya'* 21:2, translates: "The time of reckoning is drawing nigh for the people, yet they are heedless and turn away." This and subsequent translations are from *The Qur'an*, Arabic text with a new translation by Muhammad Zafrulla Khan (1991).

4. In his contribution to the collection of essays on this topic, R. Anderson Sutton asks, "How are we to know improvisation when we encounter it?" (1998, 73).

5. See Rasmussen (2004) on teaching the integrated aesthetics of performance and reception.

6. See, for example, Sawa's accounts of the *Kitab al-Aghani*, the writings of the 18th-century French researcher Villoteau as documented by Racy (2003), the 19th-century cultural explorer Edward Lane, or works by contemporary scholars Racy

(2003), Touma (1996), Rouget (1985), Danielson (1997), Rasmussen (1991, 1998), Kapchan (2003), and others.

7. See also Touma (1996, 155) for an account of audience reaction during pauses. See also Nelson on pauses (1985).

8. The concept that the music is already "out there" and that the human performer just channels it may be similar to certain Native American theories regarding the origin of music as part of the supernatural world. Both ideas contradict the Western notion of creation, with its insistence on individual authorship.

9. Sometimes *lahn* is translated as "dialect," a reference to the seven styles of reading that developed among Muhammad's followers, which will be treated in a forthcoming publication.

10. The various shades of the term *irama* were revealed to me as I shuttled regularly between gamelan musicians and reciters in Jakarta. The *irama* that gamelan teachers were teaching me and the *irama* the reciters were talking about were not one and the same.

11. Richard Wallis, Alec Jensen, Dane Harwood, and Marc Perlman, among others, contributed to a discussion I initiated on this topic via the gamelan listserv.

12. Anna Gade (2004) quotes a consultant for her project who joked, "even the mice in Indonesia can sing *lagu al-Qur'an*."

13. Javanese ethnomusicologist Sri Hastanto lists five Indonesian tuning systems but makes no mention of Arab *maqam* as a "sonic order" in Indonesia (Hastanto in 1996).

14. See Becker's discussion of Bordieu's habitus and his use of musical metaphors involving (or not) orchestration and conductors (2004, 70).

REFERENCES

Becker, Judith. 2004. *Deep Listeners: Music, Emotion, and Trancing.* Bloomington and Indianapolis: Indiana University Press.

Blum, Stephen. 1998. "The Concept and Its Ramifications." In *In the Course of Performance: Studies in the World of Musical Improvisation,* edited by Bruno Nettl with Melinda Russell, 27–46. Chicago: University of Chicago Press.

Danielson, Virginia. 1997. *The Voice of Egypt: Umm Kulthum, Arabic Song, and Egyptian Society in the Twentieth Century.* Chicago: University of Chicago Press; Cairo: American University in Cairo Press.

Danielson, Virginia, and Alexander J. Fisher. 2002. "History of Scholarship: Narratives of Middle Eastern Music History." In *The Garland Encyclopedia of World Music, Volume 6: The Middle East,* edited by Virginia Danielson, Scott Marcus, and Dwight Reynolds, 15–27. New York and London: Routledge.

Farmer, Henry George. 1929. *A History of Arabian Music to the XIIIth Century.* London: Lyzac and Co.

Faruqi, Lois Ibsen al-. 1979. "The Status of Music in Muslim Nations: Evidence from the Arab World." *Asian Music* 12(1): 56–85.

———. 1985. "Music, Musicians, and Muslim Law." *Asian Music* 17(1): 3–36.

Frischkopf, Michael. n.d. "The Sounds of Islamic Congregational Prayer in Mainstream Egyptian Practice." Unpublished manuscript.

Gade, Anna M. 2004. *Perfection Makes Practice: Learning, Emotion, and the Recited Qur'an in Indonesia.* Hilo: University of Hawai'i Press.

Hastanto, Sri. 2003. "Sonic Orders in the Musics of Indonesia." In *Sonic Orders in Asian Musics: A Field and Laboratory Study of Musical Cultures and Systems in Southeast Asia,* Vol. 1, edited by Joe Peters. Singapore: National Arts Council, Asian Committee on Culture and Information, 2003.

Kapchan, Deborah. 2003. "Nashat: the Gender of Musical Celebration in Morocco." In *Music and Gender: Perspectives from the Mediterranean,* edited by Tullia Magrini, 251–66. Chicago: University of Chicago Press.

Lambert, Jean. 1997. *La Médecine de L'ame: Le Chant de Sanaa dans la Société Yéménite [The Medicine of the Soul: San'ani Song in Yemeni Society].* Nanterre, France: Société d'Ethnologie.

Lane, Edward W. 1908 [1963]. *The Manners and Customs of the Modern Egyptians.* London: Everyman's Library.

Marcus, Scott L. 1989. "Arab Music Theory in the Modern Period." Ph.D. dissertation, University of California at Los Angeles.

———. 2002. "The Eastern Arab System of Melodic Modes in Theory and Practice: A Case Study of *Maqam Bayyati.*" In *The Garland Encyclopedia of World Music, Volume 6: The Middle East,* edited by Virginia Danielson, Scott Marcus, and Dwight Reynolds, 33–44. New York and London: Routledge.

Nasr, Seyyed Hossen. 2000. "Islam and Music: The Legal and the Spiritual Dimensions." In *Enchanting Powers: Music in the World's Religions,* edited by Laurence E. Sullivan. Cambridge, Mass.: Harvard University Press.

Nelson, Kristina. 1985. *The Art of Reciting the Qur'an.* Austin: University of Texas Press.

———1993. "The Sound of the Divine in Daily Life." In *Everyday Life in the Muslim Middle East,* edited by Donna Lee Bowen and Evelyn A. Early. Bloomington and Indianapolis: Indiana University Press.

Peacock, James L. 1990. "Ethnographic Notes on Sacred and Profane Performance." In *By Means of Performance: Intercultural Studies of Theatre and Ritual,* edited by Richard Schechner and Willa Appel, 208–35.Cambridge: Cambridge University Press.

Pressing, Jeff. 1998. "Psychological Constraints on Improvisational Expertise and Communication." In *In the Course of Performance: Studies in the World of Musical Improvisation,* edited by Bruno Nettl with Melinda Russell, 47–68. Chicago: University of Chicago Press.

Qur'an, The. 1991. Arabic text with a new translation, translated and with an introduction by Muhammad Zafrulla Khan. Brooklyn, N.Y.: Olive Branch Press.

Racy, Ali Jihad. 2003. *Making Music in the Arab World: The Culture and Artistry of Tarab.* Oxford: Oxford University Press.

Rasmussen, Anne K. 1991. "Individuality and Musical Change in the Music of Arab Americans." Ph.D. dissertation. University of California at Los Angeles.

———. 1998. "The Music of Arab Americans: Aesthetics and Performance in a New Land." In *Images of Enchantment: Visual and Performing Arts of the Middle East,* edited by Sherifa Zuhur. Cairo: American University in Cairo Press.

———. 2001. "The Qur'an in Daily Life: The Public Project of Musical Oratory." *Journal of the Society for Ethnomusicology* 45(1): 30–57.

———. 2004. "Bilateral Negotiations in Bimusicality: Insiders, Outsiders and 'the Real Version' in Middle Eastern Music Performance." In *Performing Ethnomusicology,* edited by Ted Solis, 215–28. Berkeley: University of California Press.

———. 2005. "The Arabic Aesthetic in Indonesian Islam." *The World of Music* 47(1): 65–90.

Rouget, Gilbert. 1985. *Music and Trance: A Theory of the Relations between Music and Possession.* Translation from the French revised by Brunhilde Biebuyck in collaboration with the author. Chicago: University of Chicago Press.

Sawa, George D. 1985. "The Status and Roles of the Secular Musicians in the *Kitab al-Aghani* (Book of Songs) of Abu al-Faraj al-Isbahani (D. 356 A.H./967 A.D.)." *Asian Music* 17(1).

———. 1989. *Music Performance in the Early 'Abbasid Era 132–320 AH/ 750–932 AD.* Toronto: Pontifical Institute of Mediaeval Studies.

Sells, Michael A. 1999. *Approaching the Qur'an: The Early Revelations.* Ashland, Ore: White Cloud Press.

Sutton, R. Anderson. 1998. "Do Javanese Gamelan Musicians Really Improvise?" In *In the Course of Performance: Studies in the World of Musical Improvisation,* edited by Bruno Nettl with Melinda Russell, 69–94. Chicago: University of Chicago Press.

Titon, Jeff Todd, ed. 1996. *Worlds of Music: An Introduction to Music of the World's Peoples,* 3rd ed. New York: Schirmer Books.

Touma, Habib Hassan. 1996. *The Music of the Arabs.* Translated by Laurie Schwartz. Portland, Ore.: Amadeus Press.

Wehr, Hans. 1976. *Arabic-English Dictionary: The Hans Wehr Dictionary of Modern Written Arabic,* edited by J.M. Cowan. Ithaca, N.Y.: Spoken Language Services.

～5～

GENIUS, IMPROVISATION,

AND THE NARRATIVES OF JAZZ HISTORY

Gabriel Solis

This article attempts to tie together some ideas on writing and teaching jazz history that have been weighing on my mind for the past few years. I am primarily interested in developing a historiography that is sensitive to poststructuralist critique, especially postcolonial theory, and is also informed by the ways jazz musicians individually and as a group think about their tradition. In this process, I want to draw connections between the concept of genius as it plays out in nonacademic and academic circles, the idea of musical works, and "great man" historical epistemologies in a music that is both improvisatory and situated within a heterogeneous culture that values performance over textuality. All of these ideas relate to jazz historiography, and perhaps the historiography of any music that permeates society the way jazz does, touching major antinomies of the post-Enlightenment West, of art and entertainment, of small-scale, face-to-face participatory interaction and large-scale, mass-mediated presentation. In suggesting this, I am developing some themes first suggested to me by Scott DeVeaux's article "Constructing the Jazz Tradition" (1991). Although as a historian I am sympathetic to the deconstruction of the canon (as DeVeaux suggested and as a number of writers have taken up since), as an ethnographer I am sympathetic to the profound power that a canon of "greats," "giants," or "masters" has, both for writing academic history and in the jazz community at large.

The beginning of the 21st century is very much a time of historiographical awareness and interest in jazz scholarship—partly as a lingering symptom of the postmodern condition, the "death of history," and the like, and partly as a sign of the maturation of the field. Academic jazz scholarship is only in its third or perhaps fourth generation, and many of us are interrogating the historical models that are the background for much of our work. A good deal of historiographical ink was spilled in the wake of the PBS special *Jazz*, directed by Ken Burns, because reviewers felt compelled to take issue with the extent to which the series reproduced, undigested and uncontested, the historiography of its principal consultants, Stanley Crouch and Wynton Marsalis (Kelley 2001; Pond 2003). More recently, Sherri Tucker's long entry on jazz historiography in the *Grove Music Online* (2007) and John Gennari's book *Blowin' Hot and Cool: Jazz and Its Critics* (2006) have attempted to account systematically for the shape of jazz historical writing, particularly nonacademic jazz history.

Perhaps the most notable feature of jazz history writing is its proximity in time to the music's production. As Tucker notes, "Throughout its relatively brief existence, jazz has been regarded . . . as historically significant. . . . Indeed, writers' efforts to describe, analyze, and craft coherent jazz histories have occurred nearly simultaneously with jazz music-making, itself" (2007). She notes that for a variety of reasons, not least the fact that the academic music institutions and musicologists were hostile to any sort of popular music, jazz history was written primarily by music critics and secondarily by scholars of African American culture more broadly (particularly scholars with a literary background). Gennari covers similar ground in much more detail, noting how the particular backgrounds of the various jazz critics engaged in historical writing would have led them to the particular sorts of narratives (and musicians) they championed (2006). As Tucker makes clear, this has meant not only that jazz historiography begins almost at the same time that jazz emerges as a coherent musical style (indeed, the writing of jazz history may well have helped promote the growing consensus in the 1910s that "jazz" *was* a coherent musical category) but also that until very recently jazz history was, de facto, contemporary history, written to make sense of whatever the current moment was.

A significant fact that neither Tucker nor Gennari discusses is that jazz historiography in a broad sense—as a historical consciousness or a historical imagination—has not been confined to writers and the written medium. Jazz musicians have, since early in the tradition's existence, been historically minded, and as a result jazz performance has often had a historical sensibility. I discuss this fact in detail regarding jazz in the 1980s and 1990s in my book *Monk's Music: Thelonious Monk and Jazz History in the Making* (2007), but there is good evidence that this sort of historical consciousness is much older. In particular, the model that emerged for the "jazz concert" was a sonic history that placed the music in a lineage from the old to the new, starting at least with the "Experiment in Modern Music" at Aeolian Hall in 1924 (which is historical principally because it involves the conceit that jazz developed—and could develop further—from rough, discordant, vernacular sounds into smooth, polished, high-class sounds). One fundamental tension in the teleologies of jazz historical writing is that jazz is on either an evolutionary or an entropic path, that either it is inching ever toward perfection or lives forever in danger of squandering the power of a mythic past. Three other important early jazz concerts—W. C. Handy's 1928 concert at Carnegie Hall, Benny Goodman's famous 1938 concert at the same venue, and the collaborative *Spirituals to Swing* concert promoted by John Hammond, also in 1938, which was produced in a number of locations, complete with lectures and transcriptions—all included or were entirely based on the idea of tracing the music's development in performance (see DeVeaux 1989, 8, 18–19, 20–21). These concerts were, in a sense, a systematization of the more general practice found in most jazz improvising—often glossed, following Henry Louis Gates, Jr., as "Signifyin(g)"—in which jazz performers tell a version of their music's history in performance (1988).

Duke Ellington's extended compositions were also mediums for the exercise of historiography in sound, most explicitly in *Black, Brown and Beige*, which he described as "a tone parallel to the history of the American Negro." Mark Tucker's article on Duke Ellington's "Renaissance Education" (1990) explains Ellington's lifelong interest in the history and culture of Africans and the African diaspora as a result of early educational experiences in Washington, D.C.'s black community. The academic, if not quite didactic, quality of much of Ellington's compositional output is as much a result of his youthful experience in the Negro Renaissance as is his interest in large-scale musical form and his comfort working in concert settings. Few other jazz musicians were as interested in working with African American history as Ellington, but other jazz composers and performers also came to terms with black history in their music, most recently Wynton Marsalis with the piece "Blood on the Fields" and the album *From the Plantation to the Penitentiary*. In the past 10 or 15 years the tribute album has also become a staple of the jazz recording catalogue, with musicians of every stripe playing the work of their favorites, heroes, models, and influences. These recordings become a history of sorts, or perhaps an archive of collective memory. It is my impression that this explicitly historical aspect of jazz music making at least partly accounts for the extensive jazz historical literature by nonmusicians.

As Tucker notes in her *Grove* entry, current jazz historiography (like most historiography) has become more and more critical, arguing less about what jazz is and more about what jazz has meant to specific groups of people at specific times (2007). With notable exceptions—Tucker's history of "all-girl" bands of the 1940s (2000) or Steven Isoardi's books on Horace Tapscott and the Union of God's Musicians' and Artists' Ascension in Los Angeles (Isoardi 2006; Tapscott 2001), for instance—even critical jazz scholarship that draws heavily on cultural history and anthropology has recognized, if implicitly, a core canon and focused principally on canonical musicians and their works. The rest of this essay considers why this might be so, how the concept of genius relates to the creation of a jazz canon, and why it might be useful to have a jazz historiography that is at least critical of the idea of canonicity.

I

Before launching into the big questions, I would like to expand briefly on my personal reasons for writing on this topic. A close look at my own social and intellectual history may have a direct bearing on why I find the question of historiography so interesting, and on the answers to which I have come. The story begins with the writing of my dissertation (Solis 2001), in which, strongly influenced by works in postcolonial history, especially those by Michel-Rolph Trouillot (1995) and Dipesh Chakrabarty (2000), I first settled on the idea of writing something that accounted for Thelonious Monk's place in jazz history and in the contemporary jazz scene without recourse to the sorts of hagiographical narratives that seemed so common—a deconstruction of the great man and of his great works as an expression of his genius. I wanted to understand how we come to see a figure like Monk in a particular way, and I concluded that, excellent as his music may be in and of itself, its historical importance comes from the extent to which it was taken up by others and its potentialities for improvisation were explored, developed, and used in performance. Given my penchant for social science answers to humanistic questions, the focus of my dissertation, though influenced by previous scholars in jazz, history, and anthropology (some of whom have articles in this collection), also owes much to a lingering counter-culturalism and perhaps knee-jerk reaction to authority that resulted from a hippie upbringing in northern California in the 1970s and 1980s. What I found compelling relates to what I was looking for: the pump was primed.

Since then, another aspect of my scholarly work that has pressed the issue of genius to the fore is an article of mine that was published in *Ethnomusicology*, "'A Unique Chunk of Jazz Reality'" (2004), dealing with the reissue of Monk's recordings from the Five Spot in 1958. In it I argue that our interest in hearing detritus from these (and other) jazz recording sessions says something important about how we think about authorship, musical works, and musical ownership in jazz. I thought I was expressing how important it is to me that we think about musicians as actual people, like ourselves, and resist the literary-critical approach that threatens to turn them into ciphers representing nothing but a collection of texts. I was, therefore, surprised when a number of people responded (positively) that, by giving a genius his due, I was resisting the tendency of recent musicology to reduce great composers to people just like us.

My interest in the idea of genius and the associated "great man" historiography has also come from teaching jazz history in a major school of music, especially as part of a developing program for the study of jazz and improvisatory musics (or JAIMS). In constructing courses that focus on how the contributions of great individuals have emerged in the context of dialogues on a number of levels with other musicians, sociohistorical situations, and audiences and critics who often have brought their own issues to the practice of hearing and interpreting the music, I have run into resistance in two directions. The first, and most obvious, has been from those who are deeply invested in the music and its canonic figures; the second, and perhaps more surprising, has been from those who have no prior investment in the music and find it hard to believe how central individual figures (Charlie Parker, for instance) can be in the music and the discourse around it. The former sees a kind of disrespect for the musicians, the tradition, or something like that in a non- or anticanonical historiography, and the latter seems to see a kind of naïve hero worship in my continued insistence on the incredible presence that figures like Parker (or Monk, or Coltrane . . .) have in jazz. I am convinced that the surprise and resistance expressed by the first group are important, because they indicate a feeling that is widely held by people in the jazz scene—that is, by musicians and audiences—that the canon (if a kind of vernacular, unofficial canon) is reasonable, that there are greater and lesser musicians in the music's history, and that the job of the historian is to uphold this binary interpretive framework. I take this seriously because it is representative of similar ideas held by musicians operating on pretty much all levels and in all styles of jazz today. Needless to say, there is no consensus about the membership of this canon of greater musicians (outside a handful of obvious candidates).

At the same time, I feel strongly that students, especially those in a jazz program who are thinking about a career in this music, should be asked to seriously consider why figures who are often passed over, like Stanley Turrentine or Jack McDuff, or even less visible figures like Willie Aikins, Mickey Roker, or Bootsie Barnes, are important to a historical, as well as synchronic or structural, understanding of the music, and not as "kleinmeisters." In the history of jazz, it is of signal importance to account for the significance of those who have not risen to the level of "giants" or "geniuses." Moreover, a history of jazz that sees only the contributions of individual musicians, but not the ways those contributions have been made within social, cultural, and political (that is, discursive) frameworks, misses much of what has made jazz important, powerful music for over a century or more.

II

In arguing about the specific ways the "genius" concept bears on the writing or telling of jazz history, and the grounds for its creation, it will be useful to look briefly at how the word has been marshaled vis-à-vis music and musicians in the past. Half of an insight Mikhail Bakhtin had about language, after all, was that it comes into our possession already "populated" with the thoughts and intentions of others; it comes to us already "fully historical" (1981, 293). There is an extensive literature on the concept of genius, from every conceivable discipline, focusing on such topics as definitions of the phenomenon, the supposed connection between genius and mental illness, the social construction of genius, and so forth. I am particularly interested in the work of genius's apologists in the era of postmodernism, poststructuralism, postcolonialism, and other "posts." Two books will serve as helpful examples of how genius is construed, particularly how the production of works and their "universality" are invoked.

John Briggs's book on the subject, *Fire in the Crucible: The Alchemy of Creative Genius* (1988), takes a broad view, attempting to find an understanding of genius across various contexts. Briggs uses the metaphor of an alchemist because it captures the mystery of creativity. Creative genius, like alchemy, is part science and part magic, and disentangling the two may be impossible. Briggs settles on a fairly straightforward definition: geniuses "are, for the most part, women and men who have altered in some significant way our perception of a major field of human endeavor. . . . In the case of the arts, significantly altering a field means leaving an indelible impression of vision" (1988, 12). Later, works and their universality emerge as a concern. One of the global questions for the book is: "How do certain works—the works of genius—embody 'truth,' 'beauty' and 'universality'?" In defining these taken-for-granted terms, one starts to get into slippery and problematic territory. It is not surprising that the only jazz musician to be discussed—indeed, the only African American musician of any sort even mentioned in this book— is Duke Ellington, who is arguably the first, the most accomplished, and certainly the best-known jazz composer to create music that fits most of the conventional notions of a musical work.

This book says a number of interesting things about creativity and undermines some of the worse canards about "creative" types, including the myth of the lone genius, and more basically the idea that a genius is somehow a different type of human being (Briggs 1988, 13). Nonetheless, the preconception that creative genius requires the production of works and that there is a universality to those works—universality is, perhaps mercifully, not defined in this book—means that Briggs must exclude many musicians operating outside the Western classical tradition (and, I suppose, many operating within it who are not composers) on a variety of grounds, either because the production of works is only a small part of their activity, or because their works are not perceived as "universal" from some undisclosed point of reference.

Peter Kivy's recent book *The Possessor and the Possessed: Handel, Mozart, Beethoven, and the Idea of Musical Genius* (2001), which delves more deeply into the way genius has been construed in music since the 18th century, comes to similar conclusions as Briggs and, indeed, may help us expand on some of the key issues in Briggs's definition of genius. First, Kivy also takes it as axiomatic that a musical genius produces musical works: "Musical genius is not something that can be read off someone . . . it is a 'dispositional' property, and, ordinarily, one knows that the disposition is present by its being 'expressed.' . . . We know that Beethoven was a musical genius because we know that, during his lifetime, he created musical works upon which we place the highest possible musical value." This idea is repeated many times over: "A musical genius is one who produces supremely valuable musical works," and so on (2001, 178). In insisting that the production of works is the definitive activity of a musical genius, Kivy makes it clear that to him genius is a measure of the ultimate worth of human endeavor.

The issue of universality rears its head in Kivy's discussion of Beethoven in the same problematic way that it does in Briggs. In discussing the necessary social conditions for the disposition of genius to be expressed, he notes, "Musical geniuses are able to express their genius in great musical works only in the proper social and political environment, with the requisite institutions in place. On the commonsense view, Beethoven would not have written great musical works (or any musical works at all) if he had been transported as an infant to Australia and had lived out his life in a community of Aborigines" (2001, 179). (These imagined Australian Aborigines come up again as a metaphor for nonuniversality, and in explicit contrast with Bonn, Vienna, and London and their inhabitants—apparently interchangeable expressions of culturally universal spaces and people.) Kivy can be credited with producing a flexible enough idea of musical genius to account for the different types of creativity and productivity exemplified by such varied composers as Haydn, Mozart, and Bach. Although it is hardly possible or profitable to argue against Kivy's point here, the connection between the thing of highest value, "universality," and the production of musical works is problematic because the West's others (within and without) either qualify only because they produce works that are recognizably similar to Kivy's "universal" works, or they don't qualify at all. This particular piece of illogic—the elevation of one particular to the putative status of universal—is immediately familiar to any reader of postcolonial theory in its African or South Asian forms, but it is nonetheless assumed without question far too often.

All of this is remarkably similar to the ideological underpinning for the theory of history in which Hegel presents the idea of "world historical individuals" (great men); if not the first such exposition, it is at least a good candidate for a truly influential source for much of the historiographic method that has characterized music history since the 19th century. It is noteworthy that Hegel introduces the "world historical individual" in a book in which he explicitly states that only the Germanic world is fully historical; the worlds of Aborigines and Native Americans are not at all historical, and the worlds of various others (Africans, Asians, Mediterranean people) are at various states of development, presumably locked there forever by an evolutionary paradigm ([1899] 1956). In any case, Hegel's implicit assumption that only northern Europeans could produce true world historical individuals is directly in line with Kivy's assumptions. As Kivy has defined musical genius (which amounts to essentially the world historical individual of music), it is only possible that Europeans—one fears perhaps only Germanic peoples—and others working within their paradigms could produce geniuses.

III

What are we to do with all of this? It is not sufficient to note that "great man" historiography and the attendant notion of genius are part and parcel of the racist underbelly of the Enlightenment. The question is whether they may, if stripped of that baggage, serve some use. This is the other half of that insight of Bakhtin's I alluded to earlier: that although words and ideas come to us already populated, we can and do populate them with our own intentions all the time—we are not necessarily hamstrung by their history. Either "genius" needs an intervention, or "work" does, or perhaps both need to be taken down from these lofty heights and moderated.

Someone once suggested to me that the goal of the humanities is to find and explore greatness and the goal of social science is to find and explore the common denominator. While I'm convinced that this is a problematic way of looking at the distinction between the two approaches, it is indeed common to divide human life into the normal and the exceptional. Wherever music history lies in this dialectic, I am sure I want it both ways. I want a historiography that is somehow able to see the commingling of the great and the everyday. A number of jazz scholars have suggested fruitful ways out of the canon-based historiography of geniuses and their works. Steve Pond has recently suggested that the practice of treating jazz recordings as though they were musical scores and then massively privileging melodic and harmonic "evolution" in "parade of styles" accounts of jazz history should be replaced by a jazz historiography that deals with more aspects of sound and remembers that those recordings are improvised performances (2006). Olly Wilson and Christopher Small both insisted that jazz scholars keep in mind that jazz (and in Small's case, all music) is an activity first and a set of objects second—"A way of doing something and not just something that is done" (Wilson 1974, 20; see also Small 1987). Pond notes that we need to develop this new historiography because the old historiography, in his words, produces a "massive, collective shrug" when one is attempting to understand jazz history after 1965 (2006). He suggests that if we were to take the many sounds called jazz seriously, we would find not only that our harmonic and melodic evolution narratives fail to explain the years after 1965, but that they also anachronistically limit the music we consider from before 1965, failing to account for, among others, Louis Jordan. David Ake has made a similar argument (also in favor of including Jordan in the jazz story) in *Jazz Cultures* (2002, 42–61), but in some ways Pond's work is more unsettling to the standard jazz historiography because it is not so much an argument for Jordan's inclusion as the suggestion that we should completely revamp our notion of jazz history as a succession of bounded styles.

Others have suggested that jazz historiography needs a critical intervention, but none is quite as close to what I am advocating here as the model Robin D. G. Kelley (2001) suggested in a review of Ken Burns's *Jazz* series. Kelley takes issue with several aspects of the film, especially its much-noted failure to deal with the jazz avant-garde in a serious and thoughtful way, but the most interesting and distinctive critique he suggests is that the film fails to explain jazz because of its "inability to recognize 'community'—a musician's community, an African American community, and various overlapping communities that make up the world of jazz" (2001, 9). Kelley argues that "greatness" in the music emerges through hard work and the support of a community; I would add that "greatness" emerges in the ways that a community embraces and takes possession of the work of great musicians. This, incidentally, is not far from what Tia DeNora (1995) has advocated with regard to genius and the construction of the Beethoven mythos—not that Beethoven was not great, but that his mythology, particularly as he came to be widely seen not only as *a* genius, but also as the paradigmatic representation *of* genius, was a historically contingent process that depended on Beethoven's place in a particular moment in Viennese history.

This dialectic of hard creative work and its interpretation by a community, which is also a dialectic of the exceptional and the everyday, can be seen in the ways that jazz repertoire becomes canonical. In working with Monk's music and the contemporary jazz scene, I have dealt directly with the ways repertoire is used and have come to think that there are at least two general qualities that make jazz repertoire great. The first is that it is distinctive, readily memorable—essentially the same thing that makes a great work great in the Western classical tradition. Many of Monk's compositions fit the bill, of course—"Blue Monk" seems as good an example as any: the tune uses a standard blues phrase structure and standard blues chord changes, but its rising lines in parallel thirds, and their moments of bluesy chromaticism, followed by tags that incorporate one exposed disjunct note, are immediately recognizable, as is the typically Monk-ish rhythmically displaced motivic repetition in measures 10 and 11. The piece is motivic in a way that many jazz blues are not (but, interestingly, in a way that many blues songs in the blues genre *are*). Moreover, and equally importantly, to be a truly great piece of repertoire a piece has to inspire improvisation. No amount of clarity, distinctiveness, and so forth will make a piece great if it does not create openings for musicians to bring their own thoughts, ideas, and voices to the performance. Again and again, whenever I have asked jazz musicians about this, they have commented on how much they have found Monk's pieces compelling vehicles for their own improvisations.

It would not be hard to take the example of "Blue Monk" as evidence that Monk is a genius, very much in the way that Briggs or Kivy suggested. But rather than leave it there, I would like to draw another conclusion, hopefully one that keeps intact my great respect for Monk's contribution but also creates a historiography that is true to a basic ethnographic lesson about jazz: that the scene is one of the most important social and musical units, more than the individual: that part of Monk's greatness is a direct result of the many approaches people have taken to his music over the years. Molefi Kete Asante and Olly Wilson are in agreement that the heart of African American music making is in performativity—as Wilson puts it, "the way of doing something, not simply something that is done" (1974, 20), or, as Asante puts it, "never a thing, but always an activity" (1998, 62). Although I do not agree with the complete exclusion of the "thing" in Asante's theory, my work has made it clear to me that whatever greatness the pieces or Monk's recordings of them have, much of it remained potential and was either found or created by the work of literally thousands of musicians playing it over time. What's more, I am convinced that the day-to-day performances of his music (and lots of other music) are as important as the canonical performances. And here is where these pieces differ most from the "great works of genius" of the Western classical tradition: their greatness lies in their value as "use objects" in performance settings where the principal concern is forging a sense of communalism in an exchange of sound and sentiment, in jazz's life as a participatory music.

It is not easy to accomplish a historical approach to this music that accounts for the ethnographic reality of reverence for a set of canonical figures by both musicians and audiences in jazz and yet also accounts for the equally fundamental importance of the everyday in the music. I am drawn to the social memory literature, going back at least to Maurice Halbwachs (1992) and particularly to Paul Connerton (1989), who has noted an important dialectic: cyclicity or repetition and the internalization of the past in what is often referred to as "habit memory" is in dialogue with linearity and the externalization of the past in what he calls "cognitive memory" or recollection. As in jazz practice, so in jazz history, the cyclical and the linear happen in connection with one another. Guthrie Ramsey, in his book *Race Music* (2003), has amply demonstrated the value of placing the history of canonical music in the context of family history. It would be an enormous boon for ethnographically oriented jazz historians to undertake comprehensive histories of local jazz scenes to provide detail that will ultimately be helpful in quantifying and demonstrating the significance of those everyday performances in constructing the social memory in which the history ultimately takes place, in creating the settings in which great works are forged.

If this is a goal for jazz historians, then I think genius and "great man" models of history become not so much wrong as only half the story. Yes, there are unusually good composers and performers, and they have an important place in the history, but they are neither so different from the rest of the scene nor so much more important as to be the sole topic of consideration. I hope this approach can help those who study other improvised traditions to take seriously the importance of both exceptional figures and everyday performance.

REFERENCES

Ake, David. 2002. *Jazz Cultures*. Berkeley: University of California Press.

Asante, Molefi Kete. 1998. *The Afrocentric Idea*, rev. ed. Philadelphia: Temple University Press.

Bakhtin, M. Mikhail. 1981. *The Dialogic Imagination: Four Essays*. Edited by Michael Holquist, translated by Caryl Emerson and Michael Holquist. Austin: University of Texas Press.

Briggs, John. 1988. *Fire in the Crucible: The Alchemy of Creative Genius*. New York: St. Martin's Press.

Chakrabarty, Dipesh. 2000. *Provincializing Europe: Postcolonial Thought and Historical Difference*. Princeton, N.J.: Princeton University Press.

Connerton, Paul. 1989. *How Societies Remember*. Cambridge: Cambridge University Press.

DeNora, Tia. 1995. *Beethoven and the Construction of Genius: Music and Politics in Vienna 1792–1803*. Berkeley: University of California Press.

DeVeaux, Scott. 1989. "The Emergence of the Jazz Concert, 1935–1945." *American Music* 7(1): 6–29.

———. 1991. "Constructing the Jazz Tradition: Jazz Historiography." *Black American Literature Forum* 25(3): 525–60.

Gates, Henry Louis, Jr. 1988. *The Signifying Monkey: A Theory of Afro-American Literary Criticism*. New York: Oxford University Press.

Gennari, John. 2006. *Blowin' Hot and Cool: Jazz and Its Critics*. Chicago: University of Chicago Press.

Halbwachs, Maurice. 1992. *On Collective Memory*. Edited and translated by Lewis A. Coser. Chicago: University of Chicago Press.

Hegel, G. W. F. [1899] 1956. *The Philosophy of History*. Translated by John Sibree. New York: Dover.

Isoardi, Steven L. 2006. *The Dark Tree: Jazz and the Community Arts in Los Angeles*. Berkeley: University of California Press.

Kelley, Robin D. G. 2001. "In a Mist: Thoughts on Ken Burns's *Jazz*." *ISAM Newsletter* 30(2): 8–10.

Kivy, Peter. 2001. *The Possessor and the Possessed: Handel, Mozart, Beethoven, and the Idea of Musical Genius*. New Haven, Conn., and London: Yale University Press.

Pond, Steven F. 2003. "Jamming the Reception: Ken Burns, Jazz, and the Problem of 'America's Music.'" *Notes* 60(1): 11–45.

———. 2006. "Silencing Sound: Jazz Historiography and the Sixties." Paper presented at the 51st Annual Meeting of the Society for Ethnomusicology, Honolulu, Hawaii.

Ramsey, Guthrie. 2003. *Race Music: Black Cultures from Bebop to Hip-Hop*. Berkeley: University of California Press.

Small, Christopher. 1987. *Music of the Common Tongue: Survival and Celebration in Afro-American Music*. New York: Riverrun Press.

Solis, Gabriel. 2001. "Monk's Music and the Making of a Legacy." Ph.D. dissertation, Washington University, St. Louis.

———. 2004. "'A Unique Chunk of Jazz Reality': Authorship, Musical Work Concepts, and Thelonious Monk's Live Recordings from the Five Spot, 1958." *Ethnomusicology* 48(3): 315–47.

———. 2007. *Monk's Music: Thelonious Monk and Jazz History in the Making*. Berkeley: University of California Press.

Tapscott, Horace. 2001. *Songs of the Unsung: The Musical and Social Journey of Horace Tapscott*, edited by Steven L. Isoardi. Durham, N.C.: Duke University Press.

Trouillot, Michel-Rolph. 1995. *Silencing the Past: Power and the Production of History*. Boston: Beacon Press.

Tucker, Mark. 1990. "The Renaissance Education of Duke Ellington." In *Black Music in the Harlem Renaissance: A Collection of Essays*, edited by Samuel A. Floyd, Jr., 111–28. Westport, Conn.: Greenwood Press.

Tucker, Sherri. 2000. *Swing Shift: "All-Girl" Bands of the 1940s*. Durham, N.C.: Duke University Press.

———. 2007. "Historiography (Jazz)," *Grove Music Online* (accessed April 4, 2007), *www.grovemusic.com/shared/views/article.html?section=jazz.591400*.

Wilson, Olly. 1974. "The Significance of the Relationship between Afro-American Music and West African Music." *Black Perspectives in Music* 2(1): 3–22.

❧ 6 ❧

FORMULAS AND IMPROVISATION
IN PARTICIPATORY MUSIC

Thomas Turino

Improvisation is not a concept I have specifically addressed in previous scholarly work, perhaps because I simply took it for granted as a common although not particularly focal practice in much of the music that I play and study. The conception of improvisation often varies substantially depending on the musical traditions with which a person is engaged. Here, I consider improvisation in relation to the goals and ethics of participatory music making. Because of the nature of participatory traditions, I find it useful to distinguish between *improvisation* and *formulaic performance*. After my discussion of these concepts, and *participatory music* as a distinct artistic field, my primary goal is to explain the rather minor role of highlighted improvisation in participatory traditions while at the same time indicating why some improvisatory spaces are necessary for successful participatory music, especially in relation to Csikszentmihalyi's flow theory (1988) and C. S. Peirce's basic philosophical categories of *Firstness, Secondness,* and *Thirdness* (1955). *Flow* experience is a common impetus for making music and dancing, and Peirce's categories offer additional tools for thinking about the different mental states sought and achieved through musical performance.

I address several ideas: (1) If improvisation and formulaic playing are considered distinct practices, then improvisation cannot be recognized through listening except by the musician and others who know the player's music making extremely intimately, especially consistent, longtime music partners. Thus improvisation is largely a subjective experience for the player and intimates, and it may create a particular type of pleasure precisely for this reason. (2) The experiential states produced by instances of improvisation and accident tend to differ from scripted formulaic or largely habitual performance. (3) Individuals are attracted to music making for a variety of reasons, including a range of different experiential states that can be achieved through performance. Scripted, formulaic, and improvised performances are variably attractive to specific individuals depending on the types of experiences they favor. I am interested in the comparison of formulaic and improvised performing for what it can tell us about the range of experiential states that musicians seek. (4) Successful participatory traditions accommodate a wide variety of people, welcoming different levels of expertise as well as providing different ways in which flow and other experiences can be achieved.

FORMULAS AND IMPROVISATION

I distinguish improvisation from formulaic performance along the lines suggested by Judith Becker in 1972 (in Sutton 1998, 72). By *formulaic variation*, I mean melodic, rhythmic, or harmonic paradigmatic substitutions I have made before in relation to the basic model I am performing. For most of the music that I play, such as old-time string band music, Cajun and zydeco, and mbira music, pieces and dance styles are treated by some performers as loose models with associated collections of *formulas* rather than as set, closely reproducible items. In formulaic performance a given piece is usually, although not always, easily recognizable by its sound, but any number of sonic details may vary from one repetition or performance of the piece to the next, sometimes substantially.

In formulaic performance, a "piece" is considered a platform for individual and group play rather than an art object to be faithfully reproduced. This distinction is easy to articulate and understand intellectually, but it has profound consequences for how people make and think about music. For people who operate primarily in the formulaic performance mode, the piece and associated genre are like the design and rules of a game, and formulas are like the moves and habits one has developed to play successfully. In this approach, playing music is really about *play* in the common sense of the term; it is about the doing, rather than producing, a scripted artistic form and is therefore consistent with participatory rather than presentational ethics and goals, as will be discussed further.

In traditions and approaches where the goal is to reproduce pieces faithfully as composed or played previously (e.g., classical music ensembles, tribute rock bands, traditionalist approaches to old-time), almost any significant alteration of the piece during the course of performance might be defined as improvisation. For traditions and approaches where continuous *formulaic variation* is standard practice and habitual—the baseline of what "the piece" is—it seems useful to conceptualize *improvisation* in a different way. From this vantage point, I define *improvisation* as instances in performance where I *surprise myself* with purposeful alterations, extensions, or flights away from the model and habitual formulas. For me, improvisation sometimes occurs like a spontaneous spark, and at other times I think an idea before playing it. These represent different types of experiences, but in either case the novelty of what I do and hear may be likened to the feeling of surprise. Intention distinguishes improvisation from *accidents,* which can be of an enjoyable or unacceptable nature, and both kinds create a sense of surprise (and, in the latter case, regret). Only the player can distinguish between a *happy accident* (an unintentional move, a "mistake," that worked musically) and improvisation.

Stock formulas and variations of an mbira piece or an old-time string band tune may be learned from other players. Typically, however, a person's idiosyncratic collection of formulas for a given piece or genre come from former happy accidents or improvisations enjoyed and so repeated and re-membered. If I improvise something new or make an enjoyable mistake, I purposefully try to repeat it during the next several repetitions of the piece so as to remember it; I also try to remember it and practice it later at home to make it a habit that will fall easily into place when I am playing.

In the formulaic approach, one's collection of formulas, plus the basic model, actually constitute the piece, so that with time and a sizable reper-toire of paradigmatic moves, the basic piece will vary substantially from one performance to the next. Old formulas can surprise new music partners and listeners but still be habit-based and so not surprise the player and long-term partners and fans. Often repeated formulas become part of the model, giving rise to new moments of improvisation and accident that, when enjoyed and remembered, are added to one's collection of habits for a given piece, genre, or instrument. Yesterday's improvisations and accidents become today's formulas; and today's formulas are tomorrow's models based on the gradual processes of habit formation in relation to sonic and physical icons—sounds and moves similar to those I have heard and done before. R. Anderson Sutton (1998, 76) discusses gamelan performance in much the same terms, and I would guess that this sequence of development is fairly widespread and common.

Usually, new moves—accidents as well as improvisations—are iconically related physically and sonically to things done before. Thus, in a sense they are formulaic extensions. But for me the important thing is that the novelty is substantial enough to generate surprise and thus a certain type of atten-tion that draws me out of the realm of rote habit—all of this occurring only in my own subjective experience as a player and for those who know my playing particularly well. To the extent that the novelty draws attention and creates surprise, it emerges as an index out of and for the particular moment, which, along with the intimacy indexed by recognition, is another source of pleasure. Here I am using the terms "icon" and "index" in C. S. Peirce's sense of signs that stand for something else through resemblance (icons) or co-occurrence (indices). Each instance of a specific formula (token) is iconically related—both sonically and physically—to that formula as a general type or collection of instances. As suggested immediately above, one function of indices is to "point" or draw attention to something else (the object of the sign) in the particular situation (see Turino 1999 for a discussion of Peircean semiotics).

Improvisations are also typically generated in a variety of habitual modes in response to what the people I am playing with are doing. When I play old-time music or sing with mbira music, these modes include inventing contrapuntal lines, interlocking melodic-rhythmic parts with other players or dancers, making imitations that extend or alter things my partners are doing, or shifting my part to create close rhythmic synchrony with, or alternative accents in relation to, other players or dancers.

Given the distinction I am making between improvisation and formulaic variation, it seems unlikely that we would be able to recognize a case of improvisation simply by listening to anyone but ourselves or our most intimate music partners, since we cannot know most people's complete collection of formulas. It is also difficult to distinguish between happy accidents and intended gestures for anyone but ourselves simply by listening. What seems significant, however, is that formulaic and improvised performances emerge from and create particular states of mind, types of attention, and senses of pleasure among players and dancers.

FLOW AND PEIRCE'S CATEGORIES

Because of its basis in physical and sonic habit combined with options for continual change, formulaic performance is perfect for creating extended mental states of intense concentration that Csikszentmihalyi calls *flow* (1988). Csikszentmihalyi suggests that flow states are best achieved through circumscribed activities that properly balance skill and challenge—to stave off frustration and boredom, respectively—and that provide immediate feedback on how one is doing. He suggests that these conditions allow for heightened and prolonged concentration that creates a liberating feeling of transcending oneself. When one is so deeply focused on the activity at hand, all other mundane experiences, thoughts, and concerns fall away.

Flow states correspond to what C. S. Peirce would call Secondness. Peirce (1955) has suggested that all phenomena, including states of mind and experience, are reducible to three basic philosophical categories. *Firstness* involves an entity in-and-of itself without relation to a second entity; it is the realm of pure existence and *is-ness*. *Secondness* involves relations between two entities without the mediation of a third; it is the realm of direct relations, brute fact, direct cause and effect, the slap on a face without consideration of the causes and effects of the slap. *Thirdness* involves the capacity of a mind to relate two entities, to synthesize, to generalize, to think about and conceptualize relations; it is the realm of signs. At the phenomenological level, all processes involving signs (i.e., all feeling, thought, reaction, experience) involve Thirdness. What has sometimes proven confusing is that within semiotic processes (within the phenomenological realm of Thirdness), Peirce suggests that there is relative Firstness, Secondness, and Thirdness, and he distinguishes different sign types and effects of signs accordingly. To use his best-known concepts, an icon is a First, an index a Second, and a symbol a Third. When a sign creates pure sensation or feeling (*emotional interpretant*), it is a First; when it creates a direct physical reaction (*energetic interpretant*), it is a Second; and when it creates a "more developed sign" in the mind (e.g., word-based thought or visual, sonic, or tactile image), it is a Third.

In the mental state of Secondness, there is only the individual and the activity, the two bound by intense concentration without mediating thoughts *about* what one is doing or anything else (i.e., Thirdness). For this reason mental states of Secondness, or flow, feel liberating and sometimes transcendental. As Csikszentmihalyi and his colleagues discuss (1988), people in flow, or deep Secondness, often experience time differently; hours pass like minutes, and the individual, her instrument or tools, and the activity are welded seamlessly and feel effortless, even though effort must be involved. Secondness is the directness or concreteness of the doing in the moment, one physical-sonic move causing the effect of another, resulting in a kind of "automatic pilot."

The intense concentration of Secondness can sometimes even lead to mental states of Firstness—the temporary disappearance of focal awareness itself. As an experience, Firstness is a unitary presence experienced as absence because there is only the self at such moments, without signs or thoughts relating me to a Second. The experience of Firstness can only be recognized after the fact when focal awareness returns. It is often first sensed as "waking up," with mental thoughts such as "where was I?" Such experiences disrupt flow. I have had what I believe to be a common experience of performing music in a flow state (everything clicking effortlessly along) and then having my concentration disrupted by, say, a new person coming into the room and thoughts about that person. I have also had the experience of performing in flow and then noticing how good it feels or how well things are going—those very thoughts *about* the experience disrupting it and making me stumble musically. As with disappearing into Firstness and then waking from it, mental states of Thirdness (thoughts *about* what one is doing or the person newly arrived) disrupt flow and, in my case at least, often lead to less satisfying performance.

Intentional improvisation and conscious decisions about shifting formulas also involve mental states of Thirdness, but typically they take place when one is already in this mental state and thus are not awkwardly experienced as a disruption of flow. Throughout a given performance there is a constant shifting of types of attention and mental state, and, as we shall see, different individuals seem to prefer to prolong one type of mental state over others during performance. But at least for the styles of formulaic participatory music that I play, intense prolonged experiences of Secondness, or flow, seem to be a primary goal. Achieving this state is actually what draws me and others to playing this type of music. Decision making and surprise during moments of improvisation, as well as unintended moves, tend to take me out of Secondness to mental states of Thirdness. The enjoyment of the surprise and the risk taken during improvisation offer their own rewards, but they result in a different experience and state of mind than Secondness performance.

PARTICIPATORY MUSIC

In various places I have outlined four different *fields* of music making: *participatory and presentational performance, high-fidelity* and *studio audio art recording* (e.g., 2000, 47–50; 2008). The first two fields pertain to live performance, and the second two pertain to making recorded music. Along a series of continua, each field is defined by different conceptions of what music is; by different ethics about roles, relationships, and responsibility; by different levels and types of mediation among the people involved; by different values for judging quality and success; and by different qualities and style characteristics of sound.

Although there are many types of musical participation, including silent contemplative listening, I define *participatory performance* as a special type of art in which there are only participants and potential participants in a face-to-face situation. This field is defined by the ethical priority of involving as many people as possible in the actual acts of music making and dance, as well as by a distinct set of values by which the success of a performance is significantly judged by the degree of participation achieved.

In the United States there is sometimes the mistaken notion that participatory music, like our campfire songs, must be uniformly simple. Actually, fully developed participatory traditions, such as those found in Shona and Aymara communities and in the contra dance music scene in the Midwest, involve a full range of specialization and difficulty across a variety of performance roles. Traditions that include only simple roles bore and hence ultimately exclude people who are deeply engaged with music and dance; traditions that include only highly specialized roles exclude people who want to participate but who are not engaged with music and dance beyond the social contexts of performance. Some people may be most drawn to dancing as an activity, some to instrumental performance or singing, and some to all activities equally. Successful participatory traditions allow for different types of interests and shifting between roles even within the same event.

The graded specializations of participatory roles and the variety of roles allow people who seek greater challenges to take on new things as their investment in the activity increases. Csikszentmihalyi (1988) has made a similar observation about flow activities generally. He notes that transcendental flow experience proves attractive, indeed almost addictive, bringing people back to that activity over and over again. As more time is spent in the activity, skill levels increase, requiring a corresponding increase in the level of challenge if flow is to be experienced anew. For example, it is not uncommon for people who become deeply invested in contra dancing to move from the role of beginning dancer to experienced dancer to caller; people also are sometimes moved to take up instruments, requiring an even greater time investment, so that they can play the music as well as dance as members of the scene. Within old-time musical ensembles, once the rather simple basic guitar technique is mastered, new techniques can be added or the person might take up banjo, mandolin, or fiddle, each with its own expanding horizons of challenge.

With the exception of certain uniformly simple musics (camp songs), most traditions offer this potential for expanding challenges. What is distinct about participatory traditions, however, is that people at all skill levels perform together in the same events, and maximum participation is a key criterion for judging the success of an event. In presentational performance the goals are different; ensembles tend to form with members who have relatively similar skill levels. Presentational ethics mandate an exclusion of the less skilled for the sake of the audience, whereas participatory ethics mandate an inclusion of as many people as possible. This is not to say that anything goes in participatory music making. Successful participatory performances are organized around core performers who hold the musical and (as in the case of contra dance callers) dance structures together, providing the necessary basis for a satisfying performance for all.

The fact that people at many skill levels perform together also enhances the potential for flow by simultaneously offering a variety of models for performance with different balances of skill and challenge. Neophytes can imitate and imagine themselves at the level of the intermediate performers around them, whereas they might be discouraged if the only models available were at the most advanced level. So too, intermediate participants can learn from those around them who are slightly more advanced. Within participatory traditions, circumscribed improvisatory spaces are one key way that advanced performers can continue to challenge themselves while maintaining a musical or dance style that has easy points of entry for neophytes. Successful participatory traditions (ones that draw people back again and again) have evolved to have something for everyone and seem almost specially designed to create the potential for flow for a wide variety of people.

What most fundamentally distinguishes participatory traditions from other fields is that the contributions of people at all levels of expertise are truly appreciated for what they add to the overall gestalt of sound and motion, regardless of the impact on the artistic forms. This is an ethical and aesthetic position that is difficult to grasp for musicians deeply grounded in other fields. It is not that skillfully produced sound and motion are not valued—they are in fact key to inspiring fuller participation—but the ultimate ethical priority lies in enticing people to join in. There is a tradeoff here. For example, experienced contra dancers sometimes complain, usually among themselves, that the flow (their term) of a dance is upset by too many beginners; yet the ethic remains that all are welcome, and there is even pressure for shy beginners to join in: experienced dancers often invite people to dance who have been sitting on the sidelines too long.

Because of these ethical and aesthetic values, certain sonic features commonly occur in participatory musics around the world. These include cyclical forms or short repetitive forms, intense motivic or kinesic repetition among sections, and open forms without set beginnings, middles, and ends. Charles Keil (1987) has identified dense textures and timbres and push-pull rhythmic tensions among parts as common participatory music features, and although he was focusing largely on music of the African diaspora, these key traits occur in participatory musics in many places. Unchanging rhythmic grooves are key to the "security in constancy" that inspires dancers at all levels of expertise. Other sonic features include relatively loud constant dynamics, and in general, few planned contrasts of any type. The emphasis is on a dense sound with wide intonational bands, buzzy timbres, and heterophonic fringes that contribute to a mass of sound with individual parts subdued or almost indistinguishable. This wall of sound approach provides a cloaking function so that people with different skills can enter comfortably without standing out, but I think there is more to it than this. The dense mesh of sound of participatory musics is actually a *dicent index* (Turino 2008, 9) for the social and performative integration of participants: a sign of sonic and physical merging that actually results from that same merging and thus is *experienced* as true in a space where sound and experienced social reality are the same thing.

In presentational music, performers have the responsibility of interesting and entertaining their audience. This results in an emphasis on clearer textures so that the audience can follow what individual performers are doing, as well as on planned contrasts and highlighted virtuosic solos to create variety and interest. In participatory music the dense textures, high degree of repetition, and lack of prearranged contrasts is consistent with the general lack of highlighted solos in such traditions. Moreover, formulaic variation and improvisation tend to be intensive (within or subtly layered on top of the short repetitive forms) rather than extensive (expanding or altering the form itself). In participatory traditions, formulaic variation and improvisation are usually subtle and are fitted within the overall mesh of sound. They are more about social interactions among participants—reacting sonically and kinesically with what others are doing—or about maintaining the skill-challenge balance that is key to flow experience. An emphasis on highlighted individual virtuosic display, so key to much presentational music, is actually counterproductive within participatory traditions; it would draw too much attention to the experts and place too much value on them. This, in turn, would suggest a lesser value for other contributions and create too much distance between experts and others, an impediment for the less secure to join in.

Participatory traditions offer the conditions for flow for people at all skill levels. I suggest that many people are attracted to participatory performance for this very reason. Yet even within the same participatory activity there can be a number of approaches to reaching flow. In the middle-class old-time string band tradition (Turino 2008), many fiddlers and banjoists hardly vary a tune at all from repetition to repetition, purposefully trying to keep the piece the same as the way they learned it. In my experience with such players, they are constantly learning new tunes that are not regarded as models for variation and improvisation but rather are considered set musical items. Here closely circumscribed habitual performance of a set piece provides comfort while rendering the tune precisely, and continually learning and playing new and increasingly difficult tunes provides the challenge. This approach to achieving flow, which results in the most repetitive, predictable music, seems especially popular with beginning and intermediate dancers and callers, but it is also favored by advanced performers who are concerned with maintaining a given old-time style or repertory.

My own approach, and that of other like-minded old-time players, is quite different. I have been playing clawhammer banjo for about 25 years, yet I have a relatively small repertoire of tunes. I am not interested in constantly learning new tunes unless they are substantially different from the ones I already know. Rather, I am more interested in composing tunes or in developing new formulaic variations on the tunes I regularly play. Most of the formulas I play are so habitual, as is the process of variation, that my general mental state while playing is largely "automatic pilot," even though continual variations, which almost seem to happen by themselves, usually hold my interest. When playing a single piece for a long time during a dance, however, I sometimes get bored, move out of habit, and consciously decide to vary something or try something new. I am thus initially out of Secondness, but once I have repeated or worked with the new ideas for a few repetitions, the comfort-challenge balance is restored and I get back to flow, and so the process goes. Mistakes also knock me out of Secondness, as does physical fatigue, a decision to change tunes, or noticing something that my partners are doing if their innovations inspire me to think about some type of new response. Thus my attention and state of mind shift during a long dance performance, but I would guess that on good nights I am in flow 60 to 80 percent of the time.

My main role as the banjoist in our string band is rhythmic. I particularly enjoy adding a good deal of syncopation, an overall swing feel, and playing with the time of a tune. In our local dances, where many of the dancers are inexperienced, I have received some complaints (both directly and indirectly) for (over)doing this, as well as for playing (too) fast, which I also enjoy. In this context, I find that I often have to hold back my own desires about how I enjoy playing for the sake of the dancers. By contrast, when our band has played at dance weekends or other scenes where there is a greater proportion of experienced dancers, our rhythmic approach has generated enthusiasm. The overriding participatory ethos of contra dancing requires musicians to limit their own creativity and enjoyment to match the skill levels of the callers and dancers, just as experienced dancers must limit what they do to make a partner who is a newcomer feel comfortable. Such are the priorities of participatory ethics mentioned earlier.

Having learned his old-time repertory from me, my fiddler son Matt approaches music in a thoroughly formulaic way. For a given tune he has learned my formulas and added many of his own, so that often he only vaguely remembers what the basic tune is. In contrast to my way of playing, however, Matt says that what he likes best is to continually go out on a limb by doing something he has never done before because he likes the challenge of having to find a way out of the problem he has created for himself. He consciously favors improvisation and spends more time doing it than I do. From his body language as well as things he has said to me, he is in a mental state of Thirdness when he improvises, just as I am.

We also play in presentational contexts, and Matt's improvisatory approach seems to work well for listening audiences. Significantly, however, if in our local contra dances his improvisations obscure the basic structure of the tune, especially if he blurs the A and B parts of the AABB form, we get complaints from some callers and dancers who find the music hard to follow and so lose their place in the dance. I initially had to remind him to stick closer to the tune than he normally likes to do. In these participatory events extended improvisation is a problem, whereas formulaic variation and more limited intensive improvisation—if the rhythm and basic tune structure are not altered too much—do not seem to cause a problem for dancers.

Even more than Matt, some individuals may actually prefer mental states of Thirdness when playing, such that challenge is emphasized over the comfort-challenge balance that enhances the opportunities for Secondness. Such performers, however, often gravitate to presentational contexts because of the restrictions placed on their individual desires and creativity within participatory events. In my case, I enjoy both types of settings for what they can offer, but I understand them as having fundamentally different requirements and potentials, and I still prefer the heightened possibilities for flow provided in participatory settings.

The same range of approaches described for old-time musicians also exists among Shona mbira players. One of my main teachers, Chris Mhlanga, repeatedly told me that he thinks of mbira pieces as being rather set—the basic ostinato pattern plus a limited number of stock formulaic variations—and that this material should not be altered during performances. He felt that there was little room for improvisation in mbira music, and he himself did not improvise. His reasons included the fact that if one mbira player improvises too much or plays formulas unknown to the other mbira players, the close interlocking relationship between the lead and accompanying parts would be lost. He also noted that the ancestors like the music played in the way they knew it when they were living, and if this is altered too much, they may not be attracted into their medium during a ceremony. Thus, whereas in the contra dance scene the ability of the callers and dancers limits the degree of improvisation and variation in the music, in mbira music it is the nature of interlocking parts and the desires of the ancestors that limit novelty. Mhlanga has told me, however, that in contrast to the mbira parts, there is a great deal of room for formulaic variation and improvisation in the singing that the mbira supports. When I would come up with variations on the mbira and check their acceptability with him, he would typically instruct me to play the pieces just as he had taught them. When I checked vocal lines with him, he told me that they were fine and that, in fact, each musician should have his own vocal lines to sing with the different pieces. In Mhlanga's approach, which I have adopted, mbira playing is a relatively circumscribed *core* part, and singing is a more open *elaboration* part, and the two may be combined by the same musician to achieve the comfort-challenge balance that creates flow.

Another of my mbira teachers, T. Chigamba, represents another approach; his playing involved almost constant formulaic variation with some limited improvisation—parallel to the way I play banjo. This was so habitual for him that he had difficulty playing a piece in the same way for many consecutive cycles, which made learning from him difficult. Since he typically plays with his children and they know his repertory of formulas, this did not prove to be a problem. The Chigamba case points up the importance of the longevity of musical relationships as a key variable allowing for greater variation and improvisation in participatory traditions. In the same way, my son and I know each other's moves so well that we can follow each other even in improvisatory sections, since these are typically extensions of things we have done before.

There are other mbira players who, like my son, emphasize improvisation and, in addition, virtuosic display. As Berliner noted in his book *The Soul of Mbira* (1978), however, this type of "hot" playing, typically involving younger musicians, is usually frowned upon for all the reasons expressed by Mhlanga. As I mentioned earlier, overemphasizing virtuosic display is counterproductive in participatory contexts. Likewise, other players, such as the late Dumisani Maraire, expressed the idea that formulaic variations should not be changed too quickly because this did not give other partici-pants a chance to lock in with a given variation with their own clapped, vocal, or dance parts. It would be like trying to have a meaningful dialogue with someone who kept changing the subject. Again, participatory ethics limit what musicians can do because music making is as much about social relations as it is about sound production or the creative drives of particular musicians. Those who wish to prioritize their own creative urges would do better to perform improvisational traditions in presentational contexts (e.g., jazz, bluegrass, Karnatak music).

In the least variable or improvisatory of the participatory traditions I have studied, Aymara panpipe performance, two or three pieces are collectively composed during rehearsals by a small group of musicians for the festival that will begin the following day. A given genre has a number of stock formulas that are plugged into new compositions especially as introductions and at cadences, as well as sometimes within the sections organized in AABBCC form. The use of these formulas and a great deal of internal repetition across sections allow for community members who have never heard the piece before to pick it up quickly during the festival performance itself (Turino 1993).

Musicians in this tradition explicitly state that individuals should not stand out from the ensemble sound, and as in the other traditions I have discussed, there is no place for highlighted soloing. In panpipe performance, however, there is a technique known as *requinteando* in which one member of a hocketing pair improvises or plays formulas with the melodic segments performed by his partner. These spaces for variation and improvisation are very short and must not stand out. In fact, requinteando lines make a neg-ligible contribution to the overall ensemble sound. I believe that the main reason for the practice is to provide a creative space for advanced panpipe players so that their interest and the skill-challenge balance can be maintained to enhance opportunities for *flow* within pieces that are highly repetitious and formulaic for easy access.

CONCLUSIONS

Participatory music ethics place constraints on individual freedom and creativity. The priority is on creating a comfortable performing context for people at all levels of expertise. Yet advanced players need spaces for continu-ing challenge so that they may remain engaged and experience flow, which, as I have suggested here, is a major attraction to music making in the first place. Formulaic variation and improvisation are thus essential to participa-

tory traditions, but unlike in the presentational field, the sonic result must
be subtle and *intensive* so that individual virtuosic display does not obscure
the basic model or create self-consciousness among the less experienced and
thus become an impediment to inspiring fuller participation.

REFERENCES

Berliner, Paul. 1978. *The Soul of Mbira*. Berkeley: University of California Press.
Csikszentmihalyi, Mihaly, and Isabella Selega Csikszentmihalyi, eds. 1988. *Optimal Experience: Psychological Studies of Flow in Consciousness*. New York: Cambridge University Press.
Keil, Charles. 1987. "Participatory Discrepancies and the Power of Music." *Cultural Anthropology* 2(3): 275–83.
Peirce, Charles S. 1955. *Philosophical Writings of Peirce*. Edited by Justus Buchler. New York: Dover.
Sutton, R. Anderson. 1998. "Do Javanese Gamelan Musicians Really Improvise?" In *In the Course of Performance: Studies in the World of Musical Improvisation*, edited by Bruno Nettl with Melinda Russell, 69–92. Chicago: University of Chicago Press.
Turino, Thomas. 1993. *Moving Away from Silence: Music of the Peruvian Altiplano and the Experience of Urban Migration*. Chicago: University of Chicago Press.
———. 1999. "Signs of Imagination, Identity, and Experience: A Peircean Semiotic Model for Music." *Ethnomusicology* 43: 221–55.
———. 2000. *Nationalists, Cosmopolitans, and Popular Music in Zimbabwe*. Chicago: University of Chicago Press.
———. 2008. *Music as Social Life: The Politics of Participation*. Chicago: University of Chicago Press.

PART TWO

EDUCATION

∽ 7 ∽

LEARNING TO IMPROVISE MUSIC,
IMPROVISING TO LEARN MUSIC

Patricia Shehan Campbell

Within the minds and bodies of musicians, there is sound that is born and bred, enculturated and entrained, awaiting the opportune occasion that will permit its release in expressive improvisation. With ears wide open, the improvising musician knows a rich repertoire of tunes, timbres, and textures that come from home and family, local communities, the media, and the model and mentor musicians she has known. The musician who improvises refers to structures in the sounds of her own environmental "surrounds" or "soundscape," that musical web that has enveloped her throughout her musical history. At the moment of improvisation, this backlog of sounds finds a place in expressive music making for all that she has heard, felt, and internalized from earlier experiences. The improvising musician inhabits an art world (Becker 1982) in which both recent and past experiences—from the everyday mundane practices of life to the more sublime—blend to form expressive art that pleases those who are within earshot.

WAYS OF IMPROVISATION AS EDUCATIONAL PROCESS

The route for discerning matters of improvisation and the educational process is circuitous and crowded with questions both rhetorical and real. These questions emanate from, and inform, the practice of improvisation. Is it human to improvise, and are there optimal periods for improvisation in human development? Is improvisation learned but not taught, or can it be facilitated by a teacher? What is the role and extent of improvisation in particular genres, and by what processes does the musician acquire the enabling techniques to improvise? Is there a continuum of improvisation, from high structure to low structure to free and with no premeditated plan at all, that can be studied and applied in pedagogical ways by teachers with students? Are there formal avenues to the improvisation training of musicians, music students, and the broader population of children and youth?

An examination of improvisation and the educational process is best launched through operational definitions. "Improvising to learn music" is one manifestation of the phenomenon, when the act of improvisation is embraced—or adapted, modified, and reshaped—by educators at various levels and contexts, from preschool to postgraduate studies in music. Improvising to learn music means incorporating improvisation within musical education and training, in settings where Western European art music and Western European-based pedagogical systems reign supreme. In these venues, improvisation is a means to an end, the outcome of which is the development of musicians with a more comprehensive sense of music. It is evident in music classes for children who are creating percussion pieces under the supervision of their teacher so that they may know a particular rhythm more thoroughly, as well as in aural skills classes at the tertiary level that are infused with opportunities for students to play with a motif en route to understanding it. The aim of improvising to learn music in these circumstances is to deepen the musicality of children, youth, and adults.

Improvisation may also be viewed as "learning to improvise music" in those styles that are innately rich in improvisatory material. For genres that are by design and tradition intended to be improvised, and particularly those outside the domain of Western European art music, there is embedded within the music an innate improvisatory sense and by extension an inherent process by which improvisation is learned. Jazz that is performed by professionals (rather than school jazz), certain musical practices and genres of Hindustani music, the epic and narrative songs of Serbia and Croatia, solo interpolations in the music of gospel choirs, bagpipe playing in southeastern Europe and the "northwest islands" of Ireland and Scotland, fiddle and banjo expressions of the bluegrass variety, the performance of Egyptian players of 'ud, q'anun, dombek, and riqq—these are examples of music within which improvisation is to some degree more or less naturally embedded. In these musical practices, improvisation is the ultimate goal because it is central to the music.

Running alongside conceptualizations of "improvising to learn music" and "learning to improvise music," there is a third phenomenon of "improvising music to learn." Through the process of making music up, people learn whatever can be learned of self and others and of the world beyond music. Such circumstances of music making include short forms of musical utterances, that is, "snippets" of songs and rhythms, variations on familiar songs, and progressive and evolving musical expressions. These expressions appear to be part of being human, of developing emotionally, socially, and intellectually and of responding and reacting to experiences and environments. Children are among those who "improvise music to learn" when, unprovoked and untarnished by well-meaning adults, they spontaneously chant, sing, and express themselves through rhythmic sounds and movements. As children play with music and are musically playful, they vary the songs and rhythms they have heard before. They spontaneously utter word phrases and even vocables that are loaded with melodic and rhythmic content and with semantic and emotive meaning. In the process, children improvise music to learn who they are, what their relationship may be with others, and how they may go about doing whatever it is they are doing—eating, bathing, dressing, playing with Legos and Lincoln Logs, skipping, swinging, and riding in cars. More than most people, it is children who quite regularly learn their world through the music they make.

Scholars theorize about the process of improvisation and how it is transmitted and acquired. Improvisers themselves have described the means by which they have learned their art. Improvisation may be examined through its occasional presence in formal educational settings, through a scattering of techniques and even an established method such as Dalcroze, and from a developmental standpoint that traces the early and ongoing impulse of children's explorations and creative imaginations. It may be seen as ranging from personalized renditions of standard compositions to free and unrestricted possibilities. These different perspectives are nonetheless aimed at examining principles and contexts that emerge in various parts of the educational process.

SOMETHING OUT OF SOMETHING

One of the long-enduring wonders of improvisation is its wellspring: the source(s) of the improvisational act. In understanding its place in educational contexts, it is relevant to consider first whether or not improvisational behavior is ultimately the development of something out of something heard, experienced, and felt—something that has come before. Alternately, the Latin phrase *creatio ex nihilo* (creation out of nothing) would imply that improvisation is a mysterious act. Yet if improvisation is to be understood, then a magical unfolding of musical gestures and expressions is not sufficient explanation for the complex process that it is. The act of improvisation, particularly in advanced stages of any genre, be it jazz, a Mozart cadenza, or a Hindustani khyal, requires conscious as well as unconscious selection from a reservoir of musical sound expressions that have been acquired over time. Socialization and enculturation, as well as explicit training and education,

combine to characterize the sophisticated and multifaceted process of hon-
ing the improvisational act. Even simple improvisational instances—a child's
playful decoration of a familiar song, for example—involve tapping into the
sounds that have been accumulated through experience.

The likely root of improvisation is the Latin *improvisus*, meaning "unforeseen," which argues for improvisation as a process that is not premeditated.
Music that is improvised is never fully predictable, so that the sound that
comes out at the moment of improvisation may surprise even the improvising musician herself. Whether educated within institutional settings, trained
by others, taught through some auto-didactic self-disciplined process, or
nurtured in high-approval settings where no official teacher is present but
every attempt is reinforced and valued by those who listen, an improvising
musician forges new musical expressions that are not fully planned. The
momentary phenomenon of improvisational expressions is not easily (if ever
able to be) duplicated, and the performer may not be able to verbalize what
comes tumbling out. The music of the improvising musician comes from
within—from what is already there in the body and the brain, and which
can never be entirely "foreseen."

IMPROVISATION AS HUMAN BEHAVIOR

John Blacking (1973) asserted that music "is in the body" and that musicians
who improvise are not fully in control of that which comes out as music.
The improvisatory idea awaits an appropriate catalyst or context, much like
a popcorn kernel awaiting the application of heat in order to pop, when the
hard-coated seed can then break open to the air-filled flower of corn. Suzanne
Langer (1953) noted as much in her explanation of the process of composition, reasoning that some circumstances trigger a sudden recognition by the
composer of the form that will be achieved. Implicit within the form are the
ingredients of tone, tune, and time, which may surge forward at a creative
moment in the process of composition. Likewise, improvisation emerges from
occasions that call for the sudden and spontaneous sound of music ideas. If
music already is harbored within the body and in the mind, then perhaps
the sudden recognition of expression and form is in indeed brought on by
people, places, and particular events in the personal life of the musician.

In that act of improvisation, and in re-created but personally expressive
performance as well, Blacking observed in a recorded interview that "you
become the music" (1990). T. S. Eliot, hardly the improvising musician, nonetheless offered a poetic description similar to Blacking's, suggesting that "you

are the music while it lasts" (1944). The act of improvisation is only partly predictable and wrapped in the concept of "improvisus"; it emanates from the performer's internalized musical experience that, when prompted, spills out in ways that are both intentional and free-wheeling. The music of the improvisatory act is hardly creatio ex nihilo, but is instead source-based, coming from within the improvising musician's internalized musical sensibilities.

Blacking claimed that musicians could not be taught to improvise. He clarified that this "does not mean that improvisation is random," but that "all aspects of behavior are subject to a series of interrelated, structured systems, and when a musician improvises, he is expressing these systems in relation to the reactions he picks up from his audience" (1973, 100). Blacking consistently underscored the premise that music making, including improvisation, is a social behavior, requiring social interaction, and that music is socialization made manifest in the fullest aural spectrum. Although he acknowledged learning, his postulation that improvisation cannot be taught argues against the position of those who work institutionally with students to develop this skill. Indeed, there is a consensus among educators that improvisation must be taught, as evidenced in the Handbook of the National Association of Schools of Music and the National Standards for the Arts in K-12 schools.

Edward T. Hall described improvisation as an acquired behavior. He postulated that the acquisition of culture begins with birth and is a "process (that) is automatic and, while reinforced, cannot be taught" (1992, 225). He argued further that "acquired information is so basic and so fundamental that it is almost inevitably equated with the self, and its patterns are automatic and totally out of awareness." Hall reasoned that while learning is the result of the instructional process, improvisation is more closely allied to acquisition—learning while living within the culture—than it is a conscious process of learning sequentially how to do it. Learning requires instruction, whereas acquisition is an endogenous process that is a direct consequence of environmental influences. Hall's position follows theories of enculturation and socialization that suggest that once the "material" is acquired, the songs-in-the-head and the kinetic-memory gestures have staying power. The musical repertoire and techniques find their place in the thought and behavior of improvising musicians for their later retrieval.

Blacking and Hall ride a similar thought stream in their estimation of improvisation as a human behavior whose material need not precisely be taught or even "learned" in the sense of direct teacher-to-student transmission. Rather, improvisational behaviors in music appear to be a musician's release of musical ideas, impulses, and gestures that may have arrived to improvising musicians by way of their everyday living in the world. Still, the vast store of musical information that builds from infancy onward requires the stimulation, motivation, and nurturing facilitation of a strong model, mentor, and/or master teacher to help novice musicians and musicians-in-progress tap into the treasure-load of sound sources. If the genre in which the musician wishes to work is something beyond or separate from previous musical experiences, then it stands to reason that direct rather than indirect, formal rather than informal, and explicit rather than implicit teaching may be vital—and certainly time-effective—for learning to improvise.

Among cognitive psychologists, there is widespread agreement that human behavior, including performance skills and improvisation in particular, is a direct result of repeated attempts to do it (Pressing 1988, 1998). These continued trials appear to develop grooves in the musculature where pathways of neural firings become regular, consistent, and familiar. Traces in the memory (both the mental memory and the motor memory) make these skills commonplace, even automatic. Some cognitivists refer to a pan-human principle of repeated practice as necessary for developing performance behaviors, and thus they advocate that it will take a deliberate practice regime to raise up skilled singers and instrumentalists, including improvising musicians (Sloboda 1991). There is considerable agreement among psychologists that music making and improvisatory skills are achieved by working with a teacher in a directed situation, who may facilitate repeated attempts, provide ongoing evaluation, and shape behaviors. Students should frequently or continuously absorb the performances of expert musicians, often facilitated by a teacher, to realize the potential to improvise. Research by those who study musical competence through psychological experimentation suggests that improvisation is learned through referents and models acquired from the cultural environment and that it can also be taught.

TIGHTIES AND LOOSIES

The spectrum of improvisational behaviors is wide-ranging, from those experiences that are highly structured and restricted to particular musical specifications to those with little structure and few restrictions to shape the performance. Bruce Ellis Benson (2003) proposes a hierarchy of types of improvisation (some of which more closely resemble the compositional process), from the mere "filling in" of details of tempi and dynamics that can never be fully notated in a score, all the way to performance "in the style" of a piece or genre (yet even then with freedom to gravitate away from this style). Benson suggests that improvisation divides itself into types or degrees of freedom that are distinguished quantitatively (for example, by the number of notes that are added to the notated score or that are expected by the performer), even though the quantification blurs across some levels where the extent of improvisation is not so clearly delineated. At all levels of the spectrum, which include enrichments and elaborations as found in the performance of Baroque figure bass compositions, Beethoven cadenzas, the 12–bar blues form, and even arrangements of common folk tunes, the performer reworks something that already exists. Even in the case of the far-end free improvisation, where it would seem that "anything goes," the models of what has come before still govern what the music will become.

These varied levels of improvisation may also fit on a continuum of what may be called "tighties" and "loosies" (Pline 1982). Tighties are tightly constructed performances that adhere to the parameters set by the performers themselves or by teachers in educational settings. Improvisation practices in the performance of Irish sean-nos singing, where the melody and text are mildly embellished and occasionally extended with text or melodic interpolations, are tightly linked to the requisite components of the genre's melody, rhythm, and even text. When melodies are transformed beyond the ornamentation of only a few pitches to widespread elaboration and even pitch substitution, or when the instrumentation, tempi, and considerable segments of a piece are substantially altered, the improvisation tends toward the loosie end of the continuum. Music making in South Asia, such as the improvisations of a North Indian Hindustani raga as played by sitar, is a manifestation of a more loosely constructed improvisation. The continuum stretches across a wide variety of musical possibilities, where each genre finds its niche. Within the educational process, this continuum also illustrates the range of improvisations that may be facilitated for students who want or need greater or lesser structure.

FORMULAS AND PHRASE UNITS

Improvisation has been described by oral-formula scholars as units and phrases that are spontaneously put together in the moment of performance, be it through spoken language or music. V. V. Radlov called these units and phrases of musical material Bildthiele or "idea-parts" (1967), and Bruno Nettl referred to them as "building blocks" (1974). In his study of Homeric poetry in the 1930s, Milman Parry used the word *formula* to refer to an expression that was regularly used in performance, under the same metrical conditions, to express an essential idea (A. Parry, 1971). He observed that poets and singers practiced an art that allowed expressive variation within limits. While in the strictest sense variation is not the same as improvisation, it may be seen as sitting at the high-structure end of a sliding scale of improvisation that stretches all the way from the discernible variant of a known piece to the unplanned and spontaneous nature of music that is free and unrelated to models that have come before.

Albert Lord frequently spoke of "theme" as a subject unit or group of ideas (1960). He also referred to the manner in which singing bards develop their epics and narratives, filling them with permutations of "idea-clusters," and maintained that there could be creative and imaginative expressions within the conventions of the genre (this variation within limits). These bards learned their art through a three-stage apprenticeship consisting of (a) listening in order to absorb narrative and phraseological texts, rhythms, and pitches, (b) initial attempts at singing phrases (and playing the gusle or tambura), and (c) public singing of the whole song while adding or subtracting elements to suit the situation. Questions arise as to whether the thought-units, themes, and idea-clusters are acquired automatically and outside the direct awareness of these singers (and other musicians), or whether they are consciously learned. One might expect that students of a genre can extract by themselves, or have teachers extract for them, the themes from particular works, which then become the substance of their practice sessions and lessons.

Parry and Lord's Oral Theory has affected scholarship on various types of music that are orally based and reliant on formulaic structures for generating systems that underlie styles and pieces. Leo Treitler (2003) used the approach to investigate the transmission of plainchant before the advent of musical transcription, explaining how oral formulas and formulaic systems played a role in the invention, maintenance, and passing on of melodies. Jeff Todd Titon examined the "generating systems" underlying the variety of tunes in early forms of the blues, with attention to thematic pattern as "the thought sequence that controls attitude toward human experience and selects a narrative pattern (that is, an event sequence) to illustrate those attitudes" (1977, 83). Lawrence Gushee (1981) discussed the insights gained by applying Oral Theory to the work of saxophonist Lester Young, treating the collective structure of the performance as well as formulaic structure and pointing out that composition proceeds along several tracks at once. John W. Johnson (1999) studied the West African Mande epic, noting that it is not memorized but is rather structured around formulas, formulaic expressions, and themes.

Both Timothy Rice (1994) and Michael Bakan (1999), in their studies of the performance techniques and repertoire of Bulgarian gaida (Rice) and Balinese kendang (Bakan), noted the importance of groups of ideas felt as kinesthetic or kinetic gestures rather than as separate pitches or single strokes in learning to play and to improvise. They both found that the musical structures of the genres in which they were working allowed them to compress, digress from, and enrich the phrases of those structures. Rice recognized that his own journey into gaida-playing was a discovery of what hand gestures worked, including the kinetic patterns of individual fingers over the length of a phrase. Bakan learned to play kendang by discerning the movements of the hands of the master drummer, learning by eye and ear the gestural patterns and the transitions that linked them until the entire piece came together. As in other instances of oral-theory scholarship, the themes and formulaic phrases of Bulgarian and Balinese music are the material from which expressive music making of an improvisatory nature is made.

INSIGHTS FROM THE IMPROVISERS

Insights from musicians across a wide spectrum of styles sheds light on the process of improvisation. In many traditions and genres, musicians are expected to "wing it," "make it up," "blow it out," or create it "on the spot"— "at the spur of the moment," "in imitation of (or as inspiration from) their masters." Some musicians claim that improvisation is a process in motion that cannot be easily dissected, and a few see improvisation as so integral to the music that it cannot be separated from it. Many would prefer not to talk about it. When Ali Akbar Khansahib, north Indian sarodist, was once asked to expound upon the process by which he shapes his students as improvising musicians, he replied: "Talk? Why talk? When we eat, we eat, when we sleep, we sleep, when we do music, we do music. It has nothing to do with talk" (Booth 1996, 162). Still, at times insiders to the improvisational process have spoken of teaching and learning and have paid tribute to the teachers who taught or inspired their improvisational techniques.

Outsiders or novices to the world of improvised music may perceive improvisation as a phenomenon on the edge of magic. In his opening to *Thinking in Jazz*, Paul Berliner recalls jazz bassist Calvin's explanation of improvisation: "I used to think, how could jazz musicians pick notes out of thin air? I had no idea of the knowledge it took. It was like magic to me at the time" (1994, 1). As the journey into the art and craft of improvisatory performance continues, the sense of magic dissipates, revealing an experience steeped in the musical nuts and bolts that are so primary to improvisation within a given genre. Jazzers have often maintained that musicians must be prepared in advance to gain the freedom to play with spontaneity in public performance. Duke Ellington claimed, "There has never been anybody who has blown even two bars worth listening to who didn't have some idea about what he was going to play, before he started" (Rattenbury 1990, 41). Even "free jazz" is not entirely free: Miles Davis's *Kind of Blue*, said to be the product of sketches he brought into the studio a half hour before the recording session, is governed by the "lines" or frameworks—for example, blues form—created by previous musicians and co-performers (Evans 1959). Jazz improvisations tend to bear the marks of other jazz musicians, thus keeping the jazzers within the style and culture of jazz as they pay tribute to those who have come before.

Lukas Foss, improviser and composer, advised those who would improvise in his adventures in new music to "be careful not to play safe. Play what you don't think you know. Dig deep inside, and take a chance" (Campbell 1991b, 22). His work with conservatory-trained musicians allowed him to assume expertise and yet also compelled him to move beyond the restrictions imposed by those who played by the rules and notation alone. Foss intimated that some deep-seated ideas, almost innate but certainly long internalized, may be stored inside the performer's self, waiting to be called forth to action. In his ensembles, he has advised musicians to live dangerously in the music that they have the capacity to make, and he has encouraged generations of them to develop a sense of musical risk taking in order to develop spontaneity. New music composer Elliot Schwartz clarified Foss's perspective by saying that improvisation requires musical expertise first, including performance skills and analytical understanding, and that trained musicians could then improvise by "making the most of what's there, from the instrumentation, the melodic or rhythmic subject, the social setting, and even the unforeseen accidents that are converted from mistakes to opportunities" (1982–1983, 24; cf. Campbell 1991b).

Phong Nguyen, performer of Vietnamese traditional music, discussed the essence of rao (the improvised section at the start of instrumental pieces for dan tranh or dan nguyet). He reflected on improvisation in Vietnamese style as learned by way of imitation, which then places the musician in a position of expertise and confidence to build phrases and techniques into a performance that is new and personally expressive (Nguyen and Campbell 1989). To develop the ability to improvise rao, Nguyen advised listening to live performers and recordings and examining the modal theory of Vietnamese melody. The mastery of improvisational technique in Vietnamese music is directly related to aural models, in that direct imitations of the teacher's improvisation in practice may then be recalled by artists in a public performance.

Egyptian q'anun player George Sawa recalled advice given him by his late professor, Kamil Abdallah, on how to train oneself to improvise: "Never copy completely or learn by heart an improvisation, because it will then become a pre-composed piece and will cease to be an improvisation. Listen to a lot of improvisations that are played on your instrument. . . . Sit down and play. . . . Tape your performance and leave it in a drawer for a month. Listen to it later, remove in your mind what you do not like, cherish and keep the rest" (Campbell 1991b, 24). Q'anun players who improvise must listen both to expert performances and to recordings of their own evolving style. Professional and personal models become the source of the spontaneous improvisation on q'anun, and the process of listening, performing, and comparing propels a performer through his musical development.

The way to knowledge of the modern radif, the basic repertory of Persian classical music from which musicians launch their improvisations, consists of precise procedures that are shaped by the master teacher for his students. Bruno Nettl (1984) described the teaching of Dr. Nour-Ali Boroumand, one of the few musicians who are credited with the revival of Iran's classical music. Dr. Boroumand played "short bits" in his classes, repeated them himself, and required exact repetitions by his students. They learned that every ornament and duration should be precisely reproduced, and when sufficient music (gusheh, or multiple melodies of the broader dastgah) had been introduced, students were dismissed and sent home to practice. The process in which the teacher revealed the gusheh to be learned by the students was never rushed, for the point was that every sound required contemplation. No transcription of the music was permitted in class, for the process of learning pitches and rhythms for later improvisation required a thorough connection between students and their teacher.

Sarod player Ali Akbar Khansahib once described music as "a pathway to God." He clarified that "once you really get the right sound in your soul and mind, it is a peaceful feeling, a peace that cannot be gotten anywhere" (Ruckert 2004, 88). An effective sarod teacher shows the way to this peace by guiding students to learn many songs and compositions in a single raga, so that they will "begin to see how it is constructed" and thus learn what music they can hope to make. Even prior to or alongside the task of learning compositions, students of sarod may vocalize phrases of particular pieces or brief musical gestures that constitute improvisations on the raga. Khansahib advised that "each raga [will] take a lifetime to learn . . . [and] sometimes more than one lifetime" (Ruckert 2004, 86), and it can only be learned through continued listening, repeated vocalizations, and instrumental practice. He asserted that the intricate Hindustani practice of improvisation can indeed be learned, albeit through a time-intensive process.

Experienced improvising musicians also share the sense that expertise on the instrument (or voice) must be first achieved before improvisation skills can be developed. The skilled musician can venture further afield, going beyond familiar music to make the personal music that sounds from the heart (Campbell 1991a). Improvisation across varied genres grows from the considerable effort of the performer to discover both the musical tradition itself and her personal voice. Such discovery is key to Czikszentmihalyi's concept of "Flow" (1990), in which the improvising musician becomes one with the experience, transcends the piecemeal learning that occurs in everyday lessons and practice sessions, and moves to a heightened state of awareness. Flow may be seen as integral to the performer's personal expressive self, which draws on information from the musical sources the performer has encountered and the expressive impulse from within. In sarod-playing and in new music circles, as in jazz and among bardsingers, improvisation is at its best when the phenomenon of flow is in smooth operating condition.

Far from the expertise of professional musicians, improvisation is nonetheless at play in the lives of children. Prior to school, and in spite of schooling, children are playfully musical in ways that are undeniably improvisatory. They improvise *because they must*, because of their natural propensity to do so. There is no formal educational process, either, for instilling in children the music that naturally exudes from them. Before their inhibitions grow at the onset of adolescence to diminish their spontaneity, children are lively musicians who are compelled to create, blend what they know with what they "feel," and play with the possibilities for their vocalizations, motor rhythms, and performance on musical instruments (and other assorted objects that sound). Even as there are pedagogical designs in place to train children to improvise in order to learn music, and to learn to improvise music, children may be improvising even as they play.

Children reach their first serious stage of improvisation at four months, when they are involved in vocal expansion as precursors of speech and singing. Infants have an array of sounds that adults have long abandoned: they squeal, scream, growl, and draw out vowel sounds with pitch content that can expand as much as one, or even two, octaves. Their sounds may be experimentations rather than improvisation, and yet they are imitating and personalizing what they have heard of their world even as they are offering melodic and rhythmic expressions in discovering their physical capacity to produce sounds. These early vocalizations may be a way to develop linguistic competence, and Hanus Papousek (1996) postulates that they may also be the onset of musical competence. In fact, a somewhat parallel development of linguistic and musical competence within the first two years of childhood may be a result of the intrinsic creativity that infants have from the opening days of their lives.

Research on the development of general creativity reveals a U-shaped curve that begins with a period of high creativity in early childhood (marked by children's play and freedom from conformity), is followed by a slump in the middle years, and then reemerges in a more sophisticated form of creativity, for some, in mid-adolescence and adulthood. Teachers have noted that a slump in musical creativity often emerges soon after children's entry to school, and sometimes between 9 and 12 years, in the upper intermediate grades 4 through 6. Howard Gardner referred to the slump in the U shape as the low ebb of creativity or the literal stage, a time when children enter school, and said that such slumps are "possibly in part a result of this entry" (1988, 21). This is typically when children become more aware of cultural rules and feel less comfortable breaking them in creative ways. For those who study children (and adult novices) for their improvisational behaviors, these are points in learning to improvise that are influenced by age and stage.

The musical characteristics of children's improvisations were studied as early as the 1940s by educator Gladys Moorhead and composer Donald Pond (1940–1951). They observed young children ages two to six years in their free and exploratory play both vocally and on instruments, noting the melodic and rhythmic patterns of their sung songs, chants, and performances on pitched and nonpitched percussion instruments. Common to the children's improvisations were asymmetrical rhythms, a steady beat, and both simple and compound meters. Initial improvisations on xylophones, tuned gongs, and drums were chiefly focused on exploring timbral qualities; these gave way to melodic and rhythmic qualities.

In a study of young children's improvisations, John Flohr (1979) described the behaviors of four-, six-, and eight-year-old children engaged in improvising on pentatonic Orff xylophones. The improvisations of the older children were more cohesive, oriented toward a tonal center, and replete with patterns than those of the younger children. Musical patterns were discernible in the pentatonic xylophone improvisations of children ages two to six years, evidence that young children wished to express themselves musically in a regular repeated manner to achieve some measure of unity and stability. Flohr suggested three stages of children's improvisation: motor energy stage (two to four years), in which children utilize repeated pitches and relatively equal durations; experimentation (four to six years), a time of experimentation with little regard for the overall sound; and formal properties (six to eight years), in which tonality and repetition of larger patterns indicate children's awareness of structural characteristics.

Following their study of 745 compositions of 48 children from 3 to 15 years, Keith Swanwick and June Tillman (1986) defined eight developmental stages in the creativity of British children and youth. Before schooling even begins, young children are fascinated with timbres and dynamics, which they bring into their improvisations, and work to develop a control of techniques for playing instruments. Phrasing begins to appear, and changes of speed and dynamics become important to children as they enter school (about age 5 or 6). Patterns of melody and rhythm emerge, and are repeated, by children ages 7 to 8, while 10-year-olds often show an interest in deviating from the standard patterns and sounds. By early adolescence, there is a tendency to create music with ending "tags," phrases that answer earlier phrases, and variations. A strong personal identification with particular pieces of music, and even turns of phrases, occurs at a symbolic stage for youth (age 15), followed by the emergence of systematic creativity in which older adolescents become aware of stylistic principles that underlie their chosen idioms. While compositions were analyzed to determine this stage-related sequence, the general cognitive processes of children and youth are thought to be transferable to improvisational activity. John Kratus (1991) outlined seven developmental stages in the improvisation of children, none of which are strictly age-based, that extend from "exploratory" to "personal," at which point the young composer's "voice" and style become firmly established.

Children have verbalized their perspectives on the music they improvise and how they have learned it (Campbell 1998). Responding to the question of how she had learned a seemingly improvised song, 8-year-old Lisa claimed: "I made it. Me and only me. Mostly" (Campbell 1998, 103). Such fluctuation may reflect uncertainty about the source of the music and whether the songs are in fact "new" or associated with familiar musical models and influences. Six-year-old Darryl's response to the same question, relevant to the tune he had played on his slide whistle, was "I listen and figure it out" (Campbell 1998, 87). His improvised music and the songs he was re-creating from memory required him to listen attentively, even analytically, until his musical expression could emerge. Alan, a 10-year-old player of an electronic keyboard, observed, "My inside singing is my guide to my playing" (Campbell 1998,

107), thus calling attention to his improvised music as deeply embedded in the listening process. Far beyond the framework of their formal music education, children are making music that is satisfying to them and expressive of who they are, what they are intellectually able to think, physically poised to produce, and emotionally ready to express.

IMPROVISATION FOR MUSIC MAJORS

Even as some genres require that musicians learn to improvise in performance, improvisation is also used in musical education. Engaged as they are in developing expertise in Western art music, music majors in universities, colleges, and conservatories are rarely required to study improvisation as a separate course. Students of jazz studies and organ performance are the exception, and ensembles and specific training are geared to their professional needs. Yet standard theory, aural skills, and keyboard courses are venues awaiting the infusion of improvisation training exercises, with the intent of developing comprehensive musical learning through spontaneous yet thoughtful expression. Instructional theorists believe that concepts and skills are best learned when the knowledge is "situated," or constructed from active experiences (Merrill 1991), and improvisation may be an example of real-life situated learning. More than any other experience, improvisation as an instructional technique allows music students to receive a holistic musical training in which music theory, ear training, and performance can be woven together in an information-rich context.

The phenomenological analysis of improvisation by Paul Nardone (2002) provides an insightful approach to understanding the role of improvisation music training. Nardone addressed the world of musicians and reported his analysis of improvisation as "lived meanings" for those entering the professional world. He considered both the experience and context of improvisation, noting that improvisation ensured spontaneity while also yielding to it, explored familiar and unfamiliar musical terrain, drew from corporeal and incorporeal sources of musical inspiration, and developed trust and confidence in oneself and others in musical risk taking. Likewise, Eric Clarke (2002) noted that improvisation adds an active approach to counterbalance the "arid academicism" of other formal training. He argued that improvisation encouraged a questioning approach to musical performance and explained the manner in which improvisation "brings together the skills of performing, listening and creating in contrast to the deep 'division of labour' that exists within the culture of Western classical music" (Clarke 2002, 64). Improvisation integrates the individual facets of a musician's training.

sation is used in collegiate-level theory, aural skills, and
t facilitates the conceptual learning and skill development
in the intricacies of Western art music. As students are
thmic and melodic motives, listen to them, and sing and
an also learn to play them more freely—at different pitch
levels, ___ous textures, and on various timbres. They can be encouraged
to learn phrase structures and formal designs by improvising both rhythmic
and melodic phrases in varied meters, within the scope of recommended
durations and pitches, and with one phrase complementing and contrasting another phrase. Harmonic functions may be made more coherent to
students as they start from a given melody and create a bass line for it or a
harmonic progression. Inhibitions to improvisation in standard courses are
common but are reduced by setting up students to perform on unfamiliar
instruments, to work in small groups, to express brief ideas (of four or eight
beats) followed by prearranged tutti responses, and to respond to suggestions
for preset parameters of key, length, pitch, and durational content. Improvisation may be at its best in these instructional circumstances when it is
based on models or linked to analytical listening experiences. These means
of learning-by-doing ensure that music students learn music to the fullest.

DALCROZE-DEFINED IMPROVISATION

In the search for techniques by which improvisation can be transmitted
through formal educational processes, the pedagogy known as Dalcroze
surfaces as a noteworthy practice. Particularly in schools, conservatories,
and collegiate contexts, where improvisation is usually used to develop musicianship rather than as an end in itself, Dalcroze has been used effectively
in theory, aural skills, and even piano (and piano pedagogy) courses. The
principles developed by Émile Jaques-Dalcroze, an improvising pianist, theorist, conductor, composer, and teacher, provide the single most complete
system of rhythmic training to appear in the 20th century. He is historically
remembered most for the pedagogy he evolved at the Geneva Conservatory
in Switzerland and at Hellerau, Germany, from approximately 1905 to 1920,
which features eurhythmic movement, solfege (and solfege rhythmique), and
improvisation (Spector 1990). Of these, eurhythmics is the music-and-move-
ment technique that brings students quite literally to their (stocking) feet to
respond to durational values, metric accents, melodic direction, dynamic
changes, and phrases of a musical form. Yet while his method embodied
the three components within a single entity, Jacques-Dalcroze emphasized
improvisation as prime for serious students of music.

Jaques-Dalcroze (1932) justified improvisation in the training of music students by articulating its presence in Western art music from the time of the troubadours and trouveres through the performances by J. S. Bach and Beethoven. He described the qualities of the musician who becomes more musical through improvisation, noting the improviser's need for attention, his or her adaptability and variability, instinct, the simultaneity of "conscient" (conscious) and "inconscient" (unconscious) acts, and the liaison between will and reaction, imagination, analysis, realization, and creation. His enumeration of improvisation exercises included such pedagogical ideals as "muscular contraction and relaxation," "metrical division," "study of agogic nuances," "exercises of spontaneous will and inhibition," "exercises of concentration," and "improvisation by four hands and at two pianos" (Jaques-Dalcroze 1933). He maintained that the ability to improvise is not an inborn gift but one that can be learned.

Jaques-Dalcroze based his pedagogy on the premise that learning to improvise is similar to learning a language. He was surprised that so little attention was paid to improvisation in applied music, for he believed that there was a direct connection between the brain and the body. From the spontaneous performance of a single melodic line that ticks out a steady pulse to accompany "marching soldiers" to the creation of a musical dialogue between two instruments that sound separately and then together, he intended for improvisation to be adaptable to the player's level of competence at the piano as well as to the pedagogical goals. He adamantly proclaimed, "You speak language fluently when you reach the stage of not having to think about each and every word you enunciate; you can concentrate entirely on the content of the communications. Thus it is with music, that by knowing it one no longer thinks atomistically about individual notes but rather shapes larger phrases, often in improvisatory fashion, according to what it is that one wishes to communicate" (1921). According to Jaques-Dalcroze, this skill cannot be learned sequentially or in an objectivist manner. Rather, it must be enculturated over time and through experience.

The Dalcroze method is found scattered across the globe, particularly in a selection of conservatory settings and in children's classes in Australia, Europe, Japan, and North America. It never took the world of K-12 music education by storm in the same way that the Orff-Schulwerk has drawn a massive following of American school music teachers, probably because (a) it is musically challenging to nonpianists (as the piano, with all of its harmonic as well as melodic and rhythmic possibilities, is the standard stimulus for eurhythmic movement responses), (b) it is intentionally nonsequential and

ε standard school view of stepwise procedures in music
(c) it was never designed to feed activities to teachers in
shops for their Monday morning classes but is in fact a long
g" process of many years before the musical gestures sink in and
cquired. Yet Dalcroze is a thoroughgoing pedagogy that requires
rated ear-mind-body connection in those who are drawn to it.

ch the emergence of the *National Standards for Arts* Education (1994),
musical education of children and youth in schools began to run ram-
ant with mandates for exercises in creative music making. Composition,
improvisation, and song-writing projects existed much earlier than that,
often to balance the performance-based curriculum that was the staple diet
of North American school music programs since the mid-19th century. By
the late 1950s, interest in composition led to the development of composers-
in-residence in schools that, funded by the Ford Foundation, were continued
through the 1960s. The Manhattanville Music Curriculum Project, created
in the late 1960s, was a model for developing aural acuity, creative thought,
and facility with musical sounds. Improvisation was a key component of the
project, which was replicated in many elementary school music programs
at the time.

British music education was likewise reforming its school programs in the
1960s and early 1970s, largely as a reaction to the passive "music apprecia-
tion" curriculum that was prevalent, and creative music-making experiences
became embedded in programs that had earlier been geared toward listening
lessons. Music programs in the United Kingdom had tended to emphasize
knowledge about composers and styles and thus came across to students
as courses in music history, while technical theory training had also been
developed in some schools for those with instrumental training. Progressive
educators such as John Paynter and Peter Aston were adopting an experimental approach that was influenced by the work of avant-garde composers,
artists, and writers of the era. Experimentation with vocal and instrumental
sounds, body percussion, and the sounds of found-sound objects (such as
pots, pans, forks, spoons, and other household objects) became common
in the curriculum. Popular music was studied for the ideas it might inspire
in students' composition and improvisation, and tape recorders, electronic
keyboards and synthesizers, and other electronic means were employed along
with instruments as media to be featured in student works.

Thirty years later, curricular guidelines for individual schools, statewide
curricular plans, and national policy statements have underscored the idea
that music taps into nonverbal ways of knowing and allows young people to

express themselves artistically—and musically—regardless of their verbal abilities. In North America, as in the United Kingdom, children's creative thinking in music, or musical creativity, has become the justification for music education programs (particularly in elementary schools). Since educators feel that music is multimodal, involving the eye, ear, muscle, and mind and providing a full range of emotions and deep communication, improvisation and composition have been viewed as a curricular option even for young children. Increasingly, teachers are stepping forward to provide children with creative music-making experiences that range from their teacher-directed tighties all the way to the child-centered loosies that are open to every conceivable manner of experimentation.

A considerable number of practicing teachers shun these creative activities, however, choosing to focus time and effort on developing re-creative performance skill. Their excuses for leaving improvisation aside are contained in these real-life quips: "Teach improvisation? Not when I've never improvised myself." "Improvisation is for 'jazzers,' not my students in the cello studio, or choir." "Music is one of the creative arts; isn't there enough inherent 'creativeness' in the performance of music, so that teaching improvisation becomes somewhat redundant—and thus an unnecessary addendum—in the curriculum?" "Improvisation is chaos, and that does not work in my classroom." Especially because most K-12 teachers were not trained as improvising musicians, improvisation is a vague and distant notion, and pedagogical approaches are unclear when they themselves have had no firsthand experience in the process.

Composition projects are more commonly found in schools than improvisation experiences, and classes in "general music" in elementary and secondary schools are prime venues for their occurrence. Some improvisation projects are devoted to the creative expression of individual students (often at keyboards), but far more are intended for group collaboration. There are projects with varied media, from acoustic to electronic instruments, with percussion instruments—particularly drums—being among the most commonly used in group improvisation. Creative improvisation projects for classrooms may have a specific task or a closed problem in mind, whereas others entail open tasks that are intended to trigger greater freedom of expression. Pedagogical methods such as the Orff-Schulwerk and Dalcroze support improvisation in elementary school classrooms. Their professional organizations, the American Orff-Schulwerk Association and the Dalcroze Society of America, publish quarterly newsletters and magazines that feature techniques for the implementation of improvisational strategies in lessons. Annual conferences and periodic workshops occasionally provide teachers with methods and materials to stimulate improvisatory behaviors in their students.

At the secondary level, jazz ensembles (including big band ensembles, instrumental combos, and vocal jazz groups) are the principal settings in which improvisation is taught. Guitar and keyboard classes also feature improvisatory experiences, where students are invited to improvise melodies over the chordal progressions they have learned, to pair up and create music based on motifs presented by the teacher, and even to take turns trading 8 or 12 bars of improvised music in between the tutti sections. Whereas these classes are often anchored in the performance of chords, school jazz ensembles frequently begin class sessions by warming up with blues scales. Collective and solo scale-playing is assessed by the teacher, who typically assigns solos for standards like "All the Things You Are," "Green Dolphin Street," and "Autumn Leaves" based on students' ability to play their scales well. When students are charged with leading sectional rehearsals, they follow their teacher's lead, as 15-year-old Michael describes: "I tell them, scales first. It's about scales. I make them play the G-blues, probably about 10 times. Then I show them how to take the low end of the scale, like G-Bb-C and just tongue around on those notes. Later we go to the middle and the high notes of the scale and do the same." Such an approach is reminiscent of the view of jazz pedagogue David Baker, who maintains that as long as students can play their scales, he can teach them the rest.

Like the practice of musically educating children and youth, much of the research in the field has been concentrated within the narrow frame of the so-called cognitive revolution, where developmental studies and music as cognition have dominated the professional literature. Facets critical to studies of creative musicianship—situation, process, context, and culture—have been seriously understudied. Psychomotor skill development through re-creative performance continues to be the principal thrust of K-12 music education, and policy manuals that advocate creativity in classrooms are ahead of the realities of most curricular practice. A gradual shift is now under way in research from a concentration on the personal factors of individual students to a concern for the social and cultural variables of a group, from laboratory studies to classroom contexts, and from technically scientist research to humanistically grounded methodologies and interpretative approaches. In interesting ways, the placement of improvisation in K-12 school activities may follow this pattern, reorganizing from strictly re-creative to creative experiences, from didactic to heuristic, from teacher-directed to teacher-facilitated, and from product-focused to process-oriented curricular activity. As school music is overwhelmingly focused on group interactions, aspects of context and culture will be meaningful in the further development of improvisation at elementary and secondary levels.

TOWARD A PEDAGOGY OF IMPROVISATION

Is there a pedagogical way of truth and light for the practice of improvisation? There are multiple ways of teaching and learning improvisation, and they are dependent on the culture's beliefs in the function of the musician to preserve or to create music. Just as some music is traditionally intended to be sounded exactly as the composer had envisioned it, other genres are meant to allow the performer expressive license to play with the possibilities within the form. Improvisatory styles of music are steeped in the aural capacity of performers to learn by listening to the masters (and master-teachers) and by spending long periods imitating live and recorded models. Students in this tradition learn to observe by ear and by eye and to practice repeatedly what they have observed until their teachers and mentors support them in breaking from the models to the sound of their own personal expressions within the framework of the style.

The culture of educational institutions in the West continues to maintain as its mission the conservation of Western art music. Even the "school music" genres of bands, choirs, and orchestras are decidedly Western in their orientation. Music educators in "conservatory" settings, at all levels and circumstances, work within systems where the expectation is that they serve as custodians of the theory and practice of music. Skills in the music of standard Western notation are at the center of instructional processes in applied performance studios and ensembles, as well as in theory, aural skills, and history and literature classes. Improvisation is slow to come in such venues, even as mandates from national accreditation agencies and professional organizations call for students to develop the "rudimentary capacity to create original music both extemporaneously and in written form" (National Association of Schools of Music 2004). Yet as the realization grows that it is "human to improvise," the way ahead in music courses and programs is to allow the incorporation of improvisation exercises so that students may develop a deeper and more comprehensive musical understanding. In schools and in higher education, a more thoroughgoing musical education may be achieved by setting aside time for imitating various musical styles, experimenting with a variety of sound sources, and improvising on predesigned motifs and materials.

Beyond mandates, there is the compelling belief that improvisation is an essential feature of the art of making music. Children are musically expressive until they are directed to re-create with precision only what has come before. Whereas they were once "loose" and free in their musical expressions (albeit always influenced by their sonic surrounds), improvising their tunes and grooves in learning their world, they are led to tighten their grip on what is musically acceptable—often at the risk of losing their own musical selves. In a culture where so much music is fixed and frozen and made by a "star system" of approved performers, encounters in improvisation early on and often in the educational process can allow even the youngest musicians to breathe new musical thought into their lives. Socially interactive music making can save the music, keep it alive, and place it in the possession of every musical child, adolescent, and adult. Through the process of improvisation, teachers provide ways and means for all students, of every age and experience, to find a place for the sounds within them. The ultimate aim of a musical education may be to give balance to "our music" and "their music," to the old and the new in music, to what's notated and what's not, to traditions and their potential for change. Improvisation within a musical education, whether it is learning to improvise or improvising to learn, may be central to making an expressive musician.

REFERENCES

Bakan, Michael. 1999. *Music of Death and New Creation: Experiences in the World of Balinese Gamelan Beleganjur*. Chicago: University of Chicago Press.

Becker, Howard. 1982. *Art Worlds*. Berkeley and Los Angeles: University of California Press.

Benson, Bruce Ellis. 2003. *The Improvisation of Musical Dialogue: A Phenomenology of Music*. Cambridge: Cambridge University Press.

Berliner, Paul. 1994. *Thinking in Jazz: The Infinite Art of Improvisation*. Chicago: University of Chicago Press.

Blacking, John. 1973. *How Musical Is Man?* Seattle: University of Washington Press.

———. 1990. Interview by Fiona MacGowan, John Blacking Collection Callaway Centre, The University of Western Australia.

Booth, Gregory C. 1986. "The Oral Tradition in Transition: Implications for Music Education from a Study of North Indian Tabla Transmission." Ph.D. dissertation, Kent State University.

Campbell, Patricia Shehan. 1991a. *Lessons from the World*. New York: Schirmer Books.

————. 1991b. "Unveiling the Mysteries of Creativity." *Music Educators Journal* 78(9): 21–24.

————. 1998. *Songs in Their Heads*. New York: Oxford University Press.

Clarke, Eric. 2002. "Understanding the Psychology of Performance." In *Musical Performance: A Guide to Understanding*, edited by John Rink, 59–74. Cambridge: Cambridge University Press.

Czikszentmihalyi, Mihalyi. 1990. *The Psychology of Optimal Experience*. New York: Harper & Row.

Eliot, T. S. 1944. *The Waste Land*. New York: Faber and Faber.

Evans, Bill. 1959. *Kind of Blue* (liner notes). Sound Disc Sony B0002 AIX.

Flohr, John W. 1979. "Musical Improvisation Behavior of Young Children." Ph.D. dissertation, University of Illinois at Urbana-Champaign.

Gardner, Howard. 1988. "Creativity: An Interdisciplinary Perspective." *Creativity Research Journal* 1: 8–26.

Gushee, Lawrence. 1981. "Lester Young's Shoeshine Boy." In *Report of the Twelfth Congress of the International Musicological Society, Berkeley 1977*, 151–69. Kassel: Bärenreiter.

Hall, Edward T. 1992. "Improvisation as an Acquired, Multilevel Process." *Ethnomusicology* 36(2): 223–35.

Jaques-Dalcroze, Émile. 1921. *Rhythm, Music and Education*. Translated from French by Harold F. Rubinstein. New York: G. P. Putnam's Sons.

————. 1932. "L'Improvisation au Piano." *Le Rythme* 34: 3–15.

————. 1933. "L'Improvisation Musical." *Revue musicale* 136: 344–58.

Johnson, J. W. 1999. "Dichotomy of Power and Authority in Mande Society and the Epic of Sunjata." In *In Search of Sunjata: The Mande Oral Epic as History, Literature and Performance*, edited by Ralph A. Austen, 9–24. Bloomington: Indiana University Press.

Kratus, John. 1991. "Growing with Improvisation." *Music Educators Journal* 78(9): 35–40.

Langer, Suzanne K. 1953. *Feeling and Form*. New York: Charles Scribner's Sons.

Lord, Albert. B. 1960. *The Singer of Tales*. Cambridge, Mass.: Harvard University Press.

Merrill, M. David. 1991. "Constructivism and Instructional Design." *Educational Technology* 31(5): 45–53.

Moorhead, Gladys E., and Donald Pond. 1941–1951. *Music of Young Children*. Santa Barbara, Calif.: Pillsbury Foundation for Advancement of Music Education.

National Association of Schools of Music. 2004. *National Association of Schools of Music: 2005–2006 Handbook*. Reston, Va.: Author.

National Standards for Arts Education. 1994. Reston, Va.: Music Educators National Conference.

Nettl, Bruno. 1974. "Thoughts on Improvisation: A Comparative Approach." *Musical Quarterly* 60(1): 1–19.

————. 1984. "In Honor of Our Principal Teachers." *Ethnomusicology* 28(2): 173–85.

Nguyen, Phong, and Patricia Shehan Campbell. 1989. *From Rice Paddies and Temple Yards: Traditional Music of Viet Nam.* Danbury, Conn.: World Music Press.

Papousek, Hanus. 1996. "Musicality in Infancy Research: Biological and Cultural Origins of Early Musicality." In *Musical Beginnings: Origins and Development of Musical Competence,* edited by Irene Deliege and John A. Sloboda, 37–55. New York: Oxford University Press.

Parry, Adam, ed. 1971. *The Making of Homeric Verse: The Collected Papers of Milman Parry.* Oxford: Clarendon Press.

Pline, Mary. 1982. "Tighties and Loosies." *Orff Echo* 14: 2, 3, 18.

Pressing, Jeff. 1988. "Improvisation: Methods and Models." In *Generative Processes in Music: The Psychology of Performance, Improvisation and Composition,* edited by John A. Sloboda, 129–78. New York: Oxford University Press.

————. 1998. "Psychological Constraints on Improvisational Expertise and Communication." In *In the Course of Performance: Studies in the World of Musical Improvisation,* edited by Bruno Nettl with Melinda Russell, 47–67. Chicago: University of Chicago Press.

Radlov, V. V. 1967. *South-Siberian Oral Literature, Turkic Texts,* Vol. 1., with an introduction by Denis Sinor. Bloomington: Indiana University Press.

Rattenbury, Ken. 1990. *Duke Ellington: Jazz Composer.* New Haven, Conn.: Yale University Press.

Rice, Timothy. 1994. *May It Fill Your Soul: Experiencing Bulgarian Music.* Chicago: University of Chicago Press.

Ruckert, George. 2004. *Music in North India.* New York: Oxford University Press.

Schwartz, Elliott. 1982–1983. "Forum: Improvisation." *Perspectives of New Music* 21(1–2): 69–70.

Sloboda, John A. 1991. "Musical Expertise." In *Toward a General Theory of Expertise,* edited by K. Anders Ericsson and Jacqui Smith, 153–71. Cambridge: Cambridge University Press.

Spector, Irwin. 1990. *Rhythm and Life: The Work of Émile Jaques-Dalcroze.* Stuyvesant, N.Y.: Pendragon Press.

Swanwick, Keith, and June Tillman. 1986. "The Sequence of Music Development: Creativity within Cultural Restraints." *British Journal of Music Education* 3(3): 305–39.

Titon, Jeff Todd. 1977. *Early Downhome Blues: A Musical and Cultural Analysis.* Urbana: University of Illinois Press.

Treitler, Leo. 2003. *With Voice and Pen: Coming to Know Medieval Song and How It Was Made.* New York: Oxford University Press.

⌇ 8 ⌇

IMPROVISING MOZART

Robert Levin

Classical musicians have become highly specialized. Most of today's performers practice many hours a day painstakingly learning and perfecting texts written by others. Highly skilled at reproducing music, they often have little or no training in inventing it. An actor confronted by a missed entrance or a forgotten line can often rescue the situation by inventing dialogue to bridge the gap. A memory lapse or a sudden contradiction of pronunciation or of dialect will shatter the illusion of identity between personage and actor and remind us painfully that what we are seeing is an artificial enactment of reality, not the theatrical alchemy that momentarily seems more intense than the life it imitates. Although it is difficult to ad lib dialogue in iambic pentameter, every actor has daily experience improvising conversations in his or her native tongue. This is not so for musicians; and the task of inventing within the individual languages of the great composers is daunting if not impossible for a performer who has not had extensive training in the grammar, syntax, rhetoric, and texture of music, and indeed in composition itself.

In the 18th century all composers were performers, and virtually all performers composed. Furthermore, virtually all the music performed was new. Today's gap in popular and art music did not exist then: both domains involved spontaneity within a language idiomatic to the time.

Improvisation is a given in non-art music. Present in music of all cultures, it is the central challenge in jazz. The genius of Louis Armstrong, Coleman Hawkins, Art Tatum, Miles Davis, and John Coltrane (an arbitrary sampling of past masters) has been captured on discs that document untrammeled flights of fanciful imagination. The survival of alternative takes and re-recordings reveals the complex relationship between specific elements that remain from take to take and the risky abandonment of the firm ground of preparation in the interest of truly instant creativity.

Mozart's performances were designed to display his talents as improviser, pianist, and composer (that is the order his contemporaries assigned to his gifts). His piano concertos contain contrived chasms—pauses he bridged with impulsive audacity, the so-called cadenzas and lead-ins (the shorter cadenzas that precede the return of the principal theme, as opposed to the large ones on the tonic six-four at the end of the movement). Furthermore, Mozart left many passages in sketched or schematic form, relying on the whims of live performance to fill in the specific expressive content anew at each performance.

In the 20th century musicians have been trained to try piously to observe the written testament of the composer. If the will of the performer emerges, it is often through flamboyant disregard of those instructions in order for the artist to use the composition as a mere vehicle for self-aggrandizing display. Every performer and listener of classical music has experienced the standard repertoire hundreds, even thousands of times more than the composers who wrote these works, making it ever harder to bring to them the daring of the works' initial effect. The standardization of many of today's performances reflects all these trends.

Improvisation in Mozart's case requires an intensive character study of the entire work, because a spontaneous elaboration of the written text cannot be pasted on to the musical surface. The embellishments and improvised portions must heighten the portrayal of the work's persona, not a mere series of commonplace, banal conventions (a trill here, a curlicue there). The treatises of Mozart's time emphasize that the purpose of embellishment is to deepen the character of the work; indeed, Leopold Mozart states in his violin treatise that the very tempo cannot be established until one has first determined the piece's character. Careful examination of Mozart's music shows a restless variety of rhythm and texture, with changes in accompaniment as often as every few measures. The operas clearly show the relationship between these myriad changes and the dramatic implications of the libretto. A performer of instrumental music stands to gain immensely from a study of the vocal works, in which Mozart demonstrates a virtuoso ability to mirror the society he depicts through the gestures he employs. A generalized approach beholden to notions of sonic beauty and elegance reduces this gamut to a harmless, anodyne decorousness.

The treatises of the 18th century, among them C.P.E. Bach, Quantz, Leopold Mozart, Hiller, and Türk, give explicit instruction in the kinds of embellishment and improvisation required by the music of the time; no musician can claim that the problem is a lack of available information. Such general descriptions will not suffice for idiomatic elaboration of Mozart unless they are adapted to the idiosyncrasies of his particular style, which can be gleaned from careful examination of his music. The fact is, however, that the musician desirous of learning first to prepare embellishments and cadenzas as an essential first step in learning to improvise has a vast amount of material from Mozart and his circle that reveals the type and amount of ornamentation he expected as well as the architectural shape and rhetorical content of idiomatic cadenzas. In the cases of several of the piano concertos, we possess up to three different sets of cadenzas or lead-ins, revealing not only the inexhaustibility of Mozart's invention but also the variety of possible approaches, starting from one or another of the motives heard in the movement proper, or, in the case of the A-major concerto K.488, of a free improvisation that notably eschews all of the memorable tunes of the movement in favor of a volatile flight of fancy. This remarkable cadenza leads through the fright of an unexpected diminished seventh chord (whose cry of terror is rendered in many of today's performances as a diminuendo to *pp*, demonstrating the triumph in Mozart performance today of bloodless good behavior over content) and the stammering of the disoriented protagonist to the heroic push back to the six-four and the triumphant deliverance of the final trill. Descriptions of the inner workings of these authentic cadenzas are available in modern-day treatises by Paul and Eva Badura-Skoda (2008) and Frederick Neumann (1986), as well as articles and essays by the author.

Some of Mozart's piano concertos were written for others (K.246, 271, 449, 453, 456 and possibly 488); for these concertos he needed to compose cadenzas for pupils or colleagues who lacked his quicksilver ability to improvise. He allowed his sister to perform a number of his other concertos and taught them to pupils as well, accounting for the other surviving cadenzas. (Of the six concertos for which no cadenzas survive—K.466, 467, 482, 491, 503, and 537—it would appear that he did compose cadenzas for K.466 and 467, which have been lost.) It is revealing that we do not have cadenzas for his wind and violin concertos, for which he evidently trusted the soloists to improvise. Only in the case of multiple concertos such as the *Sinfonia concertante* for violin and viola K.364 do we have a written cadenza, in order to avoid the disorder of simultaneous improvisation.

The publication history of Mozart's piano sonatas reveals that his manuscript versions contain a paucity of dynamics and eschew notation of the returns of principal themes. In the latter case Mozart simply writes Da Capo X measures, continuing only where the music deviates from the first version. When preparing such sonatas for publication or performance by pupils (cf. the C-minor fantasy K.475 and sonata K.457), Mozart added a plethora of dynamics and wrote out embellishments for key passages—not just the

principal theme of slow movements but often other passages as well (cf. the
F-major sonata K.332).

All of these materials can serve as a tutor in the art of elaboration and
embellishment from the most authentic source possible: Mozart himself.

Looking at his activities as a whole, we can see from the family corre-
spondence and surviving sources that Mozart improvised in the following
situations:

1. In the piano concertos, he improvised an accompaniment to the orchestral tuttis by doubling the string bass line (not the cello line where this
   diverges from the string bass, or the bassoon[s] where the string bass is
   silent) in his left hand and accompanying with his right. In early concertos
   the accompanimental function is indicated by figures, most often written
   in by his father, including directions to play chords, or for the right hand
   to double the left an octave higher (*unisono*), or for it to be silent (*tasto
   solo* [the key played by the left hand only]). In later scores Mozart simply
   writes *col Baßo* into the left-hand staff of the piano. It is theoretically possible that in such a situation Mozart limited the accompaniment to chords
   to mark the harmonic rhythm, as suggested by Charles Rosen, but I find it
   difficult to imagine the most imaginative musician alive playing nothing
   other than chords. The situation is not all that different from the swing
   bands of Duke Ellington or Count Basie, where the presence of the piano
   in the band need not require a lot of figuration, but merely a well-chosen
   riff or passage provoking delight or otherwise intensifying the character
   of the music, all the while preparing the audience for the piano's solo role
   still to come.
2. In the solo portions of the concertos he embellished freely, especially at
   the returns of principal themes, but also in passages whose notation is
   limited to the bare outer notes of arpeggios or other passage work (cf. the
   first movement of the C-minor piano concerto K.491, or the last movement of the E-flat concerto K.482) notated in long values. This will apply
   to concertos for other instruments, if to a lesser degree, and to other
   instrumental music as well.
3. Cadenzas and lead-ins, applicable to the concertos for other instruments
   as well.
4. When he played two works in somewhat distant keys, he improvised a
   modulating prelude to connect the tonalities. His sister Nannerl was unable to improvise and solicited pseudo-improvisations from Wolfgang on
   several occasions. These unusual compositions, principally nonmetrical,
   are constructed exactly according to the principles set down by C.P.E.
   Bach in the final chapter of his *Versuch* (1753; cf. Levin 2003).

5. When trying out a keyboard prior to formal performance, he would improvise a short piece to give him an idea of the characteristics of the instrument, which enabled him to adapt his interpretation to it.

6. During his travels Mozart often improvised on the organ when visiting churches on the route. In one case—a visit to Stralau—there is a partial protocol of such an improvisation that appears in the appendix of the second piano pieces volume of the *Neue Mozart-Ausgabe*.

That Mozart expected other musicians to improvise or at least to perform with embellishments is reflected in the vocal embellishments and cadenzas to his arias he wrote for specific singers, and to the already noted fact that the non-keyboard concertos do not contain cadenzas. Indeed, the only solo piano concerto to contain a cadenza written directly into the autograph is K.488, which strongly suggests that the work was written for performance by someone else (cf. Levin 2001).

These conventions, particularly that of the modulating preludes, may seem echoes of a distant past, but as recently as the 1930s pianists such as Josef Hofmann perpetuated this practice in their public recitals.

In light of this evidence it must be said that many of today's performances contain passages executed in a manner Mozart would have considered unacceptably incomplete. It will not matter how poetic or sonically ravishing the performance is if the utterance is not the expected "To be, or not to be: that is the question," but rather " . . . be . . . not . . . question." Furthermore, Mozart's practice of shielding audiences from abrupt and conflicting keys, each of which had a specific character as reflected in the *Affektenlehre* (the doctrine of affect), has been replaced by today's programming, in which even the most distinguished performers either neglect or deliberately disregard this principle (e.g., the interpolation of the B-minor adagio K.540 between the C-minor fantasy and sonata, as practiced by one of today's finest Mozart pianists in a Salzburg recital).

Apart from organists, few classical performers improvise any more, even though the information that would enable them to learn to do so is available. Today's performers, shaped in the crucible of competitions and recordings, learn early to avoid risk as a threat to consistency and accuracy. There is nothing more risky than improvisation, but there is nothing more devastating to music's dramatic and emotional message than avoidance of risk. This is not to say, however, that *any* kind of improvisation is better than none. It is fascinating to hear an improvised performance, but surely it matters whether the utterance is idiomatic to the language of the piece. How strange that moviemakers take great pains (at great cost) to shoot on historically accurate locations with period appurtenances, costumes, and dialogue but often are content to use music that betrays the venue at every turn. A performance of a Christopher Marlowe play in which suddenly the dialect and pronunciation of rural Alabama were interpolated for several exchanges would be perceived by an audience as grotesque or comical, yet we permit such linguistic incongruities without hesitation in music. If Mozart's language is as worthy of respect as Marlowe's, surely it is worth the time to learn it from the inside in order to invent it afresh as part of each performance.

How is it to be done? We have already seen two of the crucial tools, which are the materials surviving from Mozart's pen and those of his pupils, and the treatises of the time. In the end, however, learning to improvise is like improving one's sight-reading: one learns by doing, and above all by not becoming discouraged by initial setbacks. A budding jazz musician learns a variety of normative figures, practiced in all keys, which provide a safety net so that if the mind momentarily deserts us, the fingers still have some usable and idiomatic fodder. Such figures exist in the music of all styles, and never is the formulaic so evident as in the classical period. This means, to be sure, that a would-be improviser of Mozart needs to have considerable insight into the relationship between Mozart's melodic, rhythmic, and harmonic patterns and dramatic/emotional character portrayal; but here again we have seen how helpful study of the arias and operas can be.

Looking at Mozart's own embellishments and comparing them to the original unadorned versions is perhaps the greatest confidence-building measure we can undertake. Such comparisons immediately identify the nature of the decorations, passing tones, appoggiaturas, neighboring tones, turns, arpeggios of all kinds, and so forth. As we identify these, it becomes clearer and clearer that "Wait a minute! I can do that, too!" Having the courage to embark on the voyage may be the most crucial part of the enterprise. Once again Franklin D. Roosevelt was right: the only thing we have to fear is fear itself. The revitalization of the music through intensification of content, both lyrical and virtuosic, and the personal stake of improvisation, promises to exchange the glow of life for the humdrum conventions that have made much of classical music into something to relax to, that is, something to which we need not pay attention. If we want the audience to pay attention, we must do what actors do: invest our performances with spontaneity and danger. Improvisation guarantees both.

REFERENCES

Bach, C.P.E. 1753. *Versuch über die wahre Art das Clavier zu spielen, mit Exempeln und achtzehn Probe-Stücken in sechs Sonaten erläutert von Carl Philipp Emanuel Bach*. Berlin: In verlegung des auctoris, gedruckt bey C.F. Henning.

Badura-Skoda, Eva, and Paul Badura-Skoda. 1962. *Interpreting Mozart on the Keyboard*. Translated by Leo Black. New York: St. Martin's Press.

Levin, Robert D. 2001. "K.488: Mozart's Third Concerto for Barbara Ployer?" in *Mozartiana. The Festschrift for the Seventieth Birthday of Professor Ebisawa Bin*, edited by Yosihiko Tokumaru, 555–70. Tokyo: Tokyo Soseki.

———. 2003. "Mozart's Non-metrical Keyboard Preludes." In *The Keyboard in Baroque Europe*, edited by Christopher Hogwood, 198–216. Cambridge, N.Y.: Cambridge University Press.

Neumann, Frederick. 1986. *Ornamentation and Improvisation in Mozart*. Princeton, N.J.: Princeton University Press.

ᖱ 9 ᖱ

KEYBOARD IMPROVISATION
IN THE BAROQUE PERIOD

Charlotte Mattax Moersch

Numerous accounts from the 17th and 18th centuries document the major role improvisation played in the life of the Baroque keyboard player. Colorful anecdotes of competitions between famous players, such as that between Scarlatti and Handel at the *Palazzo della Cancelleria* in Rome, or that proposed by Bach with Marchand in 1717, attest to the universality of improvisation in the keyboard music of the Baroque (Orengia 1989, 150). Although primary sources say little about training in keyboard improvisation specifically, it is possible to give an idea of how a Baroque player learned aspects of improvisation and, by extension, how these skills might be taught to today's players. We can learn about improvisational practice from accounts of performances from the period, ornament tables and tutors of the time, and composers' own written-out embellishments.

The purpose of this essay is to introduce today's player to the stylistic subtleties of Baroque keyboard improvisation. In this aim, practical rules for embellishment will be proposed within a larger discussion of national styles of ornamentation. Evidence for the styles of both French and Italian adornments will be provided in the form of notated pieces and harpsichord transcriptions of operas. Beyond merely adding ornaments to a given piece, the Baroque player was often called upon to extemporize freely, so for this reason a discussion of the art of elaborating unmeasured preludes and free fantasias will shed light on this aspect of improvisation. Finally, the question of how to realize accompaniments in a chamber work will be addressed. Primary sources will be cited to document how the early keyboard artist learned to read figured bass, and to give insight into the style of the realization, including where to arpeggiate chords and how to add obbligato melodies to the bass.

ORNAMENTATION

The French practice consisted mainly of adding single-note ornaments, or *agréments*, including *tremblements* (trills from the upper note), *pincés* (mordents using the lower auxiliary), and *ports de voix* or *coulés* (appoggiaturas). An ornament table (Figure 9.1) by the 17th-century French harpsichordist Jean Henry d'Anglebert ([1689] 1975) summarizes these *agréments*.

In contrast to the prevailing trend of the day, which left embellishment largely up to the performer, French keyboard composers tended to be unusually explicit in indicating their *agréments*, using stenographic signs to denote the ornaments. From their music, ornament tables, and contemporary treatises such as that by Bénigne de Bacilly ([1668] 1968), the modern player can learn how to add ornaments in the French style. *Sarabande La Prude* from

FIGURE 9.1. A French ornament table. Reproduced from Jean-Henry d'Anglebert, *Pièces de clavecin, A Facsimile of the Paris, 1689 Edition*. Geneva: Minkoff, 2001. Used by permission of Editions Minkoff.

François Couperin's second suite is used by way of illustration in Figure 9.2 ([1713] 1973:22; cf. Gilbert's edition, 1972:44).[1]

The excerpt gives a snapshot of the French practice of adding embellishment. Briefly, Couperin adds *tremblements* on leading tones and in order to decorate cadences, and *pincés* at the beginning of phrases and on leaps of a fourth or fifth. He also makes liberal use of appoggiaturas, including *ports de voix*, which accent the dissonant lower note of an ascending half step, and *coulés*, to fill in descending thirds.

It is important to note that French ornaments serve not only to heighten dissonance but also to provide rhythmic accent, helping to stress the important steps of the dance. In this *Sarabande*, *tremblements* and *port-de-voix* decorate the first and second beats of the measure, in accordance with the choreography of the dance.[2]

Despite the fact that Couperin notates his ornaments, their realization

FIGURE 9.2. *Sarabande La Prude* from François Couperin's *Deuxème Ordre*. Reproduced from Couperin, *Pièces de clavecin, A Facsimile of the Paris, 1713–30 Edition*, Monuments of Music & Music Literature in Facsimile I/9, by arrangement with Broude Brothers.

is still left up to the performer who determines the speed and number of repercussions in the trill, the length of the appoggiatura, and the rhythmic placement of the ornament, which varies according to musical context and affect.

French pieces with ornaments already notated by the composer often may invite additional embellishment, especially in repeats. Accordingly, the slow movements in French style from Georg Frideric Handel's suites provide the opportunity for the addition of *agréments*. In performing the *Sarabande* from Handel's *Fourth Suite in E Minor*, the harpsichordist may use Couperin's *La Prude* as a model to extemporize single note ornaments of the French variety, including *ports de voix*, *tremblements*, *tours de gosiers* (turns), and *pincés* as illustrated in Figure 9.3 (Handel [1720] 1980, 20–21).[3] Suggested ornaments to be added by the performer are indicated in smaller type.

FREE EMBELLISHMENT

Although French practice consisted primarily of single-note ornaments, the Italian style featured diminutions, or improvised passage-work, which is generally referred to as free embellishment. Johann Quantz points to the fundamental difference between French and Italian styles, calling French *agréments* essential (*wesentliche Manieren*) and the more ornate Italian dimi-

FIGURE 9.3. Suggestions for adding French ornaments to the *Sarabande* from Georg Frideric Handel's *Fourth Suite in E Minor*, from his *Suites for Harpsichord, Book I* (London, 1720). Transcribed by the author.

nutions arbitrary (*wilkürliche Veränderungen*) (Quantz [1752] 1966, 91, 137). French ornaments were obligatory, while Italian embellishment was optional, to be supplied only if the performer could improve upon the original. Contemporary treatises give a picture of a flamboyant style of embellishment in 18th-century Italy. Although Giuseppe Tartini's method book, *Traité des agréments* ([1754] 1966), is written for the violinist, it is equally applicable to the keyboard player. He divides ornaments into natural and artificial modes. The natural mode includes figuration that can be improved by beginners, while the artificial mode features melodic variation that requires a knowledge of counterpoint. The excerpt in Figure 9.4 is one of a series of examples Tartini gives, showing how to ornament simple stepwise motion ([1754] 1966) using single-note ornaments such as appoggiaturas, cambiata figures, and trills, as well as scalar and arpeggiated passage-work.

FIGURE 9.4. An excerpt from Giuseppe Tartini's *Traité des agréments de la musique,* illustrating how to add embellishments in the Italian style. Facs. Edition by Edwin R. Jacobi, translated by Cuthbert Girdlestone, Celle, N.Y.: H. Moeck, 1961. Reprinted by permission of Bärenreiter-Verlag.

The Italian style was exported to the leading countries of Europe, as can be seen in excerpts by keyboard composers such as Pancrace Royer ([1746] 1990:2–3) in France (see Figure 9.5) and Johann Christoph Graupner (1954, 24) in Germany (see Figure 9.6).

The original edition of Handel's harpsichord suites contains two pieces in which lavish diminutions are distinguished from the principal notes of the melody by smaller type. We find this procedure used in the first *Adagio* from the *Second Suite* as illustrated in Figure 9.7 ([1720] 1980, 2–3).

A comparison of the plain and decorated versions of this melody gives today's student a useful framework for learning to improvise. A recipe for embellishing in this style can be given as follows:

1. Add single note ornaments in the form of trills, mordents, accented passing tones, cambiata figures, appoggiaturas, and acciaccaturas (dissonant chord tones).
2. Add passage-work, including scales to fill in leaps, and prefixes and suffixes to trills. Occasionally, one may leap up or down to another note of the harmony, and then fill in stepwise with improvised scales.

FIGURE 9.5. An excerpt from *La Majestueuse, Courante,* by Pancrace Royer, showing the influence of the Italian diminution style on French composers. Reproduced from Royer, *Pièces de clavecin, A Facsimile of the Paris, 1746 Edition,* Performer's Facsimiles, 122, by arrangement with Broude Brothers.

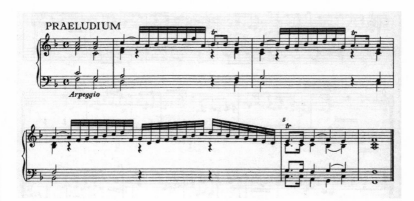

FIGURE 9.6. An excerpt from *Praeludium* from the *Partita in F Major,* by Johann Christoph Graupner. Reprinted with kind permission of Breitkopf & Haertel, Wiesbaden.

Second Suite in F major

G. F. Handel

Adagio

1) Small type in the original.

FIGURE 9.7. *Adagio* of the *Second Suite in F Major* by G.F. Handel from his *Suites for Harpsichord, Book I* (London, 1720). Reproduced by permission of Stainer & Bell Ltd, London, England. www.stainer.co.uk

3. Vary the rhythm, using even thirty-second notes, triplet figuration, and dotted notes.

The use of formulae by Handel is typical of the Baroque. George Buelow has shown how Handel used certain conventional melodic patterns analogous to the *moduli* set forth by Johann Mattheson in his *Der vollkommene Kapellmeister* (1739; Buelow 1989, 272–78; cf. Schulenberg 1995, 25). Hermann Charles Suehs used Mattheson's *moduli* as the basis for teaching improvisational techniques to music education students. He created a system of five conventions of arbitrary (free) embellishments, which coincided with those found in Mattheson's treatise: (1) "neighboring tone-related conventions," including the *trillo*, mordent, and acciaccatura; (2) "leap-retaining conventions"; (3) "motive and leap-filling conventions," including the *tirata* (scalar run) and *circolo mezzo* (turning figures); (4) "large conventions," including long ornamental figures such as *passaggi* (elaborate passage-work); and (5) "rhythmic, dynamic, and affective contrivances," including dotted rhythms (1979, 67–84).

Other examples of written-out embellishment can be found in numerous works by Johann Sebastian Bach. In addition to the frequently cited slow movement from the *Italian Concerto*, BWV 971, the *Adagio* from the *Suite in D minor*, BWV 964, provides a model for study (see Figure 9.8).

Johann Adolfe Scheibe claimed that Bach, in writing out his diminutions, encroached upon the player's right to extemporize in performance. "All embellishments, all little graces, and all that is understood by the method of playing, he [J.S. Bach] expresses in [written] notes, and not only deprives his pieces of beauty and harmony but makes the melodic line utterly unclear" (1737; quoted in Donington 1979, 155–56). Despite this, there are still opportunities for today's player to elaborate upon Bach's original. For example, Richard Troeger has shown how to extemporize a double to the courante from *Partita No. 2*, BWV 826, using Bach's own doubles to the *sarabandes* from *English Suites* Nos. 2 and 3, BWV 807, 808 as models (2003:203). Similarly, Paul Badura-Skoda adds free embellishment to the *Adagio* of the first movement of *English Suite No. 6*, BWV 811, deriving inspiration from Bach's *Chromatic Fantasy*, BWV 903 (1993:503).

OPERA TRANSCRIPTIONS

Evidence for the style of both French and Italian embellishment in Baroque keyboard music can be found in salon transcriptions of opera, which were popular throughout the 17th and 18th centuries. In France, adaptations for

Sonata nach der Violinsonate a-moll

d-moll

FIGURE 9.8. *Adagio* from the *Suite in D Minor*, BWV 964, after the *Violin Sonata in A Minor*. Copyright 1975 G. Henle Verlag, used by permission.

harpsichord of Jean-Baptiste Lully's tunes were favored. Titon du Tillet, writing in 1732, recounts that Mlle Certin, a friend of Lully's and a virtuoso harpsichordist, won the admiration of all of Paris: "This celebrated Musician [Lully] had her play on the harpsichord all the symphonies of his operas, & she executed them in the highest perfection" (1732, 637).[4] Figure 9.9 shows the opening measures of the *Ouverture de Cadmus and Hermione*, as transcribed for harpsichord by d'Anglebert and, below, as conceived by Lully. Far more ornate than Lully's plain original (1998), d'Anglebert's arrangement is replete with *coulés, tremblements, port de voix*, and freely arpeggiated chords in *style brisé* ([1689] 1975:88–89).

Similarly, in England, transcriptions for harpsichord of Handel's operas abound. William Babell's keyboard arrangements (see Figure 9.10) of the overture and airs from *Rinaldo* are heavily ornamented in the Italian style, displaying brilliant scalar passagework (210–226).

Babell played harpsichord in Handel's opera orchestra and thus would have been intimately familiar with Handel's improvisational style. Though skeptical of Babell's claim that his transcriptions represented how "Mr. Handel" himself played, Mark Kroll recognizes that these arrangements nonetheless "offer a tantalizing glimpse into Handel's extroverted playing style" (2004:79). Fol-

FIGURE 9.9. A comparison of two versions of *Ouverture de Cadmus,* by Jean-Baptise Lully. The excerpt above shows the opening measures of d'Anglebert's highly ornamented transcription for harpsichord; the excerpt below gives the first violin part of Lully's plain original. Reprinted from Graham Pont, "Handel's Overtures for Harpsichord or Organ: An Unrecognized Genre." *Early Music* Vol. 11, no. 3 (July, 1983): 309.

FIGURE 9.10. *Adagio* from *Overtures and Airs from Rinaldo* by G.F. Handel, arranged for keyboard by William Babell.

lowing Babell's lead, today's player might embellish the undecorated chords marked Adagio at the end of the *Allegro* from Handel's *Fourth Suite* as indicated in Figure 9.11.

IMPROVISING PRELUDES AND FANTASIAS

Other opportunities for improvisation in the Baroque era included the French practice of extemporizing unmeasured preludes. Titon du Tillet reports that the 15-year-old harpsichord prodigy Elizabeth Claude Jacquet de la Guerre could entertain her listeners for an entire half-hour with her brilliant improvisation of preludes (1732:636). Fortunately, many written-out preludes

FIGURE 9.11. Suggestions for ornamenting the undecorated chords at the end of the *Allegro* of the *Fourth Suite in E Minor* by G.F. Handel, from his *Suites for Harpsichord, Book I* (London, 1720). Transcribed by the author.

by Jacquet and her contemporaries survive today. They range in style from simple teaching pieces, such as the *Prelude en re* attributed to Monsieur de la Barre (n.d.; discussed in Curtis 1970, 127), to the elaborate preludes of Louis Couperin ([n.d.] 1970, ii). The unmeasured prelude's improvisational origins are reflected in the white note notation and lack of meter, which leaves the rhythmic interpretation entirely up to the performer (see Figure 9.12).[5]

Although information about the rhythmic interpretation of the preludes is well documented, the sources say next to nothing about the actual method of improvisation. In reviving this forgotten art, a useful method would be to start from a figured bass. The player can experiment with extemporizing figuration above the bass in the form of arpeggiated chords, as in the first line of the previous figure, and melodic connecting passages. The arpeggios themselves can be ornamented with passing tones between the notes of the chords. Finally, ascending appoggiaturas (*ports de voix*), trills, and mordents can be added to the melodic line to heighten expression and for accentuation.

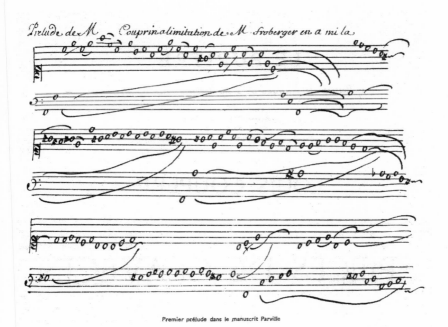

Premier prélude dans le manuscrit Parville

FIGURE 9.12. *Prélude de M. Couprin à l'imitation de M. froberger en a mi la.* Facsimile from the Parville MS. Berkeley, University of California, Music Library, MS 778.

In the same spirit, German composers later in the 18th century improvised free fantasias. Carl Philipp Emanuel Bach gives rules for the creation
of fantasias in his *Versuch über die wahre Art das Clavier zu Spielen* ([1753]
1949, 442–45). He advises the keyboard player to begin by writing a bass line,
to which harmonies are added, as indicated by figures. Melodic passages in
the form of turns, trills, arpeggios, and scales can then be elaborated over
this harmonic framework (see Figure 9.13).

It is important to view C.P.E. Bach's fantasias as part of a continuing improvising tradition. According to David Schulenberg, "J.S. Bach and his students
possessed a vocabulary of flourishes and other ornamental gestures" (1995,
20) that could be employed to improvise entire pieces or interpolated at
suitable points in pieces such as concertos. He cites George Stauffer, who has
pointed to the similarity of certain figuration in Bach's *Chromatic Fantasy* to
that in the cadenza of the first movement of the *Fifth Brandenburg Concerto*
(1989:176; cited in Schulenberg 1995, 23). Standard formulae probably formed
the basis of routine improvisations in the Bach household. As Schulenberg
observes, "notated fantasies are probably merely the visible survivals of an
improvising tradition" (1995, 26).

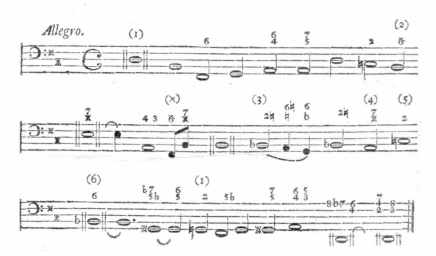

FIGURE 9.13. Excerpt from Carl Philipp Emanuel Bach, *Ver-
such über die wahre Art das Clavier zu Spielen* (Berlin, 1753).
Reproduced from the 1759 edition courtesy of the University of
Illinois at Urbana-Champaign Music Library.

FIGURE 9.13. *Cont.*

We also know that keyboard musicians, especially organists, were expected to improvise more "severe" works, such as fugal pieces, and service music, such as chorale preludes, psalm versets, and so forth. Although further discussion is beyond the scope of this paper, it is important to note that even counterpoint can be reduced to formulae. Schulenberg suggests that "various ready-made canons and strettos could be inserted into contrapuntal pieces whose subjects incorporated appropriate motives" (1995, 25).

BASSO CONTINUO REALIZATION

The most important type of improvisation for the keyboard player in the Baroque was basso continuo realization. In chamber and church music, the role of the continuo player was crucial in supplying the harmonic foundation for the ensemble. Figured bass notation evolved as a method for indicating harmonic intervals above the bass. One device used in 18th-century France for teaching figured bass realization was *la règle de l'octave* (see Figure 9.14), or the rule of the octave, a scale harmonization popularized by François Campion ([1716] 1976). Today's keyboard player could make use of the rule as an aid in learning to decipher continuo figures.

Another practical aid to learning to read figures is given by Denis Delair. He advises the player to group chords that share the same right-hand accompaniment ([1690] 1991,2). Thus, a D minor chord in the right hand yields a 5/3 chord above D in the bass; a 6/4/2 chord above C; a 7/5/3 chord above B, and a 6/4 chord above A. This procedure can be used as a teaching tool to give the modern player a quick introduction to reading figures at sight.

Numerous treatises discuss the "art" of basso continuo improvisation, addressing such topics as texture, the extemporization of right-hand melodies, ornamentation of the bass and its realization, the addition of dissonance, and the arpeggiation of chords. While these aspects depend largely on genre, period, national style, and size of the ensemble, some general principles can be presented to give the modern keyboard player some background in the different styles of realization.

For example, texture can be used as an expressive device. A full-voiced chord will give the effect of forte, and a thinner-voiced chord will give the effect of piano. "When some words express immense tenderness (which are sung very soft) a single third or a fifth with the right hand will often be sufficient: When stronger words require a louder singing, the number of the chords are also to be increased; and sometimes an octave or so with the left hand . . . and thus it may appear as if the harpsichord had the faculty of in-

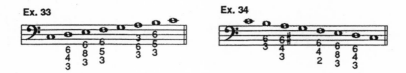

FIGURE 9.14. The "Rule of the Octave," a scale harmonization formula used for teaching figured bass in 18th-century France. Transcribed by the author.

creasing and decreasing in sound, like violoncellos, bassoons, etc" (Pasquali [1757] 1974, 43, 46).

According to Johann David Heinichen, "the more full-voiced one accompanies with both hands on the harpsichord, the more harmonious it will sound" ([1728] 1966, 72). He gives a simple procedure for forming full-voiced chords: double as many notes of the right-hand chord as the left hand can grasp, taking care to avoid parallel fifths and octaves between the outer parts.

Right-hand melodies may be extemporized as long as they do not duplicate or confuse the soloist's line. Heinichen suggests making a duet with the solo part by playing in thirds or sixths with it. He states that this is particularly useful when accompanying the voice. If the player chooses to invent a melody above the bass in cantabile pieces, the left hand may take the chordal realization, freeing the right hand to improvise ([1728] 1966, 173). Besides obbligato lines, other types of embellishment, including single-note ornaments such as the trill, slide, and mordent, may be used to give elegance, particularly in the uppermost part of the realization (Geminiani 1756–1757).

In addition to adding ornaments and varying the texture of the realization, writers such as Denis Delair give the player the freedom to alter the bass itself and to add dissonances even if they are not indicated in the figures, as long as they have been prepared ([1690] 1991, 14).

The treatise on accompaniment by Monsieur de Saint Lambert ([1707] 1991) offers clues to the actual performance of a French 18th-century continuo part. In the ninth chapter of his treatise, Saint Lambert discusses "Taste in Accompaniment." He states: "This taste principally consists of a careful handling of the harmony of one's Instrument—in such a way that one does not draw so much sound [son] from the Harpsichord that it entirely overwhelms the solo voice [la voix qui chante], or, on the contrary, that one does not draw so little [sound] that it does not support [the solo voice] enough" (61). To make more sound at the harpsichord, he recommends playing full-voiced chords by doubling all the notes of the right hand in the left hand. The accompanist can also repeat chords in large ensembles to increase the volume. For light voices, he counsels playing fewer parts and disengaging one or two stops on the harpsichord (110).

Another option Saint Lambert gives the harpsichordist is the arpeggiation of chords in recitatives. For Saint Lambert, the arpeggio is one of the embellishments most suitable for accompanying on the harpsichord: "Even when one does not double Parts, one still should arpeggiate them. One could repeat a single chord even several times, by arpeggiating it first in ascending & then in descending. But this [arpeggiated] repetition must be carefully handled, and it cannot be taught to you by a Book: rather, you must see someone actually doing it" (110).

Especially pictorial is Saint Lambert's description of recitative accompaniment. The player may linger on chords, and then re-strike a single note by itself with discretion. Conversely, "when doubling Parts one may re-strike all the notes one after another in a continual repetition—thereby drawing from the Harpsichord a crackling a bit like a volley of musket fire" (111). He concludes by emphasizing that "the greatest taste that one might display in accompaniment is to know how to adapt completely to the character . . . of the Air being sung—entering even into the spirit of the words." (112).

Delair discusses adding ornaments to arpeggiated chords. In one example, he depicts the essential notes of the chord in arpeggiated whole notes, interspersed with eighth and sixteenth notes. These *petites notes* take the form of dissonant passing tones, or *coulés*, which often fill in thirds of chords, and stepwise connecting figures of several notes, or *coulades*. Delair advises the player to hold down all the notes of the chord except the dissonances, which are to be released: "The eighth notes between the whole notes are not absolutely necessary, since they are only for ornament. Thus, one does not hold them, one only passes over them" ([1690] 1991, 30). D'Anglebert, whose *Principes* ([1689] 1975), 138–45) predate Delair's *Traité* by one year, employs ornamental notes similarly. Both authors' examples (see Figure 9.15) resemble the unmeasured prelude in style, with their arpeggiated chords and a liberal sprinkling of dissonant passing tones.

The Italian style of recitative accompaniment also featured arpeggios. Gasparini, in *L'armonico pratico al cimbalo* ([1708] 1963), shows full-voiced chords embellished by acciaccaturas, or non-chord tones. The acciaccatura can be used in chords of the sixth, diminished fifth, seventh, and 6/4/2. Encouraging the student to find his or her own method of adding acciaccaturas, Gasparini describes one he discovered in which the player strikes fourteen notes at once, the thumb and fifth finger of each hand taking two notes each

FIGURE 9.15. Reproduced from Denis Delair, *Traité d'accompagnement pour le théorbe, et le clavecin, A Facsimile of the Paris, 1690 Edition.* Geneva: Minkoff, 1972. Used by permission from Editions Minkoff.

(83–84). Despite the warnings of Italian theorists not to add too much decoration, the evidence suggests that, in practice, Italian continuo playing was rather florid: "The best French accompanists avoid the usual faults of Italian continuo playing—those unceasing, busy figurations, the broken chords, the ever-rolling arpeggios, the manual display, the disagreement between the harpsichord and bass viol, the chaotic embroidery of both left- and right-hand parts" (de la Viéville de Freneuse 1704–1706; reprinted in Bourdelot 1715; quoted in Williams [1970] 1977, 1:29).

Figure 9.16 illustrates how arpeggiation and acciaccaturas may be applied to the accompaniment of a recitative from Giovanni Maria Bononcini's cantata, *Il Lamento d'Olympia* (1721).

CONCLUSION

In sum, in the keyboard music of the Baroque, the performer's role rivaled or even exceeded that of the composer. Composers often provided only a skeletal framework to be elaborated upon *ad libitum* by the performer. Baroque keyboard players routinely extemporized melodic ornaments, passage-work, and figured bass accompaniments. Moreover, they were renowned for their brilliant opera transcriptions for keyboard, as well as their improvisation of preludes and fantasias. Scholars have noted that the music we have today

FIGURE 9.16. Recitative from *Il Lamento d'Olympia*, by Giovanni Bononcini, from *Cantate e Duetti (London, 1721)*. Recitative accompaniment realized by the author.

from this period may represent only a portion of the keyboard repertoire performed in the Baroque. Much of it may not have been written down but, rather, was improvised in performance. Players relied on standard flourishes and figuration patterns, passed down from teacher to student. The challenge for today's player is to recapture this extempore tradition as he or she seeks to recreate the lost art of Baroque keyboard improvisation in our century.

NOTES

1. I am indebted to George Houle for his lucid explanation of French ornament usage in this example.

2. For studies on *rhythmmopoeia* and dance, see Houle (1987, 65, 67, 70).

3. Scott Ross's performance of this suite served as an inspiration for the added ornamentation.

4. "*Ce célèbre Musicien lui faisoit jouer sur le Claveçin toutes les Symphonies de ses Opéra[s], & elle les executoit dans la plus grande perfection.*"

5. For information on the interpretation of the notation in unmeasured preludes, see Moroney (1976).

REFERENCES

Anglebert, Jean-Henry d'. [1689] 1975. "Principes de l'accompagnement." In *Pièces de clavecin*. Paris: the author. Reprint edited by Kenneth Gilbert, 138–45. Paris: Heugel.

Bach, Carl Philipp Emanuel. [1753] 1949. *Versuch über die wahre Art das Clavier zu*

Spielen. Original pub. in Berlin. Translated by W. J. Mitchell as *Essay on the True Art of Playing Keyboard Instruments*. New York: Norton.

Bacilly, Bénigne de. [1668] 1968. *Remarques curieuses sur l'art de bien chanter*. Original Pub. in Paris. Translated and edited by A.B. Caswell as *A Commentary upon the Art of Proper Singing*. Reprint Brooklyn, N.Y.: Institute of Medieval Music.

Badura-Skoda, Paul. 1993. *Interpreting Bach at the Keyboard*. Translated by Alfred Clayton. Oxford: Clarendon Press.

Bononcini, Giovanni. 1721. *Cantate e Duetti*. London.

Bourdelot, Pierre. 1715. *Histoire de la Musique et de ses effects*. Paris.

Buelow, George. 1989. "Mattheson's Concept of 'Moduli' as a Clue to Handel's Compositional Practice." *Göttinger Händel-beiträge* 3:272–78.

Campion, François. [1716] 1976. *Traité d'accompagnement et de composition selon la règle des octaves de musique*. Original pub. in Paris. Facs. ed. Geneva: Minkoff.

Couperin, François. [1713] 1973. *Pièces de clavecin*. Vol. 1. Facs. ed. Broude Brothers. Paris: Heugel.

Couperin, Louis. [n.d.] 1970. *Pièces de clavecin*, edited by Alan Curtis. Paris: Heugel.

Curtis, Alan. 1970. "Musique française classique à Berkeley." *Revue de musicologie* 56:123–64.

Delair, Denis. [1690] 1991. *Traité d'accompagnement pour le théorbe et le clavecin*. Orig. pub in Paris by the author. Translated by Charlotte Mattax as *Accompaniment on Theorbo & Harpsichord: Denis Delair's Treatise of 1690*. Bloomington: Indiana University Press.

Donington, Robert. 1979. *The Interpretation of Early Music, New Version*. London: Faber & Faber.

Gasparini, Francesco. [1708] 1963. *L'armonico pratico al cimbalo*. Orig. pub. Venice. Translated by F.S. Stillings and edited by D.L. Burrows as *The Practical Harmonist at the Harpsichord*. New Haven, Conn.: Yale School of Music.

Geminiani, Francesco. 1756–1957. *The Art of Accompaniment*. 2 vols. London: John Johnson.

Gilbert, Kenneth. 1972. *Francois Couperin: Pièces de clavecin, Premier livre*. Paris: Heugel.

Graupner, Johann Christoph. 1954. *Acht Partiten für Cembalo oder Klavier*, edited by Lothar Hoffmann-Erbrecht. Leipzig: Breitkopf & Härtel.

Handel, Georg Frideric. [1720] 1980. *Suites for Harpsichord, Book I*. Orig. pub. in London. Reprint edited by Christopher Kite. London: Stainer & Bell.

———. *Overtures and Airs from Rinaldo*, arranged by William Babell. *Handel Werke*, Vol. 48, 210–26.

Heinichen, Johann David. [1728] 1966. *Der Generalbass in der Komposition*. Orig. pub. in Dresden; partial translation by G.B. Buelow as *Thorough Bass Accompaniment According to Johann David Heinichen*. Berkeley: University of California Press.

Houle, George. 1987. *Meter in Music from 1600–1800: Performance, Perception, and Notation*. Bloomington: Indiana University Press.

Kroll, Mark. 2004. *Playing the Harpsichord Expressively*. Lanham: Scarecrow Press.

La Barre, Monsieur de. n.d. *Pièces de clavecin*. 11 vols. (Berkeley MS #770). Facsimile from the Bauyn MS. Reprinted in Louis Couperin, 1970.

La Viéville de Freneuse, de. 1704–1706. *Comparaison de la musique italienne et de la musique françoise*. 3 vols. Brussels.

Lully, Jean-Baptiste. 1998. *Tragédies lyriques*. Facs. ed. New York: Broude.

Mattheson, Johann. 1739. *Der vollkommene Kapellmeister*. Hamburg.

Moroney, Davitt. 1976. "The Performance of Unmeasured Harpsichord Preludes." *Early Music Journal* 4(2): 143–51.

Orengia, Jean-Louis. 1989. "L'Improvisation dans la musique de clavier de 1700 à 1750." In *Aspects de la Musique Baroque et Classique à Lyon et en France*. Under direction of Daniel Paquette, 150–57. Lyon: Presses Universitaires.

Pasquali, Nicolo. [1757] 1974. *Thorough-Bass Made Easy, or Practical Rules for Finding and Applying Its Various Chords*. Orig. pub. in Edinburgh. Facsimile edition of the 1763 edition with an introduction by John Churchill. London: Oxford University Press.

Quantz, Joachim. [1752] 1966. *Versuch einer Anweisung die Flöte traversiere zu spielen*. Original pub. in Berlin. Translated, with an introduction, by Edward R. Reilly, as *On Playing the Flute*. New York: Faber & Faber.

Royer, Joseph-Nicolas-Pancrace. [1746] 1990. *Pièces de clavecin*, Vol. 1. Paris. Reprint edited by Lisa Crawford. Paris: Heugel.

Saint Lambert, Monsieur de. [1707] 1991. *Nouveau traité de l'accompagnement du clavecin et de l'orgue*. Paris: Ballard. Translated by John Powell as *A New Treatise on Accompaniment*. Bloomington: Indiana University Press.

Scheibe, Johann Adolfe. 1737. *Critische Musicus I*. Hamburg.

Schulenberg, David. 1995. "Composition and Improvisation in the School of J.S. Bach." In *Bach Perspectives*, Vol. 1, edited by Russell Stinson, 1–42. Lincoln: University of Nebraska Press.

Stauffer, George B. 1989. "On the Enigma and Chronology of Bach's Chromatic Fantasia and Fugue in D Minor, BWV 903." In *Bach Studies*, edited by Don O. Franklin, 160–82. Cambridge: Cambridge University Press.

Suehs, Hermann Charles. 1979. "The Development, Implementation, and Assessment of a Course of Study for Instruction in Certain Improvisational Techniques in the Performance of Baroque Music from 1679–1741." D.M.A. dissertation, Catholic University of America.

Tartini, Giuseppe. [1754] 1966. *Trattato de musica*. Facsimile ed. New York: Broude Bros.

Titon du Tillet, Evrard. 1732. *Le parnasse François*. Paris: Jean-Baptiste Coignard Fils.

Troeger, Richard. 2003. *Playing Bach on the Keyboard: A Practical Guide*. Cambridge: Amadeus Press.

Williams, Peter. [1970] 1977. *Figured Bass Accompaniment*, 2 vols. Edinburgh: University Press.

BEYOND THE IMPROVISATION CLASS: LEARNING TO IMPROVISE IN A UNIVERSITY JAZZ STUDIES PROGRAM

John P. Murphy

In any study of a musical tradition centered on improvisation, the way a musician learns to improvise is an important subject because it affects the transmission and ultimately the survival of the tradition. As the jazz tradition enters its second century, there is widespread concern that the increasingly academic and codified nature of the study of jazz improvisation is promoting stylistic uniformity. Over the last several decades, the primary setting for learning to play jazz has shifted from the jam session and the gig to the university. Young people who are drawn toward the music still benefit from the early influences of family and friends and still learn about the music directly from practitioners, from recordings, and on their own. But most of them first encounter jazz, or at least the opportunity to play it with others, in secondary schools, colleges and universities, and workshops. At the same time, university jazz programs are viewed with a mixture of respect, disdain, and suspicion by some in the larger jazz community. It seems that the jazz community has not fully come to terms with this shift in the way the tradition is transmitted.

Two recent studies that situate improvisation pedagogy in a culture of academic jazz education place great emphasis on what happens in improvisation classes. David Ake (2002) argues that jazz pedagogy overstresses pitch to the detriment of rhythm and that its treatment of Coltrane overemphasizes the part of his music that works best with the chord-scale approach. Kenneth Prouty (2002, 2004) describes tensions between academic and nonacademic approaches to teaching and learning improvisation, and he questions the criteria for evaluating improvisation.

Although both studies achieve their stated goals, they have drawn conclusions on the basis of data that do not represent the diverse experiences of those who study and teach in a large jazz program. Although he is an experienced jazz pianist, Ake bases his judgments on a generalized model of the jazz improvisation curriculum, which emphasizes the chord-scale approach; on Jamey Aebersold's scale syllabus; on published critiques by other authors; and on a comment by Branford Marsalis about the Berklee College of Music program. Although Prouty did conduct fieldwork and interview faculty members in other jazz studies programs, he bases his comments regarding the University of North Texas (UNT) program on his experiences in it as a graduate student, on student comments that were gathered unsystematically, and on comments by professors that were not followed up in interviews. He focuses on the institutional structures and practices that influence the study of improvisation rather than on students' experiences within and outside those structures and practices.

As a jazz educator, I share many of the concerns expressed by Ake, Prouty, and other critics about the way academic jazz education is changing the music. As Ake writes, "Ultimately, the issue boils down to knowledge: what sorts of knowledge will be esteemed in a given setting, how will that knowledge be transmitted, by whom, and to whom?" (2002, 144). We cannot answer these questions fully without a greater understanding of how students themselves place that knowledge in a meaningful context. In this chapter I argue for more attention to student discourse as a means of understanding how they learn to improvise within and outside a university jazz curriculum. The broader significance of this question is tied to the shift from the jam session and the gig to the university jazz program as the primary site for the transmission of the jazz tradition. Rather than argue that the university jazz program is a second-rate substitute for traditional ways of learning, scholars need to consider the university jazz program as a valid musical culture that blends academic and nonacademic approaches and that is worthy of study in a holistic fashion. To begin to understand more clearly how the shift to the university as the primary training ground for young improvisers may be changing the music, I investigated the ways in which students and teachers experience their encounter with the University of North Texas curriculum.

GATHERING STUDENT REFLECTIONS

I based my study on the UNT program for three reasons: First, I know it well as a former student and current professor. Second, with frequent visits by guest artists and significant student involvement in diverse local music scenes, it is an important point of contact between the academic and nonacademic worlds of jazz. Third, it has long served as a model for best practices as well as a target for criticism. Founded in 1947, the program currently involves around 250 majors, roughly 190 of whom are undergraduates; many students with other majors in music and in other fields; 13 full-time faculty members; 9 big bands, 30 small groups, 2 vocal ensembles, 2 guitar ensembles, 1 repertory ensemble, and 20 or more visiting artists each year.[1]

I asked five questions of a diverse group of 21 students: men and women; students from the United States and international students; students of diverse racial and ethnic heritages; undergraduates, graduates, and alumni; and vocalists and instrumentalists.[2] Some of them I invited to respond, and others volunteered in response to a posted notice. I also invited professors Michael Steinel and Fred Hamilton, who regularly teach improvisation, to respond to the anonymous student comments, and I have included excerpts from their responses in this chapter along with the students' responses. I do not teach in the improvisation sequence at UNT, but I have taught improvisation at the college level elsewhere for eight years, and my graduate course in jazz style analysis includes a sustained conversation about how students learn to improvise and the most productive ways to teach it, prompted by scholarly works by Berliner (1994) and Monson (1996) and by shared experiences in the UNT program and other programs.[3]

Students responded to the following text and questions:

> The goal of my study is to understand in more detail the kinds of experiences that students have had as they learn to improvise, and what sort of relationship exists between what happens inside the improvisation class, in the rest of the jazz studies curriculum, and outside of UNT altogether.
>
> 1. Did you begin to study improvisation before coming to UNT? If so, what did you do?
> 2. What was your experience of improvisation classes at UNT?
> 3. Were there any experiences outside of improvisation classes, but within the jazz studies curriculum, that you feel affected your development as an improviser?
> 4. Were there any experiences outside of the curriculum altogether during your time at UNT that affected your development as an improviser?
> 5. Is there anything you'd like to add about your experience as a learner of improvisation?

The sections that follow present and discuss a sample of student responses to each of these prompts along with comments by Professors Steinel and Hamilton.

PREVIOUS STUDY OF IMPROVISATION

Nineteen students had studied improvisation before coming to UNT. Of the two who had not, one had played published transcriptions and the other had taken private lessons in improvisation before taking an improvisation class. Their experiences included listening to parents' record collections; playing jazz in school settings and at public jam sessions; playing blues and rock before turning to jazz; transcribing solos; playing with Aebersold records; using—and later rejecting—*The Real Book*; attending IAJE (International Association for Jazz Education) conventions; and studying at summer camps, in another prominent jazz program and at an international program modeled on it, and with a graduate of another prominent jazz program.

The students had extensive exposure to jazz before coming to UNT.[4] One student wrote, "I also sat in at many other local jazz jam sessions with players of varying abilities. At these I would play standards *without* charts, and if I didn't know the tune I was expected to learn it *real* fast or get the hell off the stand." Another comment by this student is a reminder that prior experiences may help students compensate for perceived weaknesses or omissions in the improvisation curriculum: "I have to stress that I have always felt that I have learned more from talking to other musicians about their experiences and playing with them than from learning about chords or patterns." A different student, who was introduced at a young age to the music of Miles Davis, John McLaughlin, John Coltrane, and Eric Dolphy, wrote, "These experiences encouraged me to explore the idea of improvisation from a largely emotional perspective, which left some gaps in the technical and theoretical aspects of improvisation that are emphasized at UNT." This amount of prior experience with improvisation may not be typical of the average student in the program. According to Professor Steinel, many students in improvisation classes may never have played an improvised solo in public before coming to UNT.

Other comments suggest that the chord-scale approach, in which each chord in a composition is matched with a scale that is supposedly most consonant with it, is often the first thing students learn about improvisation. Teaching this approach in an unquestioned way in middle and high schools might establish ways of relating to improvisation that are hard to change later. This suggests a comparison with the documentary project *A Private Universe*, which shows how faulty science concepts that are acquired early can be difficult to overcome.[5] In the jazz context, the concept of right and wrong notes and the use of chord outlines and scale patterns as the basis for a solo, if acquired early in a student's development, might be just as difficult to modify if a student later found them to be limiting.

IMPROVISATION CLASSES AT UNT

The undergraduate jazz improvisation curriculum at the University of North Texas consists of four sequenced classes preceded by four prerequisite courses. The prerequisites are two semesters of jazz theory, with playing exercises included in the second semester; one semester of jazz aural skills; and one semester of jazz keyboard skills. In the first level of improvisation, students improvise on blues and rhythm changes and on standard tunes such as "Satin Doll" and "There Will Never Be Another You" and study melodic, harmonic, and rhythmic strategies that are relevant to them; make and perform transcriptions of solos on tunes in those categories; and practice free improvisation using the forms they have studied. In the second level, students improvise on tunes such as "Four," "Tune Up," "Anthropology," "All the Things You Are," "Unit 7," and "What's New"; make transcriptions; and show their comprehension of theoretical concepts through playing evaluations. In the third level, students improvise on tunes such as "One Finger Snap," "Straight, No Chaser," "Windows," "Bohemia After Dark," "Driftin'," and a ballad; work on related melodic, harmonic, and rhythm strategies; and work on singing a scat solo (all students, not only vocalists). The fourth level of undergraduate improvisation classes stresses the integration of all aspects of improvisation into a personal approach, using challenging compositions such as "Upper Manhattan Medical Group," "Isfahan," "Lush Life," "Punjab," "Shade of Jade," and "Jinrikisha." Professor Stefan Karlsson's current syllabus for this course stresses creativity: "I approach this class as if you were part of my own performing group. In order to most productively prepare each tune, I expect that everyone will come well prepared and be ready to explore beyond what you typically do. In addition to paying respect to the true 'aura' of each song, taking musical chances is an important part of the learning process of improvisation and its musical saga. Rhythm, space, polytonality, patience during developmental ideas, and nonharmonic notes will be encouraged (. . . it is OK to play an A-natural on an F minor chord as long as one learns to resolve it musically!)." Students must earn an A or a B in each level to progress to the next. Required texts for the undergraduate improvisation courses include Bauer (1988), Haerle (1989, 2003), and Steinel (1995). Improvisation skills are also evaluated in undergraduate and graduate juries, which are prerequisites for performing senior and graduate recitals, respectively.

Two graduate courses complete the improvisation curriculum: an improvisation course that includes advanced theoretical materials, free improvisation, and challenging tunes; and a course on the pedagogy of improvisation. The curriculum is also subject to continual revision. For example, private study in the jazz idiom, including improvisation, recently became part of the required hours in applied music for undergraduate and graduate jazz studies majors.

Some students with extensive experience with improvisation who did not test out of the first two levels found them confining and unhelpful. One student wrote, "My early experiences with UNT's improvisation classes left me very disenchanted with the aesthetic emphasized by the jazz program. Where is the emotional and artistic fulfillment in learning patterns and plugging them into the appropriate key centers in a piece of music?" Another put it more strongly: "The bottom line with the classes is, if they were the only way I thought I could learn how to improvise I would be screwed." Students who had less experience found them informative and empowering: "The first two semesters were very educational and enjoyable to me. A lot of the things that I learned in Aebersold's books and similar materials started to make sense. I also learned new things, like the concept of articulation and chord-tone placement as applied in jazz, which, along with rhythmic concepts, were probably the things that I valued the most from those courses." Most of the students had more positive things to say about the last two levels. "My later experiences with UNT's improvisation classes were much better. [The professors] expressed more of an interest in what *I* had to say as a later participant in the continuum and gave advice that was pertinent to what I was playing, rather than what I was not."

Students' expectations play a major role in their experiences in class. If they expect it to be as satisfying musically as playing in an ensemble, they will be disappointed. "Overall, I found the improvisation classes to be marginally useful at best. This is probably due to my having approached them with the wrong attitude. I was wanting to go in there and try to make some real music. Looking back, I should have realized that it was intended more as an exercise than as an actual music-making experience, and learned what I could from 'playing by the rules' so to speak, with a better attitude."

Professors Steinel and Hamilton, like Prouty (2002, 205), emphasize that the improvisation class is a form of practice, not performance. Professor Steinel provides a useful counterbalance to some of the stronger student criticisms of the improvisation class: "In my class I stress memorization and modeling a great deal. It is my opinion that aural memory is the improviser's greatest tool (the memory of melodies, harmonies, rhythmic feels, tone qualities, etc.). When we make decisions about what and how to play the first place we go is our memory. The richer and fuller it is the more options we have. The building of this memory necessitates intense listening. The requirement of memorization of various elements insures that students spend more time listening. I am concerned but not surprised that some students may misunderstand this connection."

Requirements that seem overly prescriptive, such as memorization of patterns or transcribed solos, are intended not to produce players who are clones but to strengthen a player's memory and skill at manipulating musical materials, which can be taken in any direction a student chooses outside of class.

Professor Hamilton's comments about the limitations of the improvisation class encapsulate the argument of this chapter: "A musician learns about music in a very universal manner and isolated classes are only pieces of the larger puzzle." I contend that scholars interested in the way academic instruction may be changing the transmission of jazz tradition should study the larger puzzle: the interplay of classes, ensembles, informal listening, extracurricular playing, prior experience, and culture and ideas generally.

Steinel, Hamilton, and bassist Lynn Seaton (who also teaches improvisation at UNT) agree with the student who wrote that if the improvisation class were the only way to learn how to improvise, the student would be in bad shape. In Hamilton's words, "Unfortunately, a lot of students don't realize this. So, if they don't 'get it' in improvisation class, they may assume that either they are receiving faulty instruction or they aren't 'studying enough' as would be the case in academic classes." Just as a language student has to use the language outside of class to achieve fluency, an improvisation student is expected to take the skills that are introduced in class and apply them in a variety of musical situations.

Playing with a friend helped one student who was also a teaching assistant realize the importance of playing only what one is honestly hearing: "Ear training should be integrated into improvisation classes. I have seen many students who couldn't find the close relationship between their ears and their playing. One of my students could play Dave Holland's music but couldn't figure out the opening melody (less than 4 bars) of 'All of You' by ear. For me, it simply doesn't make any sense. We need to tell students that *if you don't hear a thing, you're cheating!!*" This connects with Day's thinking on improvisation and moral perfectionism, which he defines as "a commitment to speaking and acting true to oneself, combined with a thoroughgoing dissatisfaction with oneself as one now stands" (2000, 99).

Playing with Aebersold recordings with other people also appeared in student comments, which implies that, like video games, such recordings are not necessarily isolating but can be the setting for social interaction. This fact suggests a connection with Rasula's call for a study of private uses of recordings in jazz history (1995), which might include not only Aebersold recordings but also the 1943 recording of Charlie Parker playing along with Benny Goodman's 1937 recording of "Avalon."[6]

Improvisation class presents a common-practice approach to playing jazz. Although there are useful things to be learned from four-part writing, no thoughtful student of the common-practice approach to tonal harmony would consider it a sufficient preparation for creative work. Whereas common-practice tonal harmony has parallel fifths and octaves, common-practice jazz improvisation has so-called wrong notes. Both are temporary constraints that can safely be ignored once the student has enough experience. Common practice is the raft one uses to cross the river of inexperience. Then it can be put aside.

CURRICULAR EXPERIENCES OTHER THAN IMPROVISATION CLASS

Big bands, small groups, jam sessions, master classes by visiting artists, arranging, ear-training, graduate jazz analysis, graduate pedagogy of improvisation, advanced bass, classical music theory, transcriptions studied in private lessons, jazz history, rhythm section master classes, jazz repertory ensembles, keyboard, vocal jazz instruction and ensembles, and private study: all were cited by students as affecting their development as improvisers.

The rhythm section master class, a team-taught course, provided a more holistic approach to improvisation than the improvisation class. One student who had taken this class commented: "There are only sixteen students in the class, and four faculty to judge your playing. This has opened my mind to the idea that soloing is actually a group function. A more interesting solo involves group interaction. As a soloist now, I try to play melodies that will interact with the rest of the group, and leave more space in my soloing so that the other group members will have a place to throw ideas out to me."

Private instruction in the jazz idiom deals with improvisation. One student said: "Studying with [a jazz faculty member] has been a tremendous help. Not just in regards to improvising a solo, but about the instrument in general. [This professor] has put me in a position of thinking for myself on the instrument, which an instructor has never done for me before, and it's affected how I think about music in general, not just improvising." Jam sessions were more significant in this student's progress than improvisation classes: "I feel very strongly that the majority of my progress as an improviser and general musician was a direct result of rehearsing/performing/playing sessions with peers and more experienced faculty members in school. It is simply the difference between theorizing and participating."

Improvisation coaching can also happen in big band rehearsals. For example, Neil Slater, director of the One O'Clock Lab Band, includes both chord changes and the melody in the parts of his compositions, and he suggests that students play their solos with the melody in mind.

In smaller programs, where students take only improvisation classes and ensembles, the positive or negative effects of such classes might be magnified. Without the experiences available to students in a larger program, those in smaller programs may indeed find that the limitations of the improvisation class have a significant effect on their improvising. It is ironic, then, that critics of university improvisation teaching tend to single out UNT's large program as the source of a one-dimensional approach.

EXTRACURRICULAR EXPERIENCES

Students wrote about a wide variety of experiences outside the curriculum that influenced their development as improvisers: playing with a New Orleans–style brass band, which offers the challenge of playing an interesting solo on relatively simple chord changes; teaching, which obliges students to reflect on their own approach to improvisation; local performances; taking lessons with other teachers besides those at UNT; and professional work in Dallas, Fort Worth, and elsewhere.

Extracurricular projects helped this student connect with the emotional side of improvising: "Generally musicians at this school respond to a set of symbols that imply a series of harmonic progressions, and these progressions stimulate various responses according to the sort of vocabulary the performer has developed. The danger with this sort of improvisation is that it is very easy to go through the math or the motions of music without digging into the intuitive and emotional aspects of improvising." This student found audience responses to be more instructive than classroom feedback: "Playing solos on a professional gig really helps me to become a better soloist. When I play something that makes someone cheer or they gasp, or clap intensely at the end of my solo, then I know I have done something right. Learning to perform for a crowd really teaches you how to make a good solo more effectively than a 'sterile' classroom environment."

Professor Steinel suggests that no matter how engaging an instructional experience may be, the fact that it happens in school tends to reduce the value students attach to it. This will most likely remain one of the paradoxes of teaching such an individual activity as improvisation in a school setting. One student said: "My jazz education was all extracurricular: on gigs, jam sessions, hanging out. This still remains the best experience. I know how I reacted to 'required' courses such as music theory (even though I now recognize how important they were and wish I would have applied myself more at the time). School is always school."

Professor Hamilton reinforces the point that the student needs to assimilate what is presented in the improvisation class: "Stagnation is not brought about through the acquisition of information or repeated practicing, but through the individual's inability to bring that material to a meaningful and personal level." Here is one point where academic and nonacademic approaches to the study of improvisation converge: academic study formalizes and makes more efficient the gathering of information and stylistic models that used to be done individually or in an informal social network. In both cases, however, the individual learner has to absorb them and transform them into a personal approach to the music.

The students offered many more reflections on their learning experiences. The complete set of responses is available at the author's Web site.[7]

EVALUATING IMPROVISATION

The issue of standards for evaluating improvisation relates to a question posed by Kenneth Prouty. Reflecting on a time when a UNT professor praised one of his solos for not sounding like "university jazz," Prouty asked, "If a university jazz student shouldn't sound like 'university jazz,' what is s/he supposed to sound like?" (2004). This is another paradox of jazz improvisation pedagogy: the institution requires evaluation according to a consistent set of criteria, while the tradition requires a personal statement. Professor Hamilton summarizes the criteria this way: "Although some students will give stronger representations of certain aspects of the music, jazz faculty members are looking for swinging time, accurate intonation, good tone, infectious melodies, harmonic security with chord changes and a recognizable confidence that demonstrates the student's rapport with the music."

Having served on improvisation juries, I think these desired qualities are reasonable. A student need not play in one specific way to demonstrate them. But in a comment on a draft of this chapter, a student argued that these criteria are precisely the reason university improvisers tend to sound the same: competent, but with nothing personal to say. In this student's view, although the criteria do not strictly rule out an individual statement, they do not encourage it enough, whereas they do encourage conformity to "university" standards of what constitutes a good tone and an "appropriate" approach to melody and harmony. Originality is highly valued in the UNT program. Perhaps this difference of opinion is a problem that can be solved with clearer communication. I asked the professor who made the comment about "university jazz" what he meant by that. He replied that university jazz sounds like generic, theory-based playing, with nothing special added and with no relation to the tune that is being improvised on.

Prouty notes that "the relationship between pedagogical methodology and outcome . . . is not always clearly defined, with evaluative judgments sometimes reflecting an emphasis on areas outside the curriculum, beyond what is presented in the classroom" (2002, 162–63). This, in my view, is a good thing. It makes room for the individuality that is so highly prized in the nonacademic jazz world, and it signals the overlapping of the academic and nonacademic worlds. It necessitates that the student bring something personal to the music. Prouty expresses misgivings about the structured nature of the improvisation curriculum but is uneasy with a definition of what constitutes an acceptable solo that is less structured than he would like.

Any curriculum, no matter how comprehensive, is only a selection from many worthwhile subjects and ways to learn, and it is (or ought to be) always open to revision. Most significantly, curricula tend not to do a good job of teaching the knowledge that professionals must get from experience. This is a major theme of Schön's work on the reflective practitioner (1983, 1986), which describes what he calls the "knowing-in-action" that professionals acquire without having been explicitly taught. The situation faced by jazz improvisation students is not so different from that faced by medical students who find they must learn on their own how to talk with patients, architecture students who must learn how to collaborate with civil engineers and construction supervisors, seminary students who find that nothing in their formal training guarantees that they can preach a moving sermon, or professors who find that graduate school has not taught them how to teach effectively. All must learn by doing, through reflective practice.

The tension between academic and nonacademic approaches to the study of jazz improvisation may be a productive tension. I would be skeptical of a curriculum that presented itself as complete and totally parallel to what one might have acquired as a professional jazz musician in the past—or one that claimed to provide everything that a student needed to be successful in the future. The student's original creative effort will always be necessary. The improvisation curriculum is intended to introduce students to the practice of teaching themselves to improvise.

As jazz scholars take stock of the role of university jazz programs in the transmission of the music, now and in years to come, a more specific and individualized approach will help explain how those programs are experienced. In other words, the sort of "historical particularity" that DeVeaux advocates for the study of jazz history (1991, 553) is just as necessary to the study of the impact of jazz education as it is to the study of the transition from swing to bebop. To jazz players it seems obvious: Of course one cannot learn to improvise simply by taking a series of classes; many other experiences are necessary, and students in university jazz programs seek them out. If scholars do not contextualize the obvious, however, future accounts will have to rely on isolated opinions and overly general pronouncements, such as Kennedy's statement that the UNT program is "concerned more with creating generic professional musicians and educators than jazz musicians" (2002, 398). The only support provided for this statement is Collier's survey of jazz education programs in the United States (1994), which did not sample student views, even in the limited way this study has. There are signs, however, that university-level jazz education is getting more respect. One example is found in the introduction to a recent anthology of scholarly writing on jazz: "One of the wondrous oddities of our current moment is that the best advice to a serious jazz player in training is not to drop out and study in New York's nightclubs but to attend one of the several conservatories where excellent jazz instruction, by accomplished jazz artists, is richly available" (O'Meally et al. 2004, 1).

Perhaps future historians will study the scenes that have developed around the various schools of jazz, just as past historians have studied the regional jazz scenes that are prominent in the standard narrative of jazz history. Perhaps an oral history of the Jamey Aebersold generation in the style of *Hear Me Talkin' to Ya* (Shapiro and Hentoff 1955), or a more extensive collection of interviews in the style of *Notes and Tones* (Taylor [1977] 1993), is needed to preserve student discourse about the transmission of knowledge of the jazz tradition and to show that the improvisation class is not the only important context for learning to improvise in UNT's curriculum or others like it. That learning takes place through a variety of experiences inside and outside the curriculum; it happens privately and within a community; it happens before the student's university experience and continues after it ends; and it happens differently for each individual.

NOTES

1. The jazz studies program is located in the UNT College of Music, which has approximately 1,600 majors, 70 percent of whom are undergraduates; 105 full-time faculty, 43 adjunct faculty, 33 staff, and 130 teaching fellows and assistants; and a calendar of approximately 1,000 performances per year.

2. I treat interview data that comes exclusively from an e-mail exchange with caution if that is the only contact between the researcher and the interviewees. I did use e-mail to elicit responses in this case, however, because I had already established rapport with the students and had witnessed many of the experiences outside of improvisation classes that they described.

3. In anticipation of the objection that the arguments in this chapter are open to question as coming from an interested participant, I would counter by pointing out the importance of the insider view in any ethnomusicological inquiry. I am writing both as an ethnomusicologist and as an insider in a music culture that has been represented by researchers in a way that I find incomplete.

4. This reflects a possible bias of the sample. I invited responses from students who had a wide range of experiences and who seemed likely to have interesting things to say. Some I knew well; others I had just met. Those who were frustrated by the experience, or did not know me, may have been less likely to respond to my public invitation to participate.

5. The filmmakers visited a Harvard graduation and asked 23 graduates and faculty members two science questions: "Why are there seasons?" and "Why does the moon appear to change shape?" Twenty-one people got one or both questions wrong. One of the students who missed the second question had taken a course in the physics of planetary motion. To find out why, the filmmakers visited a nearby middle school to study how misconceptions acquired early in life can persist despite good teaching. The misconceptions may be due to misleading textbook illustrations, such as showing earth's orbit with an exaggerated ellipse, or unchallenged common-sense explanations, such as clouds obscuring the moon. One student was able to overcome her misunderstanding only when she held models of the sun and earth and thought through the problem on her own. For further information, see *www.learner.org/teacherslab/pup* (accessed May 29, 2007).

6. This can be heard on *The Complete Birth of Bebop* (Stash STCD535, 1991).

7. Since Web addresses change often, the reader is invited to reach the author's Web site via the University of North Texas College of Music, *www.music.unt.edu*, or via a search engine.

REFERENCES

Ake, David. 2002. "Jazz 'Traning: John Coltrane and the Conservatory." In *Jazz Cultures*, 112–45. Berkeley: University of California Press.

Bauer, Bob, ed. 1988. *The New Real Book*. Petaluma, Calif.: Sher Music Co.

Berliner, Paul. 1994. *Thinking in Jazz: The Infinite Art of Improvisation*. Chicago: University of Chicago Press.

Collier, Graham. 1994. "Jazz Education in America." *Jazz Changes* 1(1): 3–22.

Day, William. 2000. "Knowing as Instancing: Jazz Improvisation as Moral Perfectionism." *Journal of Aesthetics and Art Criticism* 58(2): 99–111.

DeVeaux, Scott. 1991. "Constructing the Jazz Tradition: Jazz Historiography." *Black American Literature Forum* 25(3): 525–60.

Haerle, Dan. 1989. *The Jazz Sound: A Guide to Tune Analysis Chord/Scale Choices for Improvisation*. Milwaukee, Wis.: Hal Leonard.

———. 2003. *Jazz Improvisation: A Pocket Guide*. New Albany, Ind.: Jamey Aebersold Jazz.

Kennedy, Gary. 2002. "Jazz Education." In *The New Grove Dictionary of Jazz*, 2nd ed., edited by Barry Kernfeld. Vol. 2, 396–98. New York: Grove's Dictionaries, Inc.; London: Macmillan.

Monson, Ingrid. 1996. *Saying Something: Jazz Improvisation and Interaction*. Chicago: University of Chicago Press.

O'Meally, Robert G., Brent Hayes Edwards, and Farah Jasmine Griffin, eds. 2004. *Uptown Conversation: The New Jazz Studies*. New York: Columbia University Press.

Prouty, Kenneth. 2002. "From Storyville to State University: The Intersection of Academic and Non-Academic Learning Cultures in Post-Secondary Jazz Education." Ph.D. dissertation, University of Pittsburgh.

———. 2004. "Canons in Harmony, or Canons in Conflict: A Cultural Perspective on the Curriculum and Pedagogy of Jazz Improvisation." *Research and Issues in Music Education* 2(1) (accessed May 29, 2007), *www.stthomas.edu/rimeonline/vol2/prouty1.htm*.

Rasula, Jed. 1995. "The Media of Memory: The Seductive Menace of Records in Jazz History." In *Jazz among the Discourses*, edited by Krin Gabbard, 134–62. Durham, N.C.: Duke University Press.

Schön, Donald. 1983. *The Reflective Practitioner: How Professionals Think in Action*. New York: Basic Books.

———. 1986. *Educating the Reflective Practitioner*. San Francisco: Jossey-Bass.

Shapiro, Nat, and Nat Hentoff, eds. 1955. *Hear Me Talkin' to Ya: The Story of Jazz by the Men Who Made It*. New York: Rinehart.

Steinel, Michael. 1995. *Building a Jazz Vocabulary: A Resource for Learning Jazz Improvisation*. Milwaukee, Wis.: Hal Leonard.

Taylor, Arthur. [1977] 1993. *Notes and Tones: Musician-to-Musician Interviews*. New York: Da Capo.

$\backsim$ **11** $\backsim$

ON LEARNING THE RADIF
AND IMPROVISATION IN IRAN

Bruno Nettl

THE RADIF TEACHES

A number of times I have quoted a statement made to me by my teacher of Persian music, Nour-Ali Boroumand, and have pondered its implications for years. To my question "When and how will you teach me to improvise," he replied something like "We do not teach improvisation. You learn the radif, and it teaches you to improvise" (Nettl 2002, 140). The radif is a repertory of roughly 270 short, mostly nonmetric pieces that musicians in Persian classical music memorize and that then serve as the basis for improvisation and composition. I did not question further, and over the months in which Boroumand taught me portions of the radif, he did not elaborate. The radif, it should be pointed out, consists of 12 dastgahs (units roughly parallel to Western modes, or Indian ragas); each dastgah consists of a dozen or more gushehs (melodies characterized by a typical tonality and characterizing motif, somewhat parallel to the Arabic maqam); and each dastgah has a daramad (literally "entry"), which is the dastgah's first and most characterizing part and a principal melodic motif to which a proper performer frequently refers. The following paragraphs examine the implications of Dr. Boroumand's statement in a number of contexts. How does the radif "teach"?

A logical point of entry is to consider what one learns in a musical culture in which improvisation is important: the materials on which improvisation may be based. These have been referred to as "models" (Nettl 1974), and I have also called them "points of departure" (PoD) (see Nettl 2002, 120). They include many sorts of musical phenomena—abstracted features of musical style such as collections of tones and rhythmic modes; brief motifs; sequences of harmonies; themes; compositions thoroughly worked out; general conceptions of soundscapes; or very specific models for elaboration such as forms (e.g., fugues, 12-bar blues).

The musician also learns what he or she may do with the selected PoD, the techniques used to get from the model to the final product. And then there are ways in which improvisation relates to the principles and values of culture. Thus, in one situation, it is important for the musician to know that the improvisation is central to the performance and merely accompanied by a retinue of precomposed and memorized material. In another, that improvisation is a craft outshone by the true art of precomposition. In this culture the musician learns that improvising reflects desirable values in a culture—freedom, if you will, or the ability to deal with challenges on the spot; elsewhere, it is related to deviancy, or to lack of learning. In group improvisation, the musician learns the way in which the social organization may be reflected in the music.

Moreover, the musician learns the spiritual or emotional aspects of the model and the derived techniques, the way in which different musical sounds may express moods and ideas. And surely, the aesthetic of what is an excellent, acceptable, or unsatisfactory outcome is also internalized. This is a lot to learn. Naturally, the education of the composer who does not improvise is in many ways parallel. But the things I have mentioned apply to many systems of music in which improvisation—the creation of music in the course of performance—exists alongside music that is not improvised but precomposed. It is helpful to keep these concepts in mind when considering how the Persian musician learns the art of improvising.

In considering musical cultures that distinguish between precomposition and improvisation, we also encounter different sorts of juxtaposition. Here the two are seen as totally different, whereas elsewhere there are various waystations of music making between two extremes—for example, between absolute precomposition and control of the sound in advance (e.g., much electronic music) and the almost total unpredictability of some aleatoric music. Elsewhere again, the two are thoroughly integrated, and all music making includes important components of both.

The concept of the radif as a principal tool of instruction was widely accepted by the Iranian musicians with whom I have spoken, but what does one really mean by claiming that it actually "teaches improvisation"? How does it accomplish its task? What aspects does the student internalize? And how can one evaluate whether the radif has, as it were, done its job?

RELATIONSHIPS AND CONTRASTS:
IRAN, SOUTH INDIA, AND THE ARABIC WORLD

Persian classical music, along with the classical musics of Arabic, Turkish, Central Asian, and South Asian cultures, is part of a musical world that shares important components, a group of systems that have developed in parallel fashion and share many musical, theoretical, and terminological features. The fundamental similarity of these musics is that they are based on systems of modes: composed and improvised genres (and intermediate forms) that share complex systems of rhythmic structure based on metric, pulsed, and nonmetric organization and that also involve certain types of relationships between soloist and accompanist. Each of these systems has, of course, important distinctive features, and each society sees its own music as unique. What these musics do not share is approaches to the teaching and learning of improvisation. All musicians debate over the relationship of discipline and creativity and over improvisation as a learned technique or as the result of a kind of inspiration that cannot be rationally described. But these musical cultures put different emphases on the significance of learning the PoD, on techniques, and on cultural and expressive components. Carnatic and Syrian/Lebanese Arabic music can serve as bases for comparison.

In Carnatic music (for an explanation of terminology, see Pesch 1999; Viswanathan 1977), there is a group of points of departure; it seems convenient to distinguish general from specific. "General" refers to ragas and their melodic characteristics, the collection of pitches and the order in which they should be introduced onto characteristic or typical melodic turns, motifs, or phrases and characteristic gamakas or ornaments. Similarly, rhythmic types—nonmetrically derived, it is thought, from the rhythm of ordinary speech, to music with a rhythmic pulse but no meter, to music using metric cycles, or talas—are "general" points of departure. The more specific points of departure are melodic themes, motifs, and particles derived from composed songs—usually kritis. These, when composed, use the general materials just mentioned as points of departure. Thus the musician may improvise (upon) the raga in its pure conceptual state, or upon a composed piece that in turn has been based on this same raga, a situation in which the musician has, as it were, a dual obligation.

Four main kinds of improvisation are specified and distinguished, and although they may appear in various contexts and relationships with composed pieces, they all appear in the typical pièce de résistance of a concert, the ragam-tanam-pallavi, and in a significant order. The first, alapana or

ragam, has no meter (but its rhythmic structure nevertheless has characteristics that can be described) and is based on the raga alone. It is followed by
Tanam, nonmetric but with pulse, based on the raga as well. Niraval, next,
has tala and is based on melodic material from a kriti; typically, it is a set of
improvised variations on a line from the first section (pallavi) of a composed
kriti. Kalpana svaram, finally, has tala and a somewhat predictable rhythmic
structure characterized by rapid-fire delivery of passages using the Indian
solmization syllables as text, short, equally spaced notes with occasional
reference to a line from a kriti. Thus the four kinds of improvisation appear
in the order of increased degrees of predictability. Now, the kalpana svaram
usually sounds as if it is very difficult to perform; I have no doubt that it is.
But Carnatic musicians maintain that, intellectually at least, it is the least
interesting, whereas the first, alapana, is the most valued. In fact, alapanas
performed by the same musician differ more from each other than do passages of niraval or kalpana svaram.

   Although individual masters who are teachers of Carnatic music must differ substantially in the way they introduce students to the necessary musical
knowledge and skills, and although the guru-shishya parampara may contrast
with the practices in modern music schools, some principles of teaching are
widely agreed upon (see, e.g., Pesch 1999, chapters 4 and 10). S. Ramanathan
said that his training began with a series of exercises and study pieces. The
first of these, alankaras and svaralis, required performance—melodically or
on vina—of melodic fragments consisting of segments of scales of the raga
Mayamalavagaula, a "primary" raga with four half-tones (e.g., C, D-flat, E, F,
G, A-flat, B, C). These fragments, most obviously perceived as in a quadruple
meter, would be juxtaposed first to the 8-beat Adi tala, and then to other talas
(e.g., the 6-beat Rupakam, the 7-beat Triputa, the 10-beat Jhampa). Although
this prepares a student for the performance of the metric sector of Carnatic
music generally, it leads most directly to Svara kalpana; but the various kinds
of pitch sequences help to provide an understanding of the melodic character
of the raga. Short songs with tala and devotional texts, Gitam and Padam,
are memorized, and only then is a student encouraged to try fragments of
the nonmetric alapana. Here the teacher plays short nonmetric improvised
phrases that are imitated by the student, who thereby also gets a sense of
the techniques of accompanying. The first and simplest alapanas are thus
memorized, and only after this process of imitation and memorization has
gone on for a time is the student encouraged to improvise, doing this at first
by performing embellished or elaborated versions of the memorized ones.

Typically, S. Ramanathan said, all of this material at first comes from one raga; eventually others are added.

Dr. S. Ramanathan did not claim that all Carnatic music teachers followed this approach or that his method was unique, but he did indicate that this was how he had studied. But if we say that the PoD for Carnatic music is "the raga," then we also ask in what manifestation a raga is internalized. It is these exercises, with their raga-specific melodic segments and the variations in emphasis provided by juxtaposition to contrasting talas, that provide the initial individualization of a raga, followed by memorized alapanas from the teacher's store of knowledge. Eventually, when these simple exercises and didactic pieces have been mastered, the student learns Varnams, short metric pieces in which the main characteristics and requirements of a raga are synthesized. As S. Ramanathan said, "A Varnam is the grammar of a raga."

This brief account of one teacher's method tells us that the PoD of a raga is learned by memorizing exercises of materials that may—actually, must—be used in improvisations, by quotation and reference. They are the building blocks, and an improvisor should balance referring to them with departing from them. The exercise types do not correspond precisely to the four improvisation types and to the distinction between improvisation and composition. Alankaras and Varnams lead to niraval and kalpana svaram and also undergird the ability to learn composed pieces such as kritis. But the sharp distinctions among these exercise types parallel the clear lines among the improvisatory genres. Throughout this process, as Ramanathan presented it, although devotional and spiritual issues play an important role, emotional involvement is not emphasized. Rather, the music is presented as a highly disciplined set of techniques. Musicians praise each other by emphasizing discipline, detailed knowledge, mastery of techniques, and repertory (Neuman 1979, 32–34).

Judging from the work of Ali Jihad Racy in his publications (e.g., Racy 2003) and his informal statements, the learning of the PoD in Egyptian and Lebanese Arabic music and the techniques of proceeding from PoD to improvised performance are quite different from the Carnatic model. Significantly, improvised Arabic music is largely nonmetric, and the most important forms are the instrumental nonmetric genre taqsim and the parallel but vocal mawwal. Racy's description of the tradition of learning emphasizes the relationship of teacher and student and the importance of devotional singing and chanting in the formation of musical sensitivity. Before the coming of the modern conservatory system, however, there were no standard teaching materials, and individual teachers probably had their own ways of imparting materials—for example, the typical or required content of a maqam, such as scale and motifs. According to S. Hassan (2002, 313–14), Iraqi maqam performers learn by independently imitating masters and eventually by trying out their wings in performances for a specialist audience. There appears to be no formal distinction between learning the PoD and learning what to do with it through improvisation. Both Racy and Hassan indicate that learning is an essentially private and even secret process.

Rather than giving an account of learning specific musical material of the sort used in Carnatic music, Racy (2003, 5–6, 12–13, and passim) stresses the importance of learning to perform in interaction with the audience's response, emphasizing the concepts of tarab (often glossed as "ecstasy") and saltanah (musical self-absorption). The singer "transforms the listeners and brings them to ecstasy through active and emotionally charged audience participation" (Racy 2002, 563). Understandably, this kind of interaction is not taught formally, and it can be apprehended only through observation and imitation. In the short improvised pieces known as taqsim, lasting from 1 to 15 minutes, an important part of this ecstatic component of performance, called tarab, is the customary use of modulation from the main maqam to two, three, or perhaps six or seven others for brief or extended passages, followed by a return to the home maqam. For this too, however, it seems that in the older tradition of teaching there is no systematic way of providing models for imitation. Nevertheless, certain patterns are evidently carried on through personal traditions, because the selection of maqams to which one modulates, and their order, are aspects of improvisation. Thus A. Jihad Racy (see Nettl and Riddle 1973), performing taqasim in the maqam of Nahawand, observed a group of related patterns in his performances examined in 1970:

    Rast, Hijaz, Saba, Bayati
    Bayati, Hijaz
    Rast, Bayati, Nawa Athar
    Bayati, Saba, Ajam, Kurd
    Rast, Ajam
    Bayati, Hijaz. Ajam, Saba, Nagriz
    Hijaz, Rast, Bayati
    Bayati, Saba, Aja,
    Rast, Hijaz
    Rast, Bayati
    Rast, Bayati,
    Rast, Bayati, Saba, Hijaz, Rast
    Bayati, Rast, Hijazkar

In south Indian music, my question "How do you learn to improvise?" might have been answered thus: "By studying a series of exercises," and in Arabic music: "By listening to masters improvise, imitating them, and trying out approaches to performance with audiences, determining by trial and error what works." Interestingly, too, although the concept of talent is certainly present in the two systems of musical thought, musicians in south India are mostly described as maturing through discipline, whereas in the Arabic Middle East, talent, first kept under wraps by the budding musician because of the fear of parental disapproval, is eventually recognized and plays the greater role.

In 20th-century Iran, the concepts of learning music and improvisation have similarities to both Indian and Arabic musics. To be sure, before the middle of the 19th century, a system not unlike the Arabic, with emphasis on patterned modulation, probably existed. But in the late 19th century, the concept of the radif as a fundamental repertory was developed (see Farhat 1990; Khatschi 1962; Zonis 1973, 3–40). It was created (or combined from extant elements) by a number of musicians, the most famous of them Mirza Abdollah, through their exposure to the complex but unified system of Western music and their desire to maintain a musical tradition that could compete with Western music and that was readily distinguished from the Arabic and Turkish traditions. The radif, well known to be composed of about 270 pieces, most of them nonmetric, developed variants, to the extent that each master claimed to have his own, but in fact these variants had a great deal in common. After about 1960, various attempts were made to standardize the radif (Barkechli 1963), and after a period of musical decline—1980 to 1990—there grew an interest in maintaining a radif that could be considered identical with or close to the "original" and authentic one of Mirza Abdollah (1991).

The radif was uniquely successful as a system that musically unified a musical tradition and that succeeded in rebuilding a musical culture that had lost much of its significance to its own people in the late 19th century. This fact was recognized by learned musicians such a Nour-Ali Boroumand, who said to me on various occasions, "It is really something extraordinary and fine, something quite unique, this radif that we have created in Iran." An important reason for the radif's prestige in its musical culture lies in the multiplicity of its roles: it is the macro-PoD, containing all the models acceptable for composition and performance. It comprises the techniques needed for moving from PoDs to finished performance. It includes the range of moods and spiritual values that make it possible for musicians to claim that its 12 modes express everything that music can express. Finally, it reflects important values in social organization and social life.

MUSICIANS AND SCHOLARS SPEAK

The issues of tradition, transmission, and improvisation have been the subject of debate among Iranian musicians and music scholars. If I can attempt to synthesize a large variety of opinions (from the literature and personal experience), it seems that there is concern for the authenticity of the radif; debate regarding the degree to which the content and structure of the radif must help determine improvised performance; the degree to which it is proper, in a performance, simply to quote the radif; and the importance of intellectual understanding of the radif in contrast to the significance of hal, described by Safvat as "a mental and emotional state that should come about before an artist can present his work eloquently and effectively" (During 1991, 241). Hal, glossed as "condition, health," can be recognized, according to Safvat, "by its results, the most important of which are a feeling of inner joy and elation." It is closely tied to improvisation, but learning it is not part of any training system. It can be attained by keeping company (242) with people of holy disposition and by studying poetry and mysticism. In its specifically musical connections, it seems related to tarab.

Iranian musicians who particularly associate themselves with sufism (see Safvat in During 1991, 231–50), who regard music making essentially as a mystical experience, regard the (admittedly vague) concept of hal (literally "condition," but here meaning something like "mood") as essential to learning improvisation. Knowing the radif, and having attained hal, one then improvises essentially as one is inspired at the moment. One knows the radif and has techniques at hand, but they are subordinate to the supernaturally associated inspiration.

In contrast to Safvat, Nour-Ali Boroumand maintained that the processes of Persian music making are largely cerebral, somewhat like the south Indian approach. Although he recognized the importance of making each performance unique, of not simply performing the radif as one had learned it, in his rhetoric about Persian classical music the accurate knowledge of the radif in its comprehensiveness stood out greatly above performance practice. He would constantly emphasize the greatness, the significance, of the radif, and when asked about improvisation, but he would say things like "When you have learned the radif you can play anything you wish," or "When we play we can change the order of gushehs," and he would then cast the issue somewhat impatiently aside. In an interview with Behruzi (1988, 372), he considered improvisation as something like a necessary evil, or something that is unrelated to knowledge of radif: "Improvisation has . . . been a problem in Persian music, in the sense that some musicians have been thinking and saying that you can play whatever you feel like playing." He blamed some of his contemporaries for neglecting to maintain a basic structure. Nevertheless, he praised great masters in an earlier generation for never playing (read "improvising upon") a part of the radif the same way twice. But while maintaining the importance of discipline, he also insisted on the importance of freedom at various levels—the freedom of the learned amateur musician (a state superior to the professional who makes his living performing) to play when he wishes, to then select from the radif for performance whatever he wishes, and finally to select variants of phrases and ornaments of tones.

The resistance of Iranian musicians to the concept of improvisation as a simple opposition to composition, suggested by Nooshin (2003, 262, 268), may be understood in light of the absence of this dichotomy in Persian teaching and performance practice. Musicians in the 20th century insisted on the importance of the radif as a solid and unchanging foundation. But it may be more realistic to see the entire system of Persian music as a group of continuums, of units of musical thought gradually merging into each other. There are the three levels of the radif as it is ideally learned. The concept of the radif itself contains the techniques needed for improvisation, including the notion of options, and illustrating in its content the various motivic relationships described by Zonis (1973, 104–24) as comprising a vocabulary of improvisatory techniques. Interestingly, the way in which the radif "teaches" seems to include the variety of gusheh types, from those with very generalized nonmetric melodic material with little in the way of a memorable motif (which lend themselves to far-flung improvisation) to metric materials with memorable tunes (performed with only little departure from the memorized model) and many intermediate stages. The variable relationship of performances of the various classical forms to the radif and to their precomposed versions or even written scores again fits this concept of continuums. So also does the fact that the various dastgahs (a concept somewhat similar to the Western mode or Indian raga), in their typical renditions, relate in different degrees to the radif. For example, comparisons of performances of Segah (see Nooshin 1998) and Chahargah (Nettl and Foltin 1972) typically follow the structure of gushehs as presented in the radif, separating them and devoting a section to rendering ("improvising upon") each. Performances of Shur tend to depart from the structure of the radif of Shur (though not from its content; see Babiracki and Nettl 1987).

Ella Zonis (1973, 98–148), in what has now become an early classic, provides the most detailed description of the relationship of a gusheh to the .

radif, describing and illustrating a number of techniques—repetition, ornamentation, melodic modification, and various techniques of elaboration.
Significantly, she comments on the structure of important gushehs as having
several parts, or often several versions. Thus the dastgah of Chahargah has
four "daramads," that is, four pieces that function as the basis of the dastgah,
which contain motifs to which an improvisor (and indeed the course of the
radif itself) continues to return. She suggests that the later pieces are in fact
variations of the first and that they thus constitute a model for the kind of
musical movement and musical relationship that improvisors should carry
out in performance.

Evidence of a Persian system of musical thought with various degrees of
"improvisatoriness" or departure from a PoD, impinging on performance
and teaching, is found in statements by a number of 20th-century musicians. Caron and Safvate (1966, 129) describe three levels of improvisation:
one may simply play the radif in an embellished manner; or impose on a
dastgah creativity that departs from its form in the radif; or mix materials
from several dastgahs. Boroumand suggested (as does Safvat in During 1991,
245–46) that the proper way to learn the radif was in three stages—simple,
intermediate, and complete; the simple version would contain everything of
essence, and the others would be elaborations of the simple version, an approach analogous to the concept of PoD as related to derived performance.
Nooshin (2003, 260–61) discusses the emergence in the 20th century of a
negative attitude toward the dichotomy of improvisation and composition,
as the idea of "improvisation" as used by Western musicians suggested to
their Iranian counterparts a degree of freedom that departed too greatly from
a model. Conservative musicians such as Boroumand insisted that, on the
one hand, in a true performance one never played the same thing twice but
responded to one's personal creative urges and to the audience, but, on the
other, one did not really "improvise," a term that seemed to them to suggest
rootlessness (262). One of my consultants, Nasrollah Shirinabadi, when asked
to play avaz in one dastgah a second time because, I said, each performance
was different, insisted that he did indeed play it the same way every time, a
misunderstanding that resulted from his conception that "playing it the same
way" indicated adherence to the radif as PoD.

Descriptions of teaching traditions (During 1991, 244–46; Khatschi 1962,
33–35) indicate an approach in which a master teaches certain select students
whose task it is to pass on material to a larger group. While these intermediaries (Safvat uses the term *khalife*) appear to be on the one hand superior
students, they are, on the other hand (During 1991, 245), described as musi-

cians who are uncreative and can thus be relied on to pass material along unchanged. Again, we see the separation of precise learning and improvisation mitigated by embellished, varied material. The notion of a system in which departure from a model is central is also supported by the amount of improvisation in the various genres that constituted a full-blown performance in 20th-century Persian concert music. Pishdaramad, conceived as an ensemble piece normally based on radif materials, permits no deviation from the memorized form. The avaz, based to be sure on the radif, is considered as something that need not contain any direct quotations from the radif, and that indeed is not played the same way twice. The chahar mezrab, a metric solo piece, is said to be precomposed and memorized, but in fact its various sections may often undergo variation in the sense that they may be repeated varying numbers of times, sometimes truncated, and their order may be changed. Several performances of one chahar mezrab differ more from each other than from the equivalents of pishdaramad. Tasnifs, composed songs (which may be performed instrumentally as well), are closest to pishdaramad in predictability, but musicians permit themselves somewhat greater freedom.

BUT HOW?

"But Dr. Boroumand, just how does the radif teach musicians to improvise?" I asked him this question a few times and received answers such as "You will see," "Once you have learned the gushehs you can change their order," or "We never play the same thing twice," or also, "You must listen to the nightingale; it does not repeat itself." If I suggest that a major criterion is to balance creativity with discipline, to make music that is between invention and memorization, he would wish to err on the side of discipline, saying it is better simply to take units of the radif, perhaps changing their order or selecting portions of gushehs (e.g., in a gusheh that has three sections, taking only one) and then performing variations of things readily recognizable.

I would suggest, from an analysis of music and of teaching and social behavior (but not necessarily from explicit statements by Iranian musicians), that it may be helpful to consider that the radif teaches the musician on three levels: techniques, general principles of music, and general principles of social life. Let me give some illustrations.

Principally, the radif teaches the musician that moving from memorized radif to performance involves options, but options of particular sorts. For one thing, within the radif itself a great deal of material is repeated or reappears in different contexts. For example, several dastgahs may include the same gusheh with the same name but in different tonal contexts, each time in conformity with the dastgah's scale. Thus Segah and Chahargah both include Zabol, Hesar, Mokhalef, and others. But the identical dastgah may appear in different dastgahs too, because there is overlapping between Shur and its secondary dastgahs and between Mahour and Rast-Panjgah. Indeed, one can think of some dastgahs as variations of each other—Segah and Chahargah; Shur and Dashti, Abu-Ata, Bayat-e Tork; Homayoun and Bayat-e Esfahan.

The versions of the radif presented by a musician at various times in his life may in a sense be variations of each other. Thus the name of a gusheh may refer to different content, and several identical renditions of a gusheh in different contexts may have different names. For example, in Boroumand's three radifs, the units named Daramads 1, 2, 3, and 4 are called 1, 3, 2 (with 4 lacking) in another recording, and 1, 3, 4, 2 in a third. The unit referred to here as "Daramad 4" in one recording is called "Zangouleh" in another, and "pish-e Zangouleh" in a third.

The gushehs exhibit various degrees of rhythmic and metric specificity. Many of them, however, state a norm (a motif), depart from it, and eventually return to it. As a dastgah proceeds, gusheh by gusheh, several of the gushehs will end with the main motif of the first one (daramad). But several (though definitely not all) dastgahs show the return "home" by including, about two-thirds of the way through, a gusheh that reflects (without simply repeating) the content of daramad, but an octave higher—Maqlub in Chahargah, Shur-e bala in Shur. Significantly, each dastgah has a variety of gushehs—some thematically unspecific, others with memorable themes, some metric, some (the "modulatory" gushehs) introducing accidentals. And the principle of departure from a home base and eventual return to it with the concept of forud—"descent"—to the home tonality is illustrated periodically.

Structurally, the dastgahs are not alike. For example, most of the gushehs in Chahargah are rounded off, ending with a definite close; in Shur, an ending is more typically a transition to the gusheh that follows. The concept of specific-ity balancing variety is present in the parallel yet differential structure of the dastgahs. The twelve dastgahs have important things in common, yet each has its distinctive characteristics. The radif teaches the concept of including many musics within one set of principles by its terminology. Gushehs seem to be abstracted forms of musical styles and melodies from different origins. Thus gushehs and dastgahs have names that suggest different places of ori-gin (Bayat-e Tork, Bayat-e Kord, Eragh, Hijaz, Rak-e Hendi, Rak-e Kasmir) and different places in Iran (Zabol, Esfahan, Tusi, Neshaburak). Of course, other names suggest sounds from nature (Chakovak = lark; Xzang-e shotor = camel's bell); qualities (homayoun = royal; bozorg = large; kuchek = small; golriz = filligree; khara = granite); historic individuals; and many more.

On the other hand, performances of the various dastgahs may have much in common. Certain techniques occur over and over: for example, after free-flowing invention, frequent return to basic motifs; one or two repetitions of a motif, but then, always variation; and alternation of thematically specific and general materials, of metric and nonmetric, with occasional insertion of recognized composed pieces. We see variation in the treatment of individual motifs—repetition, melodic sequence; appearance of a theme at various speeds and with different emphases.

Importantly, the radif—or a constituent dastgah—is memorized, but structurally it cannot in essence be distinguished from the improvisation that is based on it.

If learning the radif teaches the basic point of departure for improvisation and composition and the procedures for arriving at a musical product, it also teaches ways in which music reflects important guiding principles of social life. Elsewhere (Nettl 1978) I have tried to identify, on the basis of anecdotal observation but also with the support of ethnographic literature, some ways of characterizing Persian social behavior, and I have suggested three (which, to be sure, may conflict with each other): the importance of hierarchy balanced with direct access to the center of authority; the importance of a prescribed order of events or processes; and the significance of the exceptional, the unexpected, the surprising. Without here giving illustrations, I suggest that these elements are present in the radif and are transferred to the improvised avaz and to the full-blown performance that consists of five pieces, only one explicitly improvised and the others partaking of characteristics of improvisation to varying degrees.

Does the radif teach hal? No doubt musicians would maintain that it does. I can only provide two illustrations. One concerns the emotional or expressive character of each dastgah. Musicians maintain that each dastgah has its own character, but they seem to disagree on the characterization. Shur is said by some to reflect passion, and by others, resignation to fate; Mahour is gay and happy, or majestic; Chahargah is warlike, or sad. The idea that each dastgah has a mood is not disputed. But the concept of emotion in general? Dr. Boroumand considered it something very culture-specific, something that could perhaps not be understood by someone not grounded from childhood in Persian culture. "Dr. Nettl," he once said to me, "You will never understand this music. There are things that every uneducated construction worker outside here understands instinctively, but that you won't understand." He didn't mean to be discouraging; there were, after all, certain things that I could, he was sure, understand. But still . . .

Although it has been convenient to describe Persian music as consisting of two separate concepts and processes—the radif (associated with teaching and learning, and perhaps with the concept of a theory) and improvisation (performance, the "music itself")—it may be more appropriate to see the musiqi-ye asil as a group of musical phenomena that oscillate between discipline and freedom, each merging into the next. Musicians memorize the radif, which itself contains what they need to know to be proper artists, and as they proceed, in life and in a performance, they gradually let go of it, but they never abandon it entirely. Something of that sort could also be said about Carnatic and Arabic music; yet these three musical traditions, clearly related and parallel in performance structures, are taught in very different ways, and they seem to represent rather different principles of music and culture.

REFERENCES

Babiracki, Carol M., and Bruno Nettl. 1987. "Internal Interrelationships in Persian Classical Music: The Dastgah of Shur in Eighteen Radifs." *Asian Music* 19(1): 46–98.

Barkechli, Mehdi. 1963. *La Musique Traditionalle de l'Iran*. Tehran: Secretariat d'Etat aux Beaux-Arts.

Behruzi, Shahpur. 1988. *Chehre-ye Musiqi-ye Iran*. Tehran: Ketab Sara.

Caron, Nelly, and Dariouche Safvate. 1966. *Iran: Les Traditions Musicales*. Paris: Buchet/ Chastel.

During, Jean. 1991. *The Art of Persian Music*. Washington: Mage Publishers.

Farhat, Hormoz. 1990. *The Dastgâh Concept in Persian Music*. Cambridge: Cambridge University Press.

Hassan, Scheherezade Qasim. 2002. "The Iraqi Maqam and Its Transmission." In *The Garland Encyclopedia of World Music*, Vol. 6, *The Middle East*, edited by Virginia Danielson, Scott Marcus, and Dwight Reynolds, 311–16. New York: Routledge.

Khatschi, Khatschi. 1962. *Der Dastgah: Studien zur neuen Persischen Musik*. Regensburg: Bosse Verlag.

Mirza Abdollah. 1991. *Le Repertoire-Modele de la Musique Iranienne. Radif de Tar et de Setar de Mirza 'Abdollah. Version de Nur 'Ali Borumand. Introduction et Notation de Jean During*. Tehran: Editions Soroush.

Nettl, Bruno. 1974. "Thoughts on Improvisation: A Comparative Approach." *Musical Quarterly* 60(1): 1–19.

———. 1978. "Musical Values and Social Values: Symbols in Iran." *Asian Music* 12(1): 129–48.

———. 2002. *Encounters in Ethnomusicology: A Memoir.* Warren, Mich.: Harmonie Park Press.

Nettl, Bruno, with Bela Foltin, Jr. 1972. *Daramad of Chahargah, a Study in the Performance Practice of Persian Music.* Detroit: Detroit Monographs in Musicology, No.2.

Nettl, Bruno, and Ronald Riddle. 1973. "Taqsim Nahawand: A Study of Sixteen Performances by Jihad Racy." *Yearbook of the International Folk Music Council* 5:11–50.

Neuman, Daniel M. 1979. *The Life of Music in North India: The Organization of an Artistic Tradition.* Detroit: Wayne State University Press.

Nooshin, Laudan. 1998. "The Song of the Nightingale: Processes of Improvisation in Dastgah Segah." *British Journal of Ethnomusicology* 7: 69–116.

———. 2003. "Improvisation as 'Other': Creativity, Knowledge and Power—The Case of Iranian Classical Music." *Journal of the Royal Musical Association* 128(2): 242–96.

Pesch, Ludwig. 1999. *The Illustrated Companion to South Indian Classical Music.* Delhi: Oxford University Press.

Racy, Ali Jihad. 2002. "Snapshot: Sabah Fakhri." In *The Garland Encyclopedia of World Music*, Vol. 6, *The Middle East*, edited by Virginia Danielson, Scott Marcus, and Dwight Reynolds. 563–64. New York: Routledge.

———. 2003. *Making Music in the Arab World: The Culture and Artistry of Tarab.* Cambridge: Cambridge University Press.

Viswanathan, Tanjore. 1977. "The Analysis of Raga Alapana in South Indian Music." *Asian Music* 9(1): 13–71.

Zonis, Ella. 1973. *Classical Persian Music; An Introduction.* Cambridge: Harvard University Press.

$\backsim$ **12** $\backsim$

HINDUSTANI SITAR AND JAZZ GUITAR MUSIC:
A FORAY INTO COMPARATIVE IMPROVOLOGY

Stephen Slawek

When Indian musicians first began touring in the United States in the mid-1950s, their improvisational performances were often compared to jazz. Ravi Shankar, the most well-known Indian musician in the international arena, did not appreciate the analogy, as evidenced in the following passage from his autobiography: "Owing to the improvisational factor common to both Indian music and jazz, many people take it for granted that our music *is* like jazz—which is far from the truth. The improvisation in jazz is based on Western chords, harmony and a particular theme. In Indian classical music one improvises on a theme, either in the form of a song or in a gat based on a chosen raga (one of thousands!), being bound by rules and observing the complex rhythmic structures and time cycles" (1999, 149). It is apparent that Shankar recognizes a quality that is common to both jazz and Indian music—improvisation—even as he denies the similarity of the two musics on the basis of their content. In seeking to understand the nature of improvisation, Shankar's statement might be of use; he has made a distinction between the content and process of music making and implies that common features of process exist in both Indian classical music and jazz. This study probes the potential for comparing the two and aims to provide insight into the process to which Shankar alludes; in so doing, it draws from my recent research on jazz guitarists of the Philadelphia area and on my years of training in the performance of Indian music.[1] I also draw on the pedagogical materials of Mr. Joseph Sgro, a renowned guitar teacher of south Philadelphia with whom I studied for about 18 months in the mid-1960s. I explore the nature of the musical communities with which I have worked that maintain the art of musical improvisation, the codification of musical materials as a strategy for building a baseline of knowledge from which improvisational music is created, the existence of variant conceptual frameworks underpinning music making within an otherwise unified practice, and the existence of cultural tropes regarding the realization of truth and freedom through improvisational music.

MUSICAL COMMUNITIES

As a disciple of Pandit Ravi Shankar, I have had firsthand experience with the privileges one enjoys through membership in a gharana. In an earlier publication (Slawek 1991), I described the ways the Maihar gharana provided a refuge of authenticity in which its member musicians could experiment and innovate in Indian music. I also noted that the gharana consisted of two primary features, an alliance formed by the structure of the musical transmission system, and a musical style generally defined and shared by members of the alliance. An elaboration of the structure of the musical community that constitutes the Maihar gharana is not necessary here. I merely note that Ravi Shankar and Ali Akbar Khan are the two most prolific protégés of Ali Akbar Khan's father, Ustad Baba Allauddin Khan, and that Allauddin Khan was one of the best-known disciples of Ustad Wazir Khan, a maestro of the North Indian rudra vina, chief musician of the Rampur court and a descendant of Tansen. It is through their connection to Tansen that the Maihar gharana musicians claim authenticity, tracing musical materials in their repertory to those of the rudra vina, the most highly esteemed musical instrument of the Mughal courts.

A series of serendipitous events in late 2002 led me to begin a research project designed to chronicle the contributions of Joe Sgro to the guitar culture of the greater Philadelphia region.[2] In an initial presentation resulting from that research (Slawek 2003), I invoked the concept of gharana as a heuristic device to elucidate what I perceived as similarities of the Italian American guitar culture of South Philadelphia with the structure of the Indian gharana system as I had experienced it as a member of the Maihar gharana.[3] The inspiration to do so was drawn from a Web site maintained by one of Sgro's students, Sonny Troy. Troy speaks of Sgro as his revered mentor and lists numerous guitarists of the Philadelphia area, noting that they formed a brotherhood:

> I'm a Jazz Guitarist. I was born and live in the Philly/South Jersey area. I play, and have played all over this country, and some foreign countries. I have played various Jazz festivals and am currently appearing with my own trio in the Phila. Area. . . . I am currently playing a Gibson Guitar, but have advertised for Epiphone Guitars in the past while playing with

a Las Vegas based group called the "Characters." I currently reside in
Maple Shade, N.J., but was born in South Philadelphia, the birthplace of
some of the Worlds' greatest Guitarists, past and current. Here are a few
from the Philly/South Jersey area:

ANTHONY BACCARI: My Uncle and boyhood hero, who influenced me in my
playing.
CARMEN BACCARI: My Uncle and mentor who influenced me to play.
JOE SGRO: My beloved teacher and idol. Virtuoso Guitarist. Also the greatest
inspiration of my musical life. He formulated (in my opinion) the best
teaching method for Guitar ever, using studies for the Violin and Piano
and tailoring them to fit the Guitar. Great thinking, along the lines of
Albert Einstein. Before Joe, there were no set methods for playing, reading
or teaching. The true HERO of the Guitar in my eyes. Joe is also a great
Violinist, Mandolinist, theoritician [sic] and great Jazz player as well as
being a kind gentleman. He has produced more great Guitarists than
anyone on the planet. My one and only teacher and mentor.
PAT MARTINO: My all time favorite Jazz Guitarists, he and Jimmy Bruno (in
my opinion) are the best in the world. My boyhood friend.
JIMMY BRUNO: Also my all time favorite Jazz Guitarists, awesome, big time
innovative player. His Dad was great too!!
EDDIE LANG: First plectrum (pick) player. Wonderful, Wonderful!! Bing
Crosby's Guitarist.
DENNIS SANDOLE: Teacher to many great Guitarists and big time Musicians.

Guitar players in general seem to be friendly toward one another, and
seem to share a brotherhood with other Guitar players and usually become good friends. I think the Guitar leads to this. Guitar players like to
exchange ideas and thoughts about the instrument, as it has been highly
un-cultivated through the years, and only in the last 40 or 50 years have
teachers finally gotten a grasp on how to teach it. I will be adding more
to this list and page, so please stay tuned. (*www.geocities.com/bourbon-
street/1413/*)

The Web site for Jimmy Bruno, presently one of the celebrated jazz guitarists of Philadelphia, piqued my interest with the following quote from Bruno:
"There was a guy named Joe Sgro who taught all the good guitar players in
Philly at one time or another. I never got a chance to study with him, but
one of his students showed me his picking technique, which comes from a
violin bowing technique, and I adapted that when I was around 12, 13, [or]

14" (2003).[4] Sonny Troy's characterization of Philadelphia area guitarists as an alliance, together with Jimmy Bruno's statement that Joe Sgro had taught all of the good guitar players of Philadelphia, brought to my mind the socio-musical unit of gharana in Hindustani music. Another Web site, GuitarMaster.Net, advertised a series of instructional books for guitar based on the teaching method of Joseph Sgro. The home page for the site included a picture of Sgro and some quotes from Leonard Bernstein and Eugene Ormandy praising Sgro as one of the most talented musicians of the 20th century (see Figure 12.1). The primary ingredients for a gharana seemed to be in line: a great musician associated with a specific place, a long list of disciples pursuing successful musical careers, an esoteric technique, and the codification of the tradition, in this case, as a series of instructional books for guitar.

Although Sgro is a significant figure in the music culture of Philadelphia, he was not the first Italian American from south Philly to bring attention to jazz guitar. That honor is generally bestowed on Eddie Lang, whose real name was Salvatore Massaro. Jazz guitar historian Norman Mongan writes that

FIGURE 12.1.   Joe Sgro as he appeared while being interviewed by the author in January of 2003. Photo by the author.

Lang "was practically solely responsible for the creation of the jazz guitar, for until he brought his intelligence and dexterity to bear, nobody had conceived of the idea of playing guitar in a manner compatible with the demands of playing jazz solos" (1983, 29). South Philadelphia's Italian American community takes pride in their deep involvement in the growth of jazz guitar, as is evidenced by a plaque installed in Lang's neighborhood displaying the proclamation: "Eddie Lang 'Father of Jazz Guitar.' He was born Salvatore Massaro in 1902 and lived in this area as a boy. An accomplished soloist, Lang worked with Joe Venuti, Paul Whiteman, the Dorseys, and others. He was Bing Crosby's accompanist when death cut short Lang's career in 1933." Eddie Lang began his musical studies on the violin. His childhood friend and musical collaborator, Joe Venuti, was a classically trained violinist. Sgro was Venuti's younger, maternal second cousin, and he, too, was initially trained as a violinist—first by John Canciarulli, a violinist with the Philadelphia Orchestra, and later by Venuti's teacher, Isador Shapiro. The violin appears to have been an esteemed instrument within this community.

Sgro was known in his neighborhood as the "young Joe Venuti." His first major professional association was with the Victor Hugo Band, one of many offshoots of the Paul Whiteman Orchestra, which he joined when he was 15. Throughout his career, Sgro played with numerous other local trios, quartets, and bands; worked with the studio orchestras of Philadelphia affiliates of the major television networks; and was a featured soloist with the Paul Whiteman orchestra in the latter days of that band's existence. Sgro also worked as a session musician, appearing on several late 1950s and early 1960s Cameo-Parkway recordings backing up Bobby Rydell, Chubby Checker, and others, and he played mandolin with the Philadelphia Symphony under the direction of Eugene Ormandy whenever the score required. It was late in the 1950s that personal circumstances and religious beliefs led Sgro to curtail his performance activities and devote more of his energy to teaching guitar.

Dennis Sandole was the other master of jazz guitar in Philadelphia in the mid-20th century who was known as an incomparable teacher of improvisation. Sandole had worked with the Tommy Dorsey Orchestra and also appeared on several recordings backing up Billie Holiday. A few of the guitarists I consulted recalled that they had experienced a bit of Sgro/Sandole rivalry during their period of guitar studies. If that was the case, it was not apparent when Sandole arose as a topic in one of my interviews with Sgro:

> Dennis was the finest. He dwelt not so much on the instrument technically, because he taught all instruments—how to improvise harmonically. He was the

Schoenberg of the jazz world, a tremendous musician. We were very close. We really admired each other. This will show what a humble person he was: in his studio he had a great big sign, and it said, "If you ever want to really learn how to play guitar," he says, "go study with Joe Sgro" (laughs). Can you imagine? But he was excellent. He just died recently. Boy, I really miss him. We were, I'll tell you, we were together all the time. He became one of Jehovah's Witnesses. I studied the Bible with him. Musician-wise, he was tops. As far as musicians are concerned, I don't think there's anybody that's close to Dennis in the jazz field. He was very, see, he just didn't teach guitar. That's the thing. He taught, actually, jazz improvisation, principally, where I went into the classical thing. I would give the students Chopin pieces, Rachmaninoff pieces. (personal communication, July 2003)

To this, I might add that Joe Lano stated that after five years of lessons with Sgro, Sgro sent him to Sandole for advanced studies in harmony and improvisation. Tony DeCaprio also studied with both Sgro and Sandole and noted that they would have phone conversations about his progress on the instrument in the middle of a lesson. Tom Giacabetti, who teaches at Temple University and the University of the Arts in Philadelphia, is yet another example of a Sgro/Sandole product. Giacabetti stated that he combines aspects of technique and method from both Sgro and Sandole in his teaching approach. According to Joe Federico, one of Sandole's most devoted students, many of the finest jazz improvisers benefited from lessons with Sandole. Among these individuals would be John Coltrane and James Moody.[5]

THE CODIFICATION OF THE MATERIALS OF IMPROVISATION

Just as the background of vina technique provides a stylistic unity to the music of the Maihar gharana, so the influence of the classical violin method and a general reverence for the classical tradition are distinguishing factors that I believe set the south Philly style apart from other styles of jazz guitar. In characterizing Eddie Lang's style, Mongan writes: "Lang was completely original in his use of quarter tones, chord harmonics and arpeggios in solo passages, and had amazing intuition for countermelody. His uncanny dexterity was another facet of his remarkable 'gift of hand'" (1983, 29). Mongan notes that among Lang's solo recordings are a rendering of "Rachmaninoff's Prelude in C# Minor" and other nonjazz titles that "show the sheer brilliance of Lang's technique; [in which] the thirty-second note, single-string runs are played with precision and ease." He also notes Lang's European musical heritage and that Lang's idol was Andrés Segovia (ibid.).[6]

THE SGRO SCHOOL

Much of Mongan's characterization of Lang's style also applies to Sgro. Sgro himself cites Eddie Lang as the originator of jazz guitar and the Lang/Venuti duo as the originators of modern jazz: "Joe Venuti and Eddie Lang, they were the masters. By the way, those two, they started jazz the way we know it today. Before that, it was Dixieland and some of the old, uh, but the real classical musician playing classical jazz—see, that's what we were interested in, playing classical jazz. Classical means music with class. And classical, meaning the way the so-called classical musicians, the way they play concertos, that's the way we play jazz. That's what Joe Venuti was. He was a fine classical violinist. And he was a fine—he turned down the Philadelphia Orchestra and everything! And they really are the ones who are the fathers of so-called jazz. And I think that all started in Philadelphia here" (personal communication, July 23, 2003). In contrast to Lang, however, Sgro did not idolize guitarists; rather, piano players provided the inspiration for much of his style: "Did you ever hear of Art Tatum? He was my mentor really, not guitar players. Art Tatum: as far as I'm concerned, he was it. Then I followed all the other piano [players]—George Shearing came and I did all that. I was really—that's where I—guitar players never interested me because they were all playing regular Charlie Christian style, which was good. You know they were excellent players, for what they were doing. But I liked the piano chords and I liked everything about the piano because it had everything" (personal communication, January 3, 2003). By combining the jazz piano styles of Art Tatum, George Shearing, and Oscar Peterson with the systematic technical base of classical violin, Sgro created a uniquely elegant style of what he called "contemporary improvisational music" for guitar.

Common to both Indian classical music and jazz guitar playing is the great emphasis placed on achieving levels of virtuosity capable of astounding listeners. The key to virtuosic playing in both musical practices is a combination of rigorous practice and correct technique. In both traditions that I have encountered, technique is basic to producing the desired tonal quality, whether playing the guitar or the sitar. In my first class with Ravi Shankar, the initial hour was devoted to correcting what he perceived as mistakes in both my left- and right-hand techniques. For the right hand, the prescription was to lock the plectrum, the mizrab, against the second string in the follow-through from the basic inward stroke. Most sitarists do not follow such a disciplined approach to their right-hand technique, and the difference in sound between the Shankar method and that of players from other gharanas is quite apparent. This is especially so in passages known as toda, which include liberal use of paired alternate strokes at high speeds. This stroke unit, known by the mnemonic "diri," sounds loud and clear in Shankar's style, as control over the right hand prevents the open strings from sounding. In other traditions, extraneous sounds ringing out from open strings that get touched inadvertently in the follow-through of the inward part of the diri often mar the clarity of this double stroke. I should note that Shankar's teacher was primarily a sarodist, and Shankar himself has told me that he had to create his own technique to capture the finer points of Allauddin Khan's music.

Joe Sgro, being a self-taught guitarist, is also an innovator of technique. He created his own method, what he calls his "school," of guitar playing. The core of Sgro's method consists of his analysis of the physical, mental, melodic, harmonic, and rhythmic requirements of improvisation on the guitar, resulting in his development of specific techniques for the left and right hands. Among these is a picking technique that Sgro devised on the basis of ideas inspired by the games of pool he played with Jackie Gleason in between shows at the club where Sgro's band was backing up Gleason in the early 1950s. In pool, the necessity of placing the cue ball within range of the next targeted ball gave Sgro the clue needed to develop a picking technique that minimized extraneous movement. According to Sgro, continuous alternate down-up picking was standard in the early days of jazz guitar. In attempting to play like jazz pianists, with rapid runs and sweeping arpeggios, Sgro realized he needed to find a better approach, as continuous alternate picking would often take his plectrum out of range when crossing strings. He devised a system that he has termed the "slur-alternate picking technique." The unique aspect of this technique is that the pick, as much as possible, should continue in the same direction when crossing to an adjacent string. This kind of directional picking is evident in an exercise devised by Sgro/Sandole protégé Tom Giacabetti. Giacabetti combined Sgro's picking method with Sandole's insistence on developing the ability to play an arpeggio starting with each of the left-hand fingers (see Figure 12.2).

Several of the guitarists I interviewed specifically mentioned this picking technique as an important factor in their musical style, as it allows for great speed but also for smooth, legato playing (recall the quote from Jimmy Bruno). Tony DeCaprio, whose initial guitar teachers included luminaries such as Jimmy Raney and Jim Hall, told me: "When I saw [Joe Lano] play, I was just blown away by that right hand. Now here I am studying with all these heavies, but I didn't know anything about the right hand—[that it] could be put in such a scientific and exact manner—until later on in life

MAJOR 7

FIGURE 12.2. An arpeggio exercise devised by Tom Giacabetti incorporates Joe Sgro's picking method and Dennis Sandole's instruction to develop the ability to play arpeggios beginning with any finger of the left hand. Courtesy of Tom Giacabetti.

when I had encountered Joe Sgro via my interest in that technique, initially from Joe Lano. I had never seen that before and I was absolutely stunned by it. . . . When I got together with Jimmy Bruno, which was many, many years ago in Vegas, I saw he had the same right hand, so I could see that this was a Philly thing somehow . . . that's what gives him that edge" (personal communication, February 10, 2003). Regarding this picking method, Sgro student Joe Lano commented: "And I think that's what he based that whole philosophy of the picking technique on: the violin bow. And his model is great. And the thing that it does is that it gives you a legato sound—the hardest thing in the world to do on a guitar. That was the thing that amazed me when I finally heard Joe play for that first time. When I heard the sound that was coming out of the instrument, I said, 'Joe, that's what I want to sound like'" (personal communication, September 3, 2003). Lano has been based in Las Vegas since he first went there as part of the Lena Horne show several decades ago. When I visited Jimmy Bruno in July 2003, he confirmed that it was Joe Lano who taught him the Sgro picking technique.[7]

Sgro's systemization of guitar method is equally apparent in his approach to the left hand. His lesson plan included an elaborate set of fingering exercises based on permutation (see Figure 12.3) as well as exercises originally composed for the piano by the 19th-century French composer Charles-Louis Hanon. One of Sgro's jazz violin students, John Blake, Jr., remarked that Sgro's method of devising finger exercises had much in common with the exercises of Indian music that he had learned from Adrian L'Armand, a Western performer of south Indian violin. Jairazbhoy (1961), Widdess (1981), and others have described the Indian procedure of merukhand, the systematic permutation of a set of notes as a means of elaborating and extending improvisations. It is just one example of a procedure intent on exhausting all possibilities within given parameters, an element of process that appears to be present in both sitar and jazz guitar music.

Violin etudes by Wohlfahrt, Kreutzer, and others (see Figure 12.4), forms for playing major, minor, diminished, whole-tone, and other scales over three octaves, chord scales, double- and triple-stops, and chord melodies, all were important elements of Sgro's pedagogical method. Sgro devised his own system of chords arranged in basic families differentiated by string sets of four each, with four inversions of each chord. Dennis Sandole used a similar approach to chord formation, as is apparent in a brief excerpt from *Guitar Lore*, his instructional book for guitar (see Figure 12.5).

During my studies with Sgro, a typical lesson would begin with a fingering exercise followed by Hanon exercises for guitar, then a Wohlfahrt etude (Sgro

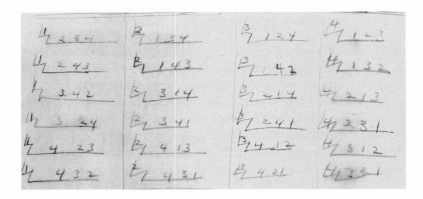

FIGURE 12.3. Sgro's system of finger exercises, as written by Sgro as part of the author's initial practical study of the Sgro guitar method in 1966 and 1967. The initial set (not shown) was to be played on four-fret blocks, one finger on each fret (1 = index; 2 = middle; 3 = ring; 4 = little finger), from the bass E string to the top e' string, starting on the first fret and moving up the fret board one fret at a time. The second set, shown here, repeats the same permutation, but the last three notes cross to the adjacent string. The same formation would eventually be repeated by skipping a string and crossing to the second string from the first note. (Reproduced from the author's personal collection.)

FIGURE 12.4. The beginning of the 26th violin etude in Wohl-fahrt book 1 with Sgro's indications of position and picking for guitar. Courtesy of Carl Fischer, Inc.

CHORD FAMILIES

The strings will be divided into five combinations:
1) 1234   2) 2346   3) 2345   4) 1235
5) 3456. This will assist the student in eventually

acquiring an extensive chord vocabulary and a fluency in adapting the top or soprano note of his melody and chords to any string.

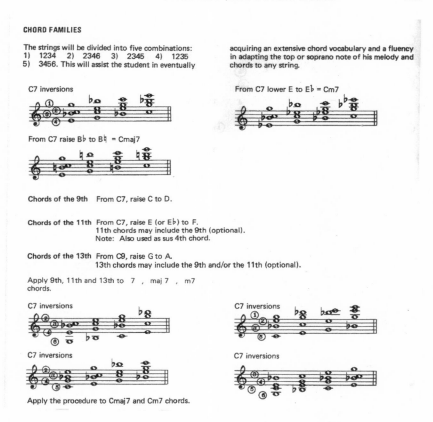

FIGURE 12.5. Guitar chord families as presented by Dennis Sandole (1981, 34). Courtesy of Carl Fischer, Inc.

always encouraged me to "make it swing"), and, in conclusion, a jazz standard written out as a chord melody. Sgro would write from memory within a few minutes songs such as "Smoke Gets in Your Eyes," "Penthouse Serenade," and "Foggy Day"—melodies (usually played at the top of the chord) in staff notation with chords indicated above in a slightly idiomatic shorthand for guitar chords (see Figure 12.6). As I advanced in Sgro's course of instruction, he procured for me a rare copy of a local fake book, *Modern Jazz*, and began to teach me how to improvise the harmonization of bebop tunes. Students who continued longer with Sgro than I went on to more advanced material, including double-stops, triple-stops, and contrapuntal techniques that Sgro termed "moving lines." Sgro, who is reluctant to play publicly now, gener-

FIGURE 12.6. "Foggy Day," as written out by Joe Sgro for the author during a guitar lesson in 1966. (Reproduced from the author's personal collection.)

ously demonstrated all of these components in a rendition of "The Shadow of Your Smile" during my interview with him in January 2003. As he played, he verbally termed each type of improvisation. Sgro's systematic taxonomy of the technique he brought to his "contemporary improvisational music" was reminiscent of a similar approach to compartmentalizing technique that I encountered in studying sitar with Pandit Ravi Shankar (see Slawek 2000).

A VARIETY OF CONCEPTS

In a previous publication, I demonstrated that the apparent unity of theoretical terminology that exists in Hindustani music actually masks the set of varying practices that take place under the rubrics of those terms (Slawek 1998). For example, the Maihar Gharana concept of raga elaboration in alap differs quite a bit from that of the Imdadkhan Gharana. I wouldn't pretend to have the kind of grounded ethnographic information necessary to determine whether a parallel condition exists among south Philly jazz guitarists. However, my preliminary work indicates that although there may not be a unified code providing an umbrella of terminology, there certainly do appear to be divergent ways of getting from the beginning of an improvisation to the end. Indeed, the two most divergent improvisational itineraries I've located to date fall along the lines of the differences between the conventional, classically oriented approach of Joe Sgro, with particular influence from violin and piano repertories, and the avant-garde, envelop-pushing approach of Dennis Sandole. Thus, you find Jimmy Bruno playing wild, virtuosic improvisations that sound firmly embedded in jazz harmonies that fit the mold of standard tunes, representing the Sgro side of things; and then you have Pat Martino venturing more toward experimental music, modal harmonies, and fusions drawing on Asian concepts of rhythm and melody, representing aspects of improvisation that were high on the agenda that Dennis Sandole advocated.[8] Pat Martino asserts that his conceptual framework derives from his realization that the structure of the guitar leads to a conception of musical organization that is fundamentally different from the piano. He sees the piano as an additive system and the guitar as a multiplicative system (see Figure 12.7a and 12.7b). He further relates the guitar system to broader aspects of the real world, such as the 12 months and the four seasons. Space does not permit further elaboration here, but interested readers can explore Martino's ideas in greater depth by perusing his Web site (*www.patmartino.com*).

ON FREEDOM THROUGH IMPROVISATION

Ingrid Monson has offered a convincing account of the commonalities that led jazz musicians of the 1950s to look eastward in their search for musical liberation from the restrictive harmonic progressions of earlier bebop. In her analysis, Monson links racial and political movements from the United States

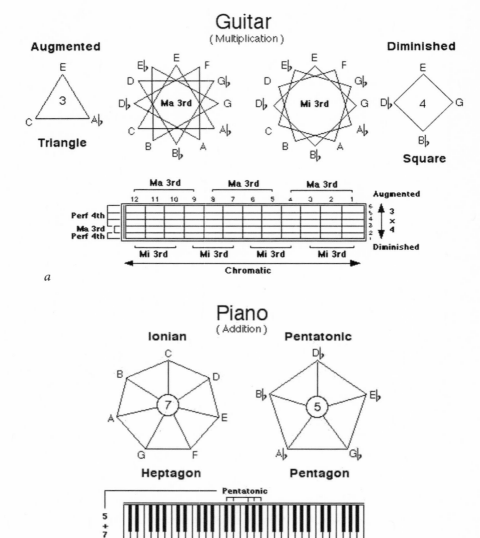

FIGURE 12.7a AND 12.7b. Pat Martino's conception of guitar and piano systems as depicted in his web publication, *The Nature of the Guitar*. Courtesy of Pat Martino.

to Africa and India by demonstrating the itinerary through which musicians such as George Russell, John Coltrane, and Miles Davis came to embrace free improvisations within modal structures as an alternative to harmonically grounded improvisations. She links these developments in jazz to broader themes such as "spirituality, anticolonialism, the civil rights movement, as well as Western aesthetic modernism and science" (1998, 163).

Although I have barely scratched the surface of the Italian American jazz guitar scene of Philadelphia, I have found little in the thinking of these musicians that would resonate with the arguments Monson has made. This is not to say that spirituality is absent from the music scene of this community of jazz guitarists. On the contrary, it is very much present. Joe Sgro became a Jehovah's Witness as a young man, and Dennis Sandole followed suit soon after. A significant number of the Italian American jazz artists emanating from south Philadelphia belong to this religion, and Sgro was particularly active in converting his students.[9] He continues his religious observances, and his musical activities are now firmly attached to his work as a Jehovah's Witness. The religion apparently is a factor in the vitality of the jazz guitar culture of the Philadelphia region. Joe Federico, a Sandole protégé, attributed the large number of excellent guitarists originating from the Philadelphia area to the fact that Sgro and Sandole gave up the life of touring musicians to devote themselves to their religious observances. Because they were living stable, domestic lives, students could count on having these premier teachers available for weekly lessons. Sgro himself suggested as much: "You know they said it's too bad—that old Joe Sgro, he's great—I hear all these things—it's too bad he became one of those Jehovah's Witnesses. You know what I told 'em? I says it's a good thing I became one of those Jehovah's Witnesses. I said because I wouldn't have been here and I wouldn't be teaching you if I wasn't one of those Jehovah's Witnesses! You know where I would have been? You never would have studied with me. I would be out playing, where I can make some money, not teaching" (personal communication, January 2003). In discussing the relationship of music and spirituality, Sgro was quick to point out that his musicality was closely related to his religious studies. For him, the Bible contains certain fundamental truths that underpin all of existence. Thus, his approach to improvisation flows from his reduction of music to certain guiding principles of melodic, rhythmic, and harmonic relationships.

While Asian and African influences were nonexistent in Sgro's music, the same cannot be said of Dennis Sandole. Sandole had an intellectual inquisitiveness that led him to carry out an extensive study of the world's musical traditions, especially scale forms. Joe Federico showed me an unpublished manuscript by Sandole called *Scale Lore* that compiled and analyzed scales from numerous foreign cultures. Some of this work appeared in Sandole's published work, *Guitar Lore* (1981), but *Scale Lore* is a much more extensive study. Still, Sandole's motivation to look outside his culture for new musical materials appears not to have arisen from political or racial issues. Rather, Sandole was seeking new materials to satisfy his creative impulses. Federico characterized Sandole as a musician ahead of his time, whose compositions from the 1950s sound avant-garde even today. Another example of musical transfer divorced from ideology is seen in Tony DeCaprio's statement to me that he used to copy Ravi Shankar's sitar licks on the guitar to develop his own technical skills (personal communication, February 2003). It is only in the music of Pat Martino that one discovers any connection to Asian spirituality in the guitar culture of Italian American jazz, and this is a single strand in the musical fabric of the area that arose well after the developments Monson elaborates. It is clear to me that numerous personalities constitute the guitar culture I experienced in the Philadelphia region, and, unlike the prominent theme of spirituality that appears to be almost universally present in Indian music discourse, no single overarching trope linking musical freedom to spiritual salvation emerged in my discussions with the musicians I interviewed.

CONCLUSION

When I first began my study of the Indian sitar, I progressed much faster than my other American classmates. I attribute much of my success to my earlier lessons on guitar with Joe Sgro. From Sgro, I learned the discipline required in improvisational music and how that translated to the systematic elaboration of ordered kernels of melody. I learned that much depended on rigorous practice that explored repetitive exercises, and I had internalized a considerably large body of systematically ordered exercises that were similar in content and concept to the basic exercises that underpin much of one's early training on the sitar. Comparing two very complex systems of music making is a complicated venture in and of itself. Here, I have only begun to unravel the commonalities of process—both social and musical—that exist in the way improvisation occurs in Hindustani music and jazz. A fuller elaboration of these is a worthy project for the future.

NOTES

1. I gratefully acknowledge the award of a Dean's Fine Arts Research Fellowship by the College of Fine Arts, the University of Texas at Austin, without which the research for this paper would not have been possible.

2. Although I had thought of Joe Sgro on occasion after discontinuing my guitar studies in 1967, I eventually lost all contact with him in 1971 when I left the United States to study sitar at the Banaras Hindu University. Slightly over three decades later I was reminded of Sgro by a high school friend who had participated in the jazz orchestra with me and whom I met after 35 years while attending (for the first time) a reunion of my high school graduating class. When my trumpet-playing colleague from the jazz orchestra saw me, what he recalled was that I had studied guitar with Joe Sgro. Impressed with the impression my guitar teacher had made on him, I was inspired to do some research on Sgro, which eventually led me to practicing jazz guitarists in the Philadelphia area who had studied with Sgro. From these individuals I learned that Sgro was still alive and well, living in the same house I visited in 1965–1967 to study with him. The absence of Sgro's name from works such as Maurice Summerfield's (1998) *The Jazz Guitar,* which includes over 300 biographical entries on jazz guitarists, including several of Sgro's students, such as Robert Conti, Tom Giacabetti, and Monnette Sudler, also compelled me to undertake this research.

3. The Italian American contribution to the Philadelphia jazz scene is curiously underplayed in the one article I have encountered in scholarly literature that has addressed jazz in Philadelphia (McMillan 2002, 158–78). However, enough information can be gleaned from the article (see, in particular, p. 166 and footnote 6) to learn that Joe Sgro was not the only classically trained Italian American imparting musical instruction to jazz players in the 1950s. Jazz trumpet player Lee Morgan received his first private instruction in the instrument from Tony Marchione, a master trumpet player of south Philadelphia who had studied with Sam Krause, then the principal trumpet player in the Philadelphia Orchestra.

4. The Web site that originally contained this quote from Jimmy Bruno has since disappeared (*www.concordrecords.com/bios/brunobio.html*). However, see note 7.

5. An Internet search will reveal that the number of professional guitarists today who have studied with Joe Sgro and Dennis Sandole is quite extensive. More than one former student left the guitar culture of southeastern Pennsylvania to delve into less common musical territory. The pedagogical activities of Sgro and Sandole also made an impact on ethnomusicologists Eric Charry, who studied with Sgro in the 1970s, and Ron Radano, who studied several years with a student of Dennis Sandole.

6. The original recording of Eddie Lang playing a guitar rendition of Rachmaninoff's Prelude in C# Minor (transposed to E minor) is included on the box set release by Mosaic Records, *The Classic Columbia and Okeh Joe Venuti and Eddie Lang Sessions.* The collection includes extensive notes by Wenzel and Peters (2002).

7. In his instructional video for jazz guitar (n.d.), Jimmy Bruno gives a detailed

explanation of his picking technique but neglects to attribute the technique to Joe Sgro. As already stated, Bruno did allude to the source of his picking style in an earlier version of his professional Web site. He also provided me with a detailed account when I interviewed him, pointing out that it was Joe Lano who showed him the basics of Sgro's slur-alternate picking method. Lano also confirmed Jimmy Bruno's account when I interviewed him.

8. Monson (1998) has examined the implications of racial and transnational aspects of the development of modal jazz in the 1950s. An intriguing missing element in her discussion is the relationship of John Coltrane and Dennis Sandole. Ratliff (2000), in his obituary of Sandole, notes that Sandole "was John Coltrane's mentor from 1946 until the early 1950's, introducing him to theory beyond chords and scales and exposing him to the music of other cultures. Mr. Sandole taught advanced harmonic techniques that were applicable to any instrument, using exotic scales and creating his own" (46).

To this, Tom Moon, music critic for *The Philadelphia Inquirer*, adds:

> Coltrane, the saxophonist whose contributions to jazz included revolutionary chord sequences, attended Mr. Sandole's clinics as a teenager and stayed in touch with him through much of his life. "When I listen to Coltrane," Dragoni [a Sandole student] said, "I can hear my lessons. . . . 'Giant Steps' is right out of the Sandole book." The guitarist was respected by several other important voices of the '50s and '60s, including saxophonists Benny Golson and James Moody, both of whom he taught. He later instructed bassist Stanley Clarke.
>
> Unlike many teachers, Mr. Sandole rarely played during lessons. Those studying with him already knew the mechanics and were seeking his insights on matters of concept, his knowledge of exotic scales, and other techniques to broaden an improvisor's range of expression. Mr. Sandole was known for his progressive approach to jazz harmony. But Martino, who studied with him for a few months in the early '60s, remembers the educator as equally adept at nurturing individuality. "He taught by not interfering with the blessings each student was given, by amplifying them in any way he could," the guitarist said.
>
> The teacher's ideas trickled down from one generation to the next. Because his approach to harmony was unconventional, he was embraced by the experimental-jazz elite, including pianist Matthew Shipp, saxophonist Bobby Zankel, and bagpiper Rufus Harley.
>
> Other students were inspired by his lyricism. In the early '60s, Mr. Sandole shaped the sensibility of the brilliant guitar melodist Joe Diorio, who went on to teach Pat Metheny. The master also taught Dale Bruning, whose students included Bill Frisell. (Moon 2000)

Sandole's interest in Asian musical traditions is clearly evidenced by his inclusion of numerous non-Western scales in his pedagogical work *Guitar Lore* (1981). Additional research would be required to determine how deeply involved Sandole was with the discourses of the spiritual, political, and musical ideas Monson links to the interracial jazz community through her study of George Russell's *Lydian Chromatic Concept* and Coltrane's modal jazz. However, the possibility exists that Sandole was a major force in the development of this important style of jazz and that he approached non-Western music more as an intellectual than as a seeker of a Utopian spirituality. If this was indeed the case, it would add a paradoxical twist to Monson's interpretation.

9. I recall seeing a table full of copies of *The Watchtower* at Sgro's residence, but I was spared any attempts at conversion while I was his student. This was not the case with several other students. Both John Blake, Jr., and Jim Tillman stated that Sgro would include religious sermons in their lessons, and Tom Giacabetti related that he had adopted the religion for a period of time but later drifted from it and consequently also discontinued his relationship with Sgro. Sonny Troy noted that several members of his family had converted to the religion and that, although he was not a practicing Witness, he was sympathetic to the religion's teachings.

REFERENCES

Bruno, Jimmy. n.d. *Jimmy Bruno: No Nonsense Jazz Guitar.* VGB 210. Pound Ridge, N.Y: Hot Licks Productions.

Jairazbhoy, Nazir. 1961. "Swaraprastara in North Indian Classical Music." *Bulletin of the School of Oriental and African Studies* 24(2): 307–25.

McMillan, Jeffrey. 2002. "A Musical Education: Lee Morgan and the Philadelphia Jazz Scene of the 1950s." *Current Musicology* 71–73: 158–78.

Mongan, Norman. 1983. *The History of the Guitar in Jazz.* New York: Oak Publications.

Monson, Ingrid. 1998. "Oh Freedom: George Russell, John Coltrane, and Modal Jazz." In *In the Course of Performance: Studies in the World of Musical Improvisation*, edited by Bruno Nettl and Melinda Russell, 149–68. Chicago and London: University of Chicago Press.

Moon, Tom. 2000. "Dennis Sandole, Educator Who Taught Giants of Jazz." *Philadelphia Inquirer*, October 4, 2000, page B06.

Ratliff, Ben. 2000. "Dennis Sandole." *New York Times*, October 8, 2000, Section 1, page 46, column 5.

Sandole, Dennis. 1981. *Guitar Lore.* King of Prussia, Pa.: Theodore Presser Co.

Shankar, Ravi. 1999. *Raga-Mala: The Autobiography of Ravi Shankar.* New York: Welcome Rain Publishers.

Slawek, Stephen. 1991. "Ravi Shankar as Mediator between a Traditional Music and Modernity." In *Ethnomusicology and Modern Music History*, edited by Stephen Blum, Philip Bohlman, and Daniel Neuman. 161–80. Urbana: University of Illinois Press.

———. 1998. "Keeping It Going": Terms, Practices and Processes of Improvisation in Hindustani Instrumental Music." In *In the Course of Performance: Studies in the World of Musical Improvisation*, edited by Bruno Nettl and Melinda Russell, 335–68. Chicago and London: University of Chicago Press.

———. 2000 (1987). *Sitar Technique in Nibaddh Forms*. Delhi: Motilal Banarsidass Publishers.

———. 2003. "'In Search of a Lost Chord': Putting Nostalgia and Memory to Work in Rediscovering Joe Sgro and the South Philly 'Gharana' of Jazz Guitar." Unpublished paper presented at the 48th Annual Meeting of the Society for Ethnomusicology, Miami, Florida, October 2–5, 2003.

Summerfield, Maurice J. 1998. *The Jazz Guitar: Its Evolution, Players and Personalities since 1900*. Newcastle upon Tyne: Ashley Mark Publishing Company.

Wenzel, Scott, and Mike Peters. 2002. *The Classic Columbia and Okeh Joe Venuti and Eddie Lang Sessions*. Mosaic Records Limited Edition #21.

Widdess, Richard. 1981. "Aspects of Form in North Indian Alap and Dhrupad." In *Music and Tradition: Essays on Asian and Other Musics Presented to Laurence Picken*, edited by D. R. Widdess and R. F. Wolpert, 143–81. Cambridge: Cambridge University Press.

WEB SITES

Sonny Troy: *www.geocities.com/BourbonStreet/1413/*
www.concordrecords.com/bios/brunobio.html
www.guitarmaster.net/
jazzinternet.com/vegasjazz/artists/joelano/
www.tonydecaprio.com/
www.patmartino.com/

INTERVIEWS

John Blake, Jr., Philadelphia, Pennsylvania, January 5, 2003
Jimmy Bruno, Willow Grove, Pennsylvania, July 20, 2003
Tony DeCaprio, Atlanta, Georgia, February 10, 2003 (by phone)
Joe Federico, Lindenwold, New Jersey, July 19, 2003
Tom Giacabetti, Stradford, New Jersey, January 4, 2003
Joe Lano, Las Vegas, Nevada, September 3, 2003 (by phone)
Pat Martino, Philadelphia, Pennsylvania, July 21, 2003
Joe Sgro, Philadelphia, Pennsylvania, January 3, 2003
Joe Sgro, Philadelphia, Pennsylvania, July 21, 2003
Allan Slutsky, Cherry Hill, New Jersey, July 20, 2003
Monnette Sudler, Chestnut Hill, Philadelphia, July 19, 2003
James Tillman, Philadelphia, Pennsylvania, January 5, 2003
Sonny Troy, Maple Shade, New Jersey, January 4, 2003

MUSICAL IMPROVISATION
IN THE MODERN DANCE CLASS:
TECHNIQUES AND APPROACHES IN
FULFILLING A MULTI-LAYERED ROLE

John Toenjes

INTRODUCTION

The modern dance class at the turn of the 21st century is a lively arena for contemporary musical improvisation. It takes place on a daily basis in a wide variety of styles in nearly every city in America and Europe (and in many other cities around the world), yet there is little study of this vast outpouring of improvised music. This essay attempts to shed light on this neglected phenomenon, describing the function of music in the dance class and the roles that musicians fulfill in the classroom, and identifying the procedures and modes of thought that go into fashioning this music.

The modern dance technique class, as generally practiced now, developed out of a marriage between ballet training and the individual needs of the artists who created modern dance in the mid-20th century.[1] It has become an avenue for artistic and technical development and is important to the establishment and continuity of a tradition in the society of modern dancers.[2] The centrality of the modern dance class to this society has led to its evolution into an entity that serves four functions. First and foremost, it is a means of training dancers' bodies. Second, it is an arena for dancers to gather and perform regularly. It also serves a ritualistic role as a site for the inner development of the individual dancer and as a repository for the retention and development of tradition. Finally, it functions as a laboratory for the development of new dance techniques and for experimentation in the relationship between music and dance.

The participation of a skilled dance musician[3] is essential if the class is to achieve its aims. The music must simultaneously serve to train bodies, inspire dance artistry and a sense of performance, and reflect the class's seriousness of purpose in its ritual function. To create such music, to make it afresh to fit the changing needs of each class and individual dance instructor, requires a skilled improviser. Through study of the small amount of writing on the subject, through interviews with accomplished practitioners of the art, and drawing from my own experience as a musician in the modern dance class, I aim to answer the following questions: What are the roles of the dance musician in the modern dance class, and how do these roles affect the music? What is the process used to create the improvised music upon which the modern dance class depends?

In the class's function as a training ground, the dance musician fills the role of training assistant to the dance instructor. Dancers need to develop a solid dancing technique. They must learn how to use rhythm to help them dance more easily and how to work with the beat. They must also learn how to shape a movement phrase and discover ways in which music and dance constructs interact. Certain musical techniques can be called upon to help dancers execute movements and to feel movement in various ways. Through fashioning music that explores various aspects of its relationship to dance, dance musicians promote "musicality" by providing the means for dancers to feel the connection between music and what is required of their bodies.

In terms of daily performance, dance musicians are composer-performers and observers, performing for and with the dance students (in the individual and collective reception of other students' performances and the group dynamic, dancers become both performers and audience at the same time) and observing the dance. In this role, concerns beyond the technical also guide musical choices. Musicians attempt to inspire artistry in the dancers through emotional intent and intriguing musical ideas.

The modern dance class involves aspects of ritual, particularly as it concerns the individual dancer's practice of the art and the development of that practice in the presence of others of like mind, according to prescribed behavior and seriousness of purpose (Beck 2003). In this sense, the musicians serve as the sacred choir to the ritual participants. They help create and maintain the proper mood to convey the earnest nature of the class, whether the music is serious or lighthearted (Moulton 2003).

In the class's laboratory function, musicians are co-experimenters with dance instructors. They can facilitate experimentation with movement and with illuminating the relationship between music and dance, both for classroom use and for the possible transferring of ideas out of the classroom and onto the stage.[4] At times instructors and musicians will take part in a dance–music dialogue during a class that leads them in radically different directions from what they expected.

Dance musicians who play music in fulfillment of these roles function at an expert level. Additionally, however, the music usually is expected to be improvised. This gives the dance instructor the freedom to experiment with innovative approaches to movement to create an excitement of the new. This is *modern* dance, and it is all that this word implies: fresh, exciting, just born. In many classes, movement combinations change daily, or at least weekly. The modern dance aesthetic assumes that the music for these changing situations will combine with the dance to create something original. And as a practical matter, musicians must be able to improvise to accommodate the mercurial needs of the modern dance class; it would be a formidable ability to have the repertoire at one's fingertips to provide appropriate music for every circumstance.

The following quotes from dance instructors illustrate the importance of dance musicians to the goals of the modern dance class.

> The role of the musician is integral to effective technique teaching. The choice of what music accompanies each dance combination informs the dancer as much as the movement itself. A great dance musician allows the student to learn on multiple levels—a kinesthetic level as well an intellectual level. The rhythm, quality, and phrasing of the music all work to support the correct use of musculature for the student. For teaching beginner-level students this is imperative! For teaching advanced students, the musician can develop and inspire a greater sense of artistry. (Lehovec 2002)

> My definition of good dance technique is "skillful phrasing" and "intimate knowledge of one's unique body characteristics." The former is a type of sophistication that is impossible for a dance teacher to transmit without the support of qualified, creative musicians who understand music's role in the technique training process. . . .
> A dance musician must also be trained to have empathy with the kinesthetic processes, to understand and to help conduct the class through subtle communication between the teacher/students/accompanist, and to play appropriate material which supports the technical agenda and point of view of the instructor. Choice of instrumentation, phrasing, accent, how complex to make something rhythmically or melodically etc., all have impact on the success or lack of success of the choreography of the class and the student's ability to learn. (Hook 2002)

In addition to fulfilling their roles, dance musicians make musical choices based on other considerations. First, there is the relationship of the improvisations to the structures of the given combinations, and to the movement within them. Second, there is the relationship of the dance musician to the individual dance instructor. And third, there is the judgment of what "works" and what doesn't in supporting the dance.

The improvisation generally fits the phrase structure of the movement combination. This can vary wildly from a standard 32-bar form to something more complicated, such as five phrases of seven bars each, to structures so complex that one must jot them down to keep them straight. The musician may need to solve a problem such as "How do I create a kinesthetically effective, inspiring, and musically satisfying improvisation that consists of five phrases of seven bars each, one that begins with a bang and includes high points at the end of the second and third phrases, then loses dynamic energy in the fourth, only to have the fifth phrase begin with two hemiolas and build in energy toward the end, leading seamlessly into a repetition of the whole piece?" Such an intricate composition must be created with only a few minutes' thought and preparation. Some musicians say that, faced with such a difficult problem, they merely start playing and somehow are able to create something with the proper form by following the dance (Attaway 2000, 35). Others are able to compute all this and quickly plan the improvisation just prior to playing.

The musician's main goal is to help each individual instructor to communicate her aesthetic and to achieve her instructional or experimental aims, through the sound of their improvisations (Beck 2003). To do this, musicians acquaint themselves with the instructor's musical preferences, both through conversation and through trial and error. At times a musician will begin an improvisation, only to have the instructor stop the exercise in favor of a different sound or emphasis, requesting the musician to, say, play the piano instead of drums or to play with more "weight." Through this process dance musicians learn each instructor's methods and tastes.

Of paramount importance to all dance musicians is that the music "work" for the purposes of the dance (Kanthak, quoted in Attaway 2000). This is usually verified by watching the dancers during the improvisation to judge if they are executing the movement correctly and with ease, and with proper stylistic and performance nuance. If the musician can think of a way to help achieve this goal by trying other musical solutions, he incorporates them into the improvisation, either immediately or in the next repetition of the movement combination.

With all these requirements, it is not surprising that relatively few musicians can improvise in this context at a high level. Because of this, some dedicated practitioners of this specialized discipline champion it as an art form in and of itself.[5]

PROCEDURES FOR IMPROVISING MUSIC

How do musicians create improvisations that fulfill these requirements? Certainly the "art" of it is unquantifiable. What distinguishes a classroom artist from a merely competent player is "kinesthetic sense" (Moulton 2003; Beck 2003; Gilbert 2003; Queen 2003), the ability to perceive how movement would feel in execution, and then to translate this perception into sound. Kinesthetic sense can be developed, but it is an innate attribute. Most dance musicians believe this to be what distinguishes a good classroom player from a poor one: kinesthetic sense is *the* prerequisite for being a dance musician. However, beyond this are other identifiable procedures and techniques for improvising music for the dance class. These have been gleaned through interviews, from analysis of my own process, and through studying videotapes of classes played by other musicians.

THE STRUCTURE OF THE MODERN DANCE CLASS

The modern dance technique class generally lasts from one and a half to two hours and has a tripartite structure. First, "center" exercises (similar to the ballet *barre*) train either specific parts of the body or focus on specific steps, such as the smooth circular movement of the legs in a *ronde de jambe* (much of the terminology used here comes from ballet). Next are longer "combinations" of movements done in the middle of the studio, followed, finally, by large movement combinations across the floor.

In a typical combination, the dance instructor first demonstrates a sequence of movements. Counting aloud as she shows what movements coincide with what beats, she comments on the movement quality and offers technical suggestions for executing the combination. The dancers learn all this as thoroughly as is possible in a short amount of time, about three or four minutes. Then the instructor "counts off" the combination (usually with the ubiquitous "five—six—seven—eight!"), and the musician begins to play as the students dance. When the combination is finished, the musician stops playing and the "dance" ends.

Dance musicians pay close attention to the demonstration, gleaning vital information from it. If they're fortunate, the instructor has shown the exercise with clear verbal and movement cues regarding tempo, meter, dynamics (as understood in the dance context, i.e., energy level), rhythmic details, movement qualities, overall feeling, and style. The musicians then decide how to interpret this information, considering whether to highlight certain rhythmic or dynamic details, how closely to match the music to the movement, and what instrumentation and style or genre might work best, keeping the instructor's preferences and the overall shape and feel of the dance class in mind (Cherry 2003). Then they get into the proper attentive/receptive state required for inspired improvisation, and let loose with the music. While playing, they study how the music is affecting the dancers, altering the music as necessary to make it more suitable, or more or less challenging, or clearer or more obfuscated, as required to support the goals of the class. If the combination is repeated, they analyze what worked and what didn't, and change the improvisation accordingly. This process is repeated for each movement combination until the class is over.

MOVEMENT ANALYSIS

During repeated demonstrations of the combination, skilled musicians take in different parts of the whole and fashion them into a complete musical picture according to a rough hierarchy. Certainly this cannot be nailed down to a precise sequence; often many clues are gathered at once, making it impossible to determine which came first, and musicians can change their original assessments in the course of watching subsequent demonstrations. If the musician is inexperienced, perhaps going through a formal educational process,[6] this hierarchy might be quite well defined, and rather rigid and circumspect. For a musician who is more experienced or who is self-taught, with perhaps a bit of help (or criticism) from dance instructors along the way, this hierarchy may be subconscious, or may appear not to be there at all. Skilled dance musicians are able to grasp the requirements of the improvisation rapidly. They seem to "hear the movement" (Kaplan 2003) and "intuit" solutions (Thackray 1966, 47). Some musicians say they are not aware of thinking; they "just see the movement and hear appropriate sounds . . . [and] allow [their] fingers to play" (Attaway 2000, 35). Yet it would be wrong to conclude that there is no analysis process, however unconscious or "intuitive" it may seem. Even musicians who at first claim they don't intellectualize (such as musician Natalie Gilbert, who said, "If I think about it too much, I can't do it!") eventually admit that there is a process, however sublimated or readily grasped through experience (Gilbert 2003).

The general sequence of gathering, analyzing, and interpreting the requirements for the improvisation seems to be:

I. 1. Watch and analyze the movement demonstration, paying attention to
   2. Tempo and meter
   3. Phrasing and overall form
   4. Dynamic, or energy quality
   5. Sense of weight and "effort quality"
   6. Mood or feeling
   7. Other details, such as specific accents and vertical space level
II. 1. Decide to play according to
   2. Kinesthetic response to movement quality
   3. Feedback
   4. Matching music to movement continuum
   5. Class skill level
   6. Style and genre
   7. Instrumentation
   8. Performance aspect

DISCUSSION OF ANALYSIS: TEMPO AND METER

All dance musicians say that tempo and meter must be the first thing known. "You have to have the tempo and the meter, then how many measures. That's a given!" (Moulton 2003). "If meter and tempo are clear, you can proceed directly to form. If not, there's a nervousness about it. You can't come up with anything" (Beck 2003).

Tempo and meter are usually straightforward, easily picked up from the demonstration (though not always). Tempo remains constant most of the time. Meter usually remains constant, though it is not too rare for it to change within a combination. Also important for the dancer is the *feel* of the meter. A compound meter, for example, has to have the right feeling of "swing"—not a jazz swing, but a modern dance swing, with a heaviness on the first note that makes dancers feel like dropping their weight and then a lightness on the second and third that helps them to rebound and recover from the drop.

PHRASING AND OVERALL FORM

The musical form of a movement combination is determined by counting the number of "dancer's counts"—where one "dancer's count" usually equates to a musician's "bar" (Cavalli 2001, 65ff)—in each movement phrase, then counting the number of phrases for each "side" (most combinations are done with an emphasis on one side of the body, and then repeated to give equal emphasis to the other side), and finally counting the number of repetitions of each side to arrive at the total length. In the case of a combination consisting of four phrases, each nine dancer's counts long, done twice on both sides, the total length of the improvisation will be sixteen phrases of nine bars each, divided into four sections with four phrases in each.

Many musicians closely match the music to the dance form. "If you can help the dancers figure out the form, they can concentrate on executing the details of the movement" (Beck 2003). But a musician sometimes alters the form slightly to challenge the dancers. The improvisation would start and end with the dance, but movement and music phrases might overlap in an attempt to challenge the dancers' sense of timing and musical sophistication, and to work on the relationship between the music and the choreography (see Figure 13.1). In this case, the musician would have to evaluate the class level and the pedagogical purpose of the combination to judge just how much challenge would benefit the class.

At the highest levels of the art, the improvisation generally will last just as long as the dance combination. If the music continues after the dance is finished, there will be formal confusion that undermines the sense of complete performance; and if the music ends too early, the dancers are left unsupported. Dancers and musician have a satisfying performance experience when the music and the dance are correlated in form and phrasing (Cherry 2003).

FIGURE 13.1. Challenging the dancers through phrasing, by first following the dance phrase built on mixed meters and then phrasing across the dance counts.

DYNAMICS, OR ENERGY QUALITY

To interpret the dynamic content of the movement, dance musicians ask themselves questions such as these: How much physical energy does it take to correctly execute the movement? Does this remain constant throughout the combination, or does it change? Do specific beats or phrases within the combination require a sudden shift of energy, or a gradual build-up of energy preparatory to them?

Musicians can use specific techniques to provide dynamic support for the dance, engaging the kinesthetic sense for their artistic application. "Dynamic," to a dancer, roughly equates to energy. "Dynamic," to most musicians, equates to volume. Raising and lowering the volume level *does* have an impact on energy level, yet other techniques are employed as well, such as increasing density, using smaller beat subdivisions, broadening or narrowing tessitura, or increasing syncopation (see Figure 13.2).

SENSE OF WEIGHT AND EFFORT QUALITY

A sense of weight and effort quality are two points of analysis that are determined primarily through kinesthetic sense and rhythmic feel. Weight is a concept with specific meaning in modern dance: a deep connection to the floor and a dropping of the weight of the body into the floor, in contrast to the perception of lightness usually desired in classical ballet. Effort quality is a term reflecting the amount of muscular tension required to perform a movement, combined with its duration (Thackray 1966, 65–67). There are different ways to respond and adapt to this kind of information. Some musicians

© 2006 John Toenjes

FIGURE 13.2. Raising the dynamic level by increasing density, using smaller beat subdivisions, widening tessitura, and increasing syncopation.

might play in a lower register of their instrument to achieve a sense of weight, and some might lead up to the moment of a weight drop with a crescendo and then suddenly back off to a soft dynamic to give the dancers an impulse to drop, not accentuating the drop itself (see Figure 13.3). Some musicians might use both of those solutions within the same improvisation.

There are also many ways to respond kinesthetically to effort qualities. In response to a forceful pushing of the arms over several seconds, a cellist might play a crescendo on a single long note while changing the timbre, say, by digging the bow of the cello so far into the string it begins to scratch; another musician might play progressively shorter note values on the conga drum. Either of these responses is valid, again, as long as it produces the desired result.

MOOD OR FEELING

The task of creating a proper mood for the combination and its place within the overall class opens up even more opportunities for different solutions. For example, in pursuit of a relaxed yet concentrated environment, a lighthearted improvisation might succeed in defusing an overly tense situation, or a more serious tone might bring closure to a humorous moment and help refocus students' attention on the task at hand. Such considerations help to keep the dancers' receptiveness and expended effort at optimal levels. Shaping the feeling of a class through judgment of the dancers' emotional and mind-body states is a function that is part of the roles of inspirational performer and ritual acolyte. An expert musician can gauge the flow and manipulate the overarching musical form of an entire class period to provide an integrated, satisfying dance class experience.

© 2006 John Toenjes

FIGURE 13.3. Influencing the sense of weight by building energy and then suddenly backing off to create an impulse to drop.

THE IMPROVISATION

Once the time comes to play, the musician adopts the receptive and open state of mind that is common to all musical improvisers, while being mindful of the movement analysis. The process then becomes a combination of intellectual and kinesthetic response, tempered and guided by means of a feedback system from musician to dancers and back (with the instructor often in the loop as well) (Cherry 2003) wherein the musician improvises and simultaneously analyzes whether or not the music is helping the dance. Based on that information, the musician either changes the improvisation to something wholly different, or to something different in part, or continues to develop the original idea if it is working well. If the instructor finds that the music is particularly inspiring, or that a certain nuance in the music has exposed some previously unseen aspect of the combination, she might even alter the movement to suit the improvisation. This feedback system is a primary influence on the improvisational process.

THE CONTINUUM OF MATCHING MUSIC TO MOVEMENT

Modern dance has developed a continuum of the relationship of music to dance that ranges from "Mickey Mousing,"[7] that is, a one-to-one relationship of sound to motion, through a general similarity, through counterpoint, to complete independence (a result of the pioneering work of John Cage and Merce Cunningham). All of these aesthetic attitudes can be played with in the improvisation. At times musicians will mirror the movement quite closely, at other times counterpoint it, and, when appropriate, stay independent from it.

The level of complexity of this relationship depends upon the dancers' musical and technical skill. Lower-level classes call for clarity of musical expression and a more direct relationship of music to dance. In higher-level classes, musicians can experiment with different solutions, as advanced dancers can benefit from negotiating more complicated and sophisticated connections. Distinctive details of the combination (see item I.6 in the Movement Analysis section above), such as specific movement accents, can be highlighted to create a direct relationship between music and dance. Emphasizing these particulars can give character and nuance to the improvisation; however, such details are often ignored in order to allow the music to have its own integrity and be a more autonomous partner with the dance.

Here is an example of mirroring a movement sequence with music. Imagine that the dancers have been instructed to reach high up into the air for four counts, strenuously stretching until finally swinging their arms down and bouncing with their knees to curl into a low swing. In response, the pianist might play a rising scale for four counts, building tension through crescendo and restless harmony, and then, at the time of the swing, play a low, loud, harmonically resolving octave in the bass register, followed by an arpeggio moving upward in the middle range to indicate the slight rise and lightness of weight at the end of the swing (see Figure 13.4). Following the movement in this way in terms of vertical space level, dynamic, and weight can inspire melodic and harmonic invention and give a shape to the improvisation that the musician probably would not have chosen without the stimulus of the dance. If done well and with taste, this type of improvisation can be effective. If overdone, it can wear thin and prove to be not a companion but rather a cloying sycophant to the dance.

STYLE AND GENRE

Style and genre are also considered in fashioning the music. Style refers to each musician's personal way of playing, which is adapted to classroom needs. For example, musician Claudia Queen likes to support the dancers with a full sound and different instrumental timbres consisting of many rhythmic subdivisions, crescendos, and filler notes, so that the dancers can "ride and fly on that magic carpet." She feels that her style "relaxes the dancers so that they can work efficiently. This helps to take the tension out of the muscles, and the dancers can be more confident because they can depend on [this full sound]" (Queen 2003). Others might employ a sparser approach that none-

FIGURE 13.4. Improvisation that musically mirrors the described choreography.

theless achieves the desired results. As dance musicians gain experience, they develop their own personal styles that work for them in the dance class.

Musical genre is sometimes chosen for its direct effect upon the dancers. Some musicians improvise in the style of a specific genre such as "impressionist" or "barrel house blues," as a way to bring out culture-based movement qualities. "What musical world am I going to play in, and how will that affect this movement?" asks musician Bill Moulton. "[Genre] can affect lots of qualities in the dancers' movements, for example, lightness and buoyancy through Baroque [music]. This also gives a sense of an ordered world [which has an] actual physical effect on the dancers" (2003). Playing in different genres is also an intellectual challenge that many dance musicians enjoy as a way to keep their improvisations fresh and to provide variety, again with the aim of shaping an entire class period (Cherry 2003).

INSTRUMENTATION

The instruments predominantly in use in dance studios today are the piano and drums (ranging from djembe to congas to trap sets, often augmented by miscellaneous small percussion), with some electronic instruments being used as well. Some dance musicians play just one instrument, some play a combination of them, and some sing while they play. Different sounds provide a variety of textures that can help shape the class by providing welcome variety. However, the choice of instrumentation is often based on how a specific timbre will affect the dancing. For example, the lack of harmonic direction and complex melodies in the drums can leave room for dancers to more freely interpret a combination. And a small drum's piercing staccato might be ideal for eliciting a sharp attack from dancers in a quick *degagé* exercise. A lyrical combination, however, might beg for a long melodic line. In this case, a percussionist might sing or play a flute while drumming. Any subtle, expert improviser will have his own methods of effecting this. But musicians who can move from one instrument to another (I have witnessed musicians in the studio play the accordion, electric guitar, cello, violin, and all sorts of homemade percussion) can pick timbres that most readily achieve the desired kinesthetic effect.

PERFORMANCE ASPECT OF THE CLASS

Dance musicians improvise with the goal of inspiring artistry in the dancers, making the class a performance in and of itself. This is simultaneously an emotionally fulfilling experience and a way to train dancers for performance rigors. And many musicians feel that the class is *their* regular outlet for performance, which heightens the intensity of the music making (Beck 2003; Kaplan 2003; Schenk 2003). With only a few minutes to plan each improvisation, dance musicians feel like they are on the spot, and so their music takes on a special urgency. Yet the repetition and the sense of safety of being part of the ritual takes the edge off the performance, which allows the musician to ease into a receptive state for a free flow of musical ideas (Moulton 2003; Beck 2003). Awkwardness or wrong turns in the spirit of experimentation are tolerated, as long as the primary goals of supporting the dance and fitting into the ritual space are not undermined.

CONCLUSION

In this article I have analyzed and attempted to demystify the process skilled musicians use to improvise in the modern dance class. Interviews and observations revealed a consensus of thought and approach, which nonetheless results in a wide variety of sounds and solutions. But in listening to this music, whatever one might hear going from class to class would be related in that the nature of each improvisation is governed by the consideration of how musical elements relate to the dance, and could be appreciated in terms of how the kinesthetic sense of each musician is expressed within the context of each of the roles he or she plays in the class. This interaction among specific musical elements, personalities, and demands particular to the modern dance class is what distinguishes this music's socializing and educational value, while its imperatives of musical originality and the ability to inspire extramusical creativity make it a rich study in the context of music making and art.

NOTES

1. This paper is an attempt to elucidate the art of improvising in the modern dance class as it is currently widely practiced. However, other dance traditions are now being folded into and influencing the modern dance class, including contact improvisation, Afro-Caribbean, and hip-hop, as well as theater arts. Already these influences are affecting the blend of dance techniques and vocabulary in the class and, consequently, musical considerations such as instrumentation, style, and genre. How they affect the overall concept of the modern dance class will be seen in time, of course.

2. A "modern dancer" in this usage is one who considers himself or herself to be part of the modern dance movement and tradition, as opposed to being a generic term for anyone dancing in the current day.

3. The term "accompanist" is not used here, as this implies a subsidiary role. The

term "dance musician" acknowledges the musician's unique and important role in the dance class. The use of this term is promoted by the International Guild of Musicians in Dance, an organization founded by a group of these artists.

4. It is not unheard of for a stage score to be developed from an improvisation originating in the classroom.

5. Most musicians interviewed for this article enthusiastically supported the notion that improvising for the modern dance class is a specialized art form and should be recognized as such.

6. Currently there are at least two degree-granting programs in playing music for dance—one at Shenandoah University, Winchester, Virginia, and one at the University of Arizona, Tucson. However, struggling through untutored experiences in the studio is the typical means of learning this art, as attested to by all the musicians interviewed.

7. "Mickey Mousing" is a somewhat pejorative term that references cartoons where the movements of animated characters are closely linked to the sound track (Teck 1994, 86).

REFERENCES

Attaway, Larry A., ed. 2000. "Improvisation: A Cyber Chat." *International Guild of Musicians in Dance Journal* 6:22–42.

Beck, Ken (Staff Musician, Department of Dance, University of Illinois at Urbana-Champaign). 2003. Interview by John Toenjes.

Cavalli, Harriet. 2001. *Dance and Music: A Guide to Dance Accompaniment for Musicians and Dance Teachers.* Gainesville: University Press of Florida

Cherry, Christian (Music Director, Dance Department, University of Oregon). 2003. Interview by John Toenjes.

Gilbert, Natalie (Director of Music, American Dance Festival). 2003. Interview by John Toenjes.

Hook, Sara (Associate Professor, Department of Dance, University of Illinois, Urbana-Champaign). 2002. Testimonial written for author's grant application to University of Illinois Provost's Office Teaching Advancement Board. Unpublished document.

Kaplan, Robert (Music Director, Dance Department, Arizona State University). 2003. Interview by John Toenjes.

Lehovec, Linda (Associate Professor, Department of Dance, University of Illinois, Urbana-Champaign). 2002. Testimonial written for author's grant application to University of Illinois Provost's Office Teaching Advancement Board. Unpublished document.

Moulton, William (Music Director, Dance Department, New York University). 2003. Interview by John Toenjes.

Queen, Claudia. (Music Director, Dance Department, Western Michigan University). 2003. Interview by John Toenjes.

Schenk, Richard (Composer and Staff Musician, Dance Department, Connecticut College). 2003. Interview by John Toenjes.

Teck, Katherine. 1994. *Ear Training for the Body: A Dancer's Guide to Music.* Pennington, N.J.: Princeton.

Thackray, Rupert M. 1966. *Playing for Dance.* London: Novello.

PART 3

CREATION

ᔢ 14 ᔢ

REPRESENTATIONS OF MUSIC MAKING

Stephen Blum

In contemplating the concept of musical improvisation, we need not only to consider how others have talked about our subject, but also to ask why many have evidently felt no need to talk about it. Those questions lead to the larger issues of how people structure their representations of music making and what purposes are served by the representations—topics that are equally pertinent to other modes of performance, such as drama, oratory, and (when experienced as performance) calligraphy and painting.

A MARKED TERM

In several areas of Western musical life over the past two centuries, two activities have often been specified as what musicians generally do: composition of a work intended for performance at a later date, and performance of a composition learned in advance—often called simply *composition* and *performance.* Used in this way both words function as unmarked terms in relation to the marked term *improvisation*—and when improvisation is defined as "composition during performance" or "composition in real time," it is explicitly distinguished from both unmarked terms.[1] The Jammy awards, initiated four years ago, are marked in relation to the Grammies, which have been around for almost half a century. People can use *composition, performance,* and *pop music* as unmarked terms when they wish to assert that some property implied by the marked term *improvisation* is absent, but also when they prefer to leave open the question of that property's presence or absence;[2] an announcement that a certain musician will perform her compositions at a particular venue does not signify that she will *not* be improvising. Nonetheless, everyday usage in many institutions of musical life continues to favor the restricted senses in which composition and performance are understood to exclude improvisation unless otherwise specified. That practice has made it easy to associate improvised music making with other markedness relations that articulate perceived differences of class, race, ethnicity, or gender. For example, sexists of the past who denied that women are capable of composing were generally more willing to grant them the ability to improvise. Influential German-speaking musicologists have argued that the idea of composition is best limited to the European practices involving notation to which the term was first applied in the 15th century, and one corollary of that argument is the suggestion—which I for one reject—that *improvisation* is a more useful term than *composition* in studies of non-European music.[3]

The differences that, for many people, have characterized these three fields and their associated roles—composer, performer, improviser—make up a system of representations centered around ideas of originality, works, notation, memory, and spontaneity. That system is a reliable source of judgments that recycle received ideas and lead people to miss out on what's happening. It encapsulates a narrative that can be briefly summarized as follows: composers produce original works, which they notate so that performers will present them in a convincing manner that may well convey an impression of spontaneity, especially when soloists or conductors perform from memory. Improvisers need not produce or remember "works," but according to the criteria of this system their music, too, should sound original as well as spontaneous. The criteria for evaluating the talents and accomplishments of individuals with an emphasis on "originality" provide a basis for identifying and promoting "stars" in all three fields.

Despite the fact that people in many parts of the world have felt inclined, even obliged, to define their acts as musicians with reference to this set of three categories, the contrasts implicit in this system are not always the most pertinent ones for understanding what musicians do in our conservatories and music departments, much less in the rest of the world.[4] The papers collected in this volume offer plenty of reasons for replacing this system with better sets of categories. A musician in an improvising ensemble can respond to events without necessarily noticing who has produced them and with no desire to demonstrate "originality" or some other merit (see Wilson 1999, 21, 31).

To the extent that the restricted senses of composition and performance became normative, people were increasingly inclined to describe too many alternatives as "improvisation," and this created a need for more specialized terms such as *aleatoric music, indeterminacy, happening,* and *open form* (see Feisst 1997; Rivest 2001). George Lewis (1996, 99–100) and Anthony Braxton have argued convincingly that white musicians in the United States found some of the specialized terms useful in their efforts to distinguish what they were doing from what African American musicians were doing. Some folklorists and music historians adopted the term *oral composition* (Lord 1960;

Treitler 1974) in response to the strong association between composition and notation, and ethnomusicologists have repeatedly asked if performers "really improvise" in one or another practice (e.g., Sutton 1998: "Do Javanese Musicians Improvise?").[5]

DIFFERENCES IN PERCEPTION AND EXPERIENCE

One way to circumvent the limitations of the system that treats improvisation as a marked category is to decide that *all* music is improvised in one way or another. That's the basic thesis of Bruce Ellis Benson in his book *The Improvisation of Musical Dialogue: A Phenomenology of Music* (2003). Benson's case centers on the second noun in his title, *dialogue*. In his conception, we improvise when we engage in any kind of dialogue with music of our predecessors or contemporaries as we compose or perform. Benson argues effectively against false conceptions of composition and performance that fail to take into account the kinds of interaction musicians engage in. He lists 11 "forms and degrees that improvisation may take," moving from "'filling in' certain details that are not notated in the score" to improvising on "the rules and expectations of a tradition." He is quick to add that his typology is far from exhaustive, inasmuch as "there are many senses and levels of improvisation" (26–30).

In this respect Benson's position as a phenomenologist interested above all in Western classical music and jazz approaches that of Bruno Nettl, who writes as a well-informed ethnomusicologist (1991, 4), "Performance practice is always in some respects an improvisatory process, and the musical thinking that goes into composition surely must always have at least a bit of the kind of thinking that goes into improvisation." The crucial difference is that Nettl's more nuanced position avoids the claim that to make music is *fundamentally* to improvise in one way or another. Usage of the term *improvisation* continues to be motivated by desires to discuss *differences* that people perceive and experience in our ways of making and interpreting music. If, as Nettl predicts (1998, 16), "we will increasingly have to look at improvisation as a group of perhaps very different phenomena," we should take his advice to study each of those phenomena "in the context of other musical processes and of cultural values and principles among which it lives" in specific communities (1991, 4). What musicians do acquires much of its meaning from what they might have done, but didn't. Different sequences of action are associated with specific roles that people adopt in performing or in preparing for performances, and people can refer to such differences in all kinds of ways—often just by naming a performance genre, or a venue where performers and listeners know what to expect.

Before the late 18th century, speakers of European languages distinguished the types of performance we now treat as improvisation by means of adverbs, adjectives, verbs, and nouns for specific genres or agents—such as the Italian *improvvisatori* who produced extemporaneous verses and the Italian distinction between "premeditated" and "improvised" theatre (Perrucci [1699] 1961). Evidently it was sufficient to mark specific types of activity as "improvised" as opposed to being carried out according to some other set of expectations, and no comprehensive term was needed. To the best of my knowledge, the generalizing noun *improvisation* and its cognates in other languages did not appear in print before the late 1790s (see Blum 1998; Bandur 2002).

The tripartite system of representations outlined above was firmly in place at the beginning of the 20th century. It served as a basis for Kandinsky's typology of three types of painting at the very same time that prominent European musicians were attempting to undermine or deconstruct it.[6] One strategy, adopted by the composer-pianist Ferruccio Busoni and the theorist Heinrich Schenker, is to insist that successful acts of composition are improvisatory (see Rink 1993 on Schenker).[7] That view is consistent with Freud's argument, in *The Interpretation of Dreams* ([1900] 2000), that "we are probably unduly inclined to overvalue the conscious character of intellectual and artistic production" rather than accepting at face value the statements of highly productive men that "what is essential and novel in their creations was given to them all of a sudden and was almost complete as they became aware of it."[8] A different strategy, commonly used by improvising musicians in the second half of the 20th century, is to argue that improvisation opens up possibilities that are not available in the process of composing.

Busoni described musical notation as "an ingenious device for capturing an improvisation, in order to allow for its rebirth" ([1916] 1974, 26).[9] In his conception, musicians should be highly interactive readers of notations, capable of reading the signs with reference to a creative process and responding appropriately.[10] On July 26, 1909, Busoni devoted six hours to making a "concertante transcription" (*Konzertmässige Interpretation*) for piano of Schoenberg's Piano Piece Op. 11, no. 2. In a prefatory note intended for the publication of his version, he remarked that performing the piece "demands of the player the greatest refinement of touch and pedalling; intimate, improvised, 'gliding,' perspicacious interpretation; affectionate immersion in its content" (1987, 398).[11] Busoni's transcription extends the duration of several harmonies and redistributes them throughout the piano's register.

For Busoni, as for millions of other musicians throughout human history, a normal relationship between two musicians involves the revision of the first musician's composition by the second. My favorite statement of this kind of relationship is the definition of melody attributed to the great 'Abbasid court musician Ishāq al-Mawsili, who died in 850 C.E.: "melodies are texts made by men and edited [or revised] by women."[12] Arabic commentaries on that definition mention such familiar techniques of editing as shortening the parts that are too long, and lengthening the parts that are too short—procedures that are evident in Busoni's numerous transcriptions. This relationship— someone makes a text or a plan in the expectation that others will alter it—has often been understood as allowing for improvisation in the making or editing of the text or plan, without necessarily requiring it.[13] Sometimes the editing is simply taken for granted as what performers do, and whether they do it before or during performance may not matter.

PHASES OF A CREATIVE PROCESS

Who performs what action at which moment in a conventional sequence is one of the main questions addressed in accounts of music making. Some systems of representation do not specify types of performers but simply list actions or events that are expected to transpire before, during, and after a performance; Figure 14.1 compares the sequences posited by Busoni and Ishāq al-Mawsili. Given enough accounts in a particular language of how people have made music, we can often detect an underlying scheme that defines an appropriate sequence of events (for a good example, see Rouget 1996, 233–36).

Busoni (1866–1924), *Entwurf einer neuen Ästhetik der Tonkunst*, 2nd ed. (Leipzig, 1916)

phase
1 musician improvises
2   improvisation captured in notation
3   improvisation reborn through appropriate responses to notated signs

Ishāq al-Mawsili (d. 850 CE), as quoted by later writers

phase
1 male musician creates melody
2   (he teaches the melody to a female musician)
3   the woman revises and renews the melody

FIGURE 14.1. Two models of music making.

Sequences that are normal are for that reason unmarked and may not need to be described in abstract terms so long as they remain unchallenged.

What may be the oldest such scheme to reach us is outlined in a well-known passage from the Chinese *Book of Documents* (Karlgren 1950), two versions of which were developed in the second century B.C.E. Figure 14.2 summarizes this scheme in Karlgren's translation: "Poetry expresses the mind, the song is a (drawing-out) chanting of its words, the notes depend upon (the mode of) the chanting, the pitch-pipes harmonize the notes" (1950, 7).[14] In other versions of this sequence the achievement of harmony (via the chain of transformations from intent to poem to song to harmonized notes) is

---

Shu ching, Book of Documents (two versions developed in 2nd century BCE)
Poetry expresses the mind, the song is a (drawing-out =) chanting of (its) words, the notes depend upon (the mode of) the chanting, the pitch-pipes harmonize the notes.   (Eng. trans. from Karlgren 1950: 7)

Li chi, Record of Rites (compiled 2nd century BCE), from ch. 27, *Yüeh chi*, Classic of Music:
[37.4a-b] As to every kind of tone [*yin*] – it is something that arises from the human heart. Feeling is moved inwardly; thus it takes shape in sound. Sound forms a pattern, and we call it 'tone.' For this reason the tone of a well-governed era is joyous and thereby peaceful. Its government is harmonious. The music of a disordered era is angry and thereby [expresses] resentment. Its government is perverse. . . . [37.8a] So one investigates sounds in order to know the tone; investigates tones in order to know music; investigates music in order to know government.   (Eng. trans. from Saussy 1993: 86, 88)

Ta-hsü [Great Preface] to the *Shih ching*, Book of Odes (25 CE):
Feeling is moved inwardly and takes form in speech. It is not enough to speak, so one sighs [the words]; it is not enough to sigh, so one draws them out and sings them; it is not enough to draw them out and sing them, so without one's willing it, one's hands dance and one's feet stamp. . . .   (ibid., 77)

Commentary on the Great Preface by K'ung Ying-ta (574-648):
what is in the heart is intent, once out of the mouth it is speech; words intoned are poetry, notes chanted are song; and when these [notes] have been distributed among the eight [kinds of instrumental] sounds, we call the result music. The differences among these are merely a matter of sequence, [different stages being] differently named. . . .   (ibid., 77-8)

FIGURE 14.2. Four versions of an ancient Chinese sequence.

understood as a sign of good government (see Saussy 1993, 63–65, 73–105). Those who wished to interpret songs as evidence of the singers' or composers' mental or spiritual state could follow the scheme in reverse, from what was heard back to the presumed stimulus.

Stories about the creation of specific compositions could flesh out this scheme—for example, by stating that a composer had first given form to an idea in a poem and had then found appropriate notes.[15] Starting with the mental or emotional experiences that are presumed to initiate a creative process, it is easy to construct stories of spontaneous music making inspired by strong emotion. A notated piece for the gu qin (seven-string zither) called *Xiaohujia* (Little Barbarian Horn) is said to have been composed by Dong Tinglan in the eighth century of our era, as a representation of music made six centuries earlier by Cai Wenji when she was moved by music played on the hujia horn of her barbarian kidnappers and made her own horn of bamboo leaves (see Yung 1997, 14–15, 45–59). As qin players develop their own ways of realizing notated works in performance, through the process known as da pu, they reflect on the implications of stories about the origins of the pieces, which are printed alongside the notations. Interpreting *Xiaohujia*, a player can imaginatively re-create the experience of an eighth-century composer attempting a representation of a second-century woman's spontaneous music making.

This story neatly illustrates what may be a rather common motive for talking about improvisation: the desire to imagine the spontaneous creation of music by someone else—perhaps from the distant past, or maybe on the other side of the tracks or south of the border, where people are said to have fewer inhibitions.[16] People speak of unpremeditated music making both as an activity we experience firsthand and as an activity we imagine happening at some remove from our own current circumstances.

The ancient Chinese scheme outlined in Figure 14.2 can be compared with European schemes describing the invention, assessment, distribution, and working out of ideas that were transferred from the pedagogy of rhetoric first to the visual arts (Baxandall 1971) and subsequently to music (Kirkendale 1979). Figure 14.3a summarizes the account of musical composition given by the author Lampadius in a textbook first published in 1537, to which Edward Lowinsky (1948) drew attention in his studies of the early use of scores.[17] Figure 14.3b outlines an argument made by Vasari in the biography of Titian written for the 1568 edition of his *Lives*: artists can proceed successfully from idea to finished painting only by drawing or sketching their "inventions" in order to judge these with their own eyes; judging one's sketches is necessary because artists are unable to visualize their inventions perfectly without the aid of their eyes (Vasari [1568] 1981, 427).[18] The relation of judgment to invention is central to both schemes, but Vasari insisted upon use of the eyes whereas Lampadius evidently assumed that composers don't need their ears or their eyes to recognize notes that should be removed from a phrase (*clausula*). Presumably, they continue to exercise judgment as they move on to the next stage, "working out" (*exercitatio*), which according to Lampadius does involve notation (see Owens 1997, 66–67). Sequences of three to five verbs or verbal nouns—such as the model *excogitare / iuditio perpendere / exercitare = in ordinem distribuere*, which we can extract from Lampadius— are rather common in European writings on musical composition from the 16th through the 19th centuries (Bent 1984 gives several examples). Some writers on rhetoric, following Quintilian, viewed judgment as inseparable from invention, and some made it a separate stage, just as Lampadius did. C.P.E. Bach's explanations of the principles that keyboardists should apply in accompanying, improvising, composing, and performing existing works show that he understood invention to be formed by judgment. Bach's statement that a keyboardist improvising a fantasia must decide "whether to take many digressions (Umwege) or none at all" (Bach 1762, 335) implies that either decision immediately produces a framework (*Gerippe*) that can be expressed as a figured bass.

Ernst Gombrich regarded Vasari's argument as the earliest formulation of an issue that Gombrich explored in his writings on the relationships between intention and feedback, and between what he called commitment and improvisation on the part of an artist. In Gombrich's view, Leonardo da Vinci's advice that artists emulate the readiness of poets to cross out lines when that would improve their poems "struck at the heart of established workshop practice" by proposing a new relationship between the artist's intention— which would formerly have been the reproduction of a conventional scheme but might now involve exploration of an original idea—and the feedback the artist receives as his or her hand moves in ways that may not fully conform to the initial intention ([1989] 1991, 103). Assessing any result of what Gombrich calls the hand's improvisations, an artist might choose "to follow the suggestion he owes to chance and to look for unintended effects" (102) rather than correcting unintended results of the hand's movements that were not compatible with a conventional scheme. In Gombrich's words, Leonardo had warned artists not "to tie their creative process down to their original commitment" but rather "to leave the possibility for corrections open to the very last moment." Associated with this advice was the maxim "Do not articulate

A.

Lampadius, *Compendium musices, tam figurati quàm plani cantus ad formam dialogi* (Bern, 1541; first ed. 1537)

phase
1 CONTRIVE notable phrases in one's mind
2   WEIGH these judiciously
3   proceed to WORKING OUT

"Sic etiam oportet Componistam prius quasdam, in animo, clausulas, sed optimas, excogitare, & quodam iuditio easdem perpendere, nè aliqua nota totam vitiet clausulam, & auditorum aures taediosas faciat. Deinde, ad exercitationem accedere, hoc est, excogitatas clausulas, in ordinem quendam distribuere, & eas, quae videntur aptiores servare."

E. Lowinsky's translation as adapted by Owens (1997: 66–67): "so also the composer ought first to think out in his mind musical phrases, indeed very good ones, and to consider them carefully with good judgment lest one note ruin the whole phrase and tire the ears of the listener, and then proceed to the working out, that is, to distribute in a certain order the phrases that have been thought out, and to save those phrases that seem more suitable."

B.

Vasari, *Le vite de' piu eccellenti pittori, scultori ed architettori*, 2nd ed., 1568 (new ed. of 1906, repr. Florence, 1981), biography of Titian:

phase
1 INVENTIONS in artist's imagination
2   DEMONSTRATION of conception to eyes of body
3   which assist in making a good JUDGMENT

"disegnare in carta . . . è necessario a chi vuol bene disporre i componimenti, ed accomodare l'invenzioni, ch' e' fa bisogno prima in più modi differenti porle in carta, per vedere come il tutto torna insieme. Conciosiachè l'idea non può vedere nè immaginare perfettamente in sè stessa l'invenzioni, se non apre e non mostra il suo concetto agli occhi corporali che l'aiutino a farne buon giudizio"

G. de Vere's translation: "for him who wishes to distribute his compositions and accomodate his inventions well, it is necessary that he should first put them down on paper in several different ways, in order to see how the whole goes together, for the reason that the eye is not able to see or imagine the inventions perfectly within herself, if she does not reveal and demonstrate her conception to the eyes of the body, that these may assist her to form a good judgment"

FIGURE 14.3. Two conceptions of the invention-judgment-distribution relationship.

too much," given that "confused things rouse the mind to new inventions"
(103–5; [1954] 1966, 60–61).[19]

The notion of improvisation that Gombrich derived from Leonardo's
writings centers on readiness to respond creatively to our perceptions of
configurations, often complex ones, that deviate from anything we might
have anticipated.[20] The situations of artists who receive visual and tactile
feedback as they manipulate utensils are not unlike those of musicians who
receive aural as well as visual and tactile feedback as they perform. Musicians
can't imagine in advance precisely how relationships among the partials of a
complex sound will change as the sound decays, how the sound will resonate
in the performance space, or how it will be perceived at various locations. In
response to feedback of this kind, musicians commonly make adjustments
in their production of sound, whether they are improvising or not. Yet the
meanings created by these adjustments, as well as the nature of the musicians' commitment to preexisting models and their understanding of how
their actions relate to those of others, are decisive factors for those who wish
to distinguish improvised performance from other types.

WELCOMING THE UNEXPECTED

Perhaps a short list of three necessary conditions for improvisation might
serve as a framework for comparing different practices: (1) performers who
are improvising respond to cues or feedback received in the course of performance; (2) sequences of cues and responses whose timing might have
been anticipated can be distinguished from cues received at unpredictable
moments, to which more than one response is possible; and (3) the balance
leans more toward unpredictable events than it would in another manner
of performance understood to be dominated by cues and responses whose
timing might have been anticipated.[21] Other performers, audience members,
instruments or implements, weather conditions, and the performers' own
physical and mental systems are all potential sources of pertinent cues and
feedback during performances. In situations where conditions (2) and (3) obtain, it is likely that interactions or events that prepare performers to improvise rather than to do something else will have preceded the performance.

These three necessary conditions are presumed to apply to other areas
of activity in which terms pertinent to the consideration of musical performances have been used, as well as to music making. Among the results of
such activities are improvised verses of poets, improvised speeches of orators,
improvised words and gestures of actors, improvised strokes of calligraphers

and painters, and improvised movements of dancers, athletes, and warriors. In various times and places, people have been interested in relationships between one or more of these categories and some other kind of performance, not necessarily improvised. The eighth-century painter Wu Tao-tsu is said to have asked General P'ei Min to perform a sword dance so that "the sight of its vigor might aid me in wielding my brush," and right after the dance Wu completed a painting "in no time . . . as though he had the help of some divinity" (Bush and Shih 1985, 64).

Terminology has often been transferred from one area to another—for example from rhetoric to painting and music making in Europe, from music theory to literary criticism in China (DeWoskin 1983, 189). But words are not always necessary in order for people to sense an affinity between, say, a calligrapher's strokes and the movements of a dancer or an instrumentalist. With little or no use of words, people may come to understand the respects in which different genres of poetry, oratory, acting, calligraphy, painting, dancing, singing, and playing instruments require, permit, or preclude one or another manner of improvising. It is often self-evident to participants that the success of a performance depends on what *we* call improvisation—perhaps to a greater extent in one genre than in another, or in one area of activity than in another. A dancer who is expected to improvise her movements might dismiss out of hand the notion of improvised painting, but neither a painter nor anyone else is likely to deny the possibility of improvised dancing.

The extent to which people expect the unexpected, and the ways in which they recognize it, are important variables in the systems of relationships among fields of activity and genres of performance that they take for granted—or that they challenge and seek to alter. An account of challenges that affected several fields of artistic activity in the United States after World War II is offered by Daniel Belgrad in his book *The Culture of Spontaneity: Improvisation and the Arts in Postwar America* (1998).[22] For other parts of the world, studies of interrelationships among several fields of activity and performance genres, with specific reference to improvisation, are few and far between.

Several questions apply to all of the fields we classify as "the arts." What sources of feedback do improvisers seek out, or otherwise encounter, and how do they interact with those sources? What kinds of preparation are thought to be necessary, carried out over what spans of time? According to Margaret Kartomi (2002, 21), puppet masters in Sulawesi and Java prepare for the multiple responsibilities they must meet during an all-night performance by meditating for hours in order to acquire "mystical power over . . . body and mind," which gives them, in Kartomi's words, "a god-like freedom to add musical ornamentation and textual allusion to [their] performances to suit the needs of the moment."

In contrast, many improvised performances are motivated by a desire to abandon, in the company of intimate friends, the kinds of control needed for some other manner of performance. Among the best examples are the gatherings at which Chinese scholars drank wine as they produced poems and paintings, perhaps to mark the departure of a friend. The script called wild cursive (*k'uang-ts'ao*), which gained popularity during the T'ang dynasty, was thought to be "commonly performed when the writer was inebriated" (Harrist and Fong 1999, xvii). When accounts of the circumstances in which texts or paintings were created are joined to the texts or paintings themselves, as has often been the case, reimagining those circumstances is potentially a vital part of a listener's or a spectator's aesthetic experience. Moreover, no supplementary information is needed for one to recognize, say, different degrees of pressure that an artist may have applied in drawing, painting, or writing: certain strokes will appear to have been produced quite rapidly (however lengthy the relevant period of preparation may have been).

In addition to the altered states attained by puppet masters through solo meditation and by Chinese scholars through shared inebriation, what other altered states are deliberately sought for purposes of improvising? In which cases, if any, should we also say that shamans who "choose to enter dissociated or semi-dissociated states" (Pegg 2001, 388) are also preparing to improvise?[23] That question links studies of musical and of dramatic improvisation. Speaking of Mongolian shamans, Carole Pegg observes that "the practitioner's performance is oral and is dramatized and improvised according to whether the ceremony is for healing, advice on hunting or divination" (388). A shaman and other participants in a ceremony might have little or no awareness of its dramatized or improvised aspects, inasmuch as shamans who seek to become the vehicles of spirits—like singers who receive songs in visions or performers who wish to serve as "the composer's voice"—understand their personal responsibility for the outcome of a performance in relation to an overriding source of authority. It may be most appropriate to speak of improvisation when performers are aware of making *personal* responses to emerging situations, which they would regard as permissible or even obligatory within the terms of whatever relationships they might wish to maintain with a given source of authority or of support. Some shamans have clearly found it possible to dramatize such personal responses.

The respects in which performers are aware of the presence of others, and the ways they dramatize those types and degrees of awareness, are variables whose importance for all studies of performance emerges clearly from the scholarly literature on improvisation. It is always appropriate, but not always easy, for ethnographers of performance to list the dramatis personae and indicate how each responds to each of the others.

TWO FAMILIES OF TERMS

Much of the terminology people use in talking about performance allows for dimensions or features we associate with improvisation. Two immense families seem most pertinent. The first is made up of terms for exchanges among participants, often though not always compared to conversation or dialogue. These include terms for instrumentalists' responses to vocalists, terms for the actions of soloists as they emerge from a relatively constant background, and terms associated with the countless performance genres that center on sung poetry exchanged between two or more partners or competitors. At the center of the second family are words for *path, road, itinerary*, and *way*, and the words for *story* that emphasize a narrative line.[24] Although neither group of terms is limited to improvisatory practices, many figures of speech in both groups carry strong associations with unscripted activities even when they are used with reference to relatively fixed structures—as in likening a string quartet to a conversation.[25] Words in the second family may have proven themselves useful precisely because of their flexibility in pointing variously to well-trodden paths, to newly discovered or newly created trails, and to odd combinations of the familiar and the freshly hewn (Blum 2001, 187). In speaking about one or another path, musicians can evoke powerful memories or anticipations of the time and effort required to discern and follow that path's course, with or without digressions, pauses, or changes of pace.

Some of the entities that are called paths are understood as models for performance, and some are understood as unique creations produced in the course of performance. In his well-known study of the vocal genres of the Kaluli people of Papua New Guinea, Steven Feld (1982) devotes a full chapter to the genre *gisalo*, which requires the lead singer to outline a path (*tok*) that will connect places associated with the person whose death he is lamenting, in a manner that activates his listeners' familiarity with these places. This requirement guarantees that each performance will be unique. In contrast, the itineraries followed by the ancestors who emerged from the earth during the time that Australian Aborigines call The Dreaming are thought to be accurately represented by the ordering of songs into fixed sequences, or "songlines."

These examples, from Papua New Guinea and Australia, serve to illustrate two of the most common motivations for making music: the need to mourn the passing of a unique individual and the need to preserve portions of the wisdom and power acquired by ancestors—in other words, a topicality constraint and a preservation constraint—which are often perceived as simultaneously present to varying degrees. Probably most of the entities that are called paths or ways consist neither of a unique way of connecting well-known locations nor of a fixed sequence of stages. The *idea* of a fixed sequence of songs is entirely compatible with a performance practice that allows or even requires performers to treat individual songs differently from one performance to the next. Likewise, the *idea* of finding a unique way in which to lament or praise someone does not exclude advance planning.

A musical practice that richly exploits multiple applications of a word for *road* is that of the Türkmen bard known as bagşy, who will shape an entire evening's performance around a theoretical conception of interlocking paths. The word *yol* (which means "road" in many Turkic languages, and also "journey" and "rule") designates any of several types of musical paths, as Zeranska-Kominek (1998), the leading scholar of Türkmen music, has shown. One type is the specialization chosen as the bagşy's vocation, which is either the path of stories or that of song. Another is the regional style, now most often distinguished as northeastern or southeastern. Each story is a journey, and so is each performance, whether it consists of a sequence of songs or concentrates on a single story. By developing a theoretical system with multiple applications of the word *yol*, Türkmen musicians retain the word's powerful associations with "shamans' ecstatic journeys to the other world" (Zeranska-Kominek 1998, 265). The bagşy may prepare for the journey of performance by taking opium. A song sung at the unpredictable moment when he or she finds the right path and the performance becomes inspired is also called *yol* (270–71). Retuning the bagşy's long-necked lute to a higher pitch level is a common way of marking various stages along the journey, and the ambitus of songs expands as the basic pitch rises, so that the bagşy moves from songs with a narrow range to those with the widest range. Each song is likewise a path, understood as a sequence of melodic segments in contrasting ranges.

The bards of northeastern Iran, neighbors of the Türkmen bagşy, exploit multiple meanings of a pair of terms meaning "question and answer." Figure 14.4 lists some of the situations that are described as exchanges of questions and answers by these bards, who are called baxši. Situations (1) and (2) are examples of improvised exchanges, whereas (3) and (4) are performances of texts that represent spontaneous exchanges.

Two baxši-s, each holding his instrument – a long-necked lute with two strings called *dutār* – sit face-to-face and answer one another's questions until one of them gains the upper hand (*bālā-dast*) when his opponent is unable to respond.

A master (*ustād*) gives instruction (*dars ta'lim*) "in phrases of this question-answer [format] (*dar ebārat-e hamuň sowāl-e javāb*)" to the pupils who are sitting before him, using poems that illustrate the format well, such as "29 Letters" (*Bist o now huruf*); two pupils may sit face-to-face and exchange questions and answers until one gains the upper hand.

In addition to "29 Letters," other poems in the baxši repertoire are structured as exchanges of questions and answers – for example, a debate between earth and sky, which is settled when God tells the sky not to boast of being superior to the earth.

In the Turkic narratives that constitute the heart of the baxši repertoire, two lovers who are sitting face-to-face may exchange questions and responses. "Apart from them, no one else [in the stories] asks such questions." Exchanges of this kind occur in the stories of *Karam and Asli, Tāher and Zohre, Ma'sum and Afruzpari, Šāh Bahrām and Banu Hosne Parizād*, among others. Like the earth and the sky in their debate, the lovers who exchange strophes are doing what a baxši has also learned how to do: they sing in response to song, using conventional melody types.

FIGURE 14.4. Four situations involving exchanges of question (*sowāl*) and answer (*javāb*), as described by one baxši in Iranian Xorasan.

In other regions of central Asia, long sequences of improvised verses exchanged between competitors are memorized and performed on subsequent occasions (Reichl 1992, 107). Paired terms equivalent to "question" and "answer," "statement" and "response," or "departure" and "return" are widely used in discussing performances of soloists that are to some extent improvised (see Čelebiev 1989, 141–44, on the Azerbaijani muğam; Slobin 1976, 144, on instrumental music of northern Afghanistan).

Attempts to describe the models used in musical improvisation have perhaps tended more toward representation of itineraries than toward representation of interactions. Important exceptions are Tullia Magrini's pathbreaking analyses (1986, 1998) of the "collective overall plans" that guide members of certain groups as they make music.

ATTENDING TO ALTERNATIVES

In his writings on mode, Harold Powers (1980, 1989) draws attention to
confusions arising from what he called the "internationalization" of that
European concept in the 20th century. As musicologists subsumed numerous technical terms in Asian languages under the general rubric of "mode,"
that term was, in Powers's words (1989, 42), "reified into a concept, as though
'mode/modal/modality' were a thing-in-itself, variously manifested in different musical cultures." With that history in mind, we can avoid a similar
reification of "improvisation" that would inspire us to look for its manifestations in different cultures. This is the essence of Bruno Nettl's advice in the
remark quoted above; my tentative list of three necessary conditions for
improvisation may go too far toward reifying the concept.

Attention to what writers and speakers in various circles have understood
as the alternatives to "modality" or "improvisation" is a first step in avoiding
an indiscriminate extension of either term; the same holds true for discussions of "creativity," "originality," "borrowing," and related terms.[26] Jeff Titon
(1992, 11) observed that many American ethnomusicologists have been interested in improvisation "because we think it exemplifies human freedom."
American ethnomusicologists are hardly alone in seeing improvisation as
an alternative to numerous forms of regimentation; the opposition between
"following orders" and "acting out your own desires" turns up in much of
the discourse that made improvisation a key topic in 20th-century musical
thought. How we can best consider that set of 20th-century interests in relation to other projects that have been described as improvisation is a question
that merits further consideration.

NOTES

1. For example, Giannattasio glosses *improvisation* as "composing in real time"
(1992, 166), and Lewis speaks of "the generation of musical structure in real time"
(1996, 91).

2. In Jakobson's definition ([1957] 1971), a marked term specifies a property, A, and
the corresponding unmarked term has both a general meaning (non-statement of A)
and a specific meaning (statement of non-A). This is the kind of situation that Bruno
Nettl memorably described in his article (1963) "A Technique of Ethnomusicology Applied to Western Culture" and has commented on in other writings and in his classes.
Looking at the categories used in library catalogues and reflecting on the relationship
of those categories to the usage of educated speakers, Nettl observed that such terms as
folk music and such categories as *Symphonies—to 1800* depend on sets of oppositions

between music that is regarded as central and normative—music by named composers rather than by "the folk" and symphonies composed after 1800—and the specialized categories whose attributes or properties may or may not be covered by the purportedly more general conception, *music*. The point is nicely summarized by Nettl: "The educational establishment, as exemplified by the terminology of library catalogues, considers 'art' music as the true and central music of the entire society, labeling it simply as 'music' while other types have distinguishing adjectives" (1983, 304).

3. "Der Begriff der Improvisation scheint, im Unterschied zu dem der Komposition, für außereuropäische Musik durchaus brauchbar zu sein, solange man sich seine partielle, eingeschränkte Nützlichkeit bewußt macht, also nicht von der vergröbernden, die Terminologie ruinierenden Vorstellung ausgeht, daß sich mündlich überlieferte Musik insgesamt und ohne Differenzierungen als Improvisation charakterisieren lasse" (Dahlhaus [1979] 2000, 415).

4. See, for example, Ruth Finnegan's account (1986) of three different ways of understanding composition in relation to performance, based on her study of music making in Milton Keynes, England.

5. Sutton's answer to this question makes a useful distinction: "Javanese musicians improvise" inasmuch as "most Javanese musicians and listeners enjoy the element of flexibility," but "Javanese music is not improvisatory" because "the aesthetic emphasis is not on originality, spontaneity, or even planned variability" (1998, 87). The same probably holds true of a great many other musical practices.

6. Kandinsky's well-known comparison of "three different originating sources" (*Ursprungsquellen*) in the final pages of his treatise *On the Spiritual in Art* is perhaps the most important adaptation by a painter of the conventional distinction between the composition and improvisation of music. Kandinsky described the compositions he called *improvisations* as "hauptsächlich unbewußte, größtenteils plötzlich entstandene Ausdrücke der Vorgänge inneren Charakters, also Eindrücke von Art 'inneren Natur'" [mainly unconscious expressions of events of an inner character that for the most part arose suddenly and are thus impressions from "inner nature"]. He distinguished these both from his *compositions*—"auf ähnliche Art (aber ganz besonders langsam) sich in ihre bildende Ausdrücke, welche lange und beinahe pedantisch nach den erste Entwürfen von mir geprüft und ausgearbeitet werden" [pictorial expressions that likewise develop within me but more slowly, which are tested at length, almost pedantically, after the first sketches, then elaborated]—and from the works he called *impressions*, which originated in "direkter Eindruck von der 'äußeren Natur' welcher in einer zeichnerisch-malerischen Form zum Ausdruck kommt" [direct impression from "external nature," expressed in graphic-painterly form] (Kandinsky [1911] 1965, 142). From the contrast he draws between the rapidity of improvisation and the sustained interrogation of sketches that precedes the elaboration of a composition, we could recognize Kandinsky's interest in music even if this passage did not follow a discussion of melodic, rhythmic, and symphonic composition in painting.

7. Rink quotes the conclusion of Schenker's essay "Die Kunst der Improvisation" (1925, 40): "Die Geistesgegenwart, mit der unsere Genies den Tonstoff in solcher Art meisterten, hat ihnen ja erst möglich gemacht, weit ausholende Synthesen zu schaffen. Ihre Werke sind eben nicht zusammengeklaubt, sondern nach Art der freien Fantasie sofort umrissen und aus einem geheimen Urgrund herausgeführt." Rink modified Ian Bent's translation of this passage: "The conscious awareness with which our geniuses mastered tonal material in this manner enabled them to create comprehensive syntheses. Their works are not merely pieced together, but are sketched out instantaneously like the free fantasy and are developed from a mysterious fundamental source" (1993, 6). Rink points out that Schenker's understanding of improvisation was based on the 18th-century practice discussed by C.P.E. Bach rather than on the models used by 19th-century pianists (and inherited by Busoni).

8. "Wir neigen wahrscheinlich in viel zu hohem Maße zur Überschätzung des bewußten Charakters auch der intellektuellen und künstlerischen Produktion. Aus den Mitteilungen einiger höchst produktiven Menschen, wie Goethe und Helmholtz, erfahren wir doch eher, daß das Wesentliche und Neue ihrer Schöpfungen ihnen einfallsartig gegeben wurde und fast fertig zu ihrer Wahrnehmung kam. Die Mithilfe der bewußten Tätigkeit in anderen Fällen hat nichts Befremdendes, wo eine Anstrengung aller Geisteskräfte vorlag. Aber es ist das viel mißbrauchte Vorrecht der bewußten Tätigkeit, daß sie uns alle anderen verdecken darf, wo immer sie mittut" (Freud [1900] 2000, 599–600).

9. "Die Notation, die Aufschreibung von Musikstücken ist zuerst ein ingeniöser Behelf, eine Improvisation festuhalten, um sie wiedererstehen zu lassen." Busoni's remark can be read as an attempt to reconcile the alternative approaches to musical performance described in Hegel's *Ästhetik*: (1) "Soll . . . noch vom Kunst die Rede sein, so hat der Künstler die Pflicht, statt den Eindruck eines musikalischen Automaten zu geben, der eine blosse Lektion hersagt und Vorgeschriebenes mechanisch wiederholt, das Werk im Sinne und Geist des Komponisten seelenvoll zu erleben"; (2) "der Künstler selbst im Vortrage komponiert, Fehlendes ergänzt, Flacheres vertieft, das Seelenlosere beseelt und in dieser Weise schlechthin selbständig und produzierend erscheint" ([1835] 1955, ii, 324).

10. Feisst quotes a remark by Roman Haubenstock-Ramati that echoes Busoni's statement: notation is "eine Art Provokation zur Improvisation, durch die wieder etwas musikalisch Wahres und Einmaliges zum Leben in unserer Zeit erweckt wird" (1997, 111).

11. "Die Wiedergabe fordert vom Spieler die verfeinertste Anschlags u. Pedalkunst; einen intimen, improvisierten, 'schwebenden,' empfundenen Vortrag; ein liebevolles Sich-Versenken in ihren Inhalt" (Theurich 1977, 178).

12. Different Arabic verbs are used when this remark is quoted in various editions of al-Farabi's *Great Book on Music* and in other writings, such as the *Kitāb-e kamāl adab al-ġinā'* of al-Hasan (trans. Shiloah 1972, 167).

13. Erlmann discusses the relationship in Ful'be praise singing between the "model"

(*taakiyaare*) that a composer "makes" or "comes up with" and the rendition (*fijirde*) of the model with appropriate variation (*sanja*) (1985, 93–95).

14. Walter Kaufmann translates this passage as follows: "Verses are the representation of various reflections and singing is the extended delivery of that representation (verses). Musical tones go together with the verses and tones are regulated by the pitch-pipes (lü)" (1976, 5).

15. Laurence Picken translates as follows Chiang K'uei's remark about one of the songs in the collection he published in 1202: "I much enjoy making songs myself. First, following the ideas, I make the long and short phrases. Afterwards I unite them with the pitches. In consequence, first and last sections (stanzas) are very different" (1966, 146).

16. A classic statement of this outlook is Rousseau's definition of *prima intenzione* in his *Dictionnaire de musique*: "Un Air, un morceau *di Prima intenzione*, est celui qui s'est formé tout d'un coup tout entier et avec toutes ses Parties dans l'esprit du Compositeur." According to Rousseau, the term had no equivalent in French "puisque l'idée que ce mot exprime n'est pas connue dans la Musique Françoise" ([1767] 1995, 994). Compare Schenker's remark on compositions that are "sketched out instantaneously," quoted in note 7 above.

17. "Sic etiam oportet Componistam prius quasdam, in animo, clausulas, sed optimas, excogitare, & quodam iuditio easdem perpendere, nè aliqua nota totam vitiet clausulam, & auditorum aures taediosas faciat. Deinde, ad exercitationem accedere, hoc est, excogitatas clausulas, in ordinem quendam distribuere, & eas, quae videntur aptiores servare."

Lowinsky's translation as adapted by Owens: "so also the composer ought first to think out in his mind musical phrases, indeed very good ones, and to consider them carefully with good judgment lest one note ruin the whole phrase and tire the ears of the listener, and then proceed to the working out, that is, to distribute in a certain order the phrases that have been thought out, and to save those phrases that seem more suitable" (Owens 1997, 66–67).

18. "disegnare in carta . . . è necessario a chi vuol bene disporre i componimenti, ed accomodare l'invenzioni, se non apre e non mostra il suo concetto agli occhi corporali che l'aiutino a farne buon giudizio"

19. "Il bozzar delle storie sia pronto, e 'l membrificare no' sia troppo finito . . ."; "perche nelle cose confuse l'ingenio si desta a' nove inventioni. . . ."

20. Gombrich argued that the art of Leonardo and his contemporaries had effected "the vital transition from drill to improvisation" ([1989] 1991, 102); acquired training in accurate reproduction of conventional schemes gave way to a process of discovery and experimentation. In constructing histories of music or of drama, we should avoid making any such claims about a transition from drill to improvisation or from improvisation to dependence on scripts or notations.

21. An important aspect of this difference in expectation, as Christopher Waterman pointed out in the discussion following the presentation of this paper at the

Urbana conference, is the awareness of participants that improvising performers are taking risks.

22. Works of the artists whom Harold Rosenberg called "The American Action Painters" ([1952] 1961), more often called "abstract expressionists"—and, somewhat later, improvised jazz—were publicized, at home and abroad, as representative products of American individualism during the first decades of the Cold War.

23. In his helpful "Remarks on the Dichotomy 'Improvised-Composed,'" Gushee observes, "The dissociation phenomenon, in which symbolic workers/creative artists understand themselves as channels through which supernatural or impersonal forces speak is common, and 'real' enough" (1982, 189).

24. David Borgo offers a similar typology, with three rather than two groups of metaphors: "Several of the most prevalent metaphors describing the musical intent, interaction, and intensification of improvising ensembles are storytelling, conversation and journey" (1996–1997, 27).

25. Finscher remarks on the frequency with which Europeans compared string quartets with conversations—the best-known instance being Goethe's remark in his letter to Zelter of November 9, 1829: "man hört vier vernünftige Leute sich untereinander unterhalten, glaubt ihren Diskursen etwas abzugewinnen und die Eigentümlichkeiten der Instrumente kennen zu lernen" (1967, 285–90).

26. Two pertinent studies of what speakers intended to accomplish in selecting one term or a group of terms over other possibilities are Tatarkiewicz ([1976] 2003), on "creativity," and Ford (2002), on the ancient Greek terminology associated with the "making" of poems.

REFERENCES

Bach, Carl Philipp Emanuel. 1762. *Versuch über die wahre Art, das Clavier zu spielen, Zweyter Theil, in welchem die Lehre von dem Accompagnement und der freyen Fantasie abgehandelt wird.* Berlin: printed by George Ludewig Winter.

Bandur, Markus. 2002. "Komposition." In *Handwörterbuch der musikalischen Terminologie.*

Baxandall, Michael. 1971. *Giotto and the Orators: Humanist Observers of Painting in Italy and the Discovery of Pictorial Composition 1350–1450.* Oxford: Clarendon Press.

Belgrad, Daniel. 1998. *The Culture of Spontaneity: Improvisation and the Arts in Postwar America.* Chicago: University of Chicago Press.

Benson, Bruce Ellis. 2003. *The Improvisation of Musical Dialogue: A Phenomenology of Music.* Cambridge: Cambridge University Press.

Bent, Ian. 1984. "The 'Compositional Process' in Music Theory 1713–1850." *Music Analysis* 3(1): 29–55.

Blum, Stephen. 1998. "Recognizing Improvisation." In *In the Course of Performance:*

Studies in the World of Musical Improvisation, edited by Bruno Nettl with Melinda Russell, 27–45. Chicago: University of Chicago Press.

———. 2001. "Composition." In *The New Grove Dictionary of Music and Musicians*, Vol. 6, edited by Stanley Sadie and John Tyrrell, 186–201. London: Macmillan.

Borgo, David. 1996–1997. "Emergent Qualities of Collectively Improvised Performance: A Study of an Egalitarian Intercultural Improvising Trio." *Pacific Review of Ethnomusicology* 8(1): 23–40.

Bush, Susan, and Hsio-yen Shi, comps., eds. 1985. *Early Chinese Texts on Painting*. Cambridge, Mass.: Harvard University Press, for the Harvard-Yenching Institute.

Busoni, Ferruccio. [1916] 1974. *Entwurf einer neuen Ästhetik der Tonkunst, mit Anmerkungen von Arnold Schönberg und einem Nachwort von H.H. Stuckenschmidt*. Frankfurt am Main: Suhrkamp. Text of the second edition of Busoni's work, first published Leipzig, 1916; first edition 1907.

———. 1987. *Selected Letters*, edited and translated by Anthony Beaumont. New York: Columbia University Press.

Čelebiev, Faık. 1989. "O morfologia mugama." In *Narodnaya muzïka: istoriya i tipologiya*, edited by I.I. Zemtsovsky, 135–56. Leningrad: Ministerstvo Kul'turï RSFSR.

Dahlhaus, Carl. [1979] 2000. "Was heißt Improvisation?" In *Gesammelte Schriften* 1: 405–17. First published in *Veröffentlichungen der Institut für Neue Musik und Musikerziehung Darmstadt* 20: 9–23.

DeWoskin, Kenneth. 1983. "Early Chinese Music and the Origins of Aesthetic Terminology." In *Theories of the Arts in China*, edited by Susan Bush and Christian Murck, 187–214. Princeton, N.J.: Princeton University Press.

Erlmann, Veit. 1985. "Model, Variation and Performance: Ful'be Praise Song in Northern Cameroon." *Yearbook for Traditional Music* 17: 88–112.

Feisst, Sabine. 1997. *Der Begriff 'Improvisation' in der neuen Musik*. Berliner Musik Studien, 14. Sinzig: Studio, Verl. Schewe.

Feld, Steven. 1982. *Sound and Sentiment: Birds, Weeping, Poetics, and Song in Kaluli Expression*. Philadelphia: University of Pennsylvania Press.

Finnegan, Ruth. 1986. "The Relation between Composition and Performance: Three Alternative Modes." In *The Oral and the Literate in Music*, edited by Tokumaru Yosihiko and Yamaguti Osamu, 73–87. Tokyo: Academia Music.

Finscher, Ludwig. 1967. *Die Entstehung des klassischen Streichquartetts: von den Vorformen zur Grundlegung durch Joseph Haydn*. Saarbrücker Studien zur Musikwissenschaft, 3. Kassel: Bärenreiter.

Ford, Andrew. 2002. *The Origins of Criticism: Literary Culture and Poetic Theory in Classical Greece*. Princeton, N.J.: Princeton University Press.

Freud, Sigmund. [1900] 2000. *Die Traumdeutung*. Frankfurt am Main: Fischer.

Giannattasio, Francesco. 1992. *Il concetto di musica: contributi e prospettive della ricerca etnomusicologica*. Rome: La Nuova Italia Scientifica.

Gombrich, E. H. [1954] 1966. "Leonardo's Method for Working Out Compositions." In *Norm and Form: Studies in the Art of the Renaissance*, 58–63. London: Phaidon. First published in *Actes du Congrès Léonard da Vinci—Études d'Art*, nos. 8–10: 177–97.

———. [1989] 1991. "Watching Artists at Work: Commitment and Improvisation in the History of Drawing." In *Topics of Our Time: Twentieth-Century Issues in Learning and in Art*, 92–130. London: Phaidon. Translation of *Wege zur Bildgestaltung: vom Einfall zur Ausführung*, 5–21. Opladen: Westdeutscher Verlag.

Gushee, Lawrence. 1982. "Analytical Method and Compositional Process in Some Thirteenth and Fourteenth-Century Music." In *Aktuelle Fragen der Musikbezogenen Mittelalterforschung*. Forum Musicologicum, 3: 165–91. Winterthur: Amadeus.

Harrist, Robert E., and Wen C. Fong. 1999. *The Embodied Image: Chinese Calligraphy from the John B. Elliott Collection*. Princeton, N.J.: Art Museum of Princeton University in association with Harry N. Abrams.

Hegel, G. W. F. [1835] 1955. *Ästhetik*, edited by Friedrich Bassenge. Frankfurt am Main: Europäische Verlagsanstalt.

Jakobson, Roman. [1957] 1971. "Shifters, Verbal Categories, and the Russian Verb." Reprinted in *Selected Writings*, 2: 130–47. The Hague: Mouton.

Kandinsky, Wassily. [1911] 1965. *Über das Geistige in der Kunst*. Bern: Benteli Verlag. First published Munich: R. Piper.

Karlgren, Bernhard. 1950. *The Book of Documents: The Shu King*. Göteborg: Elanders Boktryckeri Aktiebolag. Reprinted from *Bulletin of the Museum of Far Eastern Antiquities*.

Kartomi, Margaret J. 2002. "Meaning, Style and Change in *Gamelan* and *Wayang Kulit Banjar* since their Transplantation from Hindu-Buddhist Java to South Kalimantan." *World of Music* 44(2): 17–55.

Kaufmann, Walter. 1976. *Musical References in the Chinese Classics*. Detroit Monographs in Musicology, No. 5. Detroit: Information Coordinators.

Kirkendale, Warren. 1979. "Ciceronians versus Aristotelians on the Ricercar as Exordium." *Journal of the American Musicological Society* 32(1): 1–44.

Lampadius, Auctor. [1537] 1541. *Compendium musices, tam figurati quàm plani cantus ad formam dialogi*. Bern: Mathias Apiarius.

Lewis, George E. 1996. "Improvised Music after 1950: Afrological and Eurological Perspectives." *Black Music Research Journal* 16(1): 91–122.

Lord, Albert. 1960. *The Singer of Tales*. Cambridge, Mass.: Harvard University Press.

Lowinsky, Edward E. 1948. "On the Use of Scores by Sixteenth-Century Musicians." *Journal of the American Musicological Society* 1: 17–23.

Magrini, Tullia. 1986. *Canti d'amore e di sdegno*. Milan: Franco Angeli.

———. 1998. "Improvisation and Group Interaction in Italian Lyrical Singing." In *In the Course of Performance: Studies in the World of Musical Improvisation*, edited by Bruno Nettl with Melinda Russell, 169–98. Chicago: University of Chicago Press.

Nettl, Bruno. 1963. "A Technique of Ethnomusicology Applied to Western Culture." *Ethnomusicology* 7(3): 221–24.

———. 1983. *The Study of Ethnomusicology: Twenty-nine Issues and Concepts.* Urbana: University of Illinois Press.

———. 1991. Preface to special issue, "New Perspectives on Improvisation." *World of Music* 33(3): 3–5.

———. 1998. "Introduction: An Art Neglected in Scholarship." In *In the Course of Performance: Studies in the World of Musical Improvisation*, edited by Bruno Nettl with Melinda Russell, 1–23. Chicago: University of Chicago Press.

Owens, Jessie Ann. 1997. *Composers at Work: The Craft of Musical Composition 1450–1600.* New York: Oxford University Press.

Pegg, Carole. 2001. "Inner Asia." In *The New Grove Dictionary of Music and Musicians*, edited by Stanley Sadie and John Tyrrell, 12:385–90. London: Macmillan.

Perrucci, Andrea. [1699] 1961. *Dell'arte rappresentativa, premeditata e all'improvviso*, edited by Anton Giulio Bragaglia. Florence: Edizioni Sansoni Antiquariato.

Picken, Laurence E. R. 1966. "Secular Chinese Songs of the Twelfth Century." *Studia Musicologica Academiae Scientiarum Hungaricae* 8: 125–72.

Powers, Harold. 1980. "Mode." In *The New Grove Dictionasry of Music and Musicians*, Vol. 12, edited by Stanley Sadie, 376–450. London: Macmillan.

———. 1989. "'International Segāh' and Its Nominal Equivalents in Central Asia and Kashmir." In *Maqam-Raga-Zeilenmelodik: Konzeption und Prinzipien der Musikproduktion. Materialien der 1. Arbeitstagung der Study Group "Maqam" beim International Council for Traditional Music vom 28. Juni bis 2. Juli in Berlin*, edited by Jürgen Elsner, 40–85. Berlin: Nationalkomitee der International Council for Traditional Music.

Reichl, Karl. 1992. *Turkic Oral Epic Poetry: Traditions, Forms, Poetic Structure.* New York: Garland.

Rink, John. 1993. "Schenker and Improvisation." *Journal of Music Theory* 37: 1–54.

Rivest, Johanne. 2001. "Alea, happening, improvvisazione, opera aperta." In *Enciclopedia della musica*, I, *Il Novecento*, edited by Jean-Jacques Nattiez, 312–21.Turin: Einaudi.

Rosenberg, Harold. [1952] 1961. "The American Action Painters." In *The Tradition of the New*, 23–39. New York: Grove Press.

Rouget, Gilbert. 1996. *Un Roi africain et sa musique de cour: chants et danses du palais Porto-Novo sous le régne de Gbéfa (1948–1976).* Paris: CNRS Éditions.

Rousseau, Jean-Jacques. [1767] 1995. *Oeuvres complètes, 5. Écrits sur la musique, la langue et le théâtre*, edited by Bernard Gagnebin and Marcel Raymond. Bibliothèque de la Pléiade, 416. Paris: Gallimard. *Dictionnaire de musique* first published November 1767.

Saussy, Haun. 1993. *The Problem of a Chinese Aesthetic.* Stanford, Calif.: Stanford University Press.

Schenker, Heinrich. 1925. "Die Kunst der Improvisation." In *Das Meisterwerk in der Musik*, 1: 9–40. Munich: Drei Masken Verlag.

Shiloah, Amnon. 1972. *La perfection des connaissances musicales / Kitāb kamāl adab al-ġinā': traduction et commentaire d'un traité arabe du XI siècle.* Bibliothèque des Études Islamiques, 5. Paris: Paul Geuthner.

Slobin, Mark. 1976. *Music in the Culture of Northern Afghanistan.* Viking Fund Publications in Anthropology, No. 54. Tucson: University of Arizona Press.

Sutton, R. Anderson. 1998. "Do Javanese Musicians Improvise?" In *In the Course of Performance: Studies in the World of Musical Improvisation*, edited by Bruno Nettl with Melinda Russell, 69–92. Chicago: University of Chicago Press.

Tatarkiewicz, Wladyslaw. [1976] 2003. *Geschichte der sechs Begriffe: Kunst, Schönheit, Form, Kreativität, Mimesis, Ästhetisches Erlebnis.* Translated by Friedrich Griese. Frankfurt am Main: Suhrkamp. First published as *Dzieje szesciu pojec: sztuka—piekno—forma—twórczosc—odtwórczosc—przezycie estetyczne*, Warsaw: PWN.

Theurich, Jutta, ed. 1977. "Briefwechsel zwischen Arnold Schönberg und Ferruccio Busoni 1909–1919 (1927)." *Beiträge zur Musikwissenschaft* 19(3): 165–211.

Titon, Jeff Todd, ed. 1992. *Worlds of Music: An Introduction to the Music of the World's Peoples*, 2nd ed. New York: McGraw-Hill.

Treitler, Leo. 1974. "Homer and Gregory: The Transmission of Epic Poetry and Plainchant." *Musical Quarterly* 60(3): 333–72.

Vasari, Giorgio. [1568] 1981. *Le vite de' piu eccellenti pittori, scultori ed architettori*, ed. Gaetano Milanesi. Florence: Sansoni, VII. Reprint of 1906 edition. The Titian biography was not included in the first edition (1550) of Vasari's work.

Wilson, Peter Niklas. 1999. *Hear and Now: Gedanken zur improvisierten Musik.* Hofheim: Wolke-Verlag.

Yung, Bell. 1997. *Celestial Airs of Antiquity: Music of the Seven-String Zither of China.* Recent Researches in the Oral Traditions of Music, No. 5. Madison, Wis.: A-R Editions.

Zeranska-Kominek, Slawomira. 1998. "The Concept of Journey (*Yol*) in Turkmen Music Tradition." *Ethnomusicology* 42(2): 265–82.

IMPROVISATION AND RELATED TERMS
IN MIDDLE-PERIOD JAZZ

Lawrence Gushee

When I presented a version of this article in 2004, it was at the second con-ference I had attended within six months devoted to the mysterious art and concept of improvisation. The first one was in Germany, and its tone was very philosophical despite the focus on "jazz" (Gushee 2004); the second was assuredly ethnomusicological. In both situations I approached the topic somewhat idiosyncratically, exploring the relation between lexicography and musical practice. Actually, I had explored the lexical terrain some thirty years ago in a few pages more or less buried in a publication neither well distributed nor, apparently, much consulted (Gushee 1982). To make matters worse, no key word search on "improvisation" will find it. A German translation of a paper closely related to the present article, from the conference mentioned above, has been published, however (Gushee 2004).

In seeking to define improvisation, to be thorough, I suppose one might cast a glance at the OED or Webster's, in addition to various non-English general dictionaries. But for my purposes it would take too much time for too little profit. In any event, this can be easily done by those who wish to do so. So let's begin more or less in medias res by consulting the 1927 edition of *Grove's Dictionary of Music and Musicians*. It refers the searcher for the term to a British cousin, "extemporisation" (Colles 1927). The initial sentences are perhaps worth citing: "the art of thinking and performing music simultane-ously. It is therefore the primitive act of music-making, existing from the moment that the untutored individual obeys the impulse to relieve his feel-ings by bursting into song." Naturally, "jazz" or other kinds of "untutored" vernacular music were not mentioned in 1927; the emphasis is on French or English church organists. However, the writer avers that the learning of extempore playing is a useful adjunct in musical education. "It brings reason to the support of instinct and quickens the intelligence." These general points are, it seems to me, still of value today.

In the *New Grove Dictionary of Music,* those who consult "extemporisation" are referred to "improvisation" (Sadie 1980). As one might imagine, the entry is vastly longer and more comprehensive than the one of 1927. Nevertheless, I find the first definition, "The creation of a musical work, or the final form of a musical work, as it is being performed," to be no improvement over its predecessor, as it introduces such problematic terms as "final form" and "musical work"—incidentally making more work for the musicologist. Interestingly, the entry deals only with "art music," either Western or non-Western, referring the searcher to the separate articles on other countries or to the one on "jazz," with the rationale "By its very nature—in that improvisation is essentially evanescent—it is one of the subjects least amenable to historical research," as if the phonograph had never been invented. The "jazz" article, by the quite perceptive Max Harrison, attempts to dodge the bullet at the beginning: "Attempts at a concise—even coherent—definition of jazz have invariably failed. Initial efforts to separate it from related forms of music resulted in a false primacy of certain aspects, such as improvisation, which is neither unique nor essential to jazz."

For lack of space, I omit extended treatment here of Barry Kernfeld's lengthy and characteristically meaty article in the *New Grove Dictionary of Jazz* (Kernfeld 1988, repeated in the second edition of 2002). It is worth pointing out that the logical and theoretical structure of the article leaves little room for historical reference, especially to the 1920s, which might be considered the forge in which concepts of improvisation were hammered out. This dearth of historical reference also characterizes his interesting book *What to Listen for in Jazz* (Kernfeld 1995). I also ride roughshod over Paul Berliner's thoughtful and important book (1994), now 10 years old, subtitled "The Infinite Art of Improvisation." The bulk of its evidence comes from after 1940 or from relatively recent interviews.

Perhaps the only specialized work on jazz that covers some of the same chronological territory as I do here is Sudhalter (1999). For all its depth of discographical and biographical reference, it leaves untouched the topics here explored, concentrating almost completely on recordings. Perhaps that's only reasonable; would we be interested in jazz without the recordings that so vividly preserve the expressivity and spontaneity of the hundreds (thousands?) of bands and soloists from the 1920s and 1930s? Nonetheless, I hope to convince the reader that part of the process of dissemination and development of a primarily orally conceived music was the use of notated and published music. Written music also provides an alternative window into the thinking of musicians; an example is Louis Armstrong's transcribed solos from 1927, for which pianist-composer Elmer Schoebel apparently served as amanuensis.

A preliminary consideration is what American or English terms more vernacular than the pentasyllabic "improvisation" have been used. If we don't identify these we may fail to recognize important references to our topic. Besides, an alternative term may have a nuance of great historical or conceptual interest.

The following discussion doesn't purport to be more than a light once-over. Still, it will give an idea of the lexical thicket that preceded the eventual adoption of "improvisation" as the standard and preferred term. Without pretending to have made a search for the earliest use of some of the terms that follow—which would certainly be like looking for a needle in the haystack—I present the following mention in a 1910 West Coast boxing periodical regarding a pianist named Phil Stebbins, "who plays everything from ragtime to grand opera, reads at sight, fakes, transposes, improvises, interpolates" (Anon. 1910, 6)—in other words, an ideal entertainer and accompanist at the keyboard. Are the words "fake," "improvise," and "interpolate" synonymous? Entirely or partly? Or are they distinct but related techniques?

Seven years later, in the pages of the *Freeman*, an African American weekly published in Indianapolis but distributed nationally, a want ad by Turpin's Jazz Band sought "people who can jazz, read, improve, fake, and interpolate" (*Freeman* March 3, 1917).

More interesting, perhaps, is an excerpt from a musicians' magazine, *Jacobs Orchestra Monthly*, in which the writer of the drum column tussled with one of these words at some length:

R.H.C., New London, Conn. Q: I notice some dance drummers of my acquaintance "fake" rag-time parts and variations on the bells in place of the printed parts. They also play rag-time drum parts which are not at all as the music is written. Now, I know that, musically speaking, they are not playing correctly, but the audiences here seem to like and expect a lot of drum-work of this kind. Taking this into consideration, would it not be all right to "fake"?

A: First, last, and all the time, we are playing to our audiences, and they are the ones to please, even if we are obliged to occasionally disregard musical rules to do it. In the case that you mention, where your audiences look for "drum-work," as you say, give it to them, whatever they want, and probably they will be better satisfied than if you played the written part. But when you "fake," be sure you do so intelligently. (Stone 1912a, 67)

From countless other references, one gathers that to "fake" is frequently taken as meaning to play a part not in the written score by ear. Sometimes, however, it seems to mean simply to play by ear.

A few months later in the same source a gloss on the word "vamp" appeared: "to 'vamp' a part means to improvise or, to use a slang expression to 'fake it'" (Stone 1912b, 73). This is a term with a noble pedigree, going back at least to the 18th-century musician and lexicographer Charles Burney. These days the word, still in use in the phrase "vamp 'til ready," has clearly become a good deal more restricted in meaning.

Certainly, "fake" is itself a derogatory term, especially from the point of view of the legitimately trained, note-reading musician. One related to it is the word "routineer," derived probably from the French *routinier*, which I've encountered only from New Orleans musicians of the early 20th century. The cornetist Willie "Bunk" Johnson (1889–1949) as quoted by Alan Lomax, said that the note-reading musicians in John Robichaux's band called Buddy Bolden's band "a 'routineer' bunch, a bunch of 'fakers'" (1950, 54). The idea that the uneducated performer has to rely on habit or routine rather than rational knowledge derives from Boethius at least, if not Pythagoras, and I'm sure this is a belated echo of that dichotomy. What's interesting here is the shift in perspective. Where these days we regard improvisation as an act of creative imagination, in the past it was sometimes considered anything but, something that inadequately trained musicians did from rote or force of habit or necessity. Of course, both may be the case.

A term that surfaces in 1914 in connection with drummers is "fly." For example, a "fly drummer" can make the reputation of a band. My understanding is that such a drummer doesn't follow the written part and puts on a show that pleases the dancers and listeners (Erdmann 1914, 88). Elsewhere, around the same time, one finds a reference to a "shoo-fly" band leader, meaning one who's pretty laid-back and not a stickler for discipline. "Fly" might also mean something like "hip" or "hep"—to be in the know, perhaps to be in step with the times. One of my favorite citations comes from a 1911 ad for the publishing house Haviland: "If you're hep, nothing will hinder your having Haviland's 'Happy Hits' hanging handily about to hand out hot harmonies when holding summer 'hops'" (*Jacobs' Orchestra Monthly* May 1911, 88).

There are other related terms in musicians' argot of the early part of the century. Perhaps the most interesting one is "windjammer." A minstrel show band—probably African American—in the dispatch it sent to the *Freeman* in 1909, wrote, "Prof. Barter Reynolds is leader of the brass band and his boys certainly do some wind jamming when they parade the streets" (*Free-*

man June 26, 1909). A couple of years
Musician," written for *Jacobs' Orchestr*
stenographer and bookkeeper even th
could draw from ten to fifteen dollars
musician, I could 'jam wind' a few hour
easier time" (C.L.W. 1911, 26).

Only a few years after these citatio
"jazz"—hot ragtime played by ear, to
gun with the recordings of the Original
organization of New Orleans musiciar
frequently disparaged for the absence
cordings. As always, this is true, false, or partly each, depending on what one
means by the term "improvisation." It's interesting that the concept was not
foreign to them, whatever may be the case with their recordings. The incident
cited next comes from the copyright litigation over the piece "Barnyard Blues"
or "Livery Stable Blues" from the fall of 1917. Not only was it widely reported in
the Chicago press, where the case was heard, but members of the band, then
playing in New York City, made depositions that are found in the records of
the federal District Court, Northern District of Illinois, Eastern Division.

One exchange is of particular interest, between attorney Nathan Burkan
and Henry Ragas, the band's pianist:

Q: Are you the originator of any composition?
A: No, sir.
Q: Have you ever suggested any variations or changes in the present composi-
tion [or] any song other than the composition in question?
A: I have, yes, sir.
Q: It is nothing unusual for a musician of your calibre to make variations or
runs in the present composition, is it?
A: I don't understand what composition you mean.
Q: Any composition other than the one in question?
A: Yes.
Q: It is nothing unusual for you to put in variations or runs, something that
might strike you?
A: I could, but it don't sound well with this sort of music.
(Ragas 1917)

Granted, the word "improvisation" doesn't appear as such. Nevertheless,
I suggest that a reasonable interpretation is that, in Ragas's mind, "Livery
Stable Blues," along with other pieces in the ODJB repertory, was regarded

sition, carefully rehearsed and essentially the same from
ce to another. Many jazz historians and critics have taken the
k for their apparent failure to improvise, as demonstrated when
recorded performances of the same work are compared; this strikes
s misguided and based on a fundamental misunderstanding. Be that as
may, the impact on the youthful would-be musicians all over the country
who played the records over and over was rather different. The following account doesn't mention the ODJB, but is, I think, a reasonable summary of the
process by which many jazz neophytes learned how to play the new music.

One of the most admired and original jazz trombonists of the 1920s, Miff
Mole (1898–1961) began playing the trombone around 1916. He found that
his "improvising" was preferred to the original trombone parts and "the
members of the orchestra began encouraging me to improvise. To tell the
truth, I did not know how I accomplished it. I knew chords, but I did not
depend on this knowledge. I just let go by ear" (Grupp 1938, 41). When he
joined the Original Memphis Five, he wasn't satisfied "with improvising only
while the whole orchestra played. On my suggestion, the orchestra stopped
occasionally for two or four bars, and I filled in with whatever phrases my
ear and lip flexibility guided me to, and the stop (break) was originated. After
a while, I often played a hot chorus, with the accompaniment of the rhythm
section only" (41).

A view from the other side of the color line appeared in the distinguished
African American newspaper the *Philadelphia Tribune* in the context of a
commentary to an article hostile to jazz in the monthly newspaper of the
American Federation of Musicians: "Lie No. 2. In [the] fourth paragraph
[the author] says 'a high order of musical talent is not required to become
a jazz player.' Maybe not, but whatever musical talent the real jazz players
possess must be born in them. . . . Of course it [is] not music the way it is
played by the average white orchestra. No! Improvising is a lost art among
them. But deep down in the Negroe's soul there is music—born in—that
finds expression everytime he plays" (*Philadelphia Tribune* December 22,
1917). I understand this to mean that improvisation as a technical procedure
is inextricably linked in the writer's mind with personal expression, which
is quite characteristic of uses of the term prior to the mid-1920s.

It would take some years before the word "improvisation" separated itself
from the pack of related terms. Quite by happenstance, in the November 26,
1921, issue of the theatrical weekly *Billboard*, I came across an ad addressed
to clarinet players in which an otherwise unknown Dorsey Powers stated,
"I Make a Specialty of Jazzy Clarinet Arrangements of Dance Hits. My ar-

rangements are original, following the exact style of 'Blue' faking and improvisations as played by the Columbia, Victor and Edison Dance Clarinetists"
(page 41). Powers gives his address as the Palmer School, Davenport, Iowa.
This is perhaps the best-known school for chiropractic, founded in 1897 and
still flourishing.

Only two years later a young cornet star from Chicago, Louis Panico, put
together a remarkable work called *The Novelty Cornetist* (1924). This was offered to interested musicians in the specialized musical press of 1924 for the
then staggering sum of $10. It has four components: first, transcriptions of
Panico's playing from 25 Brunswick recordings by the Isham Jones orchestra; second, photographs of mutes and the technique of their manipulation
to produce novelty effects; third, 16 pages of breaks in nine different keys;
fourth, the author's ideas on such topics as blues, improvisation, and the
requirements of playing a jazz lead. We will treat these ideas as conforming
with Panico's beliefs, even if they, like the transcriptions, may have been set
down on paper by bandmate and virtuoso trombonist Carroll Martin, a
thoroughly literate arranger and composer.

Despite the pragmatic approach of the work, Panico nevertheless indulges
in quaintly expressed general speculations. We turn, naturally, to the section
entitled "Improvisation" (1924, 74), but the author is clearly not inclined to
make it easy for us: "A more difficult subject for explanation could scarcely
be found. To elucidate that which is metaphysical has long been an enigma to
writers of all ages, yet all have attempted, and in a measure, all have succeeded.
And, in the opinion of the writer, their success has come, usually in a moment
of relaxation from the direct effort, when impressions are conveyed which
bear the fruit of understanding. So it is likely, throughout this course, that
the essential impulse will be received from practical examples rather than the
most scientific explanations, even as parables strike bright the thought grop-
ing in a wilderness of technic." This sounds as though Panico was a devotee
of so-called "primary process" thought. Be that as it may, perhaps if the work
is reissued, it might be retitled "The Zen of Novelty Cornet Playing."

The author returns to earth with practical models for constructing both
breaks and more extended solos. A good number of the four-measure phrases
are stitched together from two-measure components taken from the anthology of breaks. Panico would prefer that breaks be used as they are supposed
to—as actual breaks, typically in measures 7–8 and 15–16 of a 16- or 32-mea-
sure form, but recognized that the student can find "himself temporarily out
of favor with the gods of inspiration" (1924, 76). He offers a number of useful
tips: the first four measures are the most important, monotony should be

avoided in any field of entertainment, and there should be a new idea about every other measure. An encouraging note appears at the end: "If the student, after studying these exercises, still does not find himself able to improvise at all, he should then look within himself, see if he actually desires as he should, increase the intensity of that desire, and the door sooner or later will open. This is one of the laws of nature, and must operate" (1924, 78).

There are many other points relating to improvisation, but perhaps we should be satisfied with a citation from the concluding "Review," in which Panico recommends the reading of a song's lyrics: "There is a great diversity in the ideas of the numerous songs which one will encounter, but usually there will come one or more suggestions from the lyrics, and you will be closer than using random novelties which have, in some instances, an opposite character" (1924, 82).

All in all, this sounds a bit weird to today's reader but it shows an attempt to deal with what, after all, is a subject that continues to defeat scholars. But it's worth considering that, in 1924, a star cornetist in the leading dance band in Chicago approached his subject with such passion and thoroughness and even, I dare say, some sophistication. One has to say that for Panico, improvisation is so mixed up with considerations of "novelty" and technical manipulation of the various mutes, as well as with adventurousness in personal music development, that his understanding of the term is really quite different from ours—not necessarily wrong, just appropriate to the musical situation of his heyday.

A work not unlike Panico's is *The Business Saxophonist* by J. Beach Cragun (1923), which in a series of 20 brief lessons is meant to acquaint the novice with some of the then fashionable tricks of the trade, such as slap tongue, flutter tongue, and the laugh. The eighth lesson is "Improvising (Faking or Filling in)." The most interesting feature of this course may be the citation of specific recordings as illustrations of the various techniques. Otherwise, it's dry as dust and schoolmasterish, very different from Panico.

Starting in 1924, dozens of publications appeared, mostly directed to piano players, showing that, as with Panico, the idea of "improvisation" was mixed up with concepts of novelty tricks. It would try the reader's patience to give a comprehensive list of these, so a few characteristic titles are provided to give the general idea:

1. Schwebel, Edwin J. 1926. *Trick piano playing: Breaks, jazz time-blue endings, fill in, when and where to apply, for the amateur and professional pianist.*

2. Shefte, Art. 1927. *Hot breaks for piano; hot but easy to play.* A collection of endings, breaks, in that style of popular music so aptly described as hot, together with the chorus of a popular song in its original form, as well as the author's version and instructions as to how and where to apply breaks, and other techniques.

3. Shefte, Art. [1925] 1927. *Up-to-the minute jazz breaks, tricks, blues, endings, etc. for the amateur and professional pianist.*

4. Waterman, Glenn R. 1924. *Piano jazz: 1001 breaks, trick endings, bass forms, space fillers, blue rhythms and syncopated effects; how to play any popular song like a player piano roll.*

5. Winn, Edward R. 1924. *Winn's how to play breaks and endings: Shows how and where to apply to popular piano music more than 100 novelty jazz and blues breaks, endings, space fillers . . .*

Not being intimately acquainted with the contents of these works, I can't comment on how they address the concept of "improvisation." However, I can speak for one work that I do know: Samuel T. Daley's *Sure System of Improvising* ([1926–1927], 2), which I suspect was offered for a wide range of instruments. (My copy is for violin.) Daley expresses the pedagogue's dislike for an art that, after all, can be thought to bypass the need for a teacher. His introduction begins: "Improvising is an art that has been credited with being born in a person and therefore, impossible, to a certain extent to teach. In this book I try to convey the idea of Improvising in a systematical manner." He continues to tussle with this contrast between system and inspiration: "Originality in improvising is an attribute that is much in demand. Copying is not harmful, providing the copying is correct from a good improvision [*sic*]. Improvising really is to play a break or a hot chorus that no one else has played. It takes a little more time and work than copying, but it is much better in the end. The idea is to have someone else copy from you, and not you copying from someone else" ([1926–1927], 12). But the way to mastery is learning how to play breaks. Once you've done this you can proceed to the "hot chorus," which sticks close to the melody with the exception of the breaks. The next step is playing "dirt choruses," in which "if played alone, the original melody can hardly be recognized." In any event, moderation is advised: "In playing for dances, it is not advisable to play too much hot stuff. It finally gets too monotonous to listen to. The idea is to play just enough to make the dancers ask for more" ([1926/1927], 47).

Authors such as Waterman, Shefte, and Daley are unknown to jazz history. But during the years when these works appeared, collections of breaks and solos by greatly admired jazz players hit the market. The degree to which they may have been ghostwritten is uncertain, yet they usually reflect the players' individual styles. The following list is offered with no claim to comprehensiveness:

Miff Mole	1925 and 1926
Jack Pettis	1926
Jimmy Dorsey	1926
Red Nichols	1926
Joe Tarto	1926
Joe Venuti	1927
Louis Armstrong	1927
Elmer Schoebel	1927
Tommy Dorsey	1927

These are mostly collections of breaks in various keys, sometimes adorned with a capsule biography (i.e., no verbal instructions and no philosophical musings a la Panico). Trombonist Mole, in his 1925 self-published collection, claimed that he was responding to numerous letters asking for a book "that will teach my original style and method of playing a trombone" (1925), going on to write, "The writing of a book does not appeal to me, but I am doing a better thing, writing a series of original breaks and hot choruses for trombone and saxophone. My style is not copied from other musicians' ideas—it is strictly original. Every break and chorus is my own improvisation and can be followed by any trombone or saxophone player" (1925). In point of fact, the breaks and solos were transcribed from records.

In Mole's 1926 collection he writes, "The player will find that by memorizing the breaks he will easily be able to fit them into the playing of popular dance melodies. . . . There are no definite rules of improvising breaks, but this should become a reality after practice and study of the construction of the breaks in this book" (1926).

At the end of the 1920s the Melrose Bros. Music Co. produced collections of breaks and hot choruses to fit into orchestrations published by them. Such is the case of the deservedly famous *Louis Armstrong's 50 Hot Choruses*, as well as *125 Jazz Breaks*, said to have been transcribed by pianist and arranger Elmer Schoebel from office Dictaphone cylinders (Armstrong 1951). There are other collections, none so extensive as Armstrong's, devoted to clarinetist Benny Goodman, saxophonist Frank Trumbauer, and trombonist Glenn Miller.

Clarinetist Drew Page (1905–1990) in his autobiography devotes a couple of pages to the topic of learning by imitation as well as using published sources: "During the twenties, a spate of books came on the market at fifty cents each, containing jazz licks and 'breaks.' . . . Those licks and breaks were supposed to be memorized and used wherever they might fit. It was a crude method, but until that time it had been thought that jazz could not be written at all. The books were probably useful to some novices." Regarding Red Nichols, Page writes, "[He] went through the whole of *Arban's Method for Trumpet*—a big thick book—marking every melodic passage that might be used as a jazz 'lick' by itself or be combined with part of another" (1980, 63).

Such a pedantic and atomistic view of improvisation, which may have worked for the earlier 1920s, did not correspond to what players were becoming capable of. Although it had been relatively simple to explain jazz improvisation in terms of two-measure phrases, accounting for coherence over eight measures or more was another matter. One of the most remarkable efforts in this direction was a four-part article by Al Davison that appeared in *Melody Maker* between April and July 1929. Davison not only possessed a bachelor of music degree from Cambridge but was also a fellow of the Royal College of Organists. Perhaps due to his legitimate training—which Davison displayed somewhat ostentatiously—he submits to analysis the entire recording by the Paul Whiteman orchestra of "Sweet Sue," including the tune itself, the arrangement, and an already famous solo by Bix Beiderbecke.

Perhaps reflecting then current British usage, he avoids the term "improvisation" for "extemporization." Generally, however, the adjective "hot" seems to cover a number of bases. He writes, "You will be safe in taking it as a fact that all the best hot solos, and very many of the novel counter-melodies and effects played by individuals, are the original, and often extemporised on the spur of the moment, ideas of their performers" (May 1929, 505).

Davison pulls out all the stops in his concluding analysis of Bix's solo: "There is no doubt that Bix is a born genius. There is probably no one in existence who has quite the same talent for transcribing a given melody in a manner which is at once rhythmical, tuneful, entertaining, novel and in fact everything a hot solo should be. All his phrases are so delightfully constructed and hang together so well. They are never cheap and there is real musical merit in his work" (July 1929, 693). Although our learned organist was able to provide from his knowledge of harmony reasons that a particular pitch is especially ingenious, he clearly is at a loss to account for why they "hang together so well."

Not only *Melody Maker*, but also *Rhythm*, begun in 1927, frequently showered praise on American players, especially those who play "hot." Perhaps this interest is due to a deeply ingrained difference between England and the United States. David Berend, in his tenor banjo column in *Metronome*, wrote, "Remember the American idea of popular music is totally different from the Continental. Here we take a popular song as the starting point and interpolate [yet another term!] it to suit our own ideas. The Continental idea is that any note printed is sacred and a musician is judged by the way he plays the notes exactly as written . . . the fact remains that the top-notchers in the profession are judged by their originality" (1929).

But it wasn't only our British cousins who were baffled by such freedom. A highly personal view was offered in the column contributed by arranger Bob Haring to *Metronome* (1929, 29).

> Now, turning from the melody field to that which is better when it is not written, we come to the torrid phase of modern music. . . . There is something very interesting in the application of the word "hot" both to a certain type of music and to the man who plays it. I have often tried to analyze in my own mind just what a "hot" musician is. Just what is implied by the expression "Get hot"? I have heard soloists get "hot" by going musically crazy. Then again, there are "hot" styles which are little more than the straight melody with slight alterations in the time values of the various notes and phrases. Still another torrid twist sounds as if every other note were a dissonant to the chord and would end in chaos were it not for the alacrity of the performer in keeping some kind of general continuity. There is fast "hot" and slow "hot" and then that particular kind of "hot" that makes an audience on the dance floor holler for more . . . in my estimation extemporaneous, dirty, low-down, "hot" jazzy rhythms must be akin to the personality of the performer (no slander intended) and cannot be imitated, for another's playing is colored by the interjection of a new personality.

Born in 1896, Haring no doubt had heard the sounds of the Original Dixieland Jazz Band when they were new. Although he was a skilled arranger, it's interesting that his eloquent words find no intellectual component whatever in jazz.

The equivalence of "improvise" (or "extemporize") with playing "hot" is evident well into the 1930s and in fact begins to spread into other genres or styles of music. At least so I judge from *Bob Miller's Simplified, Illustrated Guitar Method* (1934). Miller (1895–1955) was most active as a publisher and writer of "cowboy" songs. His brief paragraph on "Improvising" goes as follows: "By improvising is meant, making up your own melody, to play it as a solo, or as an accompaniment to another melody, but as far as Guitar playing is concerned, it means to play what is called a hot, or dirt chorus to a given harmony . . . it is really necessary to know your chords thoroughly, know what notes are in them and what you can add to it" (1934). The four examples he gives show an F-major triad, but with use of the sixth and some passing use of the second degree. (By the way, the expression "dirt chorus" was common during the late 1920s and early 1930s. It probably merits a paragraph or two of its own.)

Sometime during the late 1920s a number of terms originated that apply more to rhythmic features or techniques making for climax rather than melodic extemporization per se. This may be due to the increasing importance of "riffs" (repeated rhythmic figures). Some instances are "get off" or "get away," "wrap-up," and "ride." A quite mysterious term for taking a solo is "take a Boston," with "Boston band" used for one in which solos are especially important or prominent. None of these, however, substitutes for the term "improvise." I suspect that many of these words originated among African American musicians and later jumped the racial divide.

In 1935 saxophonist Frank Trumbauer published his *Saxophone Studies (including Method of Improvising and Technical Secrets)*. In the section on improvising there is no mention of hot or dirt choruses, but, rather, some quite modern-sounding precepts: "First in importance are the scales. One cannot know these too well and you should have each and every scale at the tips of your fingers before you attempt anything else" (1935, 39). The same applies to thirds, fourths, and so on and also to chromatic scales, which "speed up your fingers and are very handy when you are learning to improvise; sound very flashy and cover up many weak spots in your choruses" (39). He stresses the importance of exercises: "You cannot spend too much time on these exercises as they are the foundation of improvising. Constructing an improvised chorus without them is almost impossible. Many hours of practice will be necessary before you may successfully reach the finished construction of a chorus" (40). Many of the following examples make challenging use of ninths as well as passing tones, and one of my favorites uses a descending chromatic series of seventh and ninth chords, with an ascending chromatic figure for the alto sax. This is a far cry from the collections of breaks that proliferated in the previous decade.

In April 1936 David Gornston contributed a brief piece to *Metronome*, "Analyzing Some Hot Styles," which proposed the following categories for "hot styles."

1. Swing phrasing applied to melody playing.
2. Melody improvisation. This stays close to the melody but makes modest use of non-chord tones.
3. Melody variation. This uses many notes and only suggests the melody. It's advised that either the player accent melody tones or have the tune stated softly in the background.

4. Solo variation grows out of the harmony and merely suggests the original melody or spirit of the composition. (Gornston subdivides this class into melody variation, in which the performer creates a new melody, and technical variation.)
5. Obligato Hot playing, which "occurs when the improvisation is built on the harmony to the melody instead of the melody itself."
6. Novelty Hot playing, which involves peculiar tonal effects and makes unusual use of glisses, mutes, moans, corny licks, ridiculous melodic phrasing, and other devices.

Gornston's synthesis doesn't give specific examples for his categories. As an aside, it's worth mentioning that this scheme antedates by 20 years the much-cited discussion of types of improvisation by the French composer André Hodéir, published in French as *Hommes et Problèmes du Jazz* (1954) and in English as *Jazz, Its Evolution and Essence* (1956).

Gornston's concluding paragraph is noteworthy, seemingly parroting Al Davison's article: "All really good hot choruses have organization, meaning, logical construction, etc., and whether the artist realizes it or not, his rejection of an undesirable chorus is based upon his failure to find the above qualifications in the improvisation. A hot chorus must be constructed as musically as a good song" (1936). (I suspect that some of this article comes from a 1934 publication that I have not yet seen, *Improvising Simplified (The Melody Way to Hot Playing),* which includes analysis of the individual styles of ten noted jazz players.)

Toward the end of the decade, one increasingly encounters systematic chord and arpeggio studies; these were ubiquitous when I started getting interested in music in the late 1940s. And there's much anecdotal evidence for the conscious use by jazz players of such an abstract and technical approach, whether learned from a publication or from oral instruction.

But these pedagogical studies didn't begin to address an issue that would become increasingly important. As is well known, the opportunities prior to the Second World War for players to take more than one 32–measure chorus were quite limited so far as recording was concerned. On an up-tempo blues, however, one might have three 12-measure choruses, but this didn't present the same challenge to creativity and imagination that 32 measures did. Even on a dance gig, to judge from orchestrations, the chance to play for more than one chorus was virtually nonexistent. For an exception, see my article on Lester Young (Gushee 1981, or one of its republications, e.g., Gushee 1991).

Obviously, the "jam session," seen as a test or cutting contest, became sometime between 1925 and 1935 the new institution that would push players beyond the comfortable limits of published orchestrations, as well as their ingrained habits. Moreover, the creation of two or even more choruses in a row that are artistically interesting is not something that makes it into the exercise and method books. But it seems clear enough that the school in which this skill might be learned was the "jam session," the history of which, alas, has yet to be written.

The term appears to come into the formal written language sometime in the early 1930s, although the phenomenon may well go back earlier, as in such possibly related expressions as "windjammer" and to "jam wind," mentioned earlier. In any event, there's a relationship with the "cutting contest," also an occasion for display. One instance of an early jam session was the speakeasy at 222 North State St., known logically enough as the Three Deuces, which, if we're to give credence to Mezz Mezzrow, must have opened its doors in November 1927 to musicians looking for a place to play "after hours." Mezzrow contrasts these seemingly friendly jam sessions—and he appears to claim this club as the place of origin of the term—with the private sessions held by African American players, the object of which was to triumph over the opposition. These Mezzrow understands more as highly competitive "cutting contests" (Mezzrow and Wolfe 1946, 147–49). Far more notorious are the after-hours sessions of Kansas City, beginning nobody knows just when, where for example pianist Sammy Price is said to have played 111 choruses of Nagasaki, lasting 1 hour and 15 minutes. As legend has it, on a night in December 1933 the Fletcher Henderson band was playing a one-nighter in KC. Coleman Hawkins, irked by the news that Lester Young had successfully subbed for him, supposedly showed up at the Cherry Blossom club at 12th and Vine, ready to roust the local competition. By dawn only four tenor players were still standing: Hawkins, Lester Young, Ben Webster, and Herschel Evans. (By the way, one up-tempo chorus of "Nagasaki" takes about 36 seconds, so Price could have played more than 111 choruses in the time allotted.) (For a recent account, see Driggs and Haddix 2005.)

As a concluding note, it's of no small interest to look at published orchestrations with respect to instructions to the players as well as untrammeled solo space, but this would be a sizable project in its own right. Certainly for most of the 1930s and probably into the next decade, the standard designation is "solo ad lib" or "ad lib solo," sometimes with chord names or the harmonies written out. Early in the decade, instead of chord names or notation, one may find only the unadorned melody. And later in the period sometimes just the chord names appear, an indication of increasing technical sophistication among swing musicians. Of course, many hundreds of orchestrations with a jazz or swing orientation would need to be examined. By way of example consider "Tomatoes," the first published arrangement of the late Lyle "Spud" Murphy, dating from 1927. The first repetition of the 16-measure chorus is labeled for "hot sax" and the second is to be sung. After this there are three 16-measure sections on a new chord progression. The first is for solo trombone, the second is in the first trumpet part marked "solo (improvise)"—the only time I've seen the explicit use of "improvise"—and the third is for sax ensemble with brass punctuation. In any event, here, as in other orchestrations, there's no reason a skilled player couldn't play two or three choruses instead of the one allocated by the score.

CONCLUSION

What can we make of all this? Does this wealth of terminology correspond on a one-to-one basis to actual practice; that is, rather than being synonyms, are they all actually needed to designate nuances of improvisation? Or, to take the most radical alternative, are these words meaningful chiefly with respect to the way we use language but not really applicable to musical practice? The broader general question is how intellectual categories are created to describe actual practice, as formal grammar does spoken language. This paper doesn't address such ponderous questions, but it does show a kind of increasing abstraction in conceptualizing jazz improvisation, which by 1937 had resulted in a fine-grained categorization that subsumed all of the earlier terms and concepts. Perhaps it should have had as its title "From Faking to Hot Playing to Improvisation." In any event, I suspect that this progression was part of a lengthy preparation that was to result by the mid-1940s in the conversion of jazz as dance music to jazz as a rather esoteric chamber music for listening.

REFERENCES

Anon. 1910. "The Five Peaches." *Referee* April 16, 6.
———. 1911. "The Story of a Wandering Musician." *Jacobs' Orchestra Monthly* March 26.
Armstrong, Louis. 1951. *Louis Armstrong's 44 Trumpet Solos & 125 Jazz Breaks*. New York: Edwin H. Morris. (This edition is a quasi-facsimile of the 1927 publication by Melrose Bros. Music Co. but lacks six of the original fifty solos.)
Berend, David. 1929. "Tenor Banjo Questions." *Metronome* 45(1), January, 29.
Berliner, Paul. 1994. *Thinking in Jazz: The Infinite Art of Improvisation*. Chicago: University of Chicago Press.

Colles, H. C., ed. 1927. *Grove's Dictionary of Music and Musicians*, 3rd ed. New York: Macmillan.

Cragun, J. Beach. 1923. *The Business Saxophonist*. Chicago: Rubank.

C. L. W. 1911. "The Story of a Wandering Musician." *Jacobs' Orchestra Monthly* March, 26–27.

Daley, Samuel T. [1926–1927]. *Sure System of Improvising*. Akron, Ohio: Author.

Davison, Al. 1929. "An Analytical Review of 'Sweet Sue.'" Four-part series. *Melody Maker* April–July.

Driggs, Frank, and Chuck Haddix. 2005. *Kansas City Jazz*. New York: Oxford University Press.

Erdmann, Ernest F. 1914. "Erdmann's Monthly Musical Review of New York." *Jacobs' Orchestra Monthly* January, 87–94.

Gornston, David. 1936. "Analyzing Some Hot Styles." *Metronome* 52(4), April.

———. 1934. *Improvising Simplified (The Melody Way to Hot Playing)*. New York: Mills Music.

Grupp, M. 1938. "Miff Mole Started Something." *Metronome* 54(6), June, 41.

Gushee, Lawrence. 1981. "Lester Young's Shoeshine Boy." In *Report of the Twelfth Congress of the International Musicological Society, Berkeley 1977*, 151–69. Kassel: Bärenreiter.

———. 1982. "Analytical Method and Compositional Process in Some Thirteenth and Fourteenth-Century Music." In *Forum Musicologicum* [Basler Beiträge zur Musikgeschichte III], 165–91. Winterthur: Amadeus Verlag.

———. 1991. "Lester Young's Shoeshine Boy" (reprint). In *Lester Young Reader*, edited by Lewis Porter, 224–54. Washington, D.C.: Smithsonian Institution Press.

———. 2004. "Improvisation im frühen Jazz." In *Improvisieren . . .* (Darmstädter Beiträge zur Jazzforschung, band 8), 41–74. Hofheim: Wolke Verlag.

Haring, Bob. 1929. "Arranging." *Metronome* 45(7), July, 29.

Haviland. 1911. "If you're hep, nothing will hinder your having Haviland's 'Happy Hits' hanging handily about to hand out hot harmonies when holding summer 'hops.'" *Jacobs' Orchestra Monthly* May, 88.

Hodéir, André. 1954. *Hommes et Problèmes du Jazz*. Paris: Au Portulan.

———. 1956. *Jazz, Its Evolution and Essence*. New York: Grove Press.

Kernfeld, Barry. 1988. *The New Grove Dictionary of Jazz*. London: Macmillan.

———. 1995. *What to Listen for in Jazz*. New Haven, Conn.: Yale University Press.

———. 2002. *The New Grove Dictionary of Jazz*, 2nd ed. New York: Grove's Dictionaries Inc.

Lomax, Alan. 1950. *Mister Jelly Roll*. New York: Grove Press.

Mezzrow, Milton "Mezz," and Bernard Wolfe. 1946. *Really the Blues*. New York: Random House.

Miller, Bob. 1934. *Bob Miller's Simplified, Illustrated Guitar Method*. New York: Bob Miller, Inc.

Mole, "Miff." 1925. *"Original Breaks" and "Hot Choruses" for Trombone and Alto Saxophone*. (No publisher shown, but probably the author.)

———. 1926. *100 Jazz Breaks for Trombone*. New York: Alfred and Company.

Murphy, Lyle. 1927. "Tomatoes: A Low-Down." New York and Montgomery, Ala.: Chansonette.

Page, Drew. 1980. *Drew's Blues*. Baton Rouge: Louisiana State University Press.

Panico, Louis. 1924. *The Novelty Cornetist*. Chicago: Author.

Ragas, Henry W. 1917. Deposition submitted to the District Court of the United States, Northern District of Illinois, Eastern Division (*Max Hart et al. v. Roger Graham*), October 2.

Sadie, Stanley, ed. 1980. *The New Grove Dictionary of Music and Musicians*. London: Macmillan.

Schwebel, Edwin J. 1926. *Trick piano playing: breaks, jazz time-blue endings, fill in, when and where to apply, for the amateur and professional pianist*. St. Louis, Mo.: All American.

Shefte, Art. 1927. *Hot breaks for piano; hot but easy to play*. Chicago: Forster.

———. [1925] 1927. *Up-to-the-minute jazz breaks, tricks, blues, endings, etc. for the amateur and professional pianist*. Chicago: Forster.

Stone, George Burt. 1912a. Drum column. *Jacobs' Orchestra Monthly* February.

———. 1912b. Drum column. *Jacobs' Orchestra Monthly* May.

Sudhalter, Richard M. 1999. *Lost Chords: White Musicians and Their Contribution to Jazz: 1915–1945*. New York: Oxford University Press.

Trumbauer, Frank. 1935. *Saxophone Studies (including Method of Improvising and Technical Secrets)*. New York: Robbins.

Waterman, Glenn R. 1924. *Piano jazz: 1001 breaks, trick endings, bass forms, space fillers, blue rhythms and syncopated effects; how to play any popular song like a player piano roll*. Los Angeles: Waterman Piano School.

Winn, Edward R. 1924. *Winn's how to play breaks and endings: shows how and where to apply to popular piano music more than 100 novelty jazz and blues breaks, endings, space fillers. . . .* New York: Winn School of Popular Music.

⤚ 16 ⤙

OPENING THE MUSEUM WINDOW:
IMPROVISATION AND ITS INSCRIBED
VALUES IN CANONIC WORKS BY
CHOPIN AND SCHUMANN

Robert S. Hatten

Most aspects of human behavior can be understood by examining their value for an individual or social group. Practitioners and interpreters of Western art music place a primary value on artistry, or acquired knowledge and skill in one or more musical styles (see Table 16.1). Artistic improvisation—as opposed to random "noodling"—is thus valued for its grounding in a *stylistic competency* that presupposes basic principles and a vast repertoire of strategic realizations of those principles, manifested as familiar patterns (e.g., harmonic formulae), formal schemes, or even expressive genres. For artistic improvisation, even previously composed works may function as structural skeletons (in cases of improvised variations) or as intertextual sources of

Table 16.1. Values associated with improvisation (for Western art music)

I. Artistry (as informed by previously acquired knowledge and skill)
  A. Stylistic competency (playing within stylistic principles)
  B. Strategic innovation (playing with and against stylistic constraints)

II. Generativity (musical thinking in the moment, creativity as informed by intuition and the contexts of performance)
  A. Unpredictability (delight in serendipity, overcoming risk of failure)
  B. Discovery or heuristic value (leading to growth or change in the unfolding work and perhaps ultimately the style as well)

III. Spontaneity (spontaneous performance of a spontaneously creative act)
  A. Indexical relevance to a discursive situation (engagement)
  B. Grounding in the body (musical gestures as created and manifested by an improviser)
  C. Affective directness or immediacy (gesture as affective, iconic, and indexical)
  D. Authenticity (genuineness, since difficult for spontaneous gestures to "lie")
  E. A sign of the individual(s) (symbolic association)
  F. Intimate disclosure, or authentic dialogue, revealing deepest thoughts and feelings

---

meaning (in cases of quotations or allusions). Other styles may play a role as well, through either subtle allusion or outright parody. Regardless of how one acquires stylistic competency—whether by closely following instructions, by serving as an apprentice under a master teacher who may exemplify a practice, or by privately memorizing and generalizing a style from repeated listening and trial by error—that competency provides a fundamental framework for artistic improvisation. Artistry, however, cannot be reduced to stylistically normative behavior. Indeed, expressive values are often judged by how successfully the music—whether improvised or not—plays with or even against the style that ensures its coherence.[1]

If playing with and against the style is an important value in improvisation, then the *unpredictability* of that play may, by extension, form part of the performers' and listeners' delight, especially when serendipity overcomes the inherent risk of failure. This helps answer the question, from the standpoint of artistic value, why an improviser might not choose to write down an improvisation, even if she has worked it out to her satisfaction through multiple, artistically varied performances. Of course, many 20th-century jazz improvisations have been preserved, whether or not the improviser(s) intended it, through recordings or transcriptions or both.[2] But what *artistic* value might there be in something so spontaneous as to be subject to error, especially in Western musical cultures, where artistic values are often so exacting? To answer this question, one might consider the generative value of spontaneous artistic composition. Schubert improvised waltzes all night for his close circle of friends, and he later notated some of the more interesting results of his on-the-spot compositional processes. Whether or not the final result is a notated score, however, improvisation can be valued for its creativity, in the sense of its potential for *discovery* or its *heuristic* power.

But improvisers and their listeners may also value extemporaneous creation for its *spontaneity* (absorbing or forgiving those "errors" that may well be salvaged as productive turning points in a fluid discourse). Here, as in spontaneous conversation, practitioners value degrees of artistry but also enjoy the mere fact of an improvisation's *indexical relevance* to a discursive situation. Spontaneity of gesture often reveals its *grounding in the body* of a performer who is simultaneously functioning as the creator of those gestures. In my own work I have emphasized the *affective directness* or apparent *immediacy* of gesture, which I define as "communicative (whether intended or not), expressive, energetic shaping through time" (Hatten 2004, 110). This immediacy is supported by a wide range of interdisciplinary evidence from the biological to the psychological and the cultural (see Hatten 2004, 97–110).

The ensured embodiment of a performer/creator who is committed to unfolding an immediately relevant discourse may also be culturally marked as *authentic*. Interestingly, listeners may value such authenticity more highly than strict adherence to stylistic constraints—even when one might judge that the improviser has made errors within his or her own improvisational style. And if listeners in a given culture value spontaneous, embodied, directly communicative, and authentic musical gestures and discourses, then musical improvisation will also tend to be valued as a *sign* or *signature of the individual*. Furthermore, the embodiment of one's own creative gestures cannot help but expose the improviser, whose personality and inner emotional life are revealed through *intimate disclosure* (or, in the case of ensemble improvisation, through two or more individuals engaged in *authentic dialogue*). Of course, the improviser may nonetheless be wearing a mask, revealing only a persona, but this is less likely to be true for spontaneous improvisation, in which the body tends to reveal—or betray—the improviser's state of mind.[3]

It is this aspect of intimate emotional disclosure, with its complementary values of individuality and authenticity, that emerges as a powerful cross-current to Enlightenment reason in one mid-18th-century musical practice—the improvisation of fantasies. Carl Philipp Emanuel Bach's keyboard fantasies, whether improvised or later written down, were often conceived as dramatic soliloquies, as the "Hamlet" fantasy attests. Bach is unusually instructive concerning his own practice of improvising fantasies. In the final chapter of his practical treatise, *Essay on the True Art of Playing Keyboard Instruments*, he demonstrates how figured-bass ground-plans for improvisation ensure underlying coherence for the so-called free fantasy ([1753] 1949). Of course, improvisatory performances might be deemed less than individual, intimate, or authentic if overly formulaic ground-plans were heard as stifling a sense of freedom or if rhetorical effects were experienced as overly conventional.

Evidence for an improviser's intimate disclosure—and its psychic dangers—comes from a report of Beethoven's improvisations in the Viennese salons in the 1790s (a cultural practice that is admittedly hard to assess in the absence of recordings). According to Czerny, Beethoven became so engrossed in his inner world while improvising at the piano that upon glancing up and witnessing the tears of his listeners, he suddenly insulted them and charged out of the room (Kinderman 1995).[4] One need not presume that an improviser is aware of the degree of intimacy in such disclosure, or even fully aware of communication; ironically, the most profound artistic communication may happen when a performer is immersed in private reflection. A psychological interpretation for Beethoven's bad manners would be that intimate disclosure leaves an improviser psychically exposed in front of an audience of relative strangers, and sudden awareness of that vulnerability provokes a defensive response—in this case, rebuffing the very audience one has so deeply moved.

IMPLIED IMPROVISATION AND ITS VALUES
IN THE EARLY 19TH CENTURY

Having explored the range of values vested in Western improvisation, I turn now to striking evidence that during the 19th century—ironically, just when the "work concept" was becoming increasingly entrenched for both composers and performers—improvisation and its values continued to be implied by composers in works that were completely notated.[5] With Chopin we have compelling evidence for "composed-in" improvisation, as inferred from his notated works conceived for performance in intimate salon settings.[6] Here, spontaneity may be cued by several features. The Nocturne in E♭ Major, Op. 55, no. 2 (Example 16.1) features irregular subdivisions of the beat in a diminutional, varied return of the theme in m. 35, suggesting the type of rubato, also found in Mozart, where the right hand launches free of the constraints of a more regular left hand. Here, a freely asymmetrical rhythm of 7 against 6 is intensified to 7 against 3 on the fourth beat of mm. 35–6.[7]

In the Nocturne in B Major, Op. 62, no. 1 (Example 16.2), overlapping phrase structure and the effect of an endlessly evolving and recycling melody are cues of an improvisatory freedom that in turn suggests an inward and luxuriant reflectiveness. Note the progressive descents from B (m. 3), D♯ (m. 4), and F♯ (mm. 5–6) in the four-bar theme and the overlapping return of the theme when it is first recycled, with metric displacement, in B major (m. 7) and then transformed to fit into G♯ minor (m. 10). In a recent article, William Rothstein notes that this circular motion is not merely found in the overlapping of phrases but also "built into the music's phrase rhythm, its voice leading, and . . . even into its motivic structure" (2006, 21).

Later in the same nocturne (Example 16.3), improvisational 16th-note figuration suggests "melancholy rumination" over a static harmonic oscillation in mm. 21–26, disrupted by a defiant outburst in m. 26.

This passage projects an improvisatory musical style as found in a more distant culture—perhaps related to what Chopin heard during his stay on the island of Majorca seven years earlier. The 16th-note, "ruminating" figuration returns in the coda, first diatonically supporting the cadence in B major, then varied, pianissimo, with its increasingly exotic scale providing a mystical effect.

Associating improvisation with folk, primitive, or historical cultures—or improvisatory freedom as modeling an escape from the oppressive constraints of the prevailing culture—may suggest motivations for a variety of marked musical techniques. Table 16.2 presents a preliminary outline of these motivations as Romantic values and links them to particular techniques, as illustrated in my four musical examples.

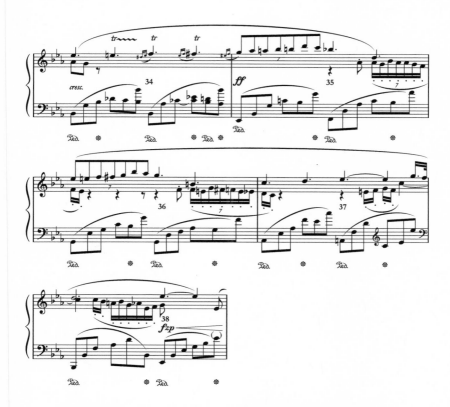

EXAMPLE 16.1. Chopin, Nocturne in E♭ Major, Op. 55, no. 2, mm. 34–38.

Note: Diminutionally varied return of theme in m. 35; freely asymmetrical rhythm of 7 against 6; intensified to 7 against 3 on fourth beat.

EXAMPLE 16.2. Chopin, Nocturne in B Major, Op. 62, no. 1, mm. 1–12.

Note: Scalar descent from B in the circular opening and closing of the four-bar theme; metric displacement as it recycles in B (m. 7) and is transformed into g♯ minor (m. 10⁴); scalar descent recycled from D♯ and F♯ within the phrase.

EXAMPLE 16.3. Chopin, Nocturne in B Major, Op. 62, no. 1.
Note: Improvisational sixteenth-note figuration as "rumination" over static harmonic oscillation in mm. 21–26; rhetorical
outburst in m. 26 akin to a Moorish flourish; the sixteenth figuration returns in the coda with more exotic scalar treatment.

Because of the high value placed on individuality and genius, the 19th
century might be considered an age especially suited for intimate improvisation, and yet improvisation can exist in any era in which one values
authenticity and sincerity of personal expression—even when individual
improvisatory freedom might threaten to go beyond social constraints. The
difference between, for example, accounts of Bach's improvisations and those
of the Romantics may be found in the degree to which individual freedom is
sought. Sebastian Bach's ability to improvise fugues on proposed subjects is
a crowning achievement of artistic spontaneous creation. Bach's spontane-

Table 16.2.   Romantic values associated with implied improvisation as notated
in a score

I. Association with folk, primitive, or historical cultures; or escape from the prevailing culture
    (viewed as urban, print-oriented, overly complex, alienating, even corrupting)
    A. Authenticity/naturalness (cueing of the "other" or the "originary")
        • Use of modes, other marked melodic/harmonic/rhythmic events not associated with
          the prevailing style (hinted at in Example 16.3; see also coda)
        • Simplicities as contrasted with the complexities of a sophisticated, score-oriented
          music culture (Example 16.3)
    B. Freedom from constraints (as willful break from oppressive social convention)
        • Improvisatory figuration or diminution as variation (Example 16.1)
        • Asymmetries, willful breaking of symmetries (Example 16.1)
        • Circular structures, less goal-oriented processes (Example 16.2)
        • Overlapping of boundaries (Example 16.2)
        • Moments of stasis for "reflection" (Example 16.3)
        • Rhetorical breaks and marked disruptions of the unmarked flow (Example 16.3)
        • Expressively motivated expansion of forms (Example 16.4)
II. Emphasis on individuality and personal expression
    A. Intimate disclosure (Examples 16.2 and 16.4)
    B. Virtuosity (Example 16.1 and end of Example 16.3)

---

ity, however, is often absorbed into the act of creativity, and the resulting, fully worked out composition may not betray improvisatory license in the calculation of its ultimate design. Should the improvisatory origins of a work be known, its organic coherence might be valued still more highly in light of its spontaneous achievement. This coherent, yet in some sense spontaneous, intuition is what Heinrich Schenker ([1926] 1977, 39, 52–53) inferred from the compositional process of those masters he placed in his exclusive canon.[8]

Even among the Romantics, the value of spontaneous creation may be tempered by another, often more ideologically compelling value, that of coherent form. In the following aphorism published in his music journal, Schumann adopts a confessional tone as he offers advice to young composers: "If heaven has gifted you with a lively imagination, you will often, in lonely hours, sit as though spellbound at the piano-forte, seeking to express your inner feelings in harmonies; and you may find yourself mysteriously drawn into a magic circle proportionate to the degree to which the realm of harmony is still vague to you. These are the happiest hours of youth. But beware of losing yourself too often in a talent that will lead you to waste strength and time on shadowy pictures. You will only obtain mastery of form and the power of clear construction by firm strokes of the pen. Therefore, write more often than improvise" (1946, 36).[9]

In spite of his instruction, Schumann finds ways to inscribe improvisatory values in his fully composed works, thereby enshrining the spontaneous
intimacy of his artistic conception. The evidence from Schumann's works
suggests that the quest for mastery of form (as in Schumann's much-discussed
"Fantasy" for piano) was not marked by slavish allegiance to received models.[10] Indeed, Schumann appears to have been strongly motivated by a need
for intimate personal disclosure (to Clara, at least) in which spontaneous
gestures as well as expressively motivated formal expansion played a role.[11]

The final dance from the first edition of the *Davidsbündlertänze*, Op. 6 (see
Example 16.4), is based on rounded binary form, but the dance only elusively
establishes C major before beginning a modulatory process toward G at the
double bar. The second strain then moves away and returns to G as tonic
(not dominant) before the thematic return coincides with a shift to C in m.
19, again occluded by its dominant seventh. Interestingly, the shift without
preparation lends C major a subdominant quality, entirely appropriate for
the pastoral connotations of this bi-chord in Schumann (compare the beginning of the coda for piano that concludes *Dichterliebe*). Only a significant
expansion after the return leads to the missing perfect authentic cadence in C
major (mm. 32–33, reinforced in mm. 40–41). In this way, Schumann achieves
a climactic affirmation that his hesitant beginning could only surmise.

The expressive freedom exemplified by the last half of this dance exceeds
the boundaries of the form and is inspired by, or at least sounds like, improvisational play. A feeling emerges, blossoms, and dies away without concern for
strict symmetries or formal schemes. Form evolves into gesture, and that gesture sounds increasingly spontaneous as it spills over the bounds of an initially
established form. Indeed, the last dance number as a whole is conceived as an
addendum to the work. The previous dance had ended with a dramatic coda in
the tragic mode of B minor—the framing key that Schumann had emphasized
by quoting the second dance, also in B minor, as a poignant memory. Thus,
from a formal perspective, Schumann is fully justified in indicating "Superflu-
ously, Eusebius added the following, and his eyes filled with tears of happiness"
above the final dance. And yet there is nothing expressively redundant in the
dance's stunning transformation to positive affirmation, with improvisatory
freedom contributing to a sense of liberating epiphany. Schumann's closural
liquidation is also poetically apt. He "tolls midnight" twice, on 12 repeated Cs
(from m. 41 in the bass, and from m. 49 on middle C), to provide an external
(and extramusical) frame—perhaps inspired by the end of the ball in Jean
Paul's influential novel *Flegeljahre*—for his internal drama.[12]

Ganz zum Überfluß meinte Eusebius noch Folgendes; dabei sprach aber viel Seligkeit aus seinen Augen.
Quite redundantly Eusebius added the following; but great happiness shone in his eyes the while.

EXAMPLE 16.4. Schumann, *Davidsbündlertänze*, Op. 6, final dance (no. 18).

Note: Rounded binary form with enormous expansion of the return section [R] to achieve a definitive and affirmative cadence in C, mm. 32–33; improvisatory freedom of form is motivated by its expressive trajectory toward epiphany of closure (mm. 40–41) and subsequent dissolution.

and progressive dissolution ⟶

EXAMPLE 16.4. *Cont.*

CONCLUSION

Competent listeners in a musical style may value spontaneous creativity within that style not only for its artistic melodic, harmonic, or formal results, but also for its potential to suggest immediate, personal, authentic, and thus intimate disclosure on the part of a performer who embodies those sonic gestures. The musical strategies in my examples from Chopin and Schumann provide evidence of an improvisational practice whose effects could be incorporated into a polished and fully notated artwork. Investigating how 19th-century composers negotiated the opposition between fixed and freer practices may help correct misconceptions of their now-canonic works. If even a "masterwork" may inscribe improvisatory values such as authenticity, individuality, and intimate disclosure, then we are less likely to view these compositions as autonomous works locked into a canonic museum, and more likely to understand them as manifestations of vital music-cultural practices.[13]

NOTES

1. This is also true of much non-Western music. The linguist Charles Bird notes that a master bard is distinguished from an apprentice among the Mande in Africa by the extent to which he goes beyond the constraints of an "aesthetic grammar" to create the tension "by which the master jostles the expectancies of his audience, to participate in his act of creation in performance" (1976, 91).

2. But jazz improvisation is not limited to the spontaneous generation of a masterpiece. Instead, it embraces the value of a spontaneity that takes risks and, though it may fail, survives the gamble by capturing (discovering, creating) a new moment of expressivity, whether or not it achieves a closed or hierarchically satisfying overall structure. However, as Steve Larson (1987) has shown in his Schenkerian analysis of Oscar Peterson's improvisations on the standard, 'Round about Midnight, these values need not be mutually exclusive. See also Larson 1998. Oscar Peterson's classical training may have been a factor here as well.

3. Umberto Eco defines semiotics as "in principle the discipline studying everything which can be used in order to lie." In the case of more spontaneous gestures, however, the effort to deceive becomes more difficult to accomplish (1976, 7). For example, we are generally able to detect the faking of emotions in those facial expressions Paul Ekman has labeled "referential expressions" (1999).

4. William Kinderman describes "Czerny's account of Beethoven's practice, after moving his listeners to tears through his improvisations, of bursting into loud laughter and mocking his hearers' emotion, saying 'You are fools!'" (1995, 261); this description draws from Alexander Wheelock Thayer's biography of Beethoven (Thayer 1964, 185).

5. The emergence of the autonomous work in the 19th century and the consequent beginning of canonization in Western music are themes developed by Lydia Goehr (1992). For an interesting example of composed improvisation in Wagner's Die Meistersinger, see Eero Tarasti (2002). This moment, when the contest song is created, is also discussed by Ernst Ferand (1938, 33). Tarasti's superb essay examines the semiotics of improvisation from the perspective of Roman Jakobson's communication model, Charles Sanders Peirce's categories of icon, index, and symbol, and A. J. Greimas's isotopies, modalities, and temporal/spatial/actorial categories.

6. John Rink (2001) addresses a related set of improvisatory features as found in Chopin's composed works. His catalogue includes structural schemata from Chopin's improvisations, adaptations of vocal improvisation (embellishments, cadenzas, and recitative-like passages), ostinato plus variation (or pedal point plus cantilena), harmonic sequences to introduce a work, preluding figuration, and even principal motives as introduced at the beginning of a work (since this was a common practice in improvisation).

The performer can contribute in still other ways toward the illusion of improvisatory spontaneity. The subtle warpings of timing, shadings of dynamic nuance, mixings of damper pedal, and discriminations of articulation are further means by which one can recreate through the body the spontaneity of gesture—as though the sounds were being heard for the first time, or captured in the moment of their birth.

7. Freedom versus constraint may be allegorized, as in Example 1, by an improvisatory right hand versus a steady left hand marking the beat. It may also be signaled by an expanded phrase that departs from the expected four-bar model. The spontaneous is typically experienced against the background of the typical—perhaps most simply as ornamental variation, and most complexly as the troping of topics or mixing of genres (see Hatten 2004, 68–89).

8. For more on Schenker's metaphor of composition as improvisation, see Rink 1993.

9. This "aphorism" appeared in the *Neue Zeitschrift für Musik* during Schumann's editorship, 1834–1844.

10. For instructive analyses of the Schumann "Fantasy," see Daverio 1993, 19–47; Marston 1992; Roesner 1991; and Rosen 1995, 100–12. Just as improvisation may be heuristic for expressive exploration within a style, it may also provide an avenue for expanding the style, perhaps leading to style change. Schumann provides clear evidence of this in his exploration of what one might call "improvisatory form" in his earlier, cyclic collections for piano, notably *Papillons* and *Carnaval*, as well as in the *Davidsbündlertänze*. Although the "system of fragments" that Daverio (1993) and Rosen (1995) discuss may not have become a standard formal option in the 19th century, it was clearly part of Schumann's evolution of tonally open forms and continuity based on hidden motivic connections, or *Witz*.

11. For more on the connections with Clara, see Daverio 1997.

12. For more on the final dance as postlude, see Rosen 1995, 233–35. Rosen concludes that "the final dance is therefore both within and without the formal structure" (235).

13. The philosopher who has gone furthest in claiming improvisation as the core of both composition and performance is Bruce Ellis Benson (2003). His list of 11 degrees of improvisation in performance reveals the breadth of a continuum of spontaneous creation, from fleshing out a score to transcription, editing, arranging, and (as in jazz) creating variations on the melody or harmony, either within a formal framework of a previous work or merely within the broader realm of a genre or style (26–30). Spontaneous creativity (or composition as impromptu selection) thus permeates both composition and performance, but to varying degrees. Benson takes this phenomenon as evidence of the instability of a work's identity: "[I]f both composition and performance result in the modification of the discourse in which they take place, then there is no escaping the conclusion that a musical work's identity is also in flux" (123). Through his extensive examination of degrees of improvisation, Benson underlines its importance across a range of current musical practices. Through his philosophical arguments he foregrounds improvisation as a crucial critical value in current discourse about the nature and status of the musical work.

REFERENCES

Bach, Carl Philipp Emanuel. [1753] 1949. *Versuch über die wahre Art das Clavier zu Spielen.* Original published in Berlin. Translated by W. J. Mitchell as *Essay on the True Art of Playing Keyboard Instruments.* New York: Norton.

Benson, Bruce Ellis. 2003. *The Improvisation of Musical Dialogue: A Phenomenology of Music.* Cambridge: Cambridge University Press.

Bird, Charles. 1976. "Poetry in the Mande: Its Form and Meaning." *Poetics* 5: 89–100.

Daverio, John. 1993. *Nineteenth-Century Music and the German Romantic Ideology.* New York: Schirmer.

———. 1997. "Musical Love Letters in the Higher and Smaller Forms." In *Robert Schumann: Herald of a "New Poetic Age,"* 105–81. New York: Oxford University Press.

Eco, Umberto. 1976. *A Theory of Semiotics.* Bloomington: Indiana University Press.

Ekman, Paul. 1999. "Emotional and Conversational Nonverbal Signals." In *Gesture, Speech, and Sign,* edited by Lynn S. Messing and Ruth Campbell, 45–55. Oxford: Oxford University Press.

Ferand, Ernst. 1938. *Die Improvisation in der Music: Eine entwicklungsgeschichtliche und psychologische Untersuchung.* Zürich: Rhein Verlag.

Goehr, Lydia. 1992. *The Imaginary Museum of Musical Works: An Essay in the Philosophy of Music.* Oxford: Clarendon Press.

Hatten, Robert S. 2004. *Interpreting Musical Gestures, Topics, and Tropes: Mozart, Beethoven, Schubert.* Bloomington: Indiana University Press.

Kinderman, William. 1995. *Beethoven.* Oxford: Oxford University Press.

Larson, Steve. 1987. "Schenkerian Analysis of Modern Jazz." Ph.D. dissertation, University of Michigan.

———. 1998. "Schenkerian Analysis of Modern Jazz: Questions about Method." *Music Theory Spectrum* 20(2): 209–41.

Marston, Nicholas. 1992. *Schumann: Fantasie, Op. 17.* Cambridge: Cambridge University Press.

Rink, John S. 1993. "Schenker and Improvisation." *Journal of Music Theory* 37(1): 1–54.

———. 2001. "The Legacy of Improvisation in Chopin." In *Muzyka w kontekcie kultury* ["Music in Cultural Context," a Festschrift in honor of Mieczyaw Tomaszewski], edited by Magorzata Janicka-Sysz, Teresa Malecka, and Krzysztof Szwajgier, 79–88. Kraków: Akademia Muzyczna.

Roesner, Linda C. 1991. "Schumann's 'Parallel' Forms." *19th-Century Music* 14(3): 265–78.

Rosen, Charles. 1995. *The Romantic Generation.* Cambridge: Harvard University Press.

Rothstein, William. 2006. "Circular Motion in Chopin's Late B-Major Nocturne." In *Structure and Meaning in Tonal Music* [Festschrift in Honor of Carl Schachter], edited by L. Poundie Burstein and David Gagné, 19–32. Hillsdale, N.Y.: Pendragon Press.

Schenker, Heinrich. [1926] 1977. "Organic Structure in Sonata Form," translated by Orin Grossman. In *Readings in Schenkerian Analysis and Other Approaches,* edited by Maury Yeston, 38–53. New Haven, Conn., and London: Yale University Press.

Schumann, Robert. 1946. *On Music and Musicians.* Edited by Konrad Wolff, translated by Paul Rosenfeld. New York: Pantheon Books.

Tarasti, Eero. 2002. "On the Semiosis of Musical Improvisation: From *Mastersingers* to Bororo Indians." In *Signs of Music: A Guide to Musical Semiotics*, 179–97. Berlin, New York: Mouton de Gruyter.

Thayer, Alexander Wheelock. 1964. *Thayer's Life of Beethoven*. Revised edition by Elliott Forbes. Princeton: Princeton University Press.

IMPROVISATION IN BEETHOVEN'S CREATIVE PROCESS

William Kinderman

Improvisation, understood as the activity of performing music spontaneously, without the aid of score, manuscript, or even sketches or memorization, might seem very different or even quite opposed to the rendering of an opus, a finished, autonomous work of musical art. According to some commentators, this disconnection between improvisation or extemporization, on the one hand, and the work-concept, on the other, came into existence at a particular historical time, a little more than two centuries ago. Lydia Goehr, in her book *The Imaginary Museum of Musical Works*, argues that "by 1800, when composition was defined as involving the predetermination of as many structural elements as possible, the notion of extemporization acquired its modern understanding. For the first time it was seen to stand in strict opposition to composition 'proper'" (1991, 234). Goehr associates this shift especially with Beethoven, so much so that she describes it as "The Beethoven Paradigm." The sense of Beethoven having predetermined many "structural elements" to create highly unified and self-sufficient works has been reinforced by analytical approaches that emphasize the coherence of motivic integration or voice-leading relations in his music. Furthermore, Beethoven's reputation as a deliberate artist, who worked so hard in composing his music, lends support to the notion that his finished pieces have a highly determined character, toward which a responsible performer might appropriately demonstrate an attitude of distanced reverence in the spirit of *Werktreue*, or "faithfulness to the work."

This essay examines the role in Beethoven's art of improvisation, or "fantasieren," to use the term the composer normally employed for extemporization. Beethoven's ability to improvise at the keyboard was regarded as extraordinary and was much commented on by his contemporaries. Indeed, some critics charged that Beethoven's approach to musical composition was harmed by its closeness to improvisation. The critic August Wendt, writing in the *Allgemeine Musikalische Zeitung* in 1815, found it unfortunate that most of Beethoven's sonatas and symphonies were spoiled by the formlessness of the fantasy (quoted in Sisman 1998, 96). Similar responses were common, and Beethoven's own propensity to inject a sense of improvisation into established musical genres is reflected in pieces like his two piano sonatas Op. 27, both of which he described as "sonata quasi fantasia." It is noteworthy too that during his long years as a piano virtuoso, Beethoven was disinclined to play his published works and preferred to extemporize. His student Ferdinand Ries reported that when they made preparations for a tour together, he was to play Beethoven's concertos and other finished compositions, whereas Beethoven "wanted only to conduct and improvise" (Thayer quoted in Forbes 1964, 367).

Eyewitness reports of Beethoven's improvisations stress his capacity for developing much out of little, seeing the world in a grain of sand by making some accidental scrap of musical material into the springboard for an astoundingly imaginative musical discourse. The composer Johann Schenk (Thayer 1917, 1: 355) described the unforgettable impression of a free fantasy more than a half-hour in length that Beethoven played in 1792. A report in the *Allgemeine musikalische Zeitung* from April 1799 emphasized that he "shows himself to the greatest advantage in improvisation, and here, indeed, it is most extraordinary with what lightness and yet firmness in the succession of ideas Beethoven not only varies a theme given him on the spur of the moment by figuration (with which many a virtuoso makes his fortune and—wind) but really develops it" (Thayer in Forbes 1964, 205; Frimmel 1906, 243–44).

Another such account stems from 1800, when Beethoven was matched with the flamboyant virtuoso pianist Daniel Steibelt in a competitive keyboard encounter. According to Ries, Steibelt responded to a performance of Beethoven's Clarinet Trio Op. 11 with polite condescension, offering in turn a showy improvisation on a popular operatic theme—the same tune chosen by Beethoven for the variations forming the finale of his trio. Beethoven retaliated by seizing the cello part of a quintet by Steibelt: after placing it upside down on the music stand, he poked out a theme with one finger from its opening bars. Offended, Steibelt walked out during Beethoven's ensuing brilliant improvisation and refused any further association with him (Thayer quoted in Forbes 1964, 257).

Beethoven's ability to transform any materials on hand into artistic coinage is illustrated in yet another story from his student Carl Czerny. Czerny reported that around 1809 the composer Ignaz Pleyel came to Vienna with his latest string quartet, which was performed at the home of Beethoven's

patron Prince Lobkowitz. Beethoven was in attendance and was urged to
perform at the piano. Rather typically, he was hesitant to play and became ir-
ritated, and then suddenly grabbed one of the parts from Pleyel's quartet—the
second violin part—and began to improvise. Czerny relates: "Never had one
heard something so ingenious, so captivating, so brilliant from him; but in
the middle of his fantasy one could still hear plainly a banal run drawn from
the violin part. . . . He had built his entire beautiful improvisation upon this
figure" (Czerny quoted in Kolneder 1968, 45). In this case, as surely in many
others, the improvised music also left its mark on one of Beethoven's major
compositions from the time, his String Quartet in E-Flat Major, Op. 74.[1]

In private situations at times when words failed, Beethoven sometimes
offered the healing power of improvised music to friends in distress. When
his former student Dorothea von Ertmann née Graumann was beset by grief
after the death of her three-year-old son in 1804, she related that he played
spontaneously for more than half an hour until "he told me everything,
and in the end even brought me comfort." Ertmann remembered that "I
felt as if I were listening to choirs of angels celebrating the entrance of my
poor child into the world of light." Another report of this kind stems from
Beethoven's intimate friend Antonia Brentano née Birkenstock, who during
her residence in Vienna between 1809 and 1812 was often ailing, suffering
to such an extent that she withdrew into solitude. She related that on such
occasions Beethoven "came in, seated himself without any further ado in
her antechamber and improvised; when he had 'said everything and given
solace' to the sufferer in his own language, he left as he had come, without
taking notice of anybody else."[2]

A natural forum for keyboard extemporization was the piano concerto,
and Beethoven's involvement with his concertos offers insight into his aesthetics of improvisation. One of his favorite devices was to reinterpret that
most indispensable of stylistic gestures, the cadence. What moment in a
classical concerto is more characteristic and predictable than that trill on
the supertonic on a dominant-seventh harmony, which signals the immi-
nent reentry of the tutti with a new ritornello statement? Beethoven paid
special attention to the solo cadenzas or lead-in passages that precede and
delay such tutti passages, and not just in concertos. Ries related an occasion
when Beethoven "played his Quintet for Pianoforte and Wind-Instruments
with [Friedrich] Ramm as [oboe] soloist. In the last Allegro there are several
holds [or pauses] before the theme is resumed. At one of these Beethoven
suddenly began to improvise, took the Rondo for a theme and entertained
himself and the others for a considerable time, but not the other players.

They were displeased and Ramm even very angry. It was really very comical to see them, momentarily expecting the performance to be resumed, put their instruments to their mouths, only to put them down again. At length Beethoven was satisfied and dropped into the Rondo. The whole company was transported with delight" (Thayer quoted in Forbes 1964, 350).

As this report indicates, Beethoven audaciously exploited the space of freedom embodied in the cadenza positioned just before a major formal articulation, the return of the main theme, as played by the full ensemble. His piano concertos make much of this juncture, and not only in rondo finales, but above all in the big solo cadenzas near the end of the opening movements. The kind of playfully or provocatively deceptive behavior that so angered Ramm becomes a source of humor and surprise. Perhaps the funniest idea in the C Major Concerto, Op. 15, is found at the end of the longest of the three solo cadenzas that Beethoven wrote out in 1809. After twice sounding the trills that would normally signal the end of the cadenza and the reentrance of the orchestra, he mischievously continues with the lengthy cadenza. In the third system of Figure 17.1, Beethoven elaborates a second-inversion tonic chord across all of the pitch registers, and a rapid descending scale into the depths of the bass, then triggers the unfolding of dominant-seventh sonorities as a protracted series of rising scales, finally unleashing a three-octave ascent to the *forte* chords at the end of measure 125. At long last, after presumably exasperating conductor, orchestra, and audience with such delaying tactics, he interpolates another surprise—a provocatively understated arpeggiated chord on the already much-emphasized dominant seventh chord, the doorstep to the cadence (Figure 17.1). This gesture in turn precedes the long-awaited—yet no longer predictable—return of the orchestra, which comes in with a bang.

Beethoven's first two piano concertos were ongoing works-in-progress, pieces that he long avoided publishing, since they underwent revision each time he had occasion to play them. The Third Concerto in C Minor also underwent a prolonged genesis, to judge from the sketches for the first and third movements with verbal indications that Beethoven made as early as 1796, during a concert tour to Prague and Berlin (Johnson 1977, 1:161, 164–65, 169–70). For the first movement he wrote down the following striking remark: "Pauke bej der Cadent" ("timpani in the cadenza"). The piece was not completed until 1803, yet this seminal idea relates to the unusual treatment of the cadenza in the finished work, as well as to a distinctive feature of his playing—the use of multiple trills.

Whereas this early sketch was presumably intended for the passage leading into the cadenza, his treatment of the end of the cadenza represents the final

FIGURE 17.1. Piano Concerto No. 1, Op. 15/I, end of cadenza, entrance of orchestra.

harvest of Beethoven's original idea. Some moments before, the precadential trill on the supertonic, D, is prolonged in the right hand without being resolved (Figure 17.2). Against this trill, a rising chromatic scale in the left hand merges into a simultaneous trill on B, the leading note. Beethoven extends the double trill for several measures, while the motive from the second bar of the opening theme is played in imitation above and below the trill on the harmony of the dominant seventh. Then G joins the trill, and the entire dominant triad is set ablaze through this unmeasured pulsation of the triple trill, a specialty of Beethoven's piano playing.

The entire passage has been poised at the threshold of the expected cadence and represents an immense internal expansion within the structural framework of the concerto cadenza. But now Beethoven again avoids reso-

FIGURE 17.2. Piano Concerto No. 3, Op. 37/I, end of cadenza, entrance of orchestra.

lution with an even more impressive effect. For the trill on the supertonic does not resolve to C; instead, it *ascends* chromatically, reaching not the tonic triad of C minor but an unstable seventh chord. This is the moment in the work as we know it that corresponds to Beethoven's original idea of "timpani in the cadenza," as the drum taps articulate the third to fourth bars of the opening theme.

Beethoven's treatment of his opening theme in the cadenza as a whole displays a vast architectural logic. After his exhaustive treatment of its first measures in the cadenza, what remains is the tail of the theme—the last two bars with their characteristic dotted rhythm. This is what Beethoven gives to the timpani, while wrapping the motive in an uncanny harmonic veil. A guiding idea of the cadenza is thus the successive treatment of the three component parts of the main theme, culminating in the mysterious drum passage. Strictly considered, the cadenza embraces not only the solo but also the timpani statements, and ends only with the long-delayed C minor cadence, where a new dialogue between the piano and strings leads to the terse close of the movement. Hence Beethoven's cadenza does indeed use "timpani in the cadenza."

In the case of the Third Concerto, we gain further insight into the relation between improvisation and formal articulation—or freedom and determination—through Beethoven's own gloss on his evolving compositional ideas. This brings us to the matter of his voluminous musical sketches and drafts, preserved in thousands of pages of surviving manuscripts. Do these sketches confirm that Beethoven labored tirelessly to create self-sufficient autonomous masterpieces? Or might they hold some significance more germane to the general issue of improvisation?

One reason for the increasing number of sketches from later stages of Beethoven's career may be that, with his increasing deafness, the composer wrote down ideas that in earlier years he would have tested at the keyboard. Some of these sketches suggest notated improvisations. Figure 17.3 shows his sketch for an "Introdutzion" to the Diabelli Variations, Op. 120. It is found near the end of an extended series of entries for the Variations in the "Wittgenstein" Sketchbook, and dates from 1819.[3] The sketch remained unused. Yet it shows a characteristic balance between figurative, rhetorical elaboration, on the one hand, and structural coherence, on the other. As in the improvisation on Pleyel's quartet as described by Czerny, Beethoven develops a motive from the theme at hand—the falling fourth interval C–G from the beginning of Diabelli's waltz. This descending fourth interval is stated five times, with the pitch levels of the second, third, and fourth statements determined by a series of descending thirds: C–G, A–E, F–C, D–A, and C–G. Each of the appearances of the motive is punctuated by a bar-line, but the open quality of the initial gesture is conveyed through a metrical repositioning of the figure; here, unlike in Diabelli's waltz, the falling fourth from C to G coincides with the bar-line, and Beethoven specifies the 6/4 position of the chord. In its subsequent appearances, an upbeat precedes the two pitches of the falling fourth motive, just as in Diabelli's theme. Fermatas over the first three sustained pitches mark points for rhetorical elaboration and improvisation, and it is obvious that not all of the implied notes are written out. The kind of detailed figurative elaboration contained in the cadenza to the C Major Concerto (see Figure 17.1) is required yet only roughly sketched here, but the structural outline of the harmonic progression and voice-leading already represents a coherent conception.

Beethoven plays here with the registral disposition of the falling-fourth motive, and he dramatizes its appearance on D-A by utilizing the lowest register in the bass. This juncture calls for an improvisatory elaboration, as is signaled by Beethoven's twofold "etc." indication, as well as by the conspicuous gap on the page itself, with space for two systems left completely empty. This gap is surely significant and implies the need for temporal expansion on D, the dominant of the dominant. If Beethoven has left ample room for elaboration, he nevertheless provides an overall framework for the progression. For as the lowest system indicates, D becomes an extended pedal point; the upward projection of the fifth of the D-minor triad marks the reemergence of the notated music. The figuration written here traces a descent from A through A flat to G, supported by a dominant seventh, and then further emphasizes the dominant of C major through trills played in different registers, leading to the theme. As this sketch shows, the falling fourth interval drawn from the waltz assumes primacy, but Beethoven has already mapped out the most important structural and registral relations of his material. His blueprint has blank spaces to be filled out with figuration, but it is not just an abstract matrix; it clearly has been imagined in sound.

Our final example examines the early genesis of the *Prestissimo* second movement of Beethoven's Sonata in E Major, Op. 109, from 1820. This example also corresponds closely to the descriptions by Ries and Czerny of Beethoven as improviser. The documentation of the compositional process is preserved in Beethoven's major sketchbook from this year, a manuscript held in the Berlin Staatsbibliothek preussischer Kulturbesitz as Artaria 195, which recently has been made available in a three-volume publication (Kinderman 2003). On page 35, immediately following sketches for the Credo of the *Missa*

FIGURE 17.3. Sketch for an unused Introduction to the Diabelli Variations, "Wittgenstein" Sketchbook, Beethoven-Haus Bonn, fol. 9 recto. Transcribed by W. Kinderman, *Beethoven's Diabelli Variations* (Oxford), pp. 210–11.

solemnis, Beethoven makes the entry shown in Figure 17.4a. This brief sketch already harbors the germinal idea of the *Prestissimo* of Op. 109. The larger linear direction of the figuration spells out a descending scalar pattern that eventually stabilizes around middle C in the lower octave. Thus the first notes of each triplet grouping of 16ths in the 12/8 meter define a descending linear contour spanning one and a half octaves. The straightforward motoric character of this figuration implies a swift tempo.

Beethoven's very next entry on this page is the draft for the beginning of the projected movement shown in Figure 17.4b. The registral span of the first sketch is taken over in the draft, whose first downbeat is placed on the same high G and which falls through the distance of a 10th to E in the following measure. Instead of unfolding in triplet patterns of 16th notes, the draft utilizes triplet groups of 8th notes; rather than scalar, stepwise descending motion, the draft spells out triadic pitches of the basic harmonies. Despite these differences, the rhythmic, textural, and registral parallels are audible

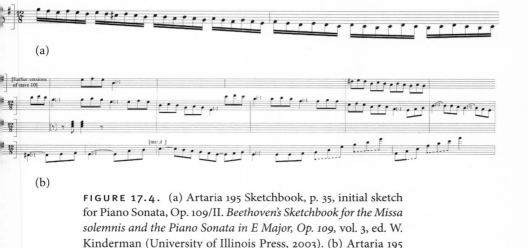

(a)

(b)

FIGURE 17.4. (a) Artaria 195 Sketchbook, p. 35, initial sketch for Piano Sonata, Op. 109/II. *Beethoven's Sketchbook for the Missa solemnis and the Piano Sonata in E Major, Op. 109,* vol. 3, ed. W. Kinderman (University of Illinois Press, 2003). (b) Artaria 195 Sketchbook, p. 35, beginning of early draft for Piano Sonata, Op. 109/II.

and compelling. These sketches catch Beethoven in the act of seizing an open-ended, improvisatory idea, which is soon transformed into a more articulate and formally shaped conception. Hence the opening two-measure phrase of the draft is sequenced upward to the dissonant harmony on the second degree. At the same time, the rhythmic pattern of two triplet-8th figures in the first measure is intensified to continuous 8ths in the first half of measure 2. One can already see in this draft how the music builds in intensity through harmonic change and rhythmic foreshortening.

The opening of the draft in Figure 17.4b is still remote from the finished work in various respects. However, a tangible connection exists. The first four 12/8 measures of the draft correspond to the first eight 6/8 measures of the completed work. The tonic orientation of the first phrase is followed by a sequential restatement of that phrase on an adjacent, subdominant-related harmony, so that an emphasis on B and G in the first phrase is answered by an emphasis on C and A in the second phrase. Meanwhile, an underlying rhythm in a continuous triplet pattern is implied. Following the first four measures of the draft, the continuation resembles the corresponding passage from the finished work still more closely. Here the rhythmic pattern enables us to recognize a precise parallel between the sketch and the completed work.

Figure 17.5 from page 41 of the sketchbook shows Beethoven having developed the elements from this preceding draft into a synoptic sonata-form design, in which the second theme area is placed in the major mode, quite unlike the finished work. The second subject is characterized by stepwise descending motion, and its realization in the recapitulation in staves 13–16 of page 41 displays a texture of falling parallel thirds reminiscent of the *first* movement of Op. 109 as we know it. The motivic material of the first system and the projected development section in staves 7–10 is recognizably close to the thematic substance of the opening section of the finished piece. In the following drafts for the *Prestissimo* in the Artaria 195 Sketchbook, the open-

1. The lower voice was written first.

FIGURE 17.5. Artaria 195 Sketchbook, p. 41, draft for Piano Sonata, Op. 109/II. *Beethoven's Sketchbook for the Missa solemnis and the Piano Sonata in E Major, Op. 109,* vol. 3, ed. W. Kinderman (University of Illinois Press, 2003).

ing section appears in close to its final form, but the movement as a whole continued to evolve through a long and complex process.

What do these examples show about the role of improvisatory currents in Beethoven's creative process? One observation is how the spontaneous impulse of improvisation is retained and nourished during various phases of the compositional process. The conventional dichotomy that opposes the fire of the initial inspiration against the cool calculation of packaging those ideas does not suffice here. Georg Sulzer, for instance, commented on sketches as "often more highly prized than works more completely realized, for all the fire of imagination, often dissipated in the execution of the work is to be met in them." He continued by saying that "the Entwurf [draft] is the product of genius. The working out, on the other hand, is primarily the doing of Art and Taste" ([1792] 1970, 80; also cited in Kramer 1991, 5). For Beethoven, however, such a categorical distinction between the spontaneous original idea and the refinement of that idea in reasoned contemplation is much too simple. The evidence from his sketches indicates that reason and imagination are not separable, and that the process of working-out could trigger further states of inspiration (Kramer 1991, 4).

This brings us back to Lydia Goehr's claim about Beethoven that because of "the predetermination of as many structural elements as possible . . . extemporization . . . was seen to stand in strict opposition to composition 'proper'" (1991, 234). What seems to support her view is that because of his deafness Beethoven had to retreat from the concert platform and curtail his performing activities. A landmark in this development came in 1809. Since he could no longer present concertos himself, he seized control as composer over the cadenzas, which in the Fifth Concerto are notated directly into the score. For this reason, the opportunity for improvisation is curtailed, and Beethoven's decision to write out cadenzas for the earlier concertos at this time might be taken as further evidence of a "predetermination of structural elements."

Nevertheless, what is also apparent is that elements suggestive of improvisation do not become less important in Beethoven's later music. The Fifth Concerto begins with a written-out cadenza, an approach that Beethoven planned as well for the unfinished Sixth Concerto in D Major from 1815.[4] Particularly in his later years, gestures evocative of improvisation assumed prominence in Beethoven's works in various genres. Stephen Rumph has claimed in this regard that "by incorporating the improvising pianist of fantasia and concerto tradition Beethoven introduces a free agent into the musical text, a subject who hovers above the formal events" (2004, 11). The wedding of such improvisatory or fantasy-like aspects with structural control is perhaps

most richly demonstrated in some of Beethoven's final works, such as the C#
Minor Quartet Op. 131. For Gustav Nottebohm, no other quartet gave such a
strong impression of improvisation (1872, 74),[5] whereas for other commentators, it was the superb integration of the work that captured attention.

This interdependence of freedom and determination reminds us of the
need to qualify the nature of what Beethoven would have regarded as successful improvisation. We know, for instance, that he did not much respect attempts at improvisation if these involved a mechanistic rehearsal of figurative
patterns or paraded technical difficulties for their own sake. For Beethoven,
such attempts fell short because they betrayed a dearth of meaning. Like
Mozart and C. P. E. Bach, Beethoven had strong convictions about music
as a rhetorical art capable of conveying a synthesis of thought and feeling.
In this respect, his reservations about improvisation as it was sometimes
practiced may have been similar to those of Mozart, who on one occasion
described even Muzio Clementi as a "mere mechanicus" (quoted in Marshall
1991, 377).[6]

The role of improvisation for Beethoven is thus double-edged. As a basic
attitude toward compositional activity it remained indispensable. For that
reason, to oppose extemporization to "composition proper" misrepresents
his creative process by ignoring the crucial interdependence of freedom and
determination in the concrete stylistic context in which Beethoven worked. In
this sense, Goehr's notion of the "Beethoven Paradigm" is at most a half-truth.
At the same time, however, Beethoven tended to regard the improvisatory
gestures in his works in very specific ways, narrowing the range of interpretative responses appropriate in performance. Ries related that when he played
Beethoven's F Major Variations, Op. 34, the composer was dissatisfied with
a little cadenza, and he remained dissatisfied, even after Ries had played the
passage for him no fewer than 17 times (Sonneck [1926] 1967, 52).

I shall close by considering two comments on improvisation by Beethoven
himself. These statements might at first seem at odds with one another, but
they can be reconciled if we embrace the notion, as Bruno Nettl has urged,
that composition and improvisation are "part of the same idea" (1974, 6).
Among some of his musical sketches from 1807–1808 Beethoven wrote that
"one improvises actually only when one doesn't pay attention to what one
plays, so if one would extemporize in the best, truest way in public, it's necessary to give oneself up freely to one's inclinations" (inscription evident in
Illustration 6, Küthen 1999; also see Löw 1962, 12; Sisman 1998, 76).[7] This
comment reflects Beethoven's proclivity to perform either without or with
a minimum of written material, even in ensemble works. We recall in this

regard Czerny's report about the very "roguish" ("muthwillig") manner in which Beethoven played his G Major Piano Concerto in 1808, incorporating difficult passages not written in the score (Nottebohm 1887, 75),[8] or Ignaz Seyfried's comments about trying to turn pages at Beethoven's performance of his C Minor Piano Concerto in 1803: "In the playing of the concerto . . . he asked me to turn the pages for him; but—heaven help me!—that was easier said than done. I saw almost nothing but empty leaves; at the most . . . a few Egyptian hieroglyphs wholly unintelligible to me scribbled down to serve as clues for him; for he played nearly all of the solo part from memory. . . . He gave me a secret glance whenever he was at the end of one of the invisible passages and my scarcely concealable anxiety not to miss the decisive moment amused him greatly and he laughed heartily at the jovial supper which we ate afterwards" (Thayer quoted in Forbes 1964, 329–30).

Clearly, then, Beethoven was fully aware of the spontaneous, unpredictable, and risky aspects of improvisation, and he embodied these features in his own performances. Yet this touches only one side of the larger issue. Nineteenth-century Europe saw a decline in the prestige of extemporized performance, and Beethoven surely shared some of the reservations about the reality of improvisation in common practice that were voiced by others after him. One thinks here of Robert Schumann's stern warning to Clara Wieck in 1838 "not to improvise too much—take care, to put everything down on paper at once" (Ferand 1957, 1126),[9] or even Richard Wagner's comment to his wife Cosima while he was composing *Parsifal* in 1878 that "to fantasize, to have ideas, is not difficult, my difficulty is always in the limitation of the material" (1977, 212). This limitation or shaping of the musical material reigns in and focuses what might otherwise become loose, additive, or incoherent.

More than most others, Beethoven was apparently quite capable in his performances of shaping his musical thoughts while "not paying attention" to what he was playing, that is, not following predictable patterns conceived in advance. At least, he was able to limit his reliance on such patterns so that his performance decisions stood out as communicative gestures made in the here-and-now. Beyond this, he insisted that such performance decisions were identical with compositional decisions appropriate in finished works. In this regard, his conviction about the interaction of improvisation and composition invites comparison with Carl Dahlhaus's assessment of the issue in relation to 20th-century music, and specifically serial composition and the rise of aleatoric technique in the 1950s: "Musical cogency is not to be expected from the disintegration of composition into improvisation, but from a compromise between the two" (Dahlhaus 1987, 273). Beethoven's clearest statement to this effect was made to his fellow musician Wenzel Johann Tomaschek in 1814. The statement seems trustworthy, since it resonates well with what we know about Beethoven's attitudes toward improvisation, so we shall close by giving Beethoven the last word: "It has always been known that the greatest pianoforte players were also the greatest composers; but how did they play? Not like the pianists of to-day, who prance up and down the keyboard with passages which they have practiced—*putsch, putsch, putsch*;—what does that mean? Nothing! When true pianoforte virtuosi played it was always something homogeneous, an entity; if written down it would appear as a well thought-out work. That is pianoforte playing; the other thing is nothing!" (Thayer quoted in Forbes 1964, 599).

NOTES

1. Hartmut Krones has identified the "banal run" in the "Rondeau" Finale of Pleyel's G Major Quartet, Op. 8, No. 2, and discovers its transformation in the trio of Beethoven's Quartet in E-Flat Major, Op. 74, from 1809 (1994, 587).

2. These two reports are cited in Solomon (2003, 229–30).

3. This sketch and all of the related sketches and drafts for the Variations from 1819 are discussed and transcribed in my book *Beethoven's Diabelli Variations* (Kinderman [1987] 1999, 210–11).

4. On the unfinished Sixth Concerto, see Lockwood (1970). Also see Cook (1989) and the exchange between Lockwood and Cook (Lockwood and Cook 1990). There also exists a sketch for a projected concerto in D minor from 1809, which begins with a series of loud, cadenza-like flourishes. This sketch is found on page 69 of the Landsberg 5 Sketchbook held in the Staatsbibliothek preussischer Kulturbesitz in Berlin; it appears in Beethoven 1993, 119.

5. Nottebohm observes that "of all the quartets the one in C♯ minor (Op. 131) makes in its form the strongest impression of an improvisation" ("Von allen Quartetten macht am meisten das in Cis-moll (Op. 131) seiner Form nach den Eindruck einer Improvisation").

6. Mozart's negative report is contained in a letter to his father Leopold Mozart from January 16, 1782.

7. "Man Fantasiert eigentlich nur, wenn man gar nicht acht giebt, was man spielt, so—würde man auch am besten, wahrsten fantasieren öffentlich—sich ungezwungen überlassen, eben was einem gefällt." A facsimile of the page containing this inscription appears as illustration 6 in *Beethoven, Goethe und Europa: Almanach zum Internationalen Beethovenfest Bonn 1999* (Laaber: Laaber Verlag, 1999), accompanying the essay by Gans-Werner Küthen, "'Was, ist, und zu welchem Ende treiben wir das virtuose Spiel?' Gedanken zum Thema Beethoven und der Reiz des Unübertrefflichen" (107–38). Also see Helmut Aloysius Löw, "Die Improvisation im Klavierwerk L. van

Beeethovens" (PhD dissertation, Saarland University, 1962), 12; and Elaine Sisman, "After the Heroic Style: Fantasia and the 'Characteristic' Sonatas of 1809," *Beethoven Forum 6 (1998): 76.*

8. This report stems from Gustav Nottebohm, who knew Czerny many years later in Vienna.

9. "Eines möchte ich Dir raten, nicht zu viel zu phantasieren . . . Nimm Dir nur vor, alles gleich auf das Papier zu bringen."

REFERENCES

Beethoven, Ludwig van. 1993. *Ludwig van Beethoven. Ein Skizzenbuch aus dem Jahre 1809 (Landsberg 5).* Transcribed with a commentary by Clemens Brenneis, 2 vols. Bonn: Beethoven-Haus.

Cook, Nicholas. 1989. "Beethoven's Unfinished Piano Concerto: A Case of Double Vision?" *Journal of the American Musicological Society* 42(2): 338–74.

Dahlhaus, Carl. 1987. "Composition and Improvisation." In *Schoenberg and the New Music,* translated by Derrick Puffert and Alfred Clayton, 265–73. Cambridge: Cambridge University Press.

Ferand, Ernest T. 1957. "Improvisation." In *Die Musik in Geschichte und Gegenwart,* edited by Friedrich Blume. Vol. 6, 1093–135. Kassel: Bärenreiter.

Forbes, Elliot, ed. 1964. *Thayer's Life of Beethoven.* Princeton: Princeton University Press.

Frimmel, Theodor von. 1906. "Der Klavierspieler Beethoven." In *Beethoven Studien.* Vol. 2, 201–71. Munich and Leipzig: Georg Müller.

Goehr, Lydia. 1991. *The Imaginary Museum of Musical Works. An Essay in the Philosophy of Music.* Oxford: Clarendon.

Johnson, Douglas. 1977. *Beethoven's Early Sketches in the "Fischhof Miscellany,"* Berlin Autograph 28. 2 vols. Ann Arbor: University of Michigan Press.

Kinderman, William, ed. and trans. 2003. *Artaria 195: Beethoven's Sketchbook for the Missa solemnis and the Piano Sonata in E Major, Opus 109.* 3 vols. with commentary, facsimile, transcription. Urbana and Chicago: University of Illinois Press.

Kinderman, William. [1987] 2008. *Beethoven's Diabelli Variations.* Oxford: Clarendon.

Kolneder, Walter, ed. 1968. *Erinnerungen aus meinem Leben* [Carl Czerny]. Strassburg and Baden-Baden.

Kramer, Richard. 1991. "The Sketch Itself." In *Beethoven's Compositional Process,* edited by William Kinderman, 3–5. Lincoln and London: University of Nebraska Press.

Krones, Hartmut. 1994. "Streichquartett Es-Dur op. 74." In *Beethoven: Interpretationen seiner Werke,* Vol. 1, edited by Albrecht Riethmüller, Carl Dahlhaus, and Alexander Ringer, 585–92. Laaber: Laaber Verlag.

Küthen, Hans-Werner. 1999. "'Was ist, und zu welchem Ende treiben wir das virtuose Spiel?' Gedanken zum Thema Beethoven und der Reiz des Unübertrefflichen."

In *Beethoven, Goethe und Europa: Almanach zum Internationalen Beethovenfest Bonn 1999*, edited by Thomas Daniel Schlee, Marcus Axt, and Annette Monheim, 107–38. Laaber: Laaber Verlag.

Lockwood, Lewis. 1970. "Beethoven's Unfinished Piano Concerto of 1815: Sources and Problems." *Musical Quarterly* 54(4): 624–46.

Lockwood, Lewis, and Nicholas Cook. 1990. Letters to the *Journal of the American Musicological Society* 43(2): 376–82, 382–85.

Löw, Helmut Aloysius. 1962. "Die Improvisation im Klavierwerk L. van Beethovens." Ph.D. dissertation, Saarland University.

Marshall, Robert, ed. 1991. *Mozart Speaks: Views on Music, Musicians, and the World.* New York: Schirmer.

Nettl, Bruno. 1974. "Thoughts on Improvisation." *Musical Quarterly* 60(1): 1–19.

Nottebohm, Gustav. 1872. *Beethoveniana.* Leipzig: Peters.

———. 1887. "Aenderungen zum Clavierconcert in G-dur." In *Zweite Beethoveniana*, 74–78. Leipzig: Peters.

Rumph, Stephen. 2004. *Beethoven after Napoleon: Political Romanticism in the Late Works.* Berkeley: University of California Press.

Schlee, Thomas Daniel, Marcus Axt, and Annette Monheim, eds. 1999. *Beethoven, Goethe und Europa: Almanach zum Internationalen Beethovenfest Bonn 1999.* Laaber: Laaber Verlag.

Sisman, Elaine. 1998. "After the Heroic Style: *Fantasia* and the 'Characteristic' Sonatas of 1809." *Beethoven Forum* 6: 67–96.

Solomon, Maynard. 2003. *Late Beethoven: Music, Thought, Imagination.* Berkeley: University of California Press.

Sonneck, O. G., ed. [1926] 1967. *Beethoven: Impressions by His Contemporaries.* New York: Schirmer. Reprint, New York: Dover.

Sulzer, Johann Georg. [1792] 1970. "Entwurf." In *Allgemeine Theorie der Schönen Künste.* Vol. 2. Leipzig: Weidmann. Reprint, Hildesheim: Georg Olms.

Thayer, Alexander Wheelock. 1917. *Ludwig van Beethovens Leben,* edited by Hermann Deiters and Hugo Riemann. Leipzig: Breitkopf & Härtel.

Wagner, Cosima. 1977. *Cosima Wagner. Die Tagebücher*, Vol. 2, edited by Martin Gregor-Dellin and Dietrich Mack. Munich: Piper.

ᕋ 18 ᕌ

WHY DO THEY IMPROVISE?
REFLECTIONS ON MEANING AND EXPERIENCE

Ali Jihad Racy

In music, the phenomena that are the most familiar are often the most elusive. This apparent paradox may reflect the very nature of music, being both an intuitive expression and, at least in some traditions, a coherent system. A case in point is improvisation, particularly as represented by the Arab taqasim, usually defined as instrumental improvisation in a particular mode, or maqam. Attempts to understand the performance modalities, and by extension the affect and cultural significance of improvising, are likely to encounter a number of epistemological challenges. In the Arab context, one such challenge is posed by the minimalist orientation of the modal theory as it exists in such eastern Arab cities as Cairo, Beirut, and Damascus. Typically, theoretical sources list a few dozen maqamat (plural of *maqam*) that together form the basis of the indigenous melodic practice as manifested in improvisatory and fixed compositions. The individual maqamat are essentially presented as scales that, in some cases, are internally divided into pentachord, tetrachord, and trichord. Occasionally added is a brief narrative, or sayr (literally, "path"), that describes the melodic movement or progression of each maqam. In the process, the narrative highlights the tonic and the notes to be emphasized, and refers to other notes that are temporarily raised or lowered or may be used as momentary resting stations in the course of improvising or composing. Obviously, the realization of the full modal essence is deferred to the realm of performance practice, for example, when improvisers provide representative as well as aesthetically moving renditions of the individual maqamat. Understandably, such a tenuous relationship between theory and practice has tended to shift the researchers' attention toward the interpretations themselves. Arab musical improvisations have been investigated in terms of their internal microprocesses (Touma 1971, 1975), in view of how they work intuitively in the case of one individual performer (Nettl and Riddle 1973, 1998), and in light of the listeners' and performers' emotional transformation that occurs in the context of performing (Racy 2003). Also considered have been the cultural and aesthetic connotations of improvisation in general and the taqasim in particular (Racy 2000), a topic that I pursue further in the present study.

More specifically, I take a closer look at why musicians improvise and how audiences interpret the phenomenon of creating music on the spot. An emphasis is placed on the taqasim as a performance genre. I write both as an improviser who comes from a tradition that values this art form, and as a Lebanese-born ethnomusicologist who is interested in improvisation cross-culturally. I posit that improvisation as a domain of musical artistry is appreciated both for its broader connotations and for its emotional content. In other words, I look at it as "a process simultaneously musical, personal, and cultural" (Monson 1998, 163). Accordingly, the significance of an Indian alap, a Persian avaz, or for that matter a free-jazz performance is intimately linked to the ways in which the performers and the listeners both conceptualize and feel the music.

When discussing improvisation, Arab musicians and musical connoisseurs often make connotative projections while recognizing the emotional efficacy of the improvised material. A few years ago, I hosted a small group of professional musicians from Aleppo, Syria, in my Arab music performance class at the University of California, Los Angeles. Happy to hear the students, most of whom were American or American-born individuals of Middle Eastern backgrounds, perform precomposed classics, they offered their compliments. However, they also requested that some students perform taqasim, stating that learning this art is a good way to experience "our true Oriental spirit." Then, when a few did improvise, or at least made an attempt to do so, the guests seemed to listen with exceptional interest, as well as with a critical ear. After the performances they offered encouraging remarks.

Obviously, cultures vary in their attitudes toward improvisation. Whereas some appreciate this art form and place a high premium upon it, others may exhibit little interest in it, or even discourage it altogether. Furthermore, within the same musical tradition attitudes toward improvising may vary considerably. In some cases, lack of interest in this art may develop in conjunction with the adoption of Western conservatory pedagogy, and with an ensuing negative attitude toward the native practice. In Egypt, for example, whereas improvisation continues to flourish in folk and Sufi contexts and among the traditionally minded urban instrumentalists, it has become increasingly rare among the mainstream vocal celebrities, especially since the mid-20th century.

The organic connection between meaning and experience, although it may apply to music in general, seems to acquire special significance in musical improvisation. Those who appreciate this form of artistry for its emotive content tend to project into it various shades of symbolic meaning. To begin with, creating music instantaneously may fascinate as well as intrigue because it seems to transcend familiar or explicit musical rules. Accordingly, it is not the application of a specific theory, but rather "the practice of practice" (Bailey 1992, xi), or in the case of Arab modal improvisation, a "procedure of variations developed upon a nonexistent theme" (Gerson-Kiwi 1970, 66).

However, this does not mean that improvisation is necessarily a random exercise. Although conceptually linked to a tersely theorized modal system, the Arab taqsim (singular of *taqasim*) embraces a culturally internalized system of rules and applications that are not always articulated by the musicians or the theorists. For that matter, experimental studies, following the Nettl-Riddle approach, which explains the modus operandi of improvisation and demonstrates the more variable and the more stable components in several of my own taqasim on the buzuq (long-necked fretted lute) and the nay (reed-flute) in maqam Nahawand (1973 and 1998), may further demystify the art of improvising. They may render the very idea of variation upon a nonexistent theme or the notion of "a version of something," instead of "improvisation upon something" (Nettl 1974, 9), more lucid and more nuanced. Such explorations could also bring to focus a cognitive grammar—implicit rules, hypothetical models, possible procedures, margins of acceptability, and so forth—that becomes operative during the improvisatory process. Paradoxically, the "nonexistent theme" does exist, but not as the theme in the theme-and-variation genre in Western art music, or for that matter as a radif, or a codified rendition of the modal repertoire in Persian classical music, but rather as a vast mental reservoir of modal directives and scenarios. In performance, such "hidden" guidelines are intuitively and selectively applied. In the case of the taqasim, they may explain, for example, where embellishments are most likely to be introduced; how the emphases on certain notes may shift along the linear progression of the melodic mode; when and how certain notes become microtonally affected in the course of performing; and ultimately, why trained listeners may feel certain performances more emotionally, or consider them aesthetically more successful, than others.

Meanwhile, improvisation is believed to entail extraordinary ability. Producing music "in the course of performance" (Nettl and Russell 1998) is known to demand exceptional skill and talent. By the same token, it can be said that improvisation is risky since the stakes, in terms of success or failure, are high. In some ways, the improviser is similar to an Olympic ice-skater. If he or she avoids the more challenging maneuvers altogether, the performance may seem quite ordinary and receive "average points"; alternatively, if more impressive feats are carried out to excess, either the performer may "shine" or, given the increased chance of mistakes happening, his or her overall performance may become seriously compromised. Comparably, musical improvisers must find the right balance between correctness and precision on the one hand, and creativity and adventure on the other. Bad improvisations are met with criticism for their aesthetic failures and at times for their symbolic aberrances.

In a related sense, improvisation is considered a highly individualized art, an ideal medium for self-expression. Similarly, improvising has been viewed as a metaphor for freedom, for example, in the jazz culture of the 1950s and 1960s (Monson 1998, 163). Especially in communities that value the soloistic idiom, the improviser becomes the center of attention, whether performing alone or playing a leading role within a musical ensemble. In this regard, the artist is expected to undergo a process of introspection that is externalized in the form of evocative musical creations.

Such dynamics of introspection and externalization are frequently associated with inspiration, which in turn leads to the creation of extraordinary musical renditions. García Lorca, in a philosophical essay on the Spanish Gypsy ethos, speaks of duende, or the creative state that inspires flamenco musicians and dancers. He refers to it as "a power and not a construct . . . a struggle and not a concept" (1955, 154). Iranian musicians who create highly affective renditions of the radif, experience a captivating mystical mood called hal, literally "state." Meanwhile, Arab musicians refer to their momentarily heightened ability to produce ecstasy in their performances as saltanah. At times, the phenomenon of inspiration acquires metaphysical or spiritual overtones, as illustrated by the Sufi concept of wajd, or the ecstatic state of mystical yearning, which may arise through the ritual practice of music and dance. In performance, the attainment of a conducive inspirational state may become a primary concern for musicians even when their music is not strictly improvised. Discussing the need to establish rapport with the audience and the challenge of performing live, Bruce Springsteen speaks of his own inspirational quest:

> Part of what the risk is, part of what I'm searching for from the moment I put my foot onstage until I walk off, is the invisible thread of energy and inspiration or soul or whatever you want to call it that is going to take me to that place where

a song can explode to life. That thread is between me and the audience every night. *Always.* I've got to grab it out of the air and physicalize it into something they can hear. Sometimes it's like catching a wave that can take you through all twenty-five songs. Sometimes it'll take you through ten and then you have to refind it. Sometimes you're looking for it again after one. A big part of what I'm experiencing when I'm performing is that search.

I don't have a piano and a sax and drums behind me on this tour. So I had to re-approach the guitar as an instrument of solo accompaniment. It becomes a bit of a new land, and I'll play it in ways I've never played it before. I'm constantly asking myself, How can I wring as much music and meaning as possible out of those six strings? One thing I do know: With the correct playing style, you can summon up an orchestra. (Springsteen 2005, 95)

The values of individuality and inspiration notwithstanding, improvisatory genres, which typically follow some traditional musical framework or "refer-ent" (Pressing 1998, 52), are frequently treated as prime representations of the culture's native idiom. Accordingly, improvisation is considered the true voice of the indigenous musical system and consequently may be cherished, or at least widely accepted as part of the cultural heritage. As virtuoso tabla player Zakir Hussain explains:

To improvise you still need certain outlines to work with. You have to have that outline, and then you improvise with that outline, so all those simple themes, or those simple patterns, which you take and then develop into something *big*, are already there, and have been given, and have been composed. You have this huge repertoire available to you, so without actually even changing anything, tradition-ally, you could do a continuous solo of a couple of hours, no problem. I mean, obviously, you have to be able to do it good enough, so that you know people enjoy it. The connoisseurs would enjoy it, however, if you're playing well, and so continuity is not the problem there. (quoted in Robinson 2001–2002, 89)

Traditionally speaking, the taqasim genre is particularly significant be-cause it is textless and essentially meterless, and "tuneless"—in other words, unbound by a fixed composition. This makes it the most direct or unencum-bered vehicle for capturing the quintessences of the maqamat. Being free of contrivances as such, modal improvisation, specifically in its solo vocal form, becomes the ideal medium for the delivery of sacred texts, as is well illustrated in the case of Qur'anic chanting.

At the same time, the improvisatory idiom, although it usually operates within some preexisting structural framework, may be directly correlated with innovation. Here the Olympic ice-skater analogy again applies. A good improviser must demonstrate good command of the musical norm, but must also present some novelties. He is expected to bring out the unexpected, or as Arab connoisseurs often explain, the music must have some "eye-catching features," but all in compliance with acceptable taste and feeling. Naturally, such spontaneous creations reflect the performance ambiance. In many cases, producing music on the spot involves the audience members directly, who in turn become partners in an active feedback process that inspires the improviser and ultimately shapes the content of his improvisation.

In light of these and other connotations we can better interpret the performances of the highly accomplished, as well as the culturally celebrated, modern Arab artists. In this regard, the taqasim of the late Egyptian composer Riyad al-Sunbati may be recognized as an exemplary union of tradition and creativity. Evoking a high level of tarab, or musical ecstasy, the delivery is both subtle and succinct. This is demonstrated by the reserved yet highly effective use of qaflat (singular, *qaflah*), or cadential patterns, and by the artful placement and timing of pauses between the musical phrases. Considered a musicians' musician, al-Sunbati also displays convincingly executed modal progressions and modulations.

Somewhat contrastive are the 'ud taqasim of the late composer, singer, actor, and 'ud player Farid al-Atrash. This artist's style appears well suited for further pleasing highly ecstatic crowds and for displaying modernisms that would appeal to his younger fans. In al-Atrash's 'ud renditions, which typically introduce his relatively long love songs, we observe very active use of the plectrum; fast modal progressions; frequent but brief modulations to other maqamat; dramatically protracted, and rather stereotypical, cadences; and an almost habitual allusion to a well-known classical Spanish theme by Albéniz, namely *Asturias*, which is known for its virtuosic pedal point passages. Al-Atrash's artistry, although deeply rooted in the Arab modal tradition, displays distinct connotations of individuality and cosmopolitanism.

A further contrast is the musical profile of the late Iraqi 'ud player Munir Bashir, who, unlike the previous two artists, led a musical career primarily as an 'ud soloist. Linked to the so-called Iraqi school of 'ud playing, Bashir's improvisations are performed on an instrument that sounds more high-strung and produces a bright resonant tone reminiscent of that of the Turkish 'ud. Furthermore, the style of playing tends to be slow, minimalist, and well suited for meditative listening. Having concertized frequently in major European cities, Bashir cultivated an improvisatory style suggestive of Indian rag music, flamenco, and blues, as well as being evocative of Iraq's traditional music. Bashir's taqasim betray a strong sense of individuality. Actually, the artist is known to have consciously refrained from playing precomposed works by others, or from emulating the more prevalent pan–East Mediterranean taqasim style in favor of producing his own renditions. Accordingly, that set him apart both as an Iraqi performer and as an individual artist in his own right.

The symbolic connotations of improvised content may vary depending upon the context of performing. For example, two of my own nay improvisations may have been interpreted differently. One of them I played in Beirut before an intimate gathering of local musical connoisseurs in the early 1980s, and the other I performed as part of a chamber piece I composed for the Kronos Quartet in 1994, which was recorded on their CD *Caravan* in 2000. In the former context, my performance may have served as a direct instigator of tarab and may have inspired a strong sense of locality and familiarity. In the latter, it may have acquired additional symbolic shades suggestive of modern stylistic fusions or cultural crossovers, or even postmodern experimentation. Within the current global environment, it is understandable that while some aesthetic features and symbolic connotations may be retained and in some cases exaggerated, others may fade out or gain new nuances and layers of significance. Naturally, this scenario extends to other musical genres.

Meanwhile, improvisation can be studied more intimately as an experience. To begin with, the improvisatory process tends to appeal directly to our senses and sensibilities. Thus, the very idea of improvising is recognized as an integral aspect of human nature. It is said that spontaneous creation represents a basic aspect of living, or to put it differently, the spirit of experimentation is inseparable from the ways in which we develop our basic skills (see Hall 1992, 231–33). Comparably, experimenting with ornaments, timbres, dynamics, and other expressive parameters may be involved in the cultivation of good musicianship.

In a related vein, the creation of music while it is being performed may have a profound transformative effect upon the improviser, as well as upon the listener. The process may evoke within the performer an elative sensation comparable to what Csikszentmihalyi (1990) calls "flow." In my own case, such a sensation can occur when I improvise on the nay or buzuq, even without the physical presence of an audience. My performance, although it may retain a modicum of cerebral control and precalculation, seems to generate its own flow. I feel that my musical intuition has taken over and set in motion a self-propelled process of creation and re-creation. Such momentary reorientation within one's musical self, what Springsteen calls "the invisible thread of energy and inspiration or soul" (2005, 95), I find to be musically liberating. When it occurs, it appears to open the gate to extraordinary mu-

sical ideas that may be totally unpremeditated and that may potentially develop into full-fledged compositions. Usually delicate, fleeting, and difficult
to retrieve after the fact, such an occurrence is often deemed transcendental
or otherworldly. Addressing the intrinsic efficacies of Indian music properly
learned from the leading gurus, Ravi Shankar provides his own reflections:

> When I myself start to perform a *raga*, the first thing I do is shut out the world
> around me and try to go down deep within myself. This starts even when I
> am concentrating on the careful tuning of the sitar and its *tarafs* (sympathetic
> strings). When, with control and concentration, I have cut myself off from the
> outside world, I step onto the threshold of the *raga* with feelings of humility,
> reverence, and awe. To me, a *raga* is like a living person, and to establish that
> intimate oneness between music and musician, one must proceed slowly. And
> when that oneness is achieved, it is the most exhilarating and ecstatic moment,
> like the supreme heights of the act of love or worship. In these miraculous mo-
> ments, when I am so much aware of the great powers surging within me and all
> around me, sympathetic and sensitive listeners are feeling the same vibrations. It
> is a strange mixture of all the intense emotions—pathos, joy, peace, spirituality,
> eroticism, all flowing together. It is like feeling God. (Shankar 1968, 57–58)

In typical performance contexts, the improviser gains certain prerogatives.
As he navigates creatively "in between the known and the unknown" (Steve
Lacy, quoted in Bailey 1992, 54) or produces expectations through stylistic
manipulations (Pressing 1998, 57), he teases the listeners' musical sensibilities.
In a sense, he refashions his immediate human environment. The improvisatory experience can perhaps be seen as a momentarily acquired form of
control or, to use García Lorca's expression, as "power" (1955) or, to quote
Shankar, as "great powers surging within" (1968, 57–58). Such an emerging
state would be generated inwardly, as well as interactively through the meeting of musical minds. Notwithstanding the challenges and perils of creating
music on the spot, musicians may improvise because they feel an internal
urge to do so and because of the exhilarating sense of musical introspection
or even adventure they derive from the process itself.

Experientially speaking, the taqsim engages us emotionally through its
organic linear motion. Needless to say, it is far from being an amorphous
or directionless impulse or—as the unfortunate and persistent stereotype
of "Islamic music" goes—a continuous mosaic-like repetition of motifs and
filigrees. Generally unbound by an explicit program outside itself, the taqsim's
modal progression resembles a coherent narrative in the way it unfolds, develops, and resolves. Yet, rather than recounting a specific "plot" or elaborating

on a fixed compositional prototype, the taqasim performer narrates his own "story" out of disparate narrative ingredients or likely musical linearities; or we might say he creates renditions of a "nonexistent narrative."

To conclude, the phenomenon of improvising music is polysemic. Such diverse connotations as creativity, individuality, inspiration, and tradition help us understand the multilayered significance and, in some cases, the ambivalence of improvising. In the Arab world today, the improvisatory tradition is threatened by Westernization and by the urge to become "modern." However, it is also esteemed for its implications of locality and its rootedness in religious practice. A comparable dimension of complexity applies to the improvisatory process. The elusive psychic space that exists between the mental or emotional mechanisms that lead to musical production, and the musical product itself, may be the very creative field that renders improvising enticing and ecstatic, as well as mystifying and technically challenging.

REFERENCES

Bailey, Derek. 1992. *Improvisation: Its Nature and Practice in Music.* New York: Da Capo Press.

Csikszentmihalyi, Mihaly. 1990. *Flow: The Psychology of Optimal Experience.* New York: Harper and Row.

García Lorca, Federico. 1955. *Poet in New York.* New York: Grove Press.

Gerson-Kiwi, Edith. 1970. "On the Technique of Arab Taqsim Composition." In *Festschrift Walter Graf*, edited by Erich Schenk, 66–73. Wiener Musikwissenschaftliche Beiträge 9. Wien: Hermann Böhlaus Nachf.

Hall, Edward T. 1992. "Improvisation as an Acquired Multilevel Process." *Ethnomusicology* 36(2): 223–35.

Monson, Ingrid. 1998. "Oh Freedom: George Russell, John Coltrane, and Modal Jazz." In *In the Course of Performance: Studies in the World of Musical Improvisation*, edited by Bruno Nettl with Melinda Russell, 149–68. Chicago: University of Chicago Press.

Nettl, Bruno. 1974. "Thoughts on Improvisation: A Comparative Approach." *Musical Quarterly* 60(1): 1–19.

Nettl, Bruno, and Ronald Riddle. 1973. "Taqsim Nahawand: A Study of Sixteen Performances by Jihad Racy." *Yearbook of the International Folk Music Council* 5: 11–49.

———. 1998. "Taqsim Nahawand Revisited: The Musicianship of Jihad Racy." In *In the Course of Performance: Studies in the World of Musical Improvisation*, edited by Bruno Nettl with Melinda Russell, 368–93. Chicago: University of Chicago Press.

Nettl, Bruno, and Melinda Russell, eds. 1998. *In the Course of Performance: Studies in the World of Musical Improvisation*. Chicago: University of Chicago Press.

Pressing, Jeff. 1998. "Psychological Constraints on Improvisational Expertise and Communication." In *In the Course of Performance: Studies in the World of Musical Improvisation*, edited by Bruno Nettl with Melinda Russell, 47–67.Chicago: University of Chicago Press.

Racy, Ali Jihad. 2000. "The Many Faces of Improvisation: The Arab Taqasim as a Musical Symbol." *Ethnomusicology* 44(2): 302–20.

———. 2003. *Making Music in the Arab World: The Culture and Artistry of Tarab*. Cambridge: Cambridge University Press.

Robinson, Michael. 2001–2002. "The Instrument Is Alive: An Interview with Ustad Zakir Hussain." *Pacific Review of Ethnomusicology* 10(1): 80–96.

Shankar, Ravi. 1968. *My Music, My Life*, with an introduction by Yehudi Menuhin. New York: Simon and Schuster.

Springsteen, Bruce. 2005. "It Happened in Jersey . . . as Told to Cal Fussman." *Esquire* August, 95–99.

Touma, Habib H. 1971. "The Maqam Phenomenon: An Improvisation Technique in the Music of the Middle East." *Ethnomusicology* 15(1): 38–48.

———. 1975. *Maqam Bayati in the Arabian Taqsim: A Study in the Phenomenology of the Maqam*. N.p.: International Monograph Publishers.

PRELUDING AT THE PIANO

Nicholas Temperley

In the Classic and early Romantic periods of European music, there was an established practice of playing an improvised prelude before a written composition. The most famous notated preludes of the period are Frédéric Chopin's 24 *Préludes* (Op. 28), published at Paris, Leipzig, and London in 1839. Today they are generally performed in concert as a single, continuous work. This article investigates the improvisation practice and seeks a new understanding of how Chopin's preludes relate to it.

Most writers on preludes have been chiefly concerned with the finished artifact. This approach is still reflected in leading reference works. Howard Ferguson, in the revised *New Grove Dictionary*, does not mention the improvised prelude (2001). He rightly calls Chopin's preludes the "prototype" of many later sets, but he has nothing to say about their immediate precursors, or their origins in improvisation. Like other scholars, he assumes that they were modeled directly on Bach's *Well-Tempered Clavier* (*WTC*), in part because they use all the major and minor keys in an orderly succession. On the other hand, Arnfried Edler in *MGG*, while listing a number of pre-Chopin sets as following in the Bach tradition, sees Chopin's preludes, in contrast, as strongly imbued with the character of French keyboard music (1997, 1801). But he too fails to consider their relationship to improvisation.

Jean-Jacques Eigeldinger, a leading authority on Chopin's life and music, acknowledges the existence of earlier published sets of preludes in all the keys; the ones he lists date from 1811 to 1828 (1988). But he claims that "Chopin was in only the slightest degree dependent on his predecessors. If some of his preludes give the impression of being improvised, it is by means that have nothing to with anything that had gone before" (1988, 173). He considers that the *WTC* was the model for all the earlier sets, and that Chopin's are even more profoundly influenced by Bach: "Ignoring the legacy of his immediate predecessors, deaf to the contemporary world, the Chopin of the preludes anchored himself in Bach so as to see himself more clearly—and, despite himself, into the future" (185).

Eigeldinger also makes a point of denying that Chopin's preludes are introductory pieces, claiming instead that they are a unified cycle. Since this is not obvious to the naked eye or ear, he tries to prove their unity by ingenious analysis. "If the Preludes are an organic whole, they must be put together according to certain structural principles: it remains to be discovered what they are and how the volume's unity is achieved over and above its diversity" (180). He thereupon "discovers" the presence of a three-note musical motive X (or another one, Y, consisting of X plus a fourth note) in each of the 24 preludes. To achieve this extraordinary feat, he allows himself to transpose, curtail, or invert the motives at will; to select their notes from different parts of the texture or from the middle of a phrase; and to ignore extraneous notes that come between those of the motive (186–93). He does not explain why, if Chopin wished to "unify" the preludes, he gave no hint of his plan and chose a method that would escape the notice of critics, performers, and analysts for nearly 150 years.

The theory is unconvincing. With the degree of freedom that Eigeldinger allows himself, one could find short melodic fragments in common between almost any two pieces. His theory is an "unfalsifiable proposition" (Popper 1959, 40). Let us suppose that Chopin actually wanted to compose and publish a set of mutually *unrelated* pieces (which their title, "24 Préludes," certainly suggests). It is hard to see how he could he have done it in a way that would defeat a determined unifier.

What is the motive behind the unifying theories? Devotees of Chopin may feel that his historical position alongside the great Germans is precarious. They may want to link him with one of them, namely Bach, over the heads of lesser men and women, and to protect him from the low status generally accorded in Western culture both to musical improvisation (Nettl 1998, 6–10) and to miniature forms (Kallberg 1992, 131–32). So they elevate the standing of his preludes by transforming them into a single, imposing composition with profound meaning and complex hidden structures.

Jeffrey Kallberg, in his study "Small 'Forms': In Defence of the Prelude," has convincingly refuted Eigeldinger's theory as "a willfully anachronistic viewpoint of the formal organisation of the preludes" endorsing "the view that smallness of form works to the aesthetic detriment of a musical work" (1992, 136). Like Kallberg I deny that large unified works are necessarily superior to miniatures, or that it is shameful to associate a composer of genius with an improvisatory convention. Further, I believe Chopin's preludes belong to a tradition of improvisation that has little connection with Bach's *WTC*. They are intended as single pieces, to be selected according to need or whim, and played either as introductions or as free-standing miniatures. This will become clearer with the following examination of their precursors.

THE PRELUDE IN EUROPEAN ART MUSIC

One might expect that the Early Music movement would have researched and revived, by this time, any practice known to have existed in the 18th or early 19th century. Indeed, some attention has been paid to improvisation in the classic period. Robert Levin in the revised *New Grove* says, "Performers and composers of the Classical period perpetuated three types of Baroque improvisation: embellishment, free fantasies and cadenzas" (2001, 112). Two of these, embellishment and cadenzas, have been taken aboard by the Early Music movement with some enthusiasm. A singer who fails to embellish an aria in certain spots, or a violinist who plays a historically inappropriate cadenza in a concerto, is now likely to run into trouble with historically aware critics. Free fantasies, on the other hand, have not been widely revived. One reason may be that the Early Music movement is directed chiefly toward performing established works of great composers in a more authentic form, whereas if you improvise a free fantasy there is no great composer in sight.

Preluding falls somewhere between the categories. It can be called a specialized free fantasy, but at the same time it is attached to a notated composition. Few musicians today (Levin himself is a possible exception) would dare, in a public concert, to perform a prelude leading into a Mozart or Beethoven sonata, though there is plenty of evidence that this was often done in their time. Even a prelude to a song, if there is not one written by the composer (for instance, in Schubert's *Heidenröslein*), is never played in conventional recitals: the singer, unless endowed with absolute pitch, has to find her note by surreptitious means. Sandra Rosenblum, in her otherwise authoritative handbook *Performing Practices in Classic Piano Music*, has a section on "Improvised Ornamentation" (1988, 287–92), but she does not mention preluding. The most complete treatment is a study by Valerie Woodring Goertzen (1996), who also wrote about Clara Schumann's preludes in Bruno Nettl's symposium *In the Course of Performance* (1998). I am indebted to her work in parts of what follows.

Preluding before a notated composition had its origins in certain practical functions. There might be a need to warm up, especially for singers and players of wind instruments. The tuning of an instrument might have to be tested. For accompanied singing the singer had to be given the pitch and perhaps the tempo of the coming song. In Protestant churches the congregation might need to be reminded of the tune it was about to sing to a hymn or metrical psalm.

In the course of time these prosaic functions were seized by players as an opportunity to display technical facility, musical learning, or creativity. This could be called a second phase of preluding. Then, in a third phase, ideal models of the prelude were written down or even printed, and so became a fixed form of composition. In the nature of things we are generally able to study only the last phase, because the earlier ones are lost.

For example, the ancient use of the organ to accompany and then also introduce voices in certain phases of the Catholic mass or office led to the Italian toccata, and then to the still grander North German präludium of the 17th century. Players' trying out the strings of a lute or harpsichord before accompanying court dances evolved into the prelude that introduced a dance suite: Louis Couperin's unmeasured preludes retained much of the improvisatory character of the older tradition, but later composers systematized the genre. The prelude or giving out of hymn tunes was for a long time improvised in Germany, Denmark, and England, but again, master organists began to write down fully worked-out examples.

Remarkably, it was one man, Johann Sebastian Bach, who brought all three of these forms of prelude to their *non plus ultra*: respectively, the prelude and fugue, the prelude to a dance suite, and the chorale prelude. In his masterly specimens little sense of spontaneous creation remains. After they were introduced to the wider public at the beginning of 19th century they became models not so much for improvisation, but for other notated compositions.

However, Bach, despite his tendency to perfectionism, was also esteemed for his skill as an improviser. At Potsdam in 1747 he astonished witnesses by his ability to improvise a fugue on a subject provided on the spot by the King. His improvisation was admired as a display of learning and knowledge of harmony, not of direct inspiration, fancy, or freedom from restraint. Similarly, Bach's son Emanuel, in a chapter on improvisation in his *Essay* of 1753, was primarily concerned with offering the student a strong harmonic framework for any free fantasy, including a prelude (Bach [1753] 1949, 430–45). He does say that the free fantasy is exceptionally well suited to stirring and stilling the passions (439). But his instructions for students contain no trace of the idea that they should follow their fancy. On the contrary, he suggests a severely methodical approach to the playing of preludes.

THE ROMANTIC PRELUDE

A new esthetic of the prelude seems to have emerged in 1765 with Jean-Jacques Rousseau's entries "Prélude" and "Préluder" in the *Encyclopédie*. After listing the practical reasons for short preludes, he continued: "But on the organ and the harpsichord, the art of preluding is something more significant: it consists of composing and playing on the spot pieces charged with the most learned aspects of composition, in fugue, imitation, and harmony. To succeed [in this art] it is not enough to be a good composer, it is not enough to master the keyboard and to possess agile and well-exercised fingers. One must also abound in that fire of genius and that liveliness of spirit that allows one at once to find subjects most suitable for harmony and melodies most pleasing to the ear" (Rousseau 1765, 287; repeated in Rousseau 1768, 383).

Charles Burney was evidently influenced by these ideas when he described Emanuel Bach's playing in 1775: "he grew so animated and possessed, that he looked like one inspired" (1775, 2: 270–71). Johann Friedrich Reichardt also professed to be spellbound by Emanuel's improvisations. Burney, when in about 1800 he wrote the article "Prelude" for Abraham Rees's *Cyclopædia* (not published until 1819), paraphrased Rousseau's words, adding: "It is above all in preluding and giving way to the imagination, that great masters, exempt from the extreme subserviency to rules which the eyes of critics require in written music, display those talents of invention and execution which ravish all hearers far beyond the written labours of meditation and study" (1819). The power to improvise an inspired prelude was increasingly treated as a mark of genius, reserved for a select few. Other prominent reference works also followed Rousseau's definition (Lichtenthal 1826, 2:133; Castil-Blaze 1828, 192).

But amateurs still wanted to learn how to do it, since it was evidently an expected part of playing a keyboard instrument, especially in private gatherings. In about 1773 Tommaso Giordani, an Italian composer living in London, published *Preludes for the Harpsichord or Piano Forte in all the Keys Flat and Sharp* (i.e., minor and major). In fact, he covered only the 14 most commonly used keys, not all 24. The preludes vary from 8 to 15 measures, all but one in common time. I believe this collection was the first of its kind.

The purpose of Giordani's collection is stated on the title page: "N.B. This is intended as an assistance to Young Performers, as the beginning any Song or lesson without Touching in the Key has a very Awkward appearance & often disconcerts the Performer." The word "lesson" meant any keyboard piece, and was sometimes used synonymously with "sonata." The phrase "touching in the key" suggests the word *toccare* in Giordani's native language, and there had always been a close connection between the prelude and the toccata.

It is extremely unlikely that Giordani was familiar with the *WTC*, which was not published until 1801, or indeed with any work by J. S. Bach (Tomita 2004, 1–6, 44–45 (Table 1.3)). His purpose, like Bach's, was didactic, but with a different goal. Bach's reason for using all the keys, shown in the title of the *WTC*, was to demonstrate the advantages of an improved form of tempered tuning in extending the tonal range of keyboard music. His preludes were not designed as introductions to any piece in the same key, since each was coupled to a fugue.

Giordani, by contrast, accepted the tonal limits of meantone tempera-ment, which was still in normal use. But preluding had evidently become a conventional practice in performance, to the point where it was "awkward" not to do it. Students and amateurs would need a prelude in every likely key, since they might have to introduce a piece in any one of these keys and could not trust themselves to improvise.

The social background to Giordani's pieces was the drawing room rather than the public concert. This was a time when young women, especially, were encouraged to learn to play the harpsichord or piano as a social grace (Sadie 1990, 315–18). In London in 1773 the trend had evidently reached the point at which a publisher, Peter Welcker, thought it worth his while to issue a collection of preludes. Significantly, he chose a fashionable Italian musician to provide them.

It is reasonable to suppose that the preludes in Giordani's collection were representative of his own spontaneous preluding and that of contemporary professional performers, but simplified to the level of young students and amateurs. Each consists of a few bars of what could well have been the be-ginning of a sonata movement, with some flourishes displaying technical virtuosity, but further exposition is soon cut off by a cadence in the tonic key (see Figure 19.1). Of course, it is likely that the printed versions are more polished and more carefully corrected than a true improvisation, but the general flavor and character are no doubt preserved. The preludes are rather routine in character: not much "fancy" is detectable at this stage.

This publication had dozens of successors—first in London, then in other European cities. Giordani himself brought out a second set of *Fourteen Pre-ludes or Capriccios and Eight Cadences* [Cadenzas] *for the Piano Forte, Harp-sichord, Harp, or Organ* in about 1785. The preludes cover the same 14 keys, but this time they are longer, unmeasured, and technically more advanced;

FIGURE 19.1. Number 12 of Tommaso Giordani's *Preludes for the Harpsichord or Piano Forte in All the Keys Flat and Sharp* (London: Welcker, [1773]).

some, headed "Arpeggio," are made up entirely of arpeggiated chords, a type found in many of these collections.

The following year Muzio Clementi issued a curious publication called *Clementi's Musical Characteristics: or A Collection of Preludes and Cadences for the Harpsichord or Piano Forte Composed in the Style of Haydn, Kozeluch, Mozart, Sterkel, Vanhal and The Author*. The purpose of this work has been disputed. Eva Badura-Skoda (1970) has suggested a partly satirical purpose, a premise questioned by Leon Plantinga (1977, 53–67). Clementi is known to have witnessed Mozart's preluding at a famous contest between the two arranged in Vienna by Emperor Joseph II in 1781.

Clementi was to become a towering figure in the musical world; he was based in London but conducted extended tours around Europe. He was a piano manufacturer, publisher, and teacher as well as a pianist and composer. His *Introduction to the Art of Playing on the Piano Forte* (1801) contained an anthology of short pieces he called lessons, many of them originally written for other media and now arranged for piano. In terms of technical demands they range from easy to intermediate, but they are grouped by key: the keys range from three flats to four sharps. Each group is preceded by a short prelude in the same key, with the implication that the prelude is suitable to introduce any of the "lessons" in the group. Figure 19.2 is a very simple prelude followed by an arrangement of a Corelli allemande, of which the first two measures are given here. Clementi studied J.S. Bach and owned a manuscript copy of the *WTC*, part 2 (Tomita 2004, 71–82), and it is possible that the shape of the arpeggiation (though in itself commonplace) was suggested by Prelude No. 1 from *WTC*, part 1.

Clementi's piano tutor was hugely influential, running to many editions in at least five languages. The fifth London edition of 1811 had an appendix that added more demanding pieces, ranging over all 24 keys, with new preludes, some of them much more substantial. Figure 19.3 is one of three preludes in G major. Here, any influence of Bach has clearly vanished. What we do find, though, is a degree of "fancy," which to the listener takes the form of surprise. The main aesthetic of the piece is one of freedom from constraint, suggesting that the player is following his inclination wherever it takes him, provided it leads him back to the main key in the end. Clementi's preludes are always barred in common time, though he often added pauses, ritardandi, accelerandi, and changes of tempo.

Two other expatriates in London, August Friedrich Christopher Kollman and Jan Ladislav Dussek, published sets of sonatas preceded by rather elaborate preludes in about 1792 and 1795, respectively (discussed in Goertzen 1996,

Clementi, 1801

Prelude in D minor by M.C.

sempre legato

Allemanda, by CORELLI

FIGURE 19.2. A prelude from Clementi's *Introduction to the Art of Playing on the Piano Forte* (London: Clementi, 1801), with the first two bars of the Corelli allemande it was designed to introduce, as arranged by Clementi. The titles are as Clementi printed them.

315, 325). Another Londoner of Italian background, Philip Anthony Corri, in 1810 published *L'anima di musica: An Original Treatise on Piano Playing*, with a section on preluding and over 200 "progressive preludes," later issued separately as *Original System of Preluding*. In it he said, "In the performance of preludes, all formality or precision of time must be avoided: they must *appear* to be the birth of the moment, the effusion of the fancy: for this reason it may be observed, that the measure of time is not always marked in preludes" (1810, 84). This is indeed the case in an 1818 collection by Clementi's Anglo-German pupil John Baptist Cramer, entitled *Twenty-Six Preludes or Short Introductions in the Principal Major and Minor Keys for the Piano Forte*.

In the German-speaking lands at this time, no pianist was more famous

FIGURE 19.3. A prelude from the appendix to the fifth edition of Clementi's *Introduction* (London, 1811): a more self-contained piece, with some elements of "fancy."

than Mozart's Czech pupil Johann Nepomuk Hummel. There are many accounts of his astonishing improvisations (Goertzen 1996, 305 n. 21). Like Clementi he decided to provide models for students, and to profit by them. He published a set of preludes in all 24 keys in the Vienna periodical *Répertoire de musique pour les dames* (1814), which were later reprinted in many cities. They are short and they follow standard harmonic progressions, but they are highly unpredictable in their affective character; some have textural contrast, and others are continuous. The dynamics are also unstandardized; some end with loud chords, others with a soft and somber cadence. In short, the aesthetic of surprise is again dominant. Figure 19.4 is one of the more exciting specimens.

Beethoven's pupil Ferdinand Ries published *Quarante préludes pour le piano-forte en plusieurs tons majeurs et mineurs* at Vienna in about 1818. The title page says they are to serve as an introduction to all kinds of movement. There is a telling detail. Although the preludes are in no particular order, they are carefully indexed by key, showing that one of their main purposes was

FIGURE 19.4. One of the more exciting short preludes from the 24 that Hummel published in the publication *Répertoire de musique pour les dames* (2. Année, cahier 9) at Vienna in 1814. This example is taken from a later reprint, *Preludes dans tous les 24 tons*, Op. 67 (Hamburg: A. Cranz, [1838]).

still a practical one: to provide suitable introductions in any key that might be wanted. Several of these give a truly improvisatory effect; they are crafted to sound like someone trying out the keyboard and freely following up an idea. Most begin with a distinct motive, which then dissolves into passage work, often reaching an emotional climax, followed by material leading quickly to the cadence. Figure 19.5 is one specimen. Below it appears the beginning of a piece by Ries's master that it might have been designed to introduce.

Carl Czerny, another famous virtuoso pianist and Beethoven pupil, offered the first comprehensive treatment of piano improvisation, published in German, English, and French as Op. 200 in 1829. In it he stated categorically that "the performer should become accustomed to improvising a prelude each time and before each piece that he studies or plays," and he repeated this instruction in his Piano School of 1839, so there can be little doubt that the practice was still customary in the year when Chopin's preludes were published (Czerny 1829, 1839, 3: 116–23).

Of the many other sets of preludes in all the keys that appeared between 1820 and 1839, an especially significant one is that of the French pianist Frédéric Kalkbrenner—if only because he was praised by Chopin, who had few kind words to say about his contemporaries. His collection was called *Twenty-Four Preludes for the Piano Forte, in All the Major and Minor Keys, being an Introduction to the Art of Preluding,* published at Paris, London, and Leipzig in 1827. The keys are in rising chromatic order, as in the *WTC.* Figure 19.6 shows the beginning of No. 3, in D flat major (the complete prelude is reproduced in facsimile in Goertzen 1996, 328–29). The whole piece is 40 measures long and, as Goertzen points out, comes closer to a finished character piece than a model for improvisation. But, like the others in the set, it is unpredictable in form. After a modulation to the dominant key, a second theme is heard (Figure 19.7), in an ascending sequence that begins to telescope and modulate through various keys; it returns in the tonic and the modulations become more remote. A virtuosic coda (Figure 19.8) preserves another tradition of the improvised prelude.

This piece, especially its final cadence, brings Chopin directly to mind, and we are getting very close to him now. Chopin's preludes, even more than Kalkbrenner's, are extraordinarily varied in character and weight. One is an impetuous flourish, another a soulful lament; one a demure 16-bar waltz, another a finished song without words. Robert Wangermée in 1950 went so far as to say that "they are preludes to nothing, and their improvisatory character is only affected, for they are a stylization of an ideal of improvisation which had already effectively ceased to be practiced" (Wangermée 1950, 242).

FIGURE 19.5. A prelude in F minor from Ries's *Quarante préludes pour le piano-forte en plusieurs tons majeurs et mineurs* (Vienna, [c.1818]). This is followed by the first two measures of Beethoven's Piano Sonata Op. 2, no. 1 (1795), which Ries's prelude might well have been designed to introduce.

FIGURE 19.6. Kalkbrenner's preludes approach Chopin's in length and complexity. This is the opening of No. 3 in D flat major from his *Twenty-four Preludes for the Piano Forte, in All the Major and Minor Keys,* Op. 88 (Paris, London, and Leipzig, [1827]).

FIGURE 19.7. Measures 9–16 of No. 3 from Kalkbrenner's *Twenty-Four Preludes for the Piano Forte, in All the Major and Minor Keys*, Op. 88 (Paris, London, and Leipzig, [1827]).

FIGURE 19.8. The conclusion of No. 3 from Kalkbrenner's
*Twenty-Four Preludes for the Piano Forte, in All the Major and
Minor Keys,* Op. 88 (Paris, London, and Leipzig, [1827]).

Yet any musician of 1839 seeing a set of preludes in all the keys could not
have failed to connect them with that practice, and both Chopin and his publishers must have been well aware of that fact. He was himself highly reputed
as an improviser (Fétis and Moscheles 1840, 73). Kallberg points out that he
often improvised preludes, and suggests that he may have used Op. 28, No.
8 in F# minor as an introduction to his Impromptu in F# major, Op. 36, at
Glasgow in 1848 (Kallberg 1992, 136–37). An English pianist, Henry Rogers, in
1850 played Chopin's Tarantella preceded by what a reviewer called "a clever
and peculiar, rather than interesting, prelude by the same composer" (*Musical
World* 25: 308)—presumably No. 17 in A flat, the key of the Tarantella. Liszt,
reviewing an 1841 concert in which Chopin played a few preludes from Op.
28, felt it necessary to point out that they were not just introductory pieces,
as the title would suggest, but were "compositions of an order entirely apart"
(*Revue et gazette musicale* 8: 246).

The idea of preluding, then, was by no means obsolete. But as Goertzen
found, it began to decline after about 1840 (Goertzen 1996, 332–37). As critical attitudes moved decisively in the direction of canonization, pianists grew
afraid to alter or add to the written notes of the masters, and even Franz Liszt
apologized for doing so. We have hardly moved away from that position

today. That is why it is healthy to remind ourselves of the historical context in which Chopin created his Op. 28.

The one prelude in Chopin's collection that clearly retains the impression of unpremeditated and fanciful improvisation is No. 2 in A minor. Very unusually for a published prelude, it begins in ambiguous tonality (Figure 19.9), continues with deepening mystery, and establishes its home key of A minor only at the final cadence.

It is obvious that Chopin's preludes transcended their predecessors in individuality and imaginative power. They were not solely models for improvised introductions. They were also artistic miniatures in their own right. Schumann, perhaps slightly baffled by their unusual character, called them "sketches, beginnings of etudes, or, so to speak, ruins, solitary eagle's wings, a wild and colourful motley of pieces" (*Neue Zeitschrift für Musik*, 11: 163). But it can hardly be doubted that they were intended as contributions to a familiar tradition, which they would transcend. Others before Chopin, notably Kalkbrenner, had taken steps to wean the prelude from its introductory function and make it work also as an independent miniature. It was Chopin who completed that process. The earlier printed sets, after all, had been devised for amateurs, whereas the Rousseau ideal for the prelude required the "fire of genius." Paradoxically, once that quality had been displayed in printed form in Chopin's preludes, it removed them from the realm of improvisation

Chopin, 1839

FIGURE 19.9. The opening of No. 2 of Chopin's 24 Préludes, Op. 39.

and brought them quickly into the fixed canon of piano music, where Bach's were already entrenched.

There is no question that Chopin admired Bach; he even had a copy of the *WTC* with him on Majorca when he was working on his preludes (Eigeldinger 1988, 174). Nevertheless, there is no perceptible link or resemblance between the two works. They are analogous only in the fact that each sums up a tradition of improvised preluding and completes its transformation into a form of premeditated composition that became a model for others. The specific tradition that lay behind Chopin's preludes was quite distinct from the one behind Bach's. It was the fanciful improvised introduction, designed to set the scene and mood for an equally romantic transmission of a work of genius.

The manner of improvised preluding in the early 19th century cannot be exactly recovered, even if it were desirable to attempt such a thing. We have only printed examples, which were not in themselves improvised and were likely to be more structured and polished, and probably also more conservative, than the practice they claimed to represent. Yet, after all, the difference may be less than it appears (see, for instance, Nettl 1998, 4–6). We have learned from two conferences on improvisation, covering cultures from all over the world, that the practice itself is typically a product of long and careful preparation, and that its aura of spontaneous creation may be more an affect or a symbol than a literal reality.

REFERENCES

Bach, Carl Philipp Emanuel. [1753] 1949. *Essay on the True Art of Playing Keyboard Instruments*. Translated and edited by William J. Mitchell. New York: W.W. Norton.

Badura-Skoda, Eva. 1970. "Clementi's 'Musical Characteristics' Opus 19." In *Studies in 18th-Century Music: A Tribute to Karl Geiringer on His 70th Birthday*, edited by H. C. Robbins Landon, 53–67. London and New York: Oxford University Press.

Burney, Charles. 1775. *The Present State of Music in Germany, The Netherlands, and United Provinces*, 2nd ed. London: T. Becket, J. Robson, and G. Robinson.

———. 1819. "Prelude, in Music." In *The Cyclopædia; or, Universal Dictionary of Arts, Sciences, and Literature*, edited by Abraham Rees, vol. 28, unpaginated. London: Longman, Hurst, Rees, Orme, & Brown.

Castil-Blaze, François Henri Joseph. 1828. *Dictionnaire de musique moderne*. Brussels: L'Académie de Musique.

Corri, Philip Anthony. 1810. *L'anima di musica: An Original Treatise on Pianoforte Playing, in which . . . the Nature of Touch and of Preluding . . . are Illustrated with Suitable Examples*. London: G. Mitchell.

Czerny, Carl. 1829. *Systematische Anleitung zum Fantasieren auf dem Pianoforte*, Op. 200. Vienna: A. Diabelli; London: Boosey; Paris: M. Schlesinger.

———. 1839. *Vollständinge theoretisch-praktische Pianoforte-Schule*. Op. 500. Translated by J.A. Hamilton as *Complete Theoretical and Practical Piano Forte School*. London: R. Cocks & Co.

Edler, Arnfried. 1997. "Präludium." In *Die Musik in Geschichte und Gegenwart*, Vol. 7: 1792–1804. Kassel: Bärenreiter.

Eigeldinger. Jean-Jacques. 1988. "Twenty-four Preludes op.28: Genre, Structure, Significance." In *Chopin Studies*, edited by Jim Samson, 167–94. Cambridge: Cambridge University Press.

Ferguson, Howard. 2001. "Prelude, §2: From 1800." In *The New Grove Dictionary of Music and Musicians*, rev. ed., Vol. 20, edited by Stanley Sadie, 292–93. London: Macmillan.

Fétis, François-Joseph, and Ignaz Moscheles. 1840. *Méthode des méthodes de piano*. Paris: Maurice Schlesinger.

Goertzen, Valerie Woodring. 1996. "By Way of Introduction: Preluding by 18th- and Early 19th-Century Pianists." *Journal of Musicology* 14(3): 299–337.

———. 1998. "Setting the Stage: Clara Schumann's Preludes." In *In the Course of Performance: Studies in the World of Musical Improvisation,* edited by Bruno Nettl with Melinda Russell, 237–59. Chicago: University of Chicago Press.

Kallberg, Jeffrey. 1992. "Small 'Forms': In Defence of the Prelude." In *The Cambridge Companion to Chopin*, edited by Jim Samson, 124–44. Cambridge: Cambridge University Press.

Levin, Robert D. 2001. "Improvisation, §II, 4: The Classical Period." In *The New Grove Dictionary of Music and Musicians*, rev. ed., Vol. 12, edited by Stanley Sadie, 112–17. London: Macmillan.

Lichtenthal, Pietro. 1826. *Dizionario e bibliografia della musica*, 4 vols. Milan: Antonio Fontana.

Nettl, Bruno. 1998. "An Art Neglected in Scholarship." In *In the Course of Performance: Studies in the World of Musical Improvisation,* edited by Bruno Nettl with Melinda Russell, 1–19. Chicago: University of Chicago Press.

Plantinga, Leon. 1977. *Clementi: His Life and Music*. London and New York: Oxford University Press.

Popper, Karl R. 1959. *The Logic of Scientific Discovery*. London: Hutchinson.

Rosenblum, Sandra. 1988. *Performance Practices in Classic Piano Music*. Bloomington and Indianapolis: Indiana University Press.

Rousseau, Jean-Jacques. 1765. "Prélude"; "Préluder." In *Encyclopédie, ou dictionnaire raisonée des sciences, des arts et des métiers*, 13: 287. Neuchâtel: S. Faulche et compagnie.

———. 1768. *Dictionnaire de musique*. Paris: la Veuve Duchesne.

Sadie, Stanley. 1990. "Music in the Home II." In *Music in Britain: The Eighteenth Century*, 313–54. Oxford: Basil Blackwell Ltd.

Tomita, Yo. 2004. "The Dawn of the English Bach Awakening Manifested in Sources of the '48.'" In *The English Bach Awakening,* edited by Michael Kassler. London: Ashgate.

Wangermée, Robert. 1950. "L'improvisation pianistique au début du XIXe siècle." In *Miscellanea musicologica Floris van der Mueren.* Ghent: L. van Melle.

CONTRIBUTORS

STEPHEN BLUM teaches ethnomusicology at the City University of New York Graduate Center. He is the author of numerous articles on the music of Iran and on issues in musicological research, and his most recent publications include the entries "Composition" and "Central Asia" in the second edition of *The New Grove Dictionary of Music and Musicians,* in which he is also the coauthor of nine other entries. He has also contributed to the volumes of *The Garland Encyclopedia of World Music* on the United States, Canada, the Middle East, and Europe.

PATRICIA SHEHAN CAMPBELL is Donald E. Peterson Professor of Music at the University of Washington, where she teaches music education and applied ethnomusicology. She is the author, coauthor, or editor of numerous books, including *Lessons from the World* and *Songs in Their Heads.* She is currently the editor of *College Music Symposium* and a frequent lecturer on world musics in education throughout the United States and abroad.

SABINE M. FEISST studied musicology at the Johann Wolfgang Goethe University in Frankfurt and at the Free University in Berlin and has taught since 2000 at Bard College, the University of Notre Dame, and Arizona State University, where she is associate professor of music. She is the author of *Der Begriff 'Improvisation' in der neuen Musik* and articles in *Archiv für Musikwissenschaft, Musical Quarterly, Journal of the Arnold Schoenberg Center,* and *Schoenberg and His World.*

LAWRENCE GUSHEE, professor emeritus of musicology at the University of Illinois at Urbana-Champaign, received postgraduate training in music and musicology at the Manhattan School of Music and Yale University. He has written about improvisation both informally (record reviews from the late 1950s) and formally with respect to medieval music, Lester Young, and Louis Armstrong. Most recently, he has published a major book, *Pioneers of Jazz: The Story behind the Creole Band.*

ROBERT S. HATTEN, professor of music theory at Indiana University, is the author of *Musical Meaning in Beethoven: Markedness, Correlation, and Interpretation* and *Interpreting Musical Gestures, Topics, and Tropes: Mozart-Beethoven-Schubert.* He has also published on Bruckner, Henze, Penderecki, temporality in music (analogues to tense and aspect), hermeneutics, style, narrativity, and deception in music.

WILLIAM KINDERMAN is professor of musicology at the University of Illinois at Urbana-Champaign. His books include *Beethoven's Diabelli Variations,* the comparative study *Beethoven,* and *Artaria 195: Beethoven's Sketchbook for the Missa solemnis and the Piano Sonata in E Major, Opus 109.* As pianist, he has recorded Beethoven's last sonatas and *Diabelli Variations* for Hyperion/Helios Records.

NATALIE KONONENKO received her PhD from Harvard University, has taught Slavic studies at the University of Virginia, and is professor of Ukrainian studies at the University of Alberta. She has done field-work in Turkey and Ukraine and has written books on Ukrainian and Turkish minstrelsy, including the prize-winning *Ukrainian Minstrels: And the Blind Shall Sing.*

ROBERT LEVIN, pianist, musicologist, composer, and editor, is also professor of music at Harvard University. A student of Wolpe, Boulanger, and Gaultier-Leon, he has also taught at Curtis, SUNY at Purchase, and the Staatliche Hochschule für Musik at Freiburg. A specialist in the performance of Mozart's works, many of which he has recorded, he has, as scholar and performer, maintained a particular interest in their improvisational aspects and in issues of authenticity. He has also championed and performed new music.

CHARLOTTE MATTAX MOERSCH holds degrees from Yale University, The Juilliard School, and Stanford University. She currently teaches harpsichord and historical performance practice at the University of Illinois at Urbana-Champaign. Since winning top prizes in the international harpsichord competitions of Bruges, Belgium, and Paris, she has performed as a solo harpsichordist and chamber musician in this country and abroad. She has recorded for Dorian, Koch International, Centaur, and Amon Ra records and is the author of *Principles of Accompaniment: Denis Delair's Treatise of 1610.*

INGRID MONSON is Quincy Jones Professor of African American music at Harvard University, where she holds a joint appointment in the departments of music and African and African American studies. She is author of *Saying Something: Jazz Improvisation and Interaction, The African Diaspora: A Musical Perspective,* and articles that have appeared in *Ethnomusicology, JAMS, Critical Inquiry, Black Music Research Journal,* and *Women Music.*

JOHN P. MURPHY is an associate professor in the jazz studies division of the University of North Texas, College of Music. He teaches jazz history and analysis and directs the Jazz Repertory Ensemble, pursues research interests in jazz and Brazilian music, and performs frequently on tenor saxophone.

BRUNO NETTL, with a PhD from Indiana University, is professor emeritus of music and anthropology at the University of Illinois, where he began teaching in 1964. He is the author of several books on ethnomusicology, including *The Study of Ethnomusicology, Blackfoot Musical Thought,* and most recently, *Encounters in Ethnomusicology: A Memoir.* He is also principal editor of *In the Course of Performance: Studies in the World of Musical Improvisation.*

ALI JIHAD RACY, a native of Lebanon, is a performer (on the Arabic bouzouq and nei) and a composer, as well as a musicologist. He received his PhD at the University of Illinois at Urbana-Champaign, taught at the universities of Hawaii and Washington, and is professor of ethnomusicology at UCLA. The author of numerous articles on the concept of tarab in Arabic music and on the role of the record industry in Egypt, and of a recent book, *Making Music in the Arab World,* he concertizes widely in the United States and abroad and has produced numerous recordings of Arabic classical music and of genres combining Arabic and Western styles.

ANNE K. RASMUSSEN is associate professor of music and ethnomusicology at the College of William and Mary, where she also directs a Middle Eastern music ensemble. Her publications and the four CD recordings she has produced address politics and gender in the culture of Qur'anic recitation and Islamic musical arts in Indonesia, the musical life of Arab Americans, and musical multiculturalism in the United States.

STEPHEN SLAWEK received his PhD at the University of Illinois and is professor of music at the University of Texas, Austin. With many years of research experience in India, he is a scholar/teacher of ethnomusicology and also a widely recognized concert artist on the sitar. His research has focused on the musical traditions of south Asia and southeast Asia, and most recently, on American popular music.

GABRIEL SOLIS studied musicology and ethnomusicology at Washington University in St. Louis, has taught at the University of Pennsylvania, and is associate professor of music at the University of Illinois at Urbana-Champaign. He is the author of *Monk's Music* and of articles on Thelonius Monk in *Musical Quarterly* and *Ethnomusicology.*

NICHOLAS TEMPERLEY was born and educated in Britain, and in 1959 he earned a PhD at Cambridge University, where he taught for five years before joining the musicology faculty at the University of Illinois in 1967. His main fields of interest are English music, especially for the church and the keyboard, and European music of the 18th and 19th centuries. The most recent of his several books is *Bound for America: Three British Composers.*

JOHN TOENJES, music director for the University of Illinois at Urbana-Champaign Department of Dance, studies early music at Stanford University and composition at the University of Missouri. He has performed as a harpsichordist with the San Francisco Symphony and the Carmel Bach Festival Orchestra, and has formed several improvisation ensembles over the years. With over 20 years of experience playing for modern dance classes in studios and universities in the United States and Europe, he has written over 30 dance scores and performed improvisation concerts with many professional dancers.

THOMAS TURINO studied ethnomusicology at the University of Texas and has been on the faculty of the University of Illinois at Urbana-Champaign since 1987. A scholar of Andean, east African, and American musical cultures, he maintains major interest in the semiotics of music and in theoretical issues of music and politics. He is the author of three books, *Moving Away from Silence: The Music of the Peruvian Altiplano and the Experience of Urban Migration; Nationalist, Cosmopolitans, and Popular Music in Zimbabwe;* and *Music as Social Life.*

INDEX

The University of Illinois Press
is a founding member of the
Association of American University Presses.

Composed in 10.5/13 Minion Pro
with Meta display
by Jim Proefrock
at the University of Illinois Press
Designed by Dennis Roberts
Manufactured by Thomson-Shore, Inc.

University of Illinois Press
1325 South Oak Street
Champaign, IL 61820-6903
www.press.uillinois.edu